SECURITY IN THE NUCLEAR AGE

Jerome H. Kahan

SECURITY IN THE NUCLEAR AGE
Developing U.S. Strategic Arms Policy

The Brookings Institution
Washington, D.C.

Library of Congress Cataloging in Publication Data:
Kahan, Jerome H
  Security in the nuclear age.
  Includes bibliographical references and index.
    1. United States—Military policy. 2. Atomic
warfare. 3. Atomic weapons and disarmament.
I. Title.
UA23.K28   355.03'35'73   75-20145
ISBN 0-8157-4818-3
ISBN 0-8157-4817-5 pbk.

9 8 7 6 5 4 3 2

THE BROOKINGS INSTITUTION is an independent organization devoted to nonpartisan research, education, and publication in economics, government, foreign policy, and the social sciences generally. Its principal purposes are to aid in the development of sound public policies and to promote public understanding of issues of national importance.

The Institution was founded on December 8, 1927, to merge the activities of the Institute for Government Research, founded in 1916, the Institute of Economics, founded in 1922, and the Robert Brookings Graduate School of Economics and Government, founded in 1924.

The Board of Trustees is responsible for the general administration of the Institution, while the immediate direction of the policies, program, and staff is vested in the President, assisted by an advisory committee of the officers and staff. The by-laws of the Institution state: "It is the function of the Trustees to make possible the conduct of scientific research, and publication, under the most favorable conditions, and to safeguard the independence of the research staff in the pursuit of their studies and in the publication of the results of such studies. It is not a part of their function to determine, control, or influence the conduct of particular investigations or the conclusions reached."

The President bears final responsibility for the decision to publish a manuscript as a Brookings book. In reaching his judgment on the competence, accuracy, and objectivity of each study, the President is advised by the director of the appropriate research program and weighs the views of a panel of expert outside readers who report to him in confidence on the quality of the work. Publication of a work signifies that it is deemed a competent treatment worthy of public consideration but does not imply endorsement of conclusions or recommendations.

The Institution maintains its position of neutrality on issues of public policy in order to safeguard the intellectual freedom of the staff. Hence interpretations or conclusions in Brookings publications should be understood to be solely those of the authors and should not be attributed to the Institution, to its trustees, officers, or other staff members, or to the organizations that support its research.

Foreword

In the late 1960s, the Soviet Union achieved parity with the United States in strategic nuclear weapons. The era of U.S. superiority had ended, and each nation possessed more than enough strategic power to inflict utter destruction on the other. As a consequence, the superpowers made their first serious attempt to control both the development of nuclear weapons and the means of delivering them by beginning the strategic arms limitation talks (SALT). After three years, these negotiations reached their climax in May 1972 with the signing of a pair of unprecedented agreements—the treaty limiting ballistic missile defenses and the five-year interim pact on offensive arms limitations; these were followed in November 1974 by the Vladivostok agreement, which specified guidelines for a treaty limiting offensive arms.

Nonetheless, many vital nuclear weapon problems remain unresolved. Mankind's hopes for checking the arms race, reducing the risk of nuclear war, and expanding international cooperation in preventing the proliferation of nuclear weapons, rest heavily on what is likely to be a continuous series of strategic arms negotiations between the Soviet Union and the United States.

These bilateral efforts in no way eliminate the need for sound unilateral decisions on U.S. strategic arms policy. If anything, the need is greater than ever as strategic parity and instabilities associated with new weapon systems continue to provoke debate over U.S. nuclear forces and strategy.

In this book, the author clarifies the origins of the nuclear weapon problems the United States now faces by outlining the history of U.S. policy in this field from the Eisenhower administration through the Nixon administration. He then analyzes the complex issues that must be considered in formulating future policies and arms control measures. His theme throughout is strategic stability, which he regards as an imperative of the nuclear age. Convinced that America's security depends on ensuring that nuclear weapons will never again be used, he concludes his analysis with policy prescriptions for deterring the use of nuclear weapons and promoting strategic stability.

Jerome H. Kahan, formerly a senior fellow in the Brookings Foreign Policy Studies program, is a member of the Policy Planning Staff of the Department of State. His book is the outcome, not only of his own research and analyses, but also of the discussions of a study group established in the spring of 1969. Both his research and the study group were sponsored jointly by the Brookings Institution and the Carnegie Endowment for International Peace.

The group comprised twenty-nine members from Congress, the executive branch, private industry, and academic and research institutions, who are listed on page 351. The chairman was Harold Brown, president of the California Institute of Technology and a former secretary of the Air Force; Franklin Lindsay, president of the Itek Corporation, served as vice-chairman. The group was directed first by Herbert Scoville, Jr., a writer and consultant on arms control issues who was formerly on the staff of the Carnegie Endowment, and later by Mr. Kahan. During a period of eighteen months, the group met to explore many of the topics pertinent to the author's study: strategic arms and arms control objectives, Soviet views on strategic policy, the effect of the nuclear balance on international crises, strategic policy and the North Atlantic Treaty Organization, and the implications of China's nuclear programs for the United States.

The Brookings Institution and Mr. Kahan are grateful to the Carnegie Endowment, to Thomas Hughes, its president, and to Thomas Halsted of its staff for encouragement and for the support that helped make possible both the study group and the author's comprehensive investigations. They are further indebted to the members of the group for their notable contributions to the development of the study.

The author wishes to thank the many friends and colleagues whose guidance proved invaluable throughout the course of this work, particularly Seyom Brown, for his creative assistance and unflagging interest, and Herbert Scoville, Jr., for his help in launching the study. He is grateful to Anne K. Long, Ruth E. Pansar, Jeannette Joseph, Louisa Thoron, and Christine Lipsey for research assistance; to Tadd Fisher for editing the manuscript; and to Florence Robinson for preparing the index.

The views expressed in this book are those of the author and should not be attributed to the study group or the other persons whose assistance is acknowledged above or to the staff members, officers, or trustees of the Brookings Institution or to the Carnegie Endowment for International Peace.

KERMIT GORDON
President

April 1975
Washington, D.C.

Contents

Introduction   1

Part One: Historical Perspectives

1. Strategic Power and Massive Retaliation: 1953–1960   9

    Nuclear Weapons and the New Look *11*
    Strategic Forces and Doctrine *26*
    Soviet Strategic Policies *47*
    Strategic Arms Control Efforts *54*
    Policy Precedents *62*

2. Assured Destruction and the Analytic Approach:
    1961–1968   74

    Defense Doctrine *74*
    Strategic Arms Policies *84*
    Soviet Strategic Policies *109*
    The Seeds of SALT *117*
    Policy Paradoxes *129*

3. Parity, Sufficiency, and SALT: 1969–1974   142

    The Nixon Defense Doctrine *143*
    The Strategy of Sufficiency *149*
    Soviet Strategic Policies *165*
    Strategic Arms Limitations *169*
    Lessons and Legacies *189*

Part Two: The Search for Stability

4. Future Strategic Policy Issues   199

    Requirements for Assured Retaliation *200*
    Flexible Strategic Options *223*
    The Numerical Balance of Forces *237*
    Strategic Forces and Overseas Commitments *244*
    Alternatives to Mutual Assured Destruction *253*

5. Arms Interaction and Arms Control   263

  Mutual Stability *264*
  Strategic Arms Control: Background Issues *276*
  Strategic Arms Limitation Possibilities *301*
  Additional SALT Issues *317*

6. Stable Deterrence: A Strategic Policy for the 1970s   328

  Principles of Stable Deterrence *330*
  Stable Deterrence in Practice *337*
  Budgetary Implications *343*

  The Brookings-Carnegie Strategic Arms Policy
  Study Group (1969–71)   351

  Index   353

Introduction

A little more than a year after the United States first tested an atomic device at Alamogordo, New Mexico, on July 16, 1945, it became starkly apparent that security in the nuclear age could not be found in sweeping solutions requiring fundamental changes in world politics and national outlooks. By that time, the United States had proposed the so-called Baruch Plan for international control of nuclear energy, and the USSR had rejected it.[1] Whether the United States was completely serious in proposing the Baruch Plan and whether the plan was technically or politically workable remain open questions to this day. Soviet resistance to the plan was understandable; Kremlin leaders could not have been expected to entrust their security to an international organization dominated by the United States, to agree to open the Soviet Union to foreign inspection, or to remain a second-class nation in the crucial field of atomic weaponry.

During the postwar years of the Truman administration, particularly after the USSR's first atomic test in 1949, U.S. leaders began to adapt their policies and programs to the realities of atomic weapons. But recognition of how profoundly these weapons had changed the traditional military characteristics and political dimensions of war took time to evolve, partly because people and institutions are reluctant to modify established thinking, plans, and procedures. Furthermore, on a practical level, in both the United States and the Soviet Union atomic destructive power and delivery potential increased slowly. Indeed, it

1. For a recent analysis, see Leneice N. Wu, *The Baruch Plan: U.S. Diplomacy Enters the Nuclear Age*, prepared for the Subcommittee on National Security Policy and Scientific Developments of the House Committee on Foreign Affairs, 92 Cong. 2 sess. (August 1972).

took ten years for the two characteristics of the contemporary strategic nuclear age—sizable nuclear arsenals and long-range delivery systems —to be reflected in the actual weapon capabilities of each nation.

Early in the Eisenhower administration, American leaders faced the problem of dealing with the unpleasant but unavoidable fact that the U.S. population had become vulnerable to Soviet intercontinental nuclear strikes. By the late 1950s the concept of deterrence had taken hold, and the procurement of retaliatory forces capable of withstanding a Soviet nuclear strike became central to American strategic doctrine. The Eisenhower administration, however, attached overriding importance to the goal of keeping military spending in check. Thus, even though nuclear arms were vital to America's basic defense posture under the controversial "massive retaliation" policy, restraint was exercised in certain strategic weapons programs.

The period 1961–68 saw an institutionalization of the doctrine of "assured destruction," the completion of the Minuteman and Polaris missile deployments, and the development of the advanced technology of multiple independently targetable reentry vehicles (MIRVs). The "flexible response" doctrine, which emphasized conventional defense, reflected the Kennedy and Johnson administrations' awareness of the limited utility of nuclear weapons and the importance of designing a strategic posture to minimize the "action-reaction" between U.S. and Soviet forces—a cycle that results in nuclear arms buildups on both sides.

After the Cuban missile crisis in 1962, the systematic expansion of the Soviet Union's strategic offensive capacity led to the loss of the overwhelming U.S. nuclear superiority that had characterized the 1950s. But this same expansion resulted in plans to begin the strategic arms limitation talks (SALT), which were then forestalled by the USSR's move into Czechoslovakia late in the summer of 1968.

SALT stemmed from the desire to dampen the cycle of U.S.-Soviet strategic arms actions and reactions that had represented a waste of resources for both nations, had become a source as well as a signal of tensions between Washington and Moscow, and had contributed to fears that the balance of terror might fail to prevent nuclear war. Neither nation, to be sure, pursued an all-out strategic arms buildup throughout the 1950s and 1960s. But the maze of mistrust between East and West, combined with the complex and constant advances in weapon technology, made sustained unilateral restraint on either side strategically questionable and politically impossible and precluded the negotiation of measures designed to reduce the risks and costs of the nuclear arms race.

By the start of the 1970s, after nearly two decades of U.S. nuclear superiority, strategic parity had been recognized as an inescapable reality of the U.S.-Soviet nuclear relationship, the Nixon administration had adopted the doctrine of "sufficiency" in response to the changed strategic environment and a reevaluation of U.S. commitments around the world after Vietnam, and SALT negotiations between the two superpowers had actually begun. In October 1972, the governments of the United States and the Soviet Union exchanged instruments of ratification officially putting into effect the strategic arms limitation accords[2] reached during President Nixon's historic visit to Moscow in May of that year. But the Moscow accords—which limited missile defenses, established a temporary offensive arms balance between U.S. and Soviet forces, and left room for unilateral arms decisions on both sides—sharpened public debate in the United States over the proper direction strategic policy should take. At the beginning of 1974 U.S. unilateral strategic policies were in a state of flux. Major new strategic programs such as Trident and the B-1 were under way, the Soviet Union was improving the quality of its nuclear forces, and the outcome of further SALT negotiations was uncertain. Toward the end of 1974 the Vladivostok agreement[3] gave some promise of successful future negotiations, but American policymakers, technical experts, and public commentators remained concerned about the problem of devising the political and military criteria needed to manage future U.S. strategic weapon programs.

Many of the basic conceptual and technical issues involved in designing a strategic arms policy for the 1970s were identified years ago and have been actively discussed for well over two decades.[4] At the present

2. Treaty between the United States of America and the Union of Soviet Socialist Republics on the Limitation of Anti-Ballistic Missile Systems; and the Interim Agreement between the United States of America and the Union of Soviet Socialist Republics on Certain Measures with Respect to the Limitation of Strategic Offensive Arms.

3. Joint Soviet-American Statement on Strategic Arms Limitation, November 24, 1974. Although the analysis presented in this book was completed in 1974 before the Vladivostok agreement, the main issues treated are still relevant and give every indication of remaining so for many years to come. References to the Vladivostok agreement appear from time to time to place these issues in proper perspective.

4. As early as 1946, a group of analysts identified many of the security premises

time, however, nuclear realities and their uncertain implications have highlighted a series of policy questions that are receiving more prominent and widespread attention than did earlier discussions. It appears that the great debate on nuclear strategy will increase in intensity during the next few years and will exert a dramatic effect on U.S. security and international stability through the coming decade.

Although currently approved programs will substantially increase U.S. strategic power, some observers fear that the Soviet Union might attempt to gain some form of nuclear advantage, even within the framework of U.S.-Soviet agreements, and argue that further increases and improvements in Soviet arms could endanger the effectiveness of important elements of our retaliatory deterrent. In addition to taking appropriate measures to prevent a serious erosion of our deterrent capability, American leaders must also deal with the issue of whether a new strategic balance might alter the perceptions of U.S. power at home and abroad and increase the propensity of Soviet leaders to risk aggressive actions. These questions are closely related to the problems associated with our policy toward SALT—the need to balance the important goal of seeking mutually stabilizing measures that can reduce nuclear costs and risks against the equally important objective of retaining the freedom and flexibility to pursue a national strategic policy consistent with our national objectives, alliance commitments, and worldwide political interests.

Among the major questions that must be addressed in deciding on a course of action for the United States in the strategic arms field are the following:

• Does the United States require a force of over 2,000 strategic delivery systems composed of a triad of invulnerable land-based missiles, sea-based missiles, and bombers to reliably deter the Soviet Union from launching a nuclear attack, or would deterrence operate safely with less than three different delivery systems and with fewer, less protected forces capable of inflicting lower levels of destruction?

• Does the numerical balance between U.S. and Soviet strategic forces exert a meaningful effect on the relative diplomatic strength of each nation and the outcome of superpower crises, or are concepts of

---

of the modern nuclear era, predicted the military and political trends of the arms competition, and prescribed principles for U.S. strategic policies that were adopted years later and that remain substantially valid today. See Bernard Brodie, ed., *The Absolute Weapon: Atomic Power and World Order* (Harcourt, Brace, 1946).

strategic "superiority" and "inferiority" largely irrelevant to international political and military issues as long as both sides retain a minimum nuclear retaliatory capability?

• Is it practical to design U.S. strategic arms policies with the goal of minimizing an action-reaction cycle between Soviet and American nuclear forces, or should the objective of nuclear stability be pursued mainly through unilateral programs to strengthen the U.S. posture, without seeking tacit or formal agreements with the USSR?

• Is the threat of mutual retaliation the most dependable answer to the question of how to live with nuclear weapons for the long term, or should our national strategy and SALT positions be shaped largely by additional or possibly alternative strategic doctrines based on selective strike options and the avoidance of attacks on population centers?

• Is there further need for strategic nuclear forces to provide a nuclear "umbrella" to our allies and to generally support America's worldwide interests, or has the presence of U.S.-Soviet strategic parity and the growth of China's nuclear forces removed the credibility and desirability of such an extended deterrence policy?

The primary purpose of this book is to explore the central issues involved in setting a U.S. strategic arms and arms control policy for the decade ahead. The pressing problems of today are amalgams containing substantial elements of previous strategic patterns as well as new technological and political ingredients Thus chapters 1, 2, and 3 provide a historical perspective through analytic descriptions of U.S. strategic policies from the early days of the Eisenhower administration in 1953 to the Nixon administration's strategic policies at the beginning of 1974. Building on these discussions, chapters 4 and 5 investigate the issues and options that will influence the fundamental features of America's future strategic posture, affect the stability of the U.S.-Soviet nuclear relationship, and determine longer-term directions for SALT. With chapter 6, the study concludes by offering guidelines for a policy of stable deterrence that can be used to shape U.S. strategic arms and arms control policies over the longer term.

A few caveats concerning the analyses are in order. To begin with, the study focuses on doctrinal and diplomatic issues related to strategic arms as seen by American policymakers and does not dwell on the details of weapon systems, the precise connection between strategic arms issues and overall American foreign policy, or the general pattern of international politics as it might influence nuclear matters. Second, discussions of Soviet strategic forces and policies are incorporated throughout the book in order to highlight the problems of threat perception and arms interactions, but there is no comprehensive treatment of the USSR's nuclear programs or attitudes. Finally, while the effects of bureaucratic and domestic political factors on U.S. strategic weapons and doctrinal decisions are often alluded to, an intensive application of these so-called nonrational models will not be found.[5] Apart from the complexity of attempting to weave such considerations into the scores of decisions and events covered by a study with as broad a sweep as the one to follow, it is the premise of this book that the *substantive merits* of alternative strategic policies have significantly influenced past U.S. courses of action in this field and will continue to do so in the future.

5. For a comprehensive treatment of the bureaucratic approach, see Morton H. Halperin, *Bureaucratic Politics and Foreign Policy* (Brookings Institution, 1974).

PART ONE

Historical Perspectives

CHAPTER ONE

Strategic Power and Massive Retaliation: 1953–1960

Throughout the late 1940s, many officials knew that the American atomic monopoly would eventually be broken and understood that Soviet acquisition of the bomb would necessitate dramatic revisions in U.S. military planning. The report of the President's Air Policy Commission, transmitted in December 1947, suggested that the USSR could obtain "substantial quantities" of atomic weapons within five years and concluded:

This means that the traditional peacetime strategy of the United States must be changed radically. We can no longer count on having our cities and the rest of our mainland untouched in a future war. . . . We must count on our homeland becoming increasingly vulnerable as the weapons increase in destructiveness and the means of delivering them are improved.[1]

Nevertheless, even after the Soviet Union's first atomic test in 1949 and the completion one year later of a National Security Council study (NSC-68) that contained cogent analyses of defense requirements in a nuclear era, U.S. doctrine continued to emphasize preatomic concepts of strategic bombing and air superiority, defense of the homeland, and victory in a war of attrition involving conventional as well as atomic forces.[2]

1. *Survival in the Air Age: A Report by the President's Air Policy Commission* (January 1, 1948), p. 12.
2. NSC-68 was the report of an ad hoc strategic reassessment study group headed by Paul H. Nitze (then director of the State Department policy planning staff) that advocated significant changes in the U.S. military posture to prevent a shift of military power. See Paul Y. Hammond, "NSC-68: Prologue to Rearmament," in Warner R. Schelling, Paul Y. Hammond, and Glenn H. Snyder, *Strategy, Politics, and Defense Budgets* (Columbia University Press, 1962), pp. 267–86. For an excellent discussion on nuclear policy issues during this period, see also George H. Quester, *Nuclear Diplomacy: The First Twenty-Five Years* (Dunellen, 1970).

9

In the early phase of the nuclear era, it was understandable that many planners contemplated atomic wars being fought along the lines of strategic bombing raids during the Second World War. Before Moscow joined the nuclear club, the United States and its allies were obviously immune to retaliation in kind, and America's nascent atomic capability served as a counterweight to the USSR's conventional military threat to Western Europe. Between 1949 and 1952, however, as the USSR began to acquire a small atomic arsenal capable of threatening Western Europe and the continental United States as well, the implications of atomic weapons were still not fully translated into operational U.S. military policies or programs. In commenting on the first American hydrogen bomb test in November 1952, President Harry S. Truman, in his last State of the Union Message, described thermonuclear power as providing a "new order of magnitude" of destruction and concluded that all-out war would "destroy the very structure of civilization."[3] But when the Truman administration ended a few weeks later, the Soviet Union had not yet tested a thermonuclear device nor flown a long-range jet bomber, while the strategic forces of the United States still consisted of medium-range B-47 bombers based abroad and a small fleet of relatively ineffective propeller-driven B-36 aircraft.

It was not until the mid-1950s that the features of the modern strategic nuclear era emerged with sufficient clarity to exert a significant effect on American defense and diplomacy. By that time, both the United States and the USSR had acquired significant arsenals of atomic weapons and had tested thermonuclear bombs, procured advanced jet-powered aircraft capable of delivering nuclear weapons over intercontinental distances, and initiated programs to develop long-range ballistic missiles. As a consequence of these technological developments, each of the major powers would gain a credible military capability to launch large-scale nuclear strikes from its own territory against the other side's homeland. The Eisenhower administration inherited the formidable task of responding to this unprecedented situation and designing practical security policies for the strategic nuclear age.

3. "Annual Message to the Congress on the State of the Union, January 7, 1953," Public Papers of the Presidents of the United States: Harry S. Truman, 1952–53 (1966), p. 1125.

Nuclear Weapons and the New Look

When President Dwight D. Eisenhower entered office, the U.S. defense budget was swollen by expenditures for the Korean war. The President and his chief advisers were firmly convinced of the need to drastically lower the level of defense spending, since they viewed a balanced federal budget as essential to a strong U.S. economy, which in turn was judged vital for national security. Indeed, the Korean experience had led to widespread public sentiment not only to bring the troops home but also to reduce U.S. armed forces generally. At the same time, the new administration saw a growing need to deal with the potential dangers posed by the Soviet Union and China, dangers heightened by the USSR's entry into the atomic age and by the potential development of Soviet thermonuclear weapons and long-range delivery systems. The problem, therefore, was how to achieve "security with solvency"—to protect the United States, contain Communism, and defend our interests abroad, while reducing defense spending.

For the Eisenhower administration, advancing and exploiting the technology of atomic and thermonuclear weapons seemed to offer the solution to this difficult equation. Hydrogen bombs of great destructive power as well as small fission weapons of low yield were becoming available in substantial numbers, along with advanced aircraft and missile delivery systems. The administration thus decided to establish a U.S. defense policy that would place increased reliance on nuclear power. Under this policy, U.S. strategic forces would supply a long-range deterrent and form the foundation of the nation's entire defense posture, while tactical nuclear weapons would support local defense needs with greater firepower. "With the shift in emphasis to the full exploitation of air power and modern weapons," President Eisenhower explained to the American people soon after entering office, "we are in a position to support strong national security programs over an indefinite period with less of a drain on our manpower, material, and financial resources."[4] The President made clear from the

4. "Annual Budget Message to the Congress: Fiscal Year 1955, January 21, 1954," *Public Papers of the Presidents of the United States: Dwight D. Eisenhower, 1954* (1960), p. 117.

outset that U.S. defense strategy, forces, and budgets should be based on the assumption that nuclear weapons would be used if necessary.[5]

Defense Doctrine and Capabilities

In a speech to the Council on Foreign Relations on January 12, 1954, Secretary of State John Foster Dulles explained that the administration had made "a basic decision" to adopt a national security policy that would "depend primarily upon a great capacity to retaliate, instantly, by means and at places of our own choosing."[6] Plans for the so-called New Look defense policy had, of course, been set in motion almost a year before Dulles's speech, and many policy pronouncements had already been made in public forums. But the speech coincided with the Eisenhower administration's need to explain its military policy publicly in the context of presenting its first official defense budget to Congress; as a result, the policy received considerable publicity. In fact, Dulles's description of the administration's defense policy created a controversy and the policy became widely known as the doctrine of "massive retaliation."

Under the New Look, U.S. strategic forces were to deter not only nuclear attacks on this nation or its allies but also a broad spectrum of potential Communist actions. During the Truman years, U.S. atomic air power was officially viewed as a deterrent to major Soviet conventional aggression against our allies in the North Atlantic Treaty Organization (NATO), although policy studies undertaken in 1950 had recognized the declining importance of atomic forces for this purpose. But the Eisenhower administration reinforced this mission and further extended the role of our strategic forces by raising the possibility that the United States might launch a nuclear attack as a response to limited aggression in Asia or throughout the so-called gray areas of the world. In this way, U.S. leaders planned to deter aggressive actions by making it known that the costs of such actions would far outweigh any potential gains. This, it was believed, would permit

5. In his State of the Union Message, January 7, 1954, President Eisenhower stated: "While determined to use atomic power to serve the usages of peace, we take into full account our great and growing number of nuclear weapons and the most effective means of using them . . . if they are needed to preserve our freedom." (*Public Papers, 1954,* pp. 10–11.)

6. John Foster Dulles, "The Evolution of Foreign Policy," *Department of State Bulletin,* vol. 30 (January 25, 1954), p. 108.

the United States to support its worldwide security interests and commitments with less emphasis on local defenses and without the need to match Communist manpower.[7]

Many critics and commentators interpreted the Eisenhower administration's doctrine to mean that the United States would automatically be prepared to launch a full-scale strategic strike against an attacker's homeland in response to all instances of aggression. But Dulles stressed that massive retaliation could not and would not be used under all circumstances and claimed that the potential for such a response did not necessarily mean turning every local war into a general war by launching atomic or hydrogen warheads against the Soviet Union or China. The secretary alluded to the possible use of U.S. nuclear forces on a limited basis and even suggested that, in certain circumstances, the United States might be prepared to accept setbacks rather than use these weapons.[8] Administration spokesmen never specified the precise conditions under which massive retaliation might be evoked or whether U.S. strategic power would be applied against an enemy's military bases or urban areas. This lack of precision could be attributed in part to an official policy that was itself unclear, but a certain degree of deliberate ambiguity may have been maintained as a means of keeping an aggressor off balance, thereby enhancing the deterrent effect of U.S. military forces.

Even as they emphasized America's strategic power, administration officials acknowledged the disadvantages of relying solely on such capabilities for deterrence or defense. Secretary Dulles spoke of the need for the United States and its allies to maintain a varied arsenal of "air, sea, and land power based on both conventional and atomic weapons" that could be applied on "a selective or massive basis as conditions may require."[9] Early descriptions of the New Look defense approach stressed the concept of a "mobile reserve" for use in small-

7. See John Foster Dulles, "Policy for Security and Peace," *Foreign Affairs*, vol. 32 (April 1954), pp. 353–64; and Arthur W. Radford, "The New Look: Defense Plans of the Nation," Speech delivered to the National Press Club, Washington, D.C., December 14, 1953, *Vital Speeches*, vol. 20 (January 1, 1954), pp. 171–73.

8. Dulles acknowledged that, although the policy of massive retaliation would provide "more basic security at less cost," it was to be expected that "at some times and some places" there might be "setbacks to the cause of freedom" under such a policy. ("The Evolution of Foreign Policy," pp. 108, 110.)

9. John F. Dulles, "Foreign Policy and National Security," Statement before the Senate Committee on Foreign Relations, March 19, 1954, *Department of State Bulletin*, vol. 30 (April 1954), p. 465.

scale conflicts, such as brushfire wars, and to handle acts of indirect aggression and subversion. The United States would maintain some forces for these purposes and would provide supportive air and sea power. But our European and Asian allies were asked to contribute the bulk of local conventional ground capabilities, which would be backed by U.S. military assistance. America's alliance structure would, of course, continue to permit the basing of U.S. nuclear systems abroad until intercontinental-range delivery systems became more widely available.

On the other hand, President Eisenhower did not wish to maintain conventional forces capable of fighting a large-scale ground war in either Europe or Asia, or even capable of coping with multiple conflicts of smaller scale.[10] Yet the President and his advisers doubted that the United States could, in fact, rely on its allies to contribute substantial levels of ground forces. Thus, to compensate for anticipated cuts in U.S. conventional strength, the administration's basic defense policy from the outset called for reliance on *tactical* nuclear weapons as well as strategic nuclear forces.[11] Selective retaliation by localized nuclear forces was to supplement massive retaliation by strategic forces.

Before the end of the administration's first term, however, the growth of Soviet strategic power threatened to undermine the credibility of the massive retaliation policy. Not only were our European allies vulnerable to nuclear attacks, but the United States itself could no longer be certain of avoiding catastrophic damage from Soviet nuclear forces—even if it struck first in an attempt to destroy Soviet delivery systems. The President and Secretary Dulles became increasingly aware that any use of nuclear weapons by either side could lead to full-scale thermonuclear war with devastating worldwide consequences. Despite the obvious vulnerability of the United States to Soviet attack, the Eisenhower administration did not renounce its

10. See Dwight D. Eisenhower, *The White House Years: Mandate for Change, 1953–1956* (Doubleday, 1963), pp. 452–54.

11. Although many commentators have suggested that it was not until the fall of 1957 that the administration first seriously considered tactical nuclear weapons, such weapons were, in fact, basic to the New Look concept. Indeed, six weeks before Dulles's speech to the Council on Foreign Relations, Admiral Arthur Radford had already alluded to this policy element in his speech to the National Press Club (see note 7). Dulles explicitly referred to technological advances permitting battlefield use of nuclear weapons on March 15, 1955. (*New York Times*, March 16, 1955.)

nuclear-oriented defense policy or modify its basic program. Official pronouncements and arms procurements continued to stress tactical and strategic nuclear weapons as a less costly alternative to larger conventional forces.

Notwithstanding this reaffirmation of the New Look defense approach, administration leaders faced the uncomfortable question of how the United States might avert nuclear war while continuing to rely on the threat of its nuclear power to contain Communism. The resolution of this dilemma was found in the strategy of "brinkmanship," most clearly and controversially espoused by Secretary Dulles but supported by President Eisenhower as well.[12] Under this strategy, the United States made clear its resolve to initiate the use of nuclear weapons if necessary to defend the nation's vital interests. The administration believed that its determination to risk *mutual* annihilation, rather than concede to Communist military moves or even diplomatic demands, would deter the Soviet Union—and the Chinese—from initiating aggression or would force them to back down under the fear of nuclear war if they did engage in aggressive acts. At the same time, by denying itself meaningful nonnuclear capabilities and by publicly rejecting the premise that tactical nuclear war or any major conflict involving the United States and the USSR could remain limited, the Eisenhower administration apparently sought to increase the likelihood of escalation in the belief that its nuclear commitment would then become more credible and its policy of deterrence would be strengthened. In this sense, tactical nuclear weapons as well as conventional forces tended to become instruments for bringing U.S. long-range nuclear power into play, and the ultimate burden of deterrence remained with our strategic forces.

The military capabilities acquired by the United States during the Eisenhower years reflected guidelines adopted in 1953 by the National Security Council, which called for the armed services to orient American forces toward nuclear weaponry.[13] Planning shortly began to move in this direction, and in 1955 President Eisenhower formally

12. Thomas Schelling, in *Arms and Influence* (Yale University Press, 1966), elaborated on the theory of brinkmanship in discussing the Eisenhower-Dulles defense policies (pp. 91–109).

13. For a discussion of the guidance report (NSC-162/2), see Seyom Brown, *The Faces of Power: Constancy and Change in United States Foreign Policy from Truman to Johnson* (Columbia University Press, 1968), pp. 72–73.

announced that the U.S. Army was to be organized into smaller, more mobile units with "greater fire power" capable of meeting "the conditions of the atomic battlefield."[14]

By the end of the decade, virtually all army divisions had been reshaped into so-called pentomic divisions, which were trained and equipped for nuclear conflict. In addition, battlefield nuclear systems, including nuclear artillery and missiles, had been introduced into U.S. forces in Europe and Asia, and the Atomic Energy Act had been amended to permit nuclear-sharing arrangements with our NATO allies. Reflecting these capabilities, NATO planning called for the early use of nuclear weapons under the "trip wire" strategy, which meant that even a low-level conventional conflict in Europe would trigger a nuclear response. U.S. tactical aircraft forces deployed in Western Europe, the Far East, and at home were primarily designed for nuclear contingencies; naval forces carried a variety of nuclear systems, and carrier-based planes were given strategic as well as tactical nuclear missions.

The character of defense budgets under the Eisenhower administration can, in principle, be used to demonstrate the emphasis placed on nuclear weapons. Owing to the lack of a program-oriented approach, it is difficult to isolate the percentage of U.S. defense spending attributable to nuclear forces during the years 1953–60. As an approximate figure, expenditures for strategic capabilities—excluding carriers but including B-47 and B-52 bombers, air-defense and warning systems, and strategic missile efforts—probably averaged $35 billion annually over this period—almost 50 percent of total yearly defense spending.[15] Attempts to allocate the remaining funds are highly speculative, since most nonstrategic air, naval, and ground units were capable of fighting in a conventional as well as a nuclear mode. But the procure-

14. "Annual Budget Message to Congress: Fiscal Year 1956, January 17, 1955," *Public Papers of the Presidents of the United States: Dwight D. Eisenhower, 1955* (1956), p. 112. In his "Atoms for Peace" speech before the U.N. General Assembly on December 8, 1953, the President remarked that atomic weapons have "virtually achieved conventional status within our armed services." (*Vital Speeches*, vol. 20 [January 1, 1954], p. 163.)

15. Author's estimate (in 1974 dollars), based on data obtained from congressional hearings during the years 1956–60 and including indirect and support costs as well as direct costs for research, development, and procurement. The estimate is consistent with that given in Edward R. Fried and others, *Setting National Priorities: The 1974 Budget* (Brookings Institution, 1973), p. 301, which puts annual direct investment costs for strategic forces during this period at $15 billion (in 1974 dollars).

ment of nonnuclear weapons and materiel was held to a minimum, and it seems reasonable to estimate that more than half of the budget for general purpose forces was nuclear-related.

In sum, military planning under the New Look—constrained by budgetary pressure and nuclear air power priorities—yielded a U.S. military posture with neither the plans nor the capacity for coping with even moderately large nonnuclear conflicts. Within a few years after the administration entered office, conventional equipment was in serious need of modernization, nonnuclear ordnance was in short supply, and logistics support for sustained conventional campaigns was inadequate. Many U.S. tactical aircraft deployed in Europe and Asia even lacked conventional bombs and bomb racks. In addition, airlift and sea-transport capabilities were gradually reduced to the point where U.S. forces abroad could not be rapidly reinforced or effectively shifted between theaters. U.S. forces were not restricted to nuclear responses alone, however, and the sheer size of U.S. land, sea, and air capabilities provided usable nonnuclear options. Nevertheless, the decline in U.S. conventional capabilities was such that it would have been difficult to avoid using nuclear weapons in any conflict involving more than a few divisions and virtually impossible to counter relatively small simultaneous attacks in Europe and Asia with nonnuclear means.[16]

Crises and Conflicts

Early in his second term, President Eisenhower concluded that tactical nuclear weapons had become "an almost routine part of our equipment" and acknowledged that the United States would almost be required to use these systems in an Asian crisis "the way our forces are organized in that area."[17] During the Berlin crisis later in the decade, Defense Secretary Neil H. McElroy affirmed that any limited conflict larger than the Quemoy or Lebanon incidents would lead to

16. For an analysis of the inadequacy of Eisenhower's conventional force capability, see Alain C. Enthoven and K. Wayne Smith, *How Much Is Enough? Shaping the Defense Program 1961–1969* (Harper and Row, 1971), pp. 120–21; Morton H. Halperin, *Defense Strategies for the Seventies* (Little, Brown, 1971), p. 109; and Robert E. Osgood, *NATO: The Entangling Alliance* (University of Chicago Press, 1961), p. 118.

17. "The President's News Conference of January 23, 1957," *Public Papers of the Presidents of the United States: Dwight D. Eisenhower, 1957* (1958), pp. 82–83.

the use of tactical nuclear weapons and in all likelihood to general war.[18]

Nuclear weapons were not used by the Eisenhower administration in Asia or Europe, but the administration's defense policy and acquired military capabilities nonetheless influenced U.S. behavior in crisis situations. A comprehensive and careful analysis of all the factors at work in the cause and conduct of the many crises faced by the United States during the Eisenhower years is beyond the scope of this investigation. On the other hand, a brief examination of the administration's actions and attitudes in these circumstances may shed light on such central issues as the propensity of U.S. leaders to consider using nuclear weapons or to threaten their use, the degree to which the nuclear character of America's defense forces may have shaped decisions in times of tension, and the effectiveness of U.S. defense policy in deterring and managing crises.

EARLY TESTS

At the outset, it might be noted that, to President Eisenhower and a number of his advisers, the lesson of Korea appeared to confirm at an early stage the validity of a defense policy that avoided the need to invest resources in preparing for conventional land wars by relying on nuclear power. In May 1953, President Eisenhower indirectly let Chinese leaders know of his willingness to resort to the use of nuclear weapons against Chinese military bases if the Korean truce negotiations broke down. As the President put it: "We intended to move decisively without inhibition in our use of weapons. . . . In India and in the Formosa Straits area, and at the truce negotiations at Panmunjom, we dropped the word, discreetly, of our intention. We felt quite sure it would reach Soviet and Chinese Communist ears."[19] While conclusive evidence cannot be produced, it is generally agreed that the threat of a possible U.S. nuclear strike was certainly an important factor in reaching a settlement in Korea. In any event, Secretary Dulles seemed convinced that U.S. strategic power was instrumental in this regard, and President Eisenhower observed that the prospects for negotia-

18. See *Missile and Space Activities*, Hearings before the Preparedness Investigating Subcommittee of the Senate Committee on Armed Services, 86 Cong. 2 sess. (1959), pp. 34–42.

19. Eisenhower, *Mandate for Change*, p. 181.

tion improved soon after the United States transmitted its veiled threat.[20]

The administration's reactions in a number of subsequent situations, on the other hand, illustrated the limits of its nuclear-oriented policy and supported the official contention that massive retaliation was not applicable in all instances. In April 1954, for example, President Eisenhower rejected Admiral Arthur Radford's suggestion to aid the French in their defense of Dien Bien Phu through the use of air power, possibly including nuclear weapons. Although Eisenhower and Dulles had issued warnings that the United States might take such action if Peking expanded its military role in Indochina, the President concluded that Radford's plan would be militarily questionable and politically inappropriate.[21] Deputy Under Secretary of State Robert Murphy, addressing the Air Force Association on August 20, 1954, observed that the fact that our enormous military capacity was not brought directly to bear in Indochina or Korea "in no way derogates from the validity of the [massive retaliation] strategy. On the contrary, it indicates the compunction with which it will be used."[22]

Faced with the Hungarian uprising in 1956, the administration was unwilling to initiate military action in Eastern Europe, having concluded that our interests were not directly challenged and that the risk of nuclear war with the Soviet Union would be too great. American spokesmen refrained from hinting at the possibility of military intervention of any type and went to great lengths to ensure that Soviet leaders would not misinterpret American intentions and take actions that could trigger a general war. Despite Khrushchev's missile threats against America's allies, the risk of conflict with the Soviet Union over the Suez crisis of that same year was not an issue for the United States, in large measure because Washington and Moscow had parallel purposes.

20. Dulles made this point in his address before the Council on Foreign Relations on January 12, 1954, and Eisenhower later recalled concluding that "it was clear that we would have to use atomic weapons" in case of a renewed conventional ground attack in Korea. (Mandate for Change, p. 180.)

21. See Eisenhower, Mandate for Change, pp. 340–73. This issue was also discussed in Roscoe Drummond and Gaston Coblentz, Duel at the Brink: John Foster Dulles' Command of American Power (Doubleday, 1960), p. 118.

22. Robert Murphy, "The Interrelationship of Military Power and Foreign Policy," Department of State Bulletin, vol. 31 (August 30, 1954), p. 293.

When American forces landed in Lebanon in 1958, they encountered no local opposition, and the risk of a wider war through
possible Soviet involvement was remote. In any event, U.S. leaders
seemed determined to avoid any display of nuclear weapons, going so
far as to prohibit American troops from landing with a nuclear-capable
Honest John rocket. President Eisenhower later claimed that this
action "demonstrated the ability of the United States to react swiftly
with conventional armed forces to meet small-scale, or 'brush fire'
situations," but expressed concern that, if a military conflict had
broken out, the United States might not have been able to cope with
the situation by using conventional forces without detracting from its
capabilities to handle other conflicts.[23]

The overall thrust of the administration's behavior in these circumstances showed the flexibility of its defense policy, reflected an
awareness of the practical limits of a massive retaliation strategy, and
dispelled fears that U.S. leaders might be unduly prone to use nuclear
weapons. But these events did not represent serious tests of the administration's policy. Either U.S. security interests were not directly
jeopardized or the actual use of U.S. military forces was not germane.
In the offshore islands and Berlin crises, on the other hand, vital U.S.
interests were judged to be at stake, direct challenges from China or
the Soviet Union were involved, and nuclear force played a more
relevant role.

OFFSHORE ISLANDS CRISIS

For six months President Eisenhower chose to pursue diplomatic
routes in dealing with Peking's political threats against Taiwan and
limited military actions against Quemoy that had begun in the fall of
1954. In March of the following year, however, President Eisenhower's
position on the use of U.S. military force began to change, and the
possible use of nuclear weapons entered the picture. Convinced that the
danger of Chinese military aggression was real, Secretary Dulles advised
the President that nuclear weapons would have to be used against
Chinese mainland airfields if the United States chose to defend Quemoy
and Matsu. President Eisenhower agreed with Dulles.[24] Within a week,
this judgment was made public. At a press conference, Secretary Dulles

23. Dwight D. Eisenhower, *The White House Years: Waging Peace, 1956–1961*
(Doubleday, 1965), p. 290.
24. See Eisenhower, *Mandate for Change,* pp. 476–77.

spoke of the U.S. land- and sea-based strategic striking power that could be brought to bear in the Far East and implied that tactical nuclear weapons might be used in the event of general war in the area.[25] Commenting the following day on Dulles's remarks, President Eisenhower explained that he saw no reason why tactical nuclear weapons should not be used "on strictly military targets and for strictly military purposes . . . exactly as you would use a bullet or anything else."[26]

The President later explained that he hoped a public allusion to nuclear options "would have some effect in persuading the Chinese of the strength of our determination."[27] Whether the President would have been prepared to actually authorize nuclear strikes in response to Chinese attacks against Taiwan or attempts to move against the islands is unknown. Although he felt strongly that the USSR would not intervene if the United States were to use military force against China, he also appreciated the risks associated with such a move.[28] As it happened, on April 2, 1955, Chou En-lai stated that China was not going to war against the United States, and on May 22 a cease-fire was instituted.

Many considerations undoubtedly influenced the Chinese decision to defuse the crisis, and Peking may have had only limited objectives at the outset. Nonetheless, given the chronology of events, it seems plausible that Chinese leaders were deterred in part from launching a military invasion in the Taiwan Strait by the desire to avoid a direct confrontation with the United States that might have led to the use of nuclear weapons against them. Public references to this possibility by the President and other officials may have had the intended effect of reminding Peking of the dangers inherent in any military conflict with the United States. Secretary Dulles seemed convinced that the threat of U.S. strategic retaliation was a crucial factor in settling the first Taiwan crisis and later referred to this episode in an attempt to highlight the success of brinkmanship tactics.[29]

The renewal of the offshore islands crisis in 1958 posed a more

25. John Foster Dulles, "Defense Commitments in Far East and Southeast Asia," *Department of State Bulletin*, vol. 32 (March 28, 1955), pp. 526–27.
26. "The President's News Conference of March 16, 1955," *Public Papers, 1955,* p. 332.
27. Eisenhower, *Mandate for Change*, p. 477.
28. See ibid., pp. 464, 471.
29. James Shepley, "How Dulles Averted War," *Life*, January 16, 1956, pp. 70–80.

serious problem. With the Kremlin on the crest of its Sputnik success, the President was concerned that Peking might be motivated to take serious military action in the belief that the United States would be deterred by the prospect of nuclear war; more important, he feared that Soviet leaders might conclude that they could exploit the "missile gap" if the United States showed a lack of resolve. President Eisenhower later claimed that, although he had not doubted the "total superiority" of the United States when the Chinese began their military buildup in August 1958, the USSR's improved strategic position had made it less likely that any large-scale conflict would remain limited and not result in general war.[30]

Although President Eisenhower and Secretary Dulles were committed to use U.S. military force if necessary to defend Quemoy against Chinese invasion or to prevent Chinese air attacks against Taiwan and the islands, they sought to reduce the risk of armed conflict and to avoid situations that could involve the actual use of nuclear weapons. To be sure, in response to heavy shelling and a Chinese blockade of Quemoy, the President had ordered the Seventh Fleet into position and had augmented U.S. air defenses on Taiwan, but great care was taken to preclude direct clashes with Chinese ships during the maneuvering that took place as U.S. ships escorted Taiwanese convoys.

Despite the effort to contain the crisis through limited military actions, however, the option of using nuclear weapons remained prominent in the administration's deliberations. Contingency plans were made for possible nuclear war, in part because some military officials questioned whether the United States could avoid the early use of nuclear arms in the event of a major military clash, since stocks of conventional weapons in the area were inadequate. Furthermore, during this resurgence of trouble in the offshore islands, the Kremlin implied that any nuclear strikes against China would be met by Soviet nuclear retaliation against the United States.[31] Fearing escalation and

---

30. Eisenhower, Waging Peace, pp. 293–95.

31. See Jonathan T. Howe, Multicrises: Sea Power and Global Politics in the Missile Age (MIT Press, 1971), p. 220. For a fuller discussion of possible Soviet motives and the timing of the Kremlin's statements, see Tang Tsou, The Embroilment over Quemoy: Mao, Chiang and Dulles, International Study Paper no. 2 (Institute of International Studies, University of Utah, 1959); Alice Langley Hsieh, Communist China's Strategy in the Nuclear Era (RAND Corporation, 1962); and Morton Halperin, China and Nuclear Proliferation (University of Chicago Center for Policy Study, 1966).

concerned about public reaction, President Eisenhower wanted to avoid the decision to use nuclear weapons. But both the President and Dulles hoped that, if the Chinese could be made to believe that the United States *might* use nuclear weapons in the event of military aggression, "the situation might quiet down, as in 1955."[32] Whether or not it was deliberately meant to convey a threat, the deployment of nuclear-capable howitzers on Quemoy may have reminded Peking of the possibility of nuclear actions by the United States.[33]

The second offshore islands crisis never reached a point of intensity that forced the Eisenhower administration to face an operational decision to use nuclear weapons. Once the United States had taken a firm stand and the USSR had refused to give Peking specific support, the Chinese avoided actions that might have resulted in U.S. retaliation and agreed to a cease-fire. It is impossible to judge whether the President would have actually used nuclear arms if the United States had attacked Chinese facilities. On the other hand, from Peking's perspective, the massive retaliation policy, although not used as a direct threat during the crisis, was apparently taken quite seriously—despite China's public denigration of nuclear power. The buildup of U.S. military strength in the area, followed by the landing of American forces on Quemoy, drove home to Chinese leaders that the United States was determined to defend the island. Obviously, the possible use of nuclear weapons by the United States was not the only important factor contributing to China's decision, but the risk of U.S. military intervention leading to nuclear escalation is viewed by many analysts as having been an important consideration in deterring Peking from making major military moves.[34]

BERLIN DANGERS

As the Quemoy situation was coming under control, a serious challenge to the Eisenhower administration was surfacing in Berlin—an area of far more importance to the United States than the Taiwan Strait. Not only were the stakes larger, but, because the Soviet Union was directly involved, nuclear risks were potentially higher.

---

32. Eisenhower, *Waging Peace*, p. 692.

33. The howitzers were conspicuously deployed on the islands, and the possibility that naval atomic capability might be used was widely publicized. See Howe, *Multicrises*, pp. 161–282.

34. See, for example, Tsou, *The Embroilment over Quemoy;* and Halperin, *China and Nuclear Proliferation.*

On November 27, 1958, Khrushchev demanded that the allied occupation of Berlin be terminated within six months—an ultimatum that President Eisenhower and Secretary Dulles feared could possibly lead to a clash of military forces. The situation became more serious when Khrushchev followed his demarche with a series of nuclear boasts often tied to the Berlin issue. By early 1959, Soviet medium-range ballistic missiles were already targeted against Western Europe, and the USSR was expected to begin deployment of intercontinental missiles within the year. To the United States and its allies, therefore, it looked as if Moscow might be trying to use its space rocket and military missile successes as diplomatic levers. But President Eisenhower seemed determined to show Kremlin leaders that they could not expect to profit from Sputnik and that neither the United States nor its NATO allies would be intimidated by missile claims and threats.[35]

When the Berlin crisis erupted, President Eisenhower conceded that the USSR's apparent lead in missilery gave it a degree of political and military advantage, but he judged overall U.S. strategic capabilities to be adequate for deterrence. Nonetheless, the President acknowledged that nuclear war was possible and that the United States would suffer tens of millions of fatalities in the event of a full-scale war over Berlin. Furthermore, he admitted publicly that the use of nuclear weapons to defend Berlin could not "free anything" and would be self-defeating.[36] Thus, President Eisenhower visualized vast destruction in Europe, as well as in Berlin itself, as the potential outcome of nuclear war. Even if the use of nuclear weapons were limited to tactical strikes against military targets, the President understood that strategic war would almost surely follow. "If resort to arms should become necessary, our troops in Berlin would be quickly overrun," he admitted, "and the conflict would almost inevitably be global war."[37] Throughout the crisis, therefore, President Eisenhower attempted to give Khrushchev room to maneuver and sought to reduce the chance of a major military conflict. The President dealt with the Kremlin

35. See Eisenhower, *Waging Peace*, pp. 338–39, for a discussion of the early phase of the Berlin crisis. Dulles's views are discussed in Drummond and Coblentz, *Duel at the Brink*, pp. 208–9.

36. "The President's News Conference of March 11, 1959," *Public Papers of the Presidents of the United States: Dwight D. Eisenhower, 1959* (1960), p. 245.

37. Eisenhower, *Waging Peace*, note on p. 336.

diplomatically—by advocating talks between foreign ministers and by meeting with Khrushchev at Camp David—and only reluctantly agreed to send U.S. convoys down the autobahn as a symbolic gesture of our resolve to defend Berlin.

Nonetheless, while seeking ways to prevent an armed clash over Berlin and to remain flexible on political settlements, President Eisenhower appeared willing to play a war of nerves with Khrushchev on the assumption that Soviet leaders would back down if the United States took a strong stance and stressed nuclear dangers. On March 16, 1959, the President suggested in a major address that Soviet leaders were well aware of the consequences of worldwide nuclear war and would therefore exercise restraint.[38] The President may have concluded that his emphasis on the possibility of nuclear war would be interpreted as a threat and would force the Soviet Union to retreat. Furthermore, as if to signal the USSR that any military conflict would in fact involve a serious risk of nuclear escalation, Eisenhower reiterated the policy that the United States would not fight a ground war in Europe and reaffirmed official plans to reduce military manpower levels.[39] Finally, speaking to the Kremlin as well as to the American people and their allies, the President documented in great detail the destructive power of U.S. strategic forces, while attempting to downplay the significance of Soviet progress in intercontinental ballistic missiles (ICBMs). Again, it is unclear whether President Eisenhower was actually prepared to resort to the use of nuclear arms if the military situation had warranted it. In discussing the Berlin crisis later, however, the President recalled concluding at the time:

Possibly we were risking the very fate of civilization on the premise that the Soviets would back down from the deadline. . . . Yet this . . . was not really gambling, for if we were not willing to take this risk, we would be certain to lose.[40]

The Kremlin withdrew its six-month deadline on March 19, 1959, and accepted the proposal for a foreign ministers' conference. Although many factors were involved, the timing of Moscow's decision suggests

38. "Radio and TV report to the American people, March 16, 1959," *Public Papers, 1959,* p. 276.

39. In a press conference, March 11, 1959, Eisenhower declared that the United States had no intention of fighting a ground war in Europe. In *Waging Peace,* he explained how he went ahead with planned reductions in conventional forces despite the mounting pressure over Berlin (p. 336).

40. Ibid., p. 342.

that the President's references to nuclear war, coupled with the firm Western stance, may have helped persuade Khrushchev to defuse the situation.[41] But the crisis remained alive throughout the remainder of 1959 as Kremlin leaders continued their strategy of indirect political intimidation by playing on the West's missile gap fears—a strategy that reached a surprising level of intensity in June of that year when Khrushchev linked a hard diplomatic position on Berlin with threats that Soviet rockets would "fly automatically" if the United States tried to defend Berlin with force.[42]

After Khrushchev and Eisenhower had met at Camp David in the fall of 1959 and agreed to hold a four-power summit meeting the following May, the Soviet leader increased his claims of ICBM strength in what appeared to be an attempt to place the USSR in a strong negotiating position for the forthcoming conference. But Khrushchev scuttled the summit—ostensibly because of the U-2 incident,[43] which may indeed have weakened the Soviet Union's bargaining position by undercutting the political power of Sputnik diplomacy—and diminished the pressure on Berlin. As it turned out, therefore, President Eisenhower not only avoided the necessity of making a nuclear weapon decision but was never forced to face the issue of making concessions regarding Berlin at the negotiating table.[44]

Strategic Forces and Doctrine

The basic features of the U.S.-Soviet strategic relationship originated during the Eisenhower administration. In both the United States and the USSR, weapon technology advanced dramatically between 1953 and 1960, progressing from atomic arsenals, propeller-driven aircraft, and medium-range jet bombers to long-range jet bombers and ballistic missiles capable of carrying thermonuclear bombs. In fact, the ICBM

41. See Arnold Horelick and Myron Rush, *Strategic Power and Soviet Foreign Policy* (University of Chicago Press, 1966), pp. 119–23.

42. Averell Harriman, "My Alarming Interview with Khrushchev," *Life*, July 13, 1959, p. 33. The interview took place in late June during the recess of the meeting of the Western foreign ministers in Geneva.

43. In May 1960, the U-2 flown by Francis Gary Powers was shot down over Soviet territory.

44. See Seyom Brown, *The Faces of Power*, pp. 154–56; and Horelick and Rush, *Strategic Power and Soviet Foreign Policy*, pp. 122–23.

and submarine-launched ballistic missile (SLBM) systems currently in existence and under development are, essentially, improved versions of missiles designed during the late 1950s, and many bombers produced in that period are still operational. By the time the Eisenhower administration left office, strategic doctrines reflecting a growing awareness of the implications of the new technologies for defense, deterrence, and diplomacy had begun to shape America's security policies.

From Superiority to Stalemate

During the early months of the Eisenhower administration, it was widely believed that the Soviet Union could not challenge U.S. superiority in atomic bombs and thermonuclear weapons for at least five years or match America's overwhelming advantage in the means of delivering these weapons. At that time, the Strategic Air Command's (SAC's) growing fleet of B-47 jet bombers numbered over 500 and could reach Soviet targets from a network of overseas bases, U.S. carrier aircraft constituted an atomic threat to the Soviet homeland, and prototypes of the intercontinental-range B-52 had already been built.

The USSR's force, on the other hand, consisted of a few hundred medium-range aircraft, comparable to the older U.S. propeller-driven B-29 bombers, which could threaten Western Europe but not seriously endanger the continental United States.[45] In addition, the size and explosive power of the USSR's atomic arsenal was vastly inferior to the stockpile available to the United States. But the strategic environment changed rather abruptly when the Soviet Union unexpectedly exploded a thermonuclear device in August 1953. Within a year, suspicions that the USSR might be developing advanced aircraft were verified when prototype intercontinental jet bombers were displayed in Moscow in 1954 in the May Day parade.

One obvious reaction to the growth of Soviet long-range striking power was to seek to protect the United States. Although official and unofficial studies had begun to question whether protection against

45. A "one-way" mission with these vintage aircraft against the United States was, of course, possible but was considered unlikely. For a discussion of this issue and other nuclear policy issues during Eisenhower's first term, see Quester, *Nuclear Diplomacy*, pp. 89–139.

nuclear strikes could actually be achieved, when the Eisenhower administration entered office the issue of whether to stress offense or defense had not been resolved in civilian or military policymaking circles.[46] In view of the Soviet Union's massive air-defense buildup, it seemed to many that strengthening defenses in an attempt to reduce the vulnerability of the United States to nuclear attack would offer psychological reassurance to the American people. Military planners, strategic experts, and the President himself saw defensive deployments as a means of maintaining strategic supremacy and preserving the credibility of the nation's deterrent policy. For these and other reasons, in early 1954 the Eisenhower administration decided to further expand the continental defense system, and within the next few years the United States deployed an integrated network of missile and aircraft interceptors, began to install the distant early warning (DEW) line, and initiated development of the semi-automatic ground environment warning and control system (SAGE).

Nonetheless, offensive force decisions remained the focal point of the administration's strategic policies throughout the decade. As indicated earlier, reliance on long-range strike capabilities was central to Eisenhower's New Look policy, which rested heavily on U.S. air power. But the emphasis on offensive power also stemmed from a growing awareness on the part of the President and his advisers that a fully effective defense of the United States against nuclear attack was neither technically possible nor economically feasible. Shortly after the initial Soviet thermonuclear test, President Eisenhower candidly informed the American people that "our former unique physical security has almost totally disappeared before the long-range bomber and the destructive power of a single bomb."[47] As the USSR further increased its intercontinental delivery capabilities, the President came to realize that U.S. invulnerability could no longer be assured.[48] This conclusion was reinforced by a comprehensive study of U.S. air-defense possibilities completed by the

46. For early analyses of strategies for the nuclear age, see *Survival in the Air Age;* and Quester, *Nuclear Diplomacy.*

47. "Address at the Sixth National Assembly of the United Church Women, Atlantic City, New Jersey, October 6, 1953," *Public Papers of the Presidents of the United States: Dwight D. Eisenhower, 1953* (1954), p. 635.

48. As early as 1950, it might be noted, Dulles had come to a similar conclusion. See Drummond and Coblentz, *Duel at the Brink,* pp. 235–36.

so-called Killian Committee in early 1955.[49] Toward the end of the administration's first term, when the Soviet threat began to shift from bombers to missiles, deterrence through the threat of reprisal became more widely accepted as the basic U.S. strategic doctrine.

As might be expected, the idea of attempting to cripple the Soviet Union's growing strategic capability through a "preventive" strike by SAC soon surfaced within the bureaucracy. But even before discussions of such a strike reached policymaking levels, it was strongly repudiated by President Eisenhower and Secretary Dulles. In November 1954, a few months after the President had publicly dismissed serious consideration of this option, Dulles proclaimed that "any idea of preventive war was wholly out of the question as far as the United States was concerned."[50] It seems certain that moral factors kept U.S. leaders from entertaining the possibility of a preventive strike; such a move would have been antithetical to the traditional American policy of eschewing surprise attack. But practical considerations undoubtedly influenced the decision as well—a U.S. counterforce strike could not be assured of completely eliminating the USSR's capability to retaliate with nuclear weapons. Even if Soviet long-range delivery capabilities could be destroyed, the United States could not be confident of preventing the USSR from inflicting substantial damage on Western Europe with its medium-range forces.

Since perfect protection was unattainable and preventive war was out of the question, the Eisenhower administration turned its attention to strengthening U.S. strategic delivery capabilities. Both the President and Secretary Dulles appreciated the importance of strategic superiority in supporting U.S. commitments, containing the Soviet Union, and offsetting the conventional forces of the Communist bloc. The New Look defense program relied heavily on B-52 intercontinental-range bombers entering the force to supplement the expanding force of B-47 medium-range aircraft. Development of the B-52 had begun under President Truman, but the Eisenhower administration authorized procurement as one of its earliest actions and announced its decision

---

49. The Killian Committee, a group of distinguished engineers and scientists, was set up by the National Security Council to reexamine U.S. strategic weapons programs.

50. *New York Times,* November 10, 1954. For a discussion of this question, see George E. Lowe, *The Age of Deterrence* (Little, Brown, 1964), p. 60.

in October 1953—only two months after the USSR's thermonuclear test. This timing was motivated by the desire to reaffirm America's strategic advantage.

BOMBER GAP

The USSR's surprising progress in acquiring the H-bomb had already called into question the premise that the United States could construct a credible policy on the threat of massive retaliation. Futhermore, the foundation of the Eisenhower administration's defense doctrine, as suggested earlier, was significantly shaken by indications that the Soviet Union had begun to produce a sophisticated strategic bomber fleet—indications that were confirmed by the famous "fly-by" of Soviet long-range jet bombers during the Moscow Aviation Day ceremonies in July 1955. This dramatic evidence of operational Soviet strategic bombers, and the fear that the Kremlin was determined to deprive the United States of its superior position, set off a short but intense "bomber gap" debate in the United States. Allen Dulles, then director of the Central Intelligence Agency (CIA), explained that intelligence analysts in the mid-1950s had no choice but to project the future USSR bomber buildup "on the basis of existing production rates and expected expansion of industrial capacity" in the USSR, since there was evidence at that time that the Soviet Union "intended to translate [its] capability into an actual program."[51] Estimates made by Air Force intelligence were substantially more pessimistic than those offered by the CIA. As a result, military spokesmen predicted that the Soviet Union could gain a two-to-one advantage in long-range bombers by the end of the decade, and an influential group of congressmen and journalists urged President Eisenhower to accelerate the B-52 program and to raise authorized force levels.

Advocates of a massive expansion of strategic forces did not simply argue that the United States should forestall an unfavorable gap from developing but claimed that America should maintain a clear position of superiority over the Soviet Union. Such pleas for superiority undoubtedly served the interests of the Air Force and gave Democratic congressmen a prominent issue for the 1956 presidential election. Indeed, these political and bureaucratic motivations became apparent

51. Allen Dulles, *The Craft of Intelligence* (Harper and Row, 1963), pp. 162–63.

during the air power hearings of the Senate Armed Services Committee in the spring of that year.[52]

But the proponents of air power superiority had a persuasive logic on their side as well. In response to the Soviet Union's growing strategic nuclear capability, they argued, it was necessary to seek vastly superior forces capable of providing the United States with the ability to substantially damage, if not to destroy entirely, Soviet strategic weapons before they were launched. Such a counterforce strategy would in turn preserve the credibility of the massive retaliation policy —developed by the Eisenhower administration itself—which rested on the threat that the United States might initiate the use of nuclear weapons in response to nonnuclear aggression. As a less extreme position, it was claimed that superior strategic forces would enable the United States to "prevail" in a strategic exchange—that is, to be able to inflict greater damage on the Soviet Union than the Soviet Union could inflict on the United States, to destroy the bulk of the USSR's nuclear forces, and to retain residual U.S. forces capable of dictating a settlement. The administration had, of course, left itself open for this line of analysis by refusing to approve a large-scale buildup of conventional forces when it appeared that the USSR might negate the U.S. advantage in strategic power.

Notwithstanding the intense attacks on his strategic policies and programs, the President fought to hold to the original B-52 force plans, but finally, when domestic pressure became unbearable, he agreed to expand the rate of long-range bomber production to twenty per month and to increase deployment levels. The rationale behind President Eisenhower's reluctance to accept the Air Force doctrine of superiority could be traced to a new strategic policy that emerged in 1955 and was given official standing early the following year—the policy of strategic "adequacy," or "sufficiency."[53]

52. For background on the bomber gap and the air power debates during 1955–56, see Lowe, *The Age of Deterrence*, pp. 121–43; and Colin S. Gray, " 'Gap' Prediction and America's Defense: Arms Race Behavior in the Eisenhower Years," *Orbis*, Spring 1972, pp. 257–74.

53. In a news conference on March 2, 1955, Eisenhower foreshadowed a revised strategic policy when he said that if you "get enough of a particular type of weapon" it may not be important "to have a lot more of it." (*Public Papers, 1955*, p. 303.) The official guidelines for adequacy were set early in 1956, and the President discussed the concept in a news conference on May 4, 1956. (*Public Papers, 1956*, pp.

Under this policy, it would not be necessary to match the Soviet Union's strategic posture weapon by weapon. Only the adequacy of U.S. deterrent power counted, and this could be provided by a variety of delivery systems—including carrier-based aircraft and medium-range bombers as well as intercontinental vehicles. By this standard, America would remain in a powerful strategic position vis-à-vis the USSR, even if the Soviet Union gained an advantage in long-range bombers. The foundation of the new strategic doctrine, according to one expert, was President Eisenhower's refusal "to make the maintenance of American strategic superiority a continuing requirement of policy."[54]

During the air power debate of 1956, many official spokesmen discussed the controversial sufficiency concept publicly, defending the President's position in the face of attacks by Democratic congressmen who accused the administration of compromising U.S. counterforce capabilities and settling for inferiority in long-range bombers. Defense Secretary Charles E. Wilson, for example, testified that "the quality of our retaliatory force is now becoming increasingly more important than its size," and Admiral Radford, chairman of the Joint Chiefs of Staff, supported this point.[55]

The most comprehensive statement of the new strategy was presented in February 1956 by Donald A. Quarles, secretary of the Air Force, in a speech appropriately entitled "How Much Is Enough?" Quarles, differing with most of his Air Force colleagues, argued that U.S. officials "must make a determination of sufficiency" after reaching a certain point in the buildup of air power and must recognize that the nation needed only to maintain a force capable of inflicting destructive levels of damage on the USSR.[56] In an even more radical departure from traditional Air Force doctrine, Quarles observed that neither

---

463–65.) Strategic adequacy is discussed in Lowe, *The Age of Deterrence*, p. 128; Samuel P. Huntington, *The Common Defense: Strategic Programs in National Politics* (Columbia University Press, 1961), pp. 100–104; and Gray, " 'Gap' Prediction and America's Defense."

54. Huntington, *The Common Defense*, p. 100.

55. *Department of Defense Appropriations for 1956*, Hearings before the Subcommittee of the House Committee on Appropriations, 84 Cong. 1 sess. (1955), p. 9.

56. Donald A. Quarles, "How Much Is Enough?" *Air Force Magazine*, September 1956, p. 51.

the United States nor the USSR could prevent the other side from maintaining the capability to inflict catastrophic damage on its homeland and then explained that such a situation could exist "even if there is a wide disparity between the offensive and defensive strengths of the opposing forces." The thrust of Quarles's remarks was summed up in the following thought:

The buildup of atomic power in the hands of the two opposed alliances of nations makes total war an unthinkable catastrophe for both sides. Neither side can hope by a mere margin of superiority in airplanes or other means of delivery of atomic weapons to escape the catastrophe of such a war. Beyond a certain point, this prospect is not the result of *relative* strength of the two opposed forces. It is the *absolute* power in the hands of each, and . . . the substantial invulnerability of this power to interdiction.[57]

The decision to adopt a policy of adequacy seemed to stem primarily from President Eisenhower's concern that superiority was simply too expensive a strategy to pursue. It had become clear that efforts to maintain superior U.S. forces with a counterforce strike potential would entail expenditures that could reach staggering proportions. Some estimates indicated that an annual SAC budget of as much as $30 billion might be required to support such a strategy.[58] But the prospect of any substantial increase in strategic costs threatened to undercut the administration's overriding objective of keeping defense spending in check and to undermine the entire concept of relying on nuclear power as an economically efficient substitute for maintaining large conventional forces. Aside from the question of cost, the President and many U.S. military officials had slowly become resigned to a strategic stalemate between the United States and the USSR as an inevitable outcome of military technology.

It should be emphasized that, in rejecting a course of clear superiority, the Eisenhower administration also rejected finite, or minimum, deterrence—a strategy advocated by the Army and the Navy that was diametrically opposed to the Air Force policy of superiority. Finite deterrence proponents claimed that U.S. strategic forces should be geared only to deter Soviet nuclear attacks, and that for this purpose a small force capable of withstanding Soviet strikes and inflicting large-scale damage in retaliation would suffice. Navy preference for this

57. Ibid., p. 52.
58. Such estimates were attributed to "high officers including President Eisenhower," in *Newsweek*, May 9, 1960, p. 27.

policy was primarily dictated by the desire to emphasize the value of
sea-based forces, including carriers and eventually the Polaris system.
The Army's motives, shared in part by the Navy, were tied to the
assumption that U.S. conventional capabilities must be drastically expanded in an era of nuclear stalemate. But President Eisenhower,
Secretary Dulles, and Admiral Radford were not prepared to reduce
strategic forces only to shift greater resources into programs designed
to improve U.S. nonnuclear capabilities. Instead, the administration
chose the brinkmanship policy of relying on the threat of nuclear
escalation to deter a wide range of conflicts. For this purpose, a powerful strategic force was still required, although massive superiority was
not.

Paradoxical as it may seem, the President saw no conflict between
acknowledging a nuclear stalemate on the strategic level and adher-
ing to the nuclear-oriented New Look defense plan. Even as Secretary
Quarles offered his analysis of mutual deterrence and the destructiveness of nuclear war, he reaffirmed the massive retaliation policy by
declaring that "the capabilities which now make total war an unacceptable proposition can also make limited aggression unacceptable"
and by recommending that the "full force" of U.S. nuclear power be used
to counter smaller-scale aggression.[59]

Thus, at the end of the Eisenhower administration's first term in
office, the United States was steering a course midway between the
options of strategic superiority and minimum deterrence while maintaining the nuclear-oriented New Look defense policy. This strategy
did not merely reflect a doctrinal choice but represented a bureaucratic
compromise between those who argued that America had too much
strategic power and those who argued that it had too little. The administration's concept of strategic adequacy was, to be sure, less a precise
set of force-planning criteria than a fairly broad doctrine that placed
upper and lower limits on the size and character of America's nuclear
posture. But the President's approach influenced the basic direction of
the U.S. reaction to the bomber gap of the mid-1950s and remained
relatively unchanged throughout the administration's second term—
forming the framework for decisions on U.S. ballistic missiles and
influencing the response to Sputnik and the missile gap of the late
1950s.

59. Quarles, "How Much Is Enough?" p. 52.

The Missile Gap and Force Vulnerability

Strategic arms issues during President Eisenhower's second term centered on missiles rather than bombers and reflected a sharpened debate over the requirements of deterrence. Signs of a shift to a new set of strategic policy concerns first appeared when U.S. projections of Soviet bomber capabilities began to be revised downward in late 1956 and early 1957. Although the Soviet Union was still credited with a large fleet of medium-range bombers, it was now claimed that the USSR would probably build only a few hundred intercontinental-range Bear and Bison aircraft. In fact, in a surprising reversal of relative strengths, it appeared certain that the United States would gain superiority in this category of arms within a few years as a consequence of the sizable B-52 program that had been authorized. This optimistic forecast regarding the U.S.-Soviet bomber balance was due in large part to advances in intelligence-gathering technology—specifically the U-2 system, which had been flying operational missions since mid-1956. High altitude photographs of airfields in the USSR had revealed no widespread deployment of long-range bombers, thus reinforcing other indications that Soviet leaders had decided not to undertake a massive bomber production program and providing hard evidence that the bomber gap was not materializing.[60]

But U-2 flights in 1957 yielded less comforting information than the data concerning Soviet bomber programs—they brought back aerial photographs of Soviet ICBM test sites. Since the beginning of the U-2 system, administration officials had been attempting to obtain more complete and credible data on Soviet ballistic missile efforts. Throughout the early 1950s, U.S. intelligence experts received indirect, uncertain, and often conflicting indications that the USSR was developing long-range ballistic missiles capable of carrying nuclear warheads. Before the end of 1955, a U.S. radar station installed in Turkey had detected tests of Soviet intermediate-range ballistic missiles (IRBMs), and deployment of these missile systems targeted against Western Europe was expected to occur shortly. Within a year, preliminary Soviet tests of what appeared to be an intercontinental ballistic missile

60. See Dulles, *Craft of Intelligence*, pp. 151–54; and Gray, "'Gap' Prediction and America's Defense," for background on the U-2 and the demise of the bomber gap. Eisenhower discussed the U-2 reconnaissance program in *Waging Peace*, pp. 543–47.

were identified. However, it was not until a U-2 mission in the spring of 1957 brought back a dramatic photographic display of the USSR's ICBM test facilities at Kapustin Yar and Tyuratam that U.S. officials concluded that the Soviet Union was making rapid progress toward the successful development of an ICBM. On the basis of this information and a series of long-range missile firings during the summer of that year, U.S. officials judged that the USSR had decided to place high priority on strategic missiles rather than produce a large force of long-range bombers.[61]

MISSILE EFFORTS

By mid-1957, of course, the United States itself was engaged in a substantial effort to develop a variety of strategic missile systems.[62] During the late 1940s and early 1950s, U.S. strategic missile efforts were barely being sustained. Although some short-range ballistic rocket and cruise missile projects were pursued, there were no serious programs to develop *long-range* ballistic missiles. A combination of technological uncertainties, bureaucratic inertia, and insufficient appreciation of the doctrine of deterrence kept U.S. strategic policies focused on the goal of producing a large bomber force. Immediately after President Eisenhower assumed office, however, evidence of Soviet ballistic missile activities prompted the new administration to review U.S. programs and to seriously study the possibility of developing an American ICBM. In early 1954, the Strategic Missile Evaluation Committee concluded that ballistic missile technology had reached the point where an ICBM system seemed feasible and recommended that the United States give the highest priority to building one. Stimulated by the committee's recommendations and by studies performed by the RAND Corporation, the Air Force accelerated work on the liquid-fueled Atlas ICBM, and in 1955 the National Security Council officially assigned top national priority to this program.

In early 1955, the Killian Committee had recommended that inter-

61. For more on the U-2 mission in 1957 and U.S. reconnaissance programs during the 1950s, see Philip J. Klass, *Secret Sentries in Space* (Random House, 1971).

62. For a history of U.S. strategic missile programs see Eugene Emme, ed., *History of Rocket Technology: Essays on Research, Development, and Utility* (Wayne State University Press, 1964); Robert L. Perry, "The Ballistic Missile Decisions," AIAA Paper no. 67-838 (American Institute of Aeronautics and Astronautics, 1967; processed); and Herbert York, *Race to Oblivion: A Participant's View of the Arms Race* (Simon and Shuster, 1970).

mediate-range missiles be pursued concurrently with ICBMs. By the end of that year the Air Force had initiated the development of a more advanced ICBM, the Titan, as well as the Thor IRBM planned for deployment in Western Europe. The Army entered the ballistic missile field and began to develop another liquid-fueled IRBM, the Jupiter, which was also to serve as a ship-launched system.[63] At that time, however, the Navy proposed a solid-fueled IRBM for use in submarines, and in late 1956 this program was authorized in the form of a major project to develop the Polaris submarine-launched ballistic missile system. Finally, throughout this period the Air Force conducted research on solid-propellant rockets capable of supporting an intercontinental-range missile—research that led to formal approval of the Minuteman ICBM program in 1958.

U.S. missile development efforts from 1954 through the middle of 1957 were largely motivated by the desire to prevent the USSR from acquiring a lead in the strategic missile field. Although such a rationale may not have been based strictly on military calculations, it did reflect the administration's concern over maintaining the credibility of its defense posture and security commitments. Despite the policy of adequacy, which denied the necessity of matching the USSR in all categories of weapons, President Eisenhower appeared to recognize the political power ICBMs could provide to Kremlin leaders and was reluctant to permit the Soviet Union to gain a monopoly in this new technology. As time passed, moreover, the military benefits of ballistic missiles began to exert a greater influence on U.S. decisions to place high priority on these programs. Military analysts and civilian leaders gradually came to recognize that ballistic missile systems afforded a more reliable deterrent capability than either bombers or cruise missiles, since ballistic missiles could penetrate Soviet air defenses with far greater certainty and could be made less vulnerable to nuclear attack.[64] The latter point was particularly crucial, for the prospect of Soviet long-range missile deployments not only focused attention on the increased vulnerability of the American population to nuclear attack but also highlighted another type of vulnerability—the risk that the U.S. strategic forces could be destroyed by a Soviet first strike.

63. See Michael H. Armacost, *The Politics of Weapons Innovation: The Thor-Jupiter Controversy* (Columbia University Press, 1969).

64. President Eisenhower particularly stressed the Polaris program as providing an "invulnerable retaliatory capability." (*Mandate for Change*, pp. 456–57.)

The potential vulnerability of nuclear delivery systems and its implications for strategic arms programs were not new issues. Academic studies and government reports produced in the late 1940s and early 1950s stressed that deterrence meant more than accumulating large numbers of weapons and that an effective deterrent posture required strategic systems capable of withstanding an initial blow while retaining sufficient penetration capability and destructive power to inflict large-scale damage on an aggressor in retaliation. Within a year after the Eisenhower administration entered office, a RAND Corporation study concluded that SAC's overseas airfields might become vulnerable to Soviet aircraft strikes and recommended that the Air Force shift its emphasis to facilities in the United States, disperse its base structure, and institute new warning and alert procedures.[65]

A second RAND study, completed in 1955 and taking into account the possibility of ballistic missile developments by the USSR, offered a far more significant evaluation of the evolving strategic environment. This analysis made the point that measures designed to protect U.S. forces against Soviet *bomber* attacks would not necessarily be capable of protecting our forces against *missile* attacks. Soviet deployment of medium- and intermediate-range ballistic missiles, it was demonstrated, posed a substantially greater potential threat to U.S. foreign-based B-47 forces than did Russian medium-range bombers. More worrisome to the authors of the study was the fear that Soviet acquisition of long-range ballistic missiles could endanger the survivability of the B-52 force located in the United States. Emphasizing that the DEW-line warning system could not detect ICBMs, RAND analysts calculated that a relatively small number of Soviet ICBMs would be capable of destroying almost all U.S. bomber forces in a surprise attack, unless American leaders undertook a broad range of programs to make our strategic deterrent less vulnerable through concealment, mobility, physical protection, and a ballistic missile warning system.

In short, even before the launching of Sputnik in October 1957 dramatized the USSR's ICBM efforts and highlighted the danger of U.S. force vulnerability, the issue had been identified and the Eisenhower administration had set in motion certain programs to minimize risks. These programs included the development of a ballistic missile

65. See Joseph Kraft, "RAND: Arsenal for Ideas," *Harper's Magazine,* July 1960, pp. 71–73. Kraft summarizes this crucial RAND study, done in 1953, and another done in 1955.

early warning radar system (BMEWS) and other actions to reduce the potential threat to SAC bombers, such as improved alert and basing techniques.

Concern over survivability was also reflected in efforts to reduce the vulnerability of the U.S. ballistic missile forces under development. For example, in the mid-1950s, the Air Force initiated programs to develop well-protected underground—or hardened—launch facilities for the soft, or relatively unprotected, Atlas ICBM; designed a second-model Titan ICBM to be housed in concrete silos; and investigated solid-fueled rocket technology that resulted in the still more survivable Minuteman silo-based system. It was perhaps most significant that the Navy Polaris project was pursued with the specific purpose of providing the United States with an extremely invulnerable retaliatory force. Polaris was judged to be a vastly more effective deterrent than the existing Regulus cruise-missile system, since it would permit underwater launching and would rely on ballistic missiles against which there were no existing defenses.

As implied above, the administration was not totally surprised by the Sputnik launching, since intelligence information had provided evidence of Soviet progress in the missile field. Earlier claims by Kremlin leaders of the success of their long-range missile program, while initially greeted with disbelief, were given credibility when U.S. radars verified Khrushchev's boast of having tested an ICBM in August 1957, two months before the October space feat. Nevertheless, to the administration, Sputnik represented more than a psychological setback for the United States and its allies; it highlighted the technical potential of Soviet rockets and suggested that the USSR might be moving even more rapidly than anticipated toward an operational ICBM capability. National intelligence estimates prepared in late 1957 had in fact been revised to reflect recent Soviet ICBM activities and the Sputnik launch. These estimates, based on Soviet technical capabilities and production potential, showed that the Soviet Union could deploy a small number of ICBMs, perhaps 10, by early 1959, and had the capacity to deploy as many as 100 ICBMs by 1960 and 500 by 1961.[66]

66. For a detailed discussion of intelligence estimates during this period, see Roy Licklider, "The Missile Gap Controversy," *Political Science Quarterly*, vol. 85 (December 1970), pp. 600–15.

THE GAITHER REPORT

Despite the revised estimates of Soviet missile efforts and the political impact of Sputnik, President Eisenhower seemed satisfied that the pace and character of U.S. strategic programs were sufficient to guard America's security. But the orbiting of Sputnik had created the missile gap controversy, which abruptly turned the Eisenhower administration's strategic programs into a prominent public issue as the President's arms plans were attacked from a number of quarters. Beginning immediately after Sputnik and lasting throughout the final three years of the administration's second term, the missile gap controversy far surpassed the earlier one over the bomber gap in its intensity, international significance, and effect on U.S. strategic arms decisions.[67]

The earliest series of criticisms appeared in a top secret report, "Deterrence and Survival in the Nuclear Age," known as the Gaither Report, which was presented to the National Security Council on November 7, 1957, one month after Sputnik. Although the report was not formally declassified until fifteen years later, its substance was leaked to the press almost immediately after it was transmitted to President Eisenhower and became an important element of the public debate. Composed of a number of distinguished nongovernmental experts, the Gaither Committee was originally formed in the spring of 1957 as an advisory group to study the problem of protecting civilian populations in the event of a nuclear attack. But its mission was soon expanded to include an investigation of the deterrent value of U.S. retaliatory forces and of broader questions related to American defense programs.[68] In its report, the Gaither Committee painted a grim picture of the administration's defense posture and recommended increased across-the-board spending for improvements in U.S. defense capabilities, including strengthened conventional forces and enlarged civil defense programs. Particular attention, however, was paid to the potential vulnerability of America's strategic forces—a problem that became the central theme of the committee's report because of the debate stimulated by the Sputnik launch.

67. For the most comprehensive study of this issue, see Edgar M. Bottome, *The Missile Gap: A Study of the Formulation of Military and Political Policy* (Fairleigh Dickenson University Press, 1971).

68. See Morton H. Halperin, "The Gaither Committee and the Policy Process," *World Politics*, April 1961, pp. 360–84.

Expressing serious concern over the state of the U.S.-Soviet nuclear balance and its implications, the committee concluded in its report that "by 1959, the USSR may be able to launch an attack with ICBMs carrying megaton warheads, against which SAC will be almost completely vulnerable under present programs."[69] In order to minimize the risk of having such a situation arise, the committee proposed a series of measures to enhance the survivability of U.S. strategic bombers, including a shortened reaction time, further base dispersion, the protection of SAC bases through active and passive defense, and the deployment of a ballistic missile warning net. Many of these measures were either being undertaken or planned, but the committee apparently believed that a considerably more rapid and expanded effort was required. Some members reportedly thought that the President and his advisers did not fully appreciate the principles of nuclear deterrence and were placing undue importance on the development of a total destruction capability without focusing on the crucial question of second-strike capabilities. In a similar vein, the report recommended that U.S. missile programs be accelerated to provide earlier operational dates, that the authorized number of IRBMs for overseas deployment be increased fourfold from 60 to 240, and that the level of Atlas and Titan ICBM procurement be raised from 80 to 600. The committee justified this expanded program as required "by the prospects of an early Russian ICBM capability," but emphasized the need for acquiring the highly survivable Polaris system as soon as possible and for rapid installation of hardened sites for land-based missiles.[70]

The Gaither Committee's concern about the U.S.-Soviet nuclear balance was widely shared. Following the launching of Sputnik and Khrushchev's "rocket rattling" statements, the question of U.S. force vulnerability and the relative position of Soviet and American strategic missile capabilities dominated the domestic political scene. In 1958, for example, estimates attributed to the Air Force were cited by journalists as a means of demonstrating that the Soviet Union would soon gain a substantial lead in long-range ballistic missiles. These figures, which were considerably higher than the official national estimates, showed that the Soviet Union could have as many as 100 operational ICBMs by the end of 1959, 500 by the end of 1960, and 1,000 by the end of 1961. It was pointed out that, under plans at that

69. Security Resources Panel of the Science Advisory Committee, *Deterrence and Survival in the Nuclear Age* (November 7, 1957), p. 14.
70. Ibid., p. 5.

time, U.S. missile deployments would remain inferior to these Soviet force levels by as much as a six-to-one ratio during the critical period of the early 1960s before the gap would begin to close. Congressional and academic spokesmen repeated this theme and accused the administration of following a policy that not only would result in U.S. numerical inferiority in the missile field but could raise the dangerous possibility of a Soviet "knock-out blow" against our strategic forces. Supporting the thrust of the Gaither Report, these critics called for an acceleration of U.S. missile programs, an increase in the planned force size, and greater emphasis on making U.S. weapons survivable.

Unable to ignore these demands but perhaps also influenced by a reappraisal of U.S. strategic needs after the shock of Sputnik, President Eisenhower requested over $1 billion in supplementary funds in early 1958 to speed up the dispersal of SAC aircraft, place a greater fraction of SAC's bombers on fifteen-minute alert, accelerate and expand ICBM and IRBM programs, commence construction of the BMEWS system, and put still higher priority on the Polaris project. Thus, while rejecting those proposals that would have led to major increases in U.S. defense spending for conventional forces and dismissing a proposal for stepped-up civil defense, the President accepted many of the recommendations of the Gaither Committee. Nevertheless, many outside experts continued to attack the administration's strategic policies, and in the summer of 1958 Congress, on its own initiative, appropriated additional funds for the ICBM and Polaris programs.

The ensuing battle between the administration and the Democrat-controlled Congress over the missile gap was obviously influenced by partisan politics, but many senators with expertise on military matters disagreed strongly on substantive grounds with the President's strategic arms policy. In hearings held by the Senate Preparedness Subcommittee in 1958, in speeches, and in interviews, prominent senators accused the Eisenhower administration of endangering U.S. security by refusing to allocate the resources necessary to maintain a reliable American deterrent and of seeking "economic security at the expense of military security."[71]

Not surprisingly, the sudden public prominence of strategic issues forced administration leaders to explain and defend their policies. In a speech in November 1957 shortly after the Sputnik launching, Presi-

71. See Senator John F. Kennedy's statements in the *Congressional Record*, vol. 104, pt. 14, 85 Cong. 1 sess. (1958), p. 1757.

dent Eisenhower reassured the American people that U.S. military capabilities were more than adequate to protect the nation and its allies. The President said he was convinced "that, although the Soviets are quite likely ahead in some missile and special areas . . . as of today the overall military strength of the free world is distinctly greater than that of the Communist countries."[72] Behind this statement and similar declarations was the obvious concern of President Eisenhower and his advisers that perceived deficiencies in the U.S. nuclear posture might lead to a large-scale expansion of strategic programs to the point of undercutting the administration's goal of keeping defense spending under control. Budgetary considerations thus were important in shaping the administration's programs during its final years in office. In responding to critics throughout the missile gap debate of 1958 and 1959, however, President Eisenhower, Defense Secretary Neil McElroy, and other senior spokesmen justified their strategic policies on technical, military, and doctrinal grounds.

To begin with, administration spokesmen denied that any possible missile gap in the future would create a "deterrent gap." Even if the Soviet Union were to gain an advantage in ballistic missiles, they argued, America's total strategic arsenal—which would consist of over 600 B-52 and 1,400 B-47 bombers by late 1959, and which also included carrier-based aircraft and the Regulus and Snark cruise missiles —would be more than adequate to deter a nuclear attack. President Eisenhower pointed out that Kremlin leaders could not be confident of launching a successful counterforce first strike, because of the difficulty of mounting a coordinated attack against all U.S. forces and doubts over the reliability of Soviet missiles. Even if a surprise attack on American bases substantially reduced our available striking power, the President explained, "our [remaining] bombers would immediately be on their way in sufficient strength to accomplish . . . retaliation."[73]

Defense Secretary McElroy testified to Congress in support of the President's programs by indicating that it was neither the intention nor the policy of the administration to attempt to match the Soviet Union "missile for missile in the ICBM category" and arguing that the United

72. "Radio and Television Address to the American People on Science in National Security, November 7, 1957," *Public Papers, 1957*, p. 794.
73. "Annual Message to the Congress on the State of the Union, January 9, 1958," *Public Papers of the Presidents of the United States: Dwight D. Eisenhower, 1958* (1959), p. 4.

States would rely on its diversified capability to deliver nuclear weapons to maintain its deterrent.[74] This line of reasoning was, of course, the same as that behind the policy of adequacy used by the Eisenhower administration to contain pressures for expanding U.S. strategic programs when the bomber gap became an issue during the mid-1950s.

As a secondary yet significant theme, administration officials stressed the progress being made in developing U.S. ballistic missile capabilities. America's position was clearly strengthened psychologically as well as technologically when the first U.S. earth-orbiting space satellite was launched on January 31, 1958—only a few months after the Soviet launching. However, the President underscored the variety of *military* missile programs that had been instituted before Sputnik, maintaining that these programs were progressing as fast as was technologically feasible and claiming that additional funding could not be effectively absorbed.[75]

President Eisenhower indicated that U.S. IRBMs, scheduled for initial installation in Western Europe before the end of 1958, could reach the USSR and would temporarily offset Soviet missiles until America's ICBMs became available. The parallel Thor and Jupiter IRBM programs, recognized for their potential vulnerability to surprise attack, were nonetheless justified as serving deterrence as well as diplomatic objectives over the near term until a substantial American ICBM force became available. In regard to intercontinental missiles, administration officials stressed the progress of the Navy Polaris project and of Air Force programs to develop hardened ICBMs but also argued the necessity of pressing forward with the soft Atlas system— on the grounds that it made military sense to add still another complicating factor to the execution of a Soviet first-strike attack and that political benefits would result from the early achievement of an American ICBM system.

Finally, administration spokesmen observed that the Soviet Union's successful Sputnik shots and missile flight tests did not necessarily imply that the Kremlin was about to deploy a force of operational ICBMs. In any event, even if the USSR were to gain a temporary advantage in numbers, it was claimed, U.S. ballistic missiles would ultimately be more effective. After the first successful full-range flight test of an Atlas ICBM

74. *New York Times,* January 30, 1959.
75. Eisenhower, *Waging Peace,* p. 208.

in November 1958, increased confidence was expressed that the United States would indeed acquire reliable strategic missiles in time to minimize the adverse impact of any potential gap.

MISSILE ESTIMATES

Even as the administration strove to defend its strategic policies, official projections of Soviet ICBM levels were downgraded because national intelligence estimates in 1959 began to reflect evidence that the Soviet Union might not be engaged in a crash missile production effort. But congressional critics remained skeptical of the administration's policies, and Air Force projections of Soviet ICBM strength continued to remain high. Despite lowered estimates, official spokesmen admitted that the USSR would have a three-to-one advantage over the United States in deployed ICBMs by the early 1960s. In January 1960, however, national estimates dropped sharply; the new secretary of defense, Thomas Gates, indicated that the Soviet Union would be expected to enjoy only a "moderate numerical superiority" in strategic missiles during the next three years.[76] Gates justified these revised figures by alluding to new intelligence that enabled the United States to estimate the USSR's ICBM inventory and expected deployment rates on the basis of *probable* Soviet programs rather than on what the USSR might be *capable* of accomplishing using its maximum capacity for missile production.

For security reasons, Secretary Gates refused to elaborate on his remarks or to clarify his cryptic hints of "new intelligence" to congressmen who accused the administration of playing politics with national estimates in an election year. The secretary was, of course, referring to the failure of U-2 flights to show evidence of Soviet operational ICBM deployments throughout 1958 and 1959. Although the Soviet Union was deploying a sizable force of intermediate- and medium-range ballistic missiles (IR/MRBMs) and was continuing to test and talk about ICBMs, the lack of positive information confirming extensive production and construction efforts led administration leaders to conclude that Moscow

76. *Department of Defense Appropriations for 1961*, Hearings before the Subcommittee of the House Committee on Appropriations, 86 Cong. 2 sess. (1960), pt. 1, p. 4. The congressional hearing in which Secretary of Defense McElroy first estimated the three-to-one advantage was never released to the public, but reports of it were never denied by the secretary. For a discussion of this issue, see Bottome, *The Missile Gap*.

had refrained from moving ahead full speed with intercontinental missile programs and that future U.S. force planning could therefore be based on less pessimistic threat projections. It is questionable in retrospect, however, whether U-2 information was of sufficient coverage and confidence to have permitted such conclusions to be drawn. The U.S. intelligence community itself seriously disagreed about the utility of U-2 data in forming reliable estimates of Soviet ICBM programs.

After the U-2 incident in May 1960, President Eisenhower decided to terminate the program of aerial flights over the Soviet Union, partly for political reasons but also because of the obvious threat posed by Soviet ground-to-air missiles. The last set of U-2 data, gleaned from an April mission, still showed no evidence of widespread missile deployments—although by that time the USSR may have initiated construction of a small number of operational ICBM sites at locations not covered by overflights.[77]

At the time of the U-2 incident, the United States was already engaged in an active program to develop a more secure and sophisticated overflight capability using reconnaissance satellites, but reliable data would not become available until 1961. Consequently, during its final eight months in office, the Eisenhower administration lost the ability to monitor USSR missile efforts through aerial photography. On the other hand, throughout 1960 the United States made substantial progress on its own missile program, thus diminishing still further the danger that an unfavorable gap would develop—regardless of progress on the Soviet side. In addition to the Thor and Jupiter IRBMs deployed in Europe, an Atlas ICBM squadron was officially activated at a U.S. military base in August 1960. By the end of 1960, a Titan ICBM had been successfully flight-tested, the Minuteman development program was proceeding ahead of schedule, and two Polaris submarines were at sea. With the success of the Polaris and Minuteman programs, it might be noted, the Eisenhower administration decided to concentrate on these second-generation systems and to limit the production of first-generation ICBMs to only a few hundred missiles. This decision was motivated both by the desire to avoid the expense of building large numbers of costly Atlas and Titan missiles and by the recognition that solid-fueled systems could be made more survivable than liquid-fueled systems.

77. See Klass, *Secret Sentries in Space*, p. 50.

Notwithstanding mounting evidence that the relative strategic position of the United States was improving and that the danger of a Soviet surprise attack was becoming increasingly remote, the missile gap remained a salient issue during the presidential campaign of 1960. Democratic candidate John F. Kennedy, for example, highlighted the failures in U.S. missile tests and claimed that the missile gap was growing larger.[78] In an apparent response to domestic political pressures, President Eisenhower in his defense budget for fiscal year 1961 requested increased funding for missile programs and later in the year released additional funds for missile programs that Congress had already appropriated. The President finished his term of office with the conviction that his administration had left the United States in an extremely sound strategic position. In his last State of the Union Message, President Eisenhower told the American people that "the 'bomber gap' of several years ago was always a fiction, and the missile gap shows every sign of being the same."[79]

The President proved to be correct. By the end of 1960, the Soviet Union had fewer than thirty-five operational ICBMs, while the United States had already deployed thirty-two Polaris and nine long-range Atlas missiles. Of more importance, however, was the massive ongoing U.S. production and construction program that would lead to a *reverse* missile gap decidedly unfavorable to the Soviet Union. Defense plans left by the Eisenhower administration called for a total of 250 Atlas and Titan ICBMs to be deployed by 1962 and included specific authorization for the procurement of 450 Minuteman missiles and 19 Polaris submarines. When combined with the force of more than 600 B-52 and nearly 1,400 B-47 bombers, the relative strategic position of the United States as it entered the new decade was one of overwhelming dominance.

Soviet Strategic Policies

The Eisenhower administration's nuclear policies were devised to counter what was believed to be the Soviet strategic threat. But early

78. Ibid., p. 54.
79. "Annual Message to the Congress on the State of the Union, January 12, 1961," *Public Papers of the Presidents of the United States: Dwight D. Eisenhower, 1960–61* (1961), p. 919.

U.S. force and policy decisions had an important effect on the evolution of Soviet strategic policies that, in turn, influenced later U.S. decisions and the prospects for curbing the emerging nuclear arms competition.

There is little doubt that Soviet leaders were fearful of the Eisenhower administration's massive retaliation policy, which threatened a nuclear first strike against the USSR in the event of serious Soviet aggression against the United States or its allies. Pronouncements of U.S. counterforce first-strike aims by American military leaders fueled Soviet fears still further. During 1954, for example, Defense Minister Nikolai Bulganin warned against the danger of a surprise nuclear attack by the United States in a series of public statements.[80] Looking back on the 1953–60 period, Khrushchev later remarked that Secretary Dulles's policy amounted to "barefaced atomic blackmail."[81]

The actual state of the U.S.-Soviet strategic balance in the early and mid-1950s contributed to the Soviet Union's alarm. In 1953, it should be recalled, the USSR possessed only small numbers of medium-range propeller-driven bombers, while the growing U.S. B-47 bomber force deployed overseas and U.S. carrier-based aircraft posed threats to the Soviet homeland. By 1955, the Soviet Union had acquired a small intercontinental bomber force and was introducing medium-range jet bombers into its fleet. These weapons gave Kremlin leaders the capability of inflicting damage against the U.S. homeland in addition to holding Western Europe hostage with shorter-range systems. But the United States had also begun to deploy the intercontinental B-52 bomber and, equally important from the Soviet standpoint, was continuing to expand its B-47 force. America's overseas basing facilities and aerial refueling techniques enabled the use of the U.S. medium-range bomber force for strategic missions, thus giving the nation an overwhelming strategic advantage over the USSR—even though the numerical balance of bomber forces on both sides was approximately equal and despite a large-scale air-defense network throughout the Soviet Union.

Although President Eisenhower and other officials came to accept

80. *Izvestiya*, July 22, 1954, cited in Horelick and Rush, *Strategic Power and Soviet Foreign Policy*, p. 22. For background on Soviet reactions to massive retaliation and on Soviet strategic policies in the 1950s, see V. D. Sokolovskii, *Soviet Military Strategy* (Prentice-Hall, 1966).

81. Cited in Chalmers Roberts, *The Nuclear Years: The Arms Race and Arms Control 1945–70* (Praeger, 1970), p. 41.

the proposition that it was impossible to prevent the Soviet Union from inflicting severe damage on the United States or its Western European allies, it is possible to argue that the United States could have launched a first strike against the USSR in the mid-1950s and sustained only minimal damage from a retaliatory attack. Whatever the actual conditions, Kremlin leaders at that time seemed to believe that this was the situation, and Khrushchev himself acknowledged that during this period the USSR "did not possess sufficient means of retaliation."[82]

To be sure, Soviet leaders apparently believed that the United States would be extremely reluctant to deliberately initiate a nuclear attack against the USSR. The atomic bomb was not used against the Soviet Union when the United States had a monopoly, and President Eisenhower had publicly eschewed preventive war. But Moscow could not trust America's good intentions, and uncertainties over future U.S. strategic deployments seemed to trigger "worst-case" interpretations by Soviet officials. Kremlin leaders heard a chorus of mixed voices in the United States commenting on our strategic doctrine, making it difficult for the USSR to dismiss the possibility that the United States might seek overwhelming superiority, or perhaps a first-strike capability designed to destroy Soviet forces, in order to support the massive retaliation policy. At a minimum, the Kremlin feared that the United States might use its strategic power inadvertently or accidentally in a crisis. Finally, Soviet leaders must have realized that the USSR not only was inferior on the strategic level but also lacked a counter to the expanding U.S. tactical nuclear weapons arsenal that threatened to negate Soviet conventional superiority in the European theater.

Moscow's strategic policies in the 1950s were shaped by the internal debates over defense strategy and the role of nuclear weapons that erupted after Stalin's death. In early 1954, Premier Georgi Malenkov, echoing President Eisenhower, stated publicly that the availability of thermonuclear weapons on both sides meant that a world war would lead to "the destruction of world civilization."[83] Khrushchev and Bulganin, on the other hand, initially expressed the traditional Soviet view that only the West would be destroyed in a major conflict, but they soon came to accept Malenkov's concept as a reality of the nuclear age.

82. Ibid.
83. *Pravda*, March 13, 1954, cited in Horelick and Rush, *Strategic Power and Soviet Foreign Policy*, p. 19.

Primarily for this reason, Khrushchev abandoned the idea that war between Communist and capitalist nations was inevitable and in 1956 set forth the principle of peaceful coexistence.[84]

For the reasons suggested above, however, neither Khrushchev nor Bulganin were prepared to assume that nuclear deterrence would operate automatically or to trust the United States to refrain from using its strategic power for purposes detrimental to Soviet security. The Kremlin leadership therefore faced the issue of how to respond to the Eisenhower administration's defense program—more specifically, how to avoid nuclear inferiority, gain a credible deterrent, and blunt U.S. military and political threats. The ensuing Soviet strategic policy was constrained by the state of technology and by bureaucratic pressures. Nevertheless, motivated by a strong personal conviction that defense spending should not be permitted to interfere with necessary domestic economic needs, Khrushchev managed to forge a strategy that seemed to follow a logic based on three principles.

First, rather than compete against SAC's B-52 force and the U.S. lead in bombers, Khrushchev decided to offset U.S. strategic superiority by emphasizing Russia's lead in missilery. Long-range bombers were expensive to build and operate, and the lack of overseas bases denied the USSR the option of using medium-range bombers for strategic purposes. Moreover, many Soviet officials were rapidly recognizing that ballistic missiles could make bombers obsolete; consequently, they saw substantial economic and security advantages to be gained by forgoing major investments in bombers and moving immediately to acquire a strategic missile force. Thus, while Kremlin leaders sought to create the opposite impression, and even as bomber gap fears were raised, the USSR did not produce the large fleet of intercontinental bombers predicted by the West. But the Soviet Union continued to enlarge its air-defense network in an attempt to diminish the U.S. bomber threat and to maintain the traditional Soviet emphasis on defense.

A second element in Khrushchev's strategy initially was to develop a powerful nuclear capability against Western Europe and then to acquire a substantial long-range capability against the United States. This was reflected in the decision to build a sizable medium-range bomber force rather than a long-range fleet and by the emphasis

84. Khrushchev did this at the Twentieth Communist Party Congress, February 1956. For background, see Thomas W. Wolfe, *Soviet Power and Europe, 1945–1970* (Johns Hopkins Press, 1970), pp. 128–59.

placed on the deployment of MR/IRBMs during the second half of the decade. Despite the obvious interest of Soviet leaders in attaining the capacity to extend the reach of Soviet nuclear forces to intercontinental distances, a temporary regional priority could be justified. For one thing, medium-range systems were less costly and difficult to produce than longer-range systems, and technical experience could be gained from constructing such systems. In addition, Soviet medium-range systems would not only provide an effective deterrent to the United States through the threat posed to its West European allies but would also enable the USSR to target the large network of U.S. overseas SAC bases. Finally, the deployment of nuclear systems aimed at Western Europe represented a military counter to NATO's tactical atomic forces and could serve the USSR's political objective of disrupting relations between the United States and its European allies.

The third and most distinctive dimension of Khrushchev's strategy was the use of rhetoric to create a false impression of Soviet strategic capabilities—the "Sputnik diplomacy" policy. This policy was foreshadowed soon after the USSR deployed MRBMs when Khrushchev directed threats against Western Europe, particularly during the Suez crisis in 1956. But the detection by the United States of Soviet long-range missile tests in the summer of 1957, followed by the Sputnik launchings later that year, provided Khrushchev with a unique opportunity to dramatize the power of Soviet ICBM forces through a series of claims and threats.[85]

The basic Soviet approach was to avoid specifics and to play on the uncertainties in U.S. intelligence estimates as USSR capabilities became exaggerated during the course of the missile gap debate. Accordingly, Khrushchev and other Soviet officials spoke only in vague terms of their ability to deliver "crushing blows" against the United States when alluding to "shifts" in the balance of power. Kremlin leaders issued general statements to the effect that any Western use of nuclear weapons would be countered in kind, dropped hints that the USSR might initiate a nuclear exchange under certain circumstances, made broad assertions that neither the United States nor NATO could escape destruction in the event of a nuclear war, and reiterated amorphous demands for the West to cease provocative acts. Soviet

85. For a systematic discussion of Soviet threats and claims during the years 1956–60, see Horelick and Rush, *Strategic Power and Soviet Foreign Policy*, pp. 42–102.

missile claims were equally vague. After the Sputnik launch, Khrushchev first asserted that the USSR had successfully developed long-range missiles, then announced in November 1958 that "serial production" of ICBMs had been initiated, and finally claimed one year later, without citing facts or figures, that the USSR possessed a substantial operational capability of intercontinental missiles.

Once the United States and its allies showed evidence of fear that the strategic balance might begin to favor the USSR, Khrushchev, as noted, tried to exploit the West's concern by attempting to exert influence during the offshore islands crisis in 1958, putting pressure on Berlin, and generally seeking to intimidate the United States and its allies. On the other hand, most experts agree that Khrushchev throughout this period sought to extract maximum political and psychological benefits *without* running unnecessary risks of nuclear conflict with the United States—risks that Soviet leaders were clearly not prepared to take, given their actual position of strategic inferiority.

In retrospect, it is unclear whether Khrushchev's strategy was deliberately designed for aggressive purposes or whether it reflected a desire to neutralize U.S. superiority.[86] One line of reasoning suggests that the unexpectedly intense U.S. reactions to Sputnik provided Khrushchev with the opportunity to avoid the appearance of inferiority without investing resources in a major effort to deploy the costly and cumbersome first-generation ICBMs that had been developed. According to this theory, only then did Khrushchev decide that a continued fueling of missile gap fears might permit the USSR to defuse the U.S. nuclear threat while concealing the modest scope of its existing missile programs and gaining time to redress the strategic balance more efficiently with improved ICBM systems. An opposite view holds that the entire Soviet effort—from the earlier bomber gap to the missile gap—represented a systematic plan on the part of Khrushchev to exploit Soviet power by creating uncertainty in the West. The actual justifications for Khrushchev's policy obviously contained elements of both interpretations—as well as other domestic and international political factors. But whatever the mixture of motivations, Sputnik diplomacy influenced U.S.-Soviet relations, played a role in the crises of the late 1950s, and exerted an important effect on U.S. strategic policies and perceptions for almost three years.

86. See Wolfe, *Soviet Power and Europe*, pp. 84–89.

Toward the end of 1960—after the U-2 incident—Khrushchev's claims diminished. The Kremlin had been aware of the U-2 flights, and, as the Berlin crisis developed during 1959 and early 1960, Khrushchev probably suspected that President Eisenhower was beginning to regard the missile gap as a myth. Projections of Soviet missile strength were dropping, and American missile programs were proceeding on schedule. But the public exposure of the U-2 program in May 1960 finally undermined the military credibility and political value of Soviet missile claims. In dealing with the West and in maintaining a worldwide image, the USSR could no longer be confident of relying on deception to mask its lack of ICBM deployments.

While possibly gaining some political benefits, Khrushchev failed in his attempts to use the apparent shift in the nuclear balance to extract major concessions from the West. In one sense, however, his strategy could be considered a success, since it helped counter the perceived threat of the massive retaliation policy by placing the Eisenhower administration on the defensive and diminishing the intensity of America's claims of strategic superiority. But this short-term gain was offset by the fact that Khrushchev's policies had the effect of stimulating U.S. missile programs and ultimately leading to a *widening* of America's strategic advantage. Ironically, Sputnik diplomacy had backfired, and the USSR faced an extremely disadvantageous and potentially dangerous situation as the United States moved toward a position of clear strategic superiority in the 1960s.

It is interesting to note that in many respects Khrushchev shared President Eisenhower's military objectives and, during the latter part of the 1950s, pursued a defense policy somewhat similar to that of the Eisenhower administration.[87] Khrushchev recognized that a nuclear exchange would be catastrophic for both sides; for this very reason he came to believe, as did President Eisenhower, that a general war was unlikely and that the prospect of nuclear escalation would deter a lower-scale conflict. Therefore, in seeking to keep military spending in check, Khrushchev, like President Eisenhower, began to look to strategic power to provide a substitute for further expansions of conventional forces. Yet budget concerns also led Khrushchev to find a second-best position acceptable and to reject the goal of nuclear superiority for the USSR, much as President Eisenhower turned to the

87. This point is discussed in Roman Kolkowitz and others, *The Soviet Union and Arms Control: A Superpower Dilemma* (Johns Hopkins Press, 1970), pp. 27–29.

concept of adequacy. Finally, to the extent that it emphasized bluff and rhetoric, Khrushchev's Sputnik diplomacy resembled Dulles's strategy of brinkmanship. While the USSR may not have responded to U.S. strategic programs by building large-scale forces of its own, Soviet leaders seemed to have responded in kind to U.S. policy pronouncements.

Strategic Arms Control Efforts

The strategic arms race during the years 1953–60 did not follow a simple action-reaction pattern, with each nation responding to potential threats against its nuclear retaliatory capability, stimulating its adversary to take countermeasures, and causing the weapon cycle to continue at higher force levels. To some extent, this mechanism operated on the American side when concern over Soviet ICBMs triggered a series of programs to enhance the survivability of U.S. strategic forces. But the Soviet Union refrained from procuring large numbers of long-range systems in response to U.S. strategic force buildups. Although the Soviet air-defense program was undoubtedly a reaction to America's bomber threat, the USSR's strategic offensive arms policies were motivated by factors unique to that nation's political and technological position—factors that led the Kremlin to emphasize medium-range systems and to turn to a diplomacy of deception rather than to undertake a substantial ICBM production program.

On the other hand, there were interplays between U.S. and Soviet strategic postures and policies throughout this period that influenced nuclear stability and affected relations between the two nations. Perceptions were distorted, for example, as each nation miscalculated the other's strategic capabilities and misjudged its intentions. Reading Dulles's massive retaliation doctrine literally, Soviet leaders expected the United States to seek a counterforce first-strike capability, while U.S. leaders, reacting to the USSR's early technological lead and missile claims, expected the Soviet Union to gain a significant edge in ICBMs. Both estimates proved to be incorrect, but not until each side had responded with hostility and increased tension. In addition, changes in weapon technology introduced potential instabilities into the U.S.-Soviet strategic balance by raising the prospect that force vulnerabilities might lead to a breakdown in nuclear deterrence. Because of the long flight time of aircraft launched between the United States and the Soviet Union, the bomber forces of both sides during the early and mid-1950s posed relatively little danger of a successful surprise attack by either nation. The development of ballistic missiles later in the decade, however, brought this problem into focus when Soviet ICBM activities created concern in the United States over maintaining the survivability of SAC's bombers. More worrisome in the view of some was the possibility that the deployment of large numbers of first-generation ICBMs on both sides would lead to strategic instabilities far more severe than those present in a situation where missiles threatened bombers. Slow-reacting ICBMs installed on soft launching pads and incapable of being recalled could create what one analyst described as "the reciprocal fear of surprise attack" and consequently could increase the risk of preemptive strikes or accidental firings.[88]

Some form of U.S.-Soviet cooperative effort to reduce the risks and costs of the emerging strategic competition would have been valuable in this period. But the international environment seemed to preclude early progress in strategic arms control. When the Eisenhower administration took office, multilateral disarmament negotiations were being conducted within the framework of the United Nations Disarmament Commission. The proposals then being discussed by East and West called for complete disarmament covering all categories of weapons and forces, conventional as well as atomic. Despite the interest of all parties in the goal of disarmament, the United States, the USSR, and their respective allies seemed to be using these negotiations as political tools by offering unrealistic plans of high propaganda value containing "jokers" that would automatically prevent acceptance by the other side.[89]

During the following few years, the growth of U.S. and Soviet capabilities for mass destruction focused attention on the dangers of nuclear weaponry. In an attempt to reduce the military risks of nuclear power and to improve the climate for East-West negotiations, Presi-

88. The coined phrase is a chapter title in Thomas C. Schelling, *The Strategy of Conflict* (Oxford University Press, 1963), p. 207. For a discussion of strategic stability issues during the Eisenhower years see Quester, *Nuclear Diplomacy*.

89. See John W. Spanier and Joseph L. Nogee, *The Politics of Disarmament: A Study in Soviet-American Gamesmanship* (Praeger, 1962). For a comprehensive discussion of disarmament plans during the 1950s, see Bernhard G. Bechhoefer, *Postwar Negotiations for Arms Control* (Brookings Institution, 1961).

dent Eisenhower proposed the Atoms for Peace plan in the spring of
1953. But disarmament discussions in 1954 and 1955 continued to
center on comprehensive agreements encompassing prohibitions on
the use, manufacture, and ownership of nuclear weapons, as well as
severe restrictions on nonnuclear armed forces.

Both U.S. and Soviet disarmament approaches, however, soon
showed signs of shifting away from comprehensive schemes to the
consideration of more limited arms control possibilities. The increasing
interest in these partial measures was based on the recognition that
reliable verification of general disarmament was simply not feasible
and that limited measures might help reduce the danger of nuclear
war and build confidence. Soviet negotiators took the lead in proposing
partial plans, including a ban on nuclear testing, ground control posts
in Europe, and budget restrictions, but U.S. proposals also began to
contain similar elements. Indeed, because of this new policy direction,
the United States established a Disarmament Commission under
Harold Stassen to formulate and negotiate proposals.

Open Skies Proposal

One widely publicized U.S. plan of the period was President Eisenhower's Open Skies proposal, presented at the Geneva summit conference in July 1955.[90] The goal of the Open Skies proposal was to
reduce the risk of surprise attack through bilateral U.S.-Soviet exchanges of "blueprints" of military forces and installations, combined
with a broad-gauged system of verification through aerial reconnaissance and ground inspection. Included in the information to be exchanged were "weapons and delivery systems suitable for surprise
attack," but the U.S. proposal also called for data on *all* armed forces
and facilities. President Eisenhower was personally interested in reducing nuclear dangers and developing mutual confidence, consistent with
the "spirit of Geneva." But the Soviet Union rebelled against U.S.
demands for inspection and rejected the plan as "nothing more than a
bald espionage plot."[91]

It is difficult to judge whether Open Skies was offered as a serious

90. "United States Outline Plan for the Implementation of President Eisenhower's
Aerial Inspection Proposal," *Documents on Disarmament, 1945–59* (U.S. Arms Control and Disarmament Agency, 1960), p. 502.

91. Eisenhower, *Mandate for Change*, p. 521.

proposal to diminish the risks associated with the U.S.-Soviet nuclear relationship or was put forth for political and propagandistic purposes. Perhaps, as the USSR feared, the United States deliberately developed the plan in order to obtain information regarding Soviet nuclear facilities, bomber programs, and missile activities. In any case, the proposal was prepared in haste and could be questioned on its merits as a sound arms control measure. For example, it is not clear how additional military information or the comprehensive inspection system proposed would have reduced the risk of strategic surprise attack, since rapid launchings of bombers and missiles would still have been possible. Moreover, despite the official rationale that more knowledge would result in less danger, the aerial and on-site inspection requirements could have enabled each side to pinpoint the other's soft strategic deployments and to gain knowledge of its adversary's vulnerability—knowledge that could have increased the danger of a nuclear first strike by one side or the other. In other words, the Open Skies plan could have had the paradoxical effect of increasing the risk of war and heightening tensions. From this perspective, Soviet objections seemed valid, and even the United States might well have refused to follow through with its own plan.

Notwithstanding its failure, Open Skies raised a number of fundamental issues that continued to affect the policies, proposals, and prospects for strategic arms control throughout the remainder of the decade. U.S. awareness of the risk of nuclear surprise attack increased as the Soviet Union made progress in its ICBM developments, and U.S. leaders began to express concern about the potential vulnerability of SAC bombers to a missile strike. For this reason—and also as a means of checking the Soviet Union's missile momentum—the Eisenhower administration decided to propose measures designed to curtail ballistic rocket developments and applications. Thus, before Sputnik, the U.S. delegation to the London Disarmament Conference in early 1957 had already introduced a plan for controls over conventional and nuclear arms that included international inspection of missile testing. In addition, attempts to reduce the danger of a first strike through the use of aerial inspection and ground control measures within agreed zones remained a salient element of the comprehensive proposal put forth by the four Western powers in August 1957. In July, despite a somewhat cynical attitude toward negotiations with the Soviet bloc, Secretary Dulles had specifically mentioned intercontinental missiles when he said it was possible that a "mutually reinforcing combination of aerial inspection and ground control" could "reduce the risk and degree of surprise [attack]."[92]

Throughout 1956 and 1957, the Soviet Union opposed Western plans while proposing that all nations issue declarations banning the use of nuclear arms and calling for the complete elimination of such weapons. These proposals were unrealistic, ran counter to U.S. defense policy, and could only have been designed to be rejected. At one point, the Kremlin seemed to adopt a positive stance toward aerial inspection, but further discussion revealed that the USSR's inspection plan dealt only with zones in Central Europe, and this would have led to asymmetric restrictions clearly unfavorable to NATO. Aside from Moscow's basic objection to the intrusiveness of any Open Skies arrangement involving inspection of the Soviet Union, Kremlin leaders at that time were hopeful of redressing the U.S. bomber advantage by exploiting their lead in ICBM technology and could not have been expected to consider missile limitation measures. Whether or not the United States was serious in setting forth its plans, therefore, the relative technical and strategic positions of Washington and Moscow seemed to preclude practical negotiations involving controls on long-range delivery systems.

Surprise Attack Conference

In September 1958, however, Khrushchev moved away from purely propagandistic proposals by finally agreeing to President Eisenhower's suggestion that a conference of experts be convened to study the technical aspects of reducing the possibility of surprise attack. This Soviet decision, which led to the Surprise Attack Conference held in Geneva later that year, was apparently influenced by two factors. First, Soviet leaders seemed to have developed a genuine concern over the danger of accidental or inadvertent nuclear war. The Soviet Union had already accused the United States of increasing the danger of unintended global conflict through its practice of flying nuclear-armed SAC bombers toward the USSR's borders, and in accepting the President's proposal Khrushchev explained that such actions made the problem of

92. "Radio and Television Address by Secretary of State Dulles, July 22, 1957," *Department of State Bulletin*, vol. 37 (August 12, 1957), p. 269.

preventing surprise attack "especially acute."[93] Second, Khrushchev may have thought that a positive outlook toward arms control would support his broader policy goal of avoiding a serious Soviet-American confrontation and would further attempts to slow down the expansion of U.S. strategic programs. After all, even though Khrushchev had continued to make extravagant claims about Soviet progress in mis-silery, the USSR was still in an extremely vulnerable strategic position.

At the conference, the basic differences in U.S. and Soviet interests in, and approaches to, the problem of surprise attack reappeared.[94] Harking back to the Open Skies philosophy, the U.S. representatives again stressed data exchange, technical aids, and comprehensive inspection to reduce suspicions of surprise attack preparation and to provide early warning in the event of an attack. They suggested the possible use of aerial overflights with a variety of sensory devices as well as the possibility of stationing observers at air fields, naval bases, transportation centers, and virtually all important military installations in each country. As in the case of Open Skies, the "objects of control" were to include long-range aircraft and conventional forces, but particular attention was to be placed on developing a system of observations at missile sites with special radars and communication links installed to assist inspectors in detecting firings and in transmitting warning signals.

The USSR responded by reasserting that surprise attack was primarily a political problem, involving intentions more than military capabilities, and arguing that the problem could not be solved by technical means outside the framework of genuine disarmament. On a more practical level, Soviet representatives again questioned the value of the U.S. proposals in actually lowering the likelihood of a surprise attack, pointing out that disclosure of information could increase the susceptibility of systems to attack and consequently improve the chances for successful first strikes. Finally, the Soviet Union claimed that the most serious danger of surprise attack was to be found in the European theater and that emphasis should be placed on minimizing the prospect of conventional conflict in that area.

93. "Premier Khrushchev's Letter to the President," *Department of State Bulletin*, vol. 39 (August 18, 1958), p. 280.

94. For a fully documented account of the Surprise Attack Conference, see Johan J. Holst, "Strategic Arms Control and Stability: A Retrospective Look," in Johan J. Holst and William Schneider, Jr., eds., *Why ABM? Policy Issues in the Missile Defense Controversy* (Pergamon Press, 1969), pp. 245–84.

In essence, the issues discussed at the Surprise Attack Conference were updated and more sophisticated versions of the issues associated with discussions of the Open Skies plan in 1955. The U.S. approach was excessively geared to technical schemes of dubious effectiveness, and it is doubtful that the United States would have agreed to its own inspection requirements. Because the U-2 program was under way, it can even be argued that the United States had far less need for agreed verification procedures in 1958 than it did in 1955—although a legitimization and extension of aerial inspection of the USSR would clearly have served American interests. For its part, the Soviet Union seemed reluctant to find ways of reducing mutual military risks unless it could settle outstanding political problems at the same time. The fear that Khrushchev's missile bluffing might be exposed undoubtedly further inhibited the USSR's agreement to inspection. It was not surprising therefore that the conference ended after only six weeks of discussion without an agreement having been reached. In contrast to the failure to obtain agreements limiting strategic delivery systems, technical negotiations on the problem of banning nuclear weapon tests were successfully conducted during the late 1950s, paving the way for the U.S.-Soviet moratorium on nuclear testing and the partial test ban treaty of 1963.[95]

It is of course possible to find persuasive arguments to explain the lack of progress in strategic arms limitations during the Eisenhower years. For one thing, the nature of the U.S.-Soviet nuclear relationship made it difficult to define or to design sensible schemes for bringing the strategic competition under control. The initial U.S. advantage in medium-range and carrier-based aircraft and America's subsequent superiority in long-range bombers precluded an equitable agreement on arms limitations. The uncertainties associated with ballistic missiles complicated efforts to contain rocket technology, and rapidly changing strategic inventories on both sides made it especially difficult for either the United States or the Soviet Union to grasp the potential benefits of strategic arms control. Furthermore, Washington and Moscow were slow in seeing the need for "separable" arrangements that would affect only nuclear delivery systems. Both East and West issued proposals for control over the testing and use of ballistic missiles and rockets but usually as elements in comprehensive and complicated multistage plans encompassing all weapon categories. On the other hand, even if both sides had

95. Treaty Banning Nuclear Weapon Tests in the Atmosphere, in Outer Space and under Water, signed at Moscow, August 5, 1963.

set their sights on such arrangements, negotiations would have been complicated because a variety of medium- as well as long-range aircraft and missile systems served "strategic" missions for both nations. Inspection would have presented further problems, since observation satellites capable of nonintrusive verification were not yet in operation. The use of agreed aerial overflights, which many experts viewed as an inefficient verification technique, was unacceptable to the USSR, and unilateral reliance by the United States on its U-2 flights would undoubtedly have been out of the question. Finally, the basic mistrust between the two nations, combined with the policies of massive retaliation and Sputnik diplomacy, kept tension between Washington and Moscow at a level too high for productive negotiations.

Nothwithstanding the formidable technical obstacles to strategic limitations and the hostile international environment, it is important to recognize that, in general, neither nation placed top priority on arms control during the 1950s. Political will and serious commitment in themselves would not have guaranteed success, but their absence removed all possibility of progress in containing the emerging strategic competition. Although real differences in disarmament perspectives and purposes existed between the United States and the USSR, the evidence suggests that both sides used negotiations as political tools and not as mechanisms for increasing their security. The Soviet Union, for example, stressed the political preconditions to disarmament and proposed measures to outlaw and ban the use of nuclear weapons, while the United States presented equally unacceptable plans that focused on technical issues and mandatory inspection.

Kremlin leaders seemed to view negotiations mainly as a means of disguising the USSR's military deficiencies, acquiring prestige through the illusion of sincerity, and reducing the risk of U.S. attack as they slowly built a reliable deterrent. President Eisenhower expressed sincere interest in disarmament as a means of limiting expenditures and lowering the danger of nuclear war, yet, in direct contradiction of these goals, he supported an overall defense posture built on strategic weaponry and atomic threats. Despite occasional public statements supporting disarmament plans, Secretary Dulles was skeptical about serious arms control discussions with the Soviet Union and sought to undercut many of Stassen's efforts.

In a more positive vein, it can be argued that both sides profited from the brief negotiating experience of the Surprise Attack Conference—the United States by gaining a better understanding of the Soviet views toward secrecy and the political prerequisites for arms control and the USSR through an exposure to American views on deterrence and stability. These contacts may have helped sensitize leaders and experts in each nation to the danger of nuclear war and may have moved the United States and the USSR somewhat closer to an appreciation of the need for bilateral negotiations specifically geared to the limitation of strategic weapon systems. Toward the end of the Eisenhower administration's second term, perhaps because of the stimulus of the conference, the United States seemed to display a renewed awareness of the need to halt the spiraling competition in strategic delivery vehicles. But it was not until a decade later that the evolution of U.S.-Soviet political relations, the appreciation of the security benefits of arms control, and the character of the arms balance permitted Washington and Moscow to undertake meaningful strategic limitation negotiations.

Policy Precedents

Without attempting to resolve the question of how serious President Eisenhower may have been in contemplating the military use of nuclear weapons during particular crises, it is possible to conclude that his administration's defense policy of threatening to employ nuclear weapons or implying that any armed conflict would escalate to strategic war was successful. There were, after all, no serious military conflicts during Eisenhower's presidency and the few potentially dangerous situations—in the Taiwan Strait and Berlin—were settled without losses to U.S. security. While many factors obviously contributed to the cause and outcome of these crises, it can be plausibly argued that the administration's policy of alluding to the possible use of atomic weapons contributed to the final Korean settlement, inhibited the Chinese from pressing further in the offshore islands, and diminished Khrushchev's demands in Berlin. U.S. responses to these situations signaled willingness to risk an all-out conflict, and the fear of nuclear war exerted an inhibiting effect on Communist leaders.

On the other hand, had the crises faced by the administration evolved along somewhat different lines, the disadvantages of the New Look defense posture and the doctrine of brinkmanship could have been exposed. Instead of being deterred by the threat of massive retaliation, Peking and Moscow might have called America's bluff and acted on the assumption that the United States would refrain from using nuclear weapons in the event of a more intense confrontation. Part of the motivation behind Peking's offshore island probe in 1958 and Moscow's stance on Berlin, it should be recalled, was the belief that the United States might not respond effectively to small-scale military actions or diplomatic probes once the Soviet Union had acquired a long-range strategic capability. It is possible, therefore, that the Chinese could have decided to attack Quemoy or that the USSR could have chosen to engage U.S. forces in Berlin in the belief that these moves would not lead to a major conflict. Because of its relatively narrow range of conventional military alternatives, however, the United States might have felt compelled to use atomic weapons in a limited fashion, even at the risk of triggering a global war. Although President Eisenhower assumed that the other side would not take potentially dangerous actions, this was not a risk-free technique for making decisions in managing conflicts, for it placed the burden of avoiding actions that could lead to nuclear war on the USSR and China.

The propensity of the Eisenhower administration to pursue diplomatic rather than military routes during the offshore islands and Berlin crises can be considered a strong point of its defense policy. Nevertheless, a case can be made that the United States was pressured into adopting conciliatory positions and avoiding armed conflict on any level because of its serious lack of nonnuclear options. Whether or not certain U.S. concessions might have been warranted in these particular crises, this approach represents a form of diplomacy that may not always serve the security interests of the nation or its allies. In this sense, the Eisenhower administration's defense policy not only encouraged Moscow and Peking to test the U.S. deterrent but provided unreliable political and military tools for dealing with conflicts when they arose.

On a broader basis, the Eisenhower administration's defense policy can be faulted for its adverse effect on U.S.-Soviet relations and its basic incompatibility with arms control. Massive retaliation was perceived by Kremlin leaders as a provocative policy that suggested the specter of a U.S. first strike and raised the very real possibility of nuclear blackmail by American leaders. These fears contributed to Khrushchev's rocket rattling strategy and the high level of tension between Washington and Moscow. As a consequence, the international political environment was not conducive to progress in limiting nuclear delivery systems. It is difficult to reconcile the administration's proclaimed interest in nuclear disarmament measures with a defense policy and a military force posture so heavily oriented toward nuclear arms. Indeed, some analysts have criticized the Eisenhower administration, first, for spreading nuclear technology through the Atoms for Peace program, and then for increasing the incentives for other nations to acquire nuclear weapons by advocating a NATO atomic strategy involving nuclear-sharing arrangements with U.S. allies.[96]

The New Look defense posture, ironically, differed little in total costs and manpower levels from the conventionally oriented defense posture subsequently developed under Presidents Kennedy and Johnson. Measured in real dollars, for example, annual U.S. defense budgets in the mid-1960s—excluding Vietnam—averaged only $3 billion higher than those of the late 1950s, and total military manpower during these years was only slightly above the 2.5 million level reached in Eisenhower's second term.[97] This was partly because the development of a nuclear-oriented defense posture required greater resources than originally anticipated. During the late 1950s, the increasingly costly U.S. strategic programs competed against demands for general purpose force improvements, and studies showed that the establishment of a serious tactical atomic posture necessitated budgets almost as large as those for maintaining sizable conventional forces.[98] In addition, the Eisenhower administration's approach to defense planning, which gave the military services considerable freedom of decision, resulted in inefficiency. With less stress on nuclear power in force procurements and more efficient defense management procedures, budget levels for strategic and tactical nuclear programs could have been reduced and more resources could have been applied to improving and organizing the conventional forces.

Turning to the more general questions raised by the Eisenhower administration's strategic arms policies, two related issues might be

96. See William B. Bader, *The United States and the Spread of Nuclear Weapons* (Pegasus, 1968).

97. Estimates are drawn from *The Military Budget and National Economic Priorities,* Hearings before the Subcommittee on Economy in Government of the Joint Economic Committee, 91 Cong. 1 sess. (1969), pt. 1, pp. 374–75.

98. See Robert Osgood, *NATO, The Entangling Alliance* (University of Chicago Press, 1962), pp. 106–7, 151–58.

considered. The first issue concerns the information available to the administration at any given time regarding the USSR's long-range strategic weapon programs and how such information was translated into estimates of existing operational forces as well as projected future Soviet deployments. The second issue deals with the question of whether the programs instituted by the administration provided an effective deterrent that also stabilized the Soviet-American strategic relationship.

Reliability of Intelligence Estimates

During the early years of the administration's first term, U.S. intelligence analysts lacked reliable information about the Soviet Union's strategic nuclear programs and were forced to rely on imperfect, indirect, or obsolete sources. Before the end of 1956, however, U.S. radars were providing technical data on Soviet missile testing, and more important, U-2 photoreconnaissance aircraft had begun to fly missions in an attempt to obtain hard information on a variety of Soviet strategic activities. Defense Secretary Gates later explained that, during its four years of operation, the U-2 program yielded information on "airfields, aircraft, missiles, missile testing and training, special weapons storage, submarine production, atomic production, and aircraft deployments."[99] President Eisenhower praised this program as providing critical "negative information" that disproved the "horrors" of the alleged bomber and missile gaps.[100] It certainly seems plausible that material gathered from the U-2, when combined with that from other sources, showed rather reliably that the USSR had refrained from building a large inventory of intercontinental-range strategic *bombers*. But it is questionable whether available U-2 information was sufficiently trustworthy to permit administration officials to first dismiss the possibility that the Kremlin would mount a major long-range *missile* construction program or to later conclude that the USSR had not deployed an ICBM force.[101]

When initial Soviet ICBM tests in 1957 were followed by the

99. *Events Incident to the Summit Conference,* Hearings before the Senate Committee on Foreign Relations, 86 Cong. 2 sess. (1960), p. 124.

100. Eisenhower, *Waging Peace,* note on p. 547.

101. There is intense disagreement in the scholarly community on the effectiveness of the U-2. Quester and Gray, for example, fully support Eisenhower's optimistic assessment, while Bottome questions whether the U-2 provided complete coverage and Klass concludes that aerial overflights were not able to dismiss the missile gap.

Sputnik launchings, U.S. leaders thought it likely that the USSR would translate these technological successes into an operational ballistic missile capability. The existence of an ICBM test site in the USSR and plants throughout the Soviet Union capable of producing large numbers of long-range missiles suggested that Soviet leaders might have decided to forgo long-range bomber buildups in favor of a massive missile construction program. National intelligence estimates in late 1957 indicated that the Soviet Union would be able to fully test and initially deploy ICBMs within two years after the test in August 1957 and to subsequently install hundreds of long-range missiles. These projections were based on production capacity estimates and calculations of the total floorspace available for possible missile fabrication and assembly.

By 1959, however, the official administration position was that the USSR had *not* pursued an all-out ICBM program, and, when President Eisenhower left office, he dismissed the missile gap as well as the earlier bomber gap as a myth. The administration's conclusion regarding Soviet missile programs was attributed to the fact that none of the 200 U-2 missions had brought back evidence of operational ICBM sites in the Soviet Union. It is doubtful, however, that the coverage of the flights was sufficiently complete to confirm the total absence of ICBMs throughout the USSR. In theory, the U-2 system was capable of photographing over 20,000 square miles of Russian territory in one pass, but, in practice, military risks and diplomatic inhibitions prevented the President from approving deep and sustained missions. Moreover, requirements for favorable weather free of cloud cover further restricted the frequency and target areas of the U-2 flights. For these reasons, it is estimated that fewer than thirty "extended penetrations" of the Soviet Union took place in four years, and each of these flights was limited in time and scope.[102]

As a consequence of the data derived from the relatively small number of deep-penetration U-2 missions, the Eisenhower administration may well have been in a position to conclude that the USSR had not installed ICBMs near the Trans-Siberian Railroad. Flights were aimed at this area because it seemed the most logical location for deploying the Soviet Union's cumbersome liquid-fueled ICBMs, which were

102. Charles J. V. Murphy, "Khrushchev's Paper Bear," *Fortune*, December 1964, p. 227. A number of former technical intelligence analysts have suggested that as few as a *half-dozen* deep U-2 missions were flown.

difficult to transport by road or air. On the other hand, the USSR could have constructed ICBMs at less suitable sites, particularly in the northern regions, that had not been monitored by the U-2, and many intelligence experts at the time feared this possibility. Despite the difficulties associated with building ICBM installations, the USSR had far more flexibility in locating missile sites than in deploying bombers. The network of USSR airbases was known to many U.S. officials because of U-2 data and other evidence. The construction of bomber bases in remote areas was extremely difficult, and the construction of new military airfields could not be easily disguised. This helps explain why the U-2 flights could disprove the presence of long-range bombers with confidence but could not provide comparable assurance regarding Soviet ICBMs.

To make matters worse, after U-2 overflights were discontinued in mid-1960, the United States was unable to continue the search for Soviet ICBM sites in remote regions or to verify that deployment had not been initiated in areas already surveyed. In itself, the fact that the USSR had tested over twenty-five ICBMs suggested to many that a substantial production line existed, and a resurgence of Soviet missile firings earlier that year had contributed to concern within the intelligence community that ICBM deployments might be imminent. The last set of photographs returned from the U-2 flights had raised suspicions of possible operational sites in southern Russia. Although Discoverer satellites may have been yielding data toward the end of 1960, the quality and comprehensiveness of this information was insufficient for analysts to dismiss the possibility of Soviet ICBM deployments at that time. It was necessary to obtain data from additional operational satellites scheduled to be launched the following year for the remaining uncertainties to be resolved.

Some observers claim that Kennedy administration officials in early 1961 were certain that the USSR had few if any operational ICBMs, but such conclusions could not be drawn with confidence until the fall of 1961 when the cumulative results of a series of satellite missions provided credible and accurate information on all potential missile sites and enabled U.S. intelligence agencies to reach a consensus that the Soviet Union had deployed only a "handful" of ICBMs.[103]

103. Philip J. Klass, "Keeping the Nuclear Peace: Spies in the Sky," *New York Times Magazine*, September 3, 1972, p. 7. See also Herbert Scoville, Jr., "A Leap Forward in Verification," in Mason Willrich and John B. Rhinelander, eds., *SALT: The Moscow Agreement and Beyond* (Free Press, 1974), pp. 160–84.

Notwithstanding its limitations, U-2 information showing the lack of operational Soviet ICBMs, at least in obvious deployment areas, made plausible the gradual lowering of intelligence estimates and the use of more realistic premises in projecting the size of the Soviet Union's strategic missile force. But reconnaissance satellites, which entered the scene as the Eisenhower administration ended, offered advantages over the U-2 that went beyond the question of vulnerability to surface-to-air missiles and the issue of intrusion over a nation's airspace. For example, one satellite, remaining in orbit for many days and circling the USSR, could provide expanded surveillance of the Soviet Union's landmass and take thousands of pictures with a resolution adequate to discern missile sites as well as a host of additional strategic installations and activities. During the 1960s, U.S. satellites improved, and the USSR began to photograph the United States from space. This new method of obtaining technical intelligence information was to play a significant role in planning U.S. strategic programs and in facilitating progress in Soviet-American arms control negotiations.

Criteria for Deterrence and Stability

It is difficult to dispute the fact that at no time during the Eisenhower years was the United States in serious danger of a Soviet counterforce attack nor was America's strategically superior position ever challenged by the Soviet Union. Yet experts disagree in retrospect about the hypothetical but relevant issue of the degree to which this powerful U.S. strategic position could be attributed to the sound policies of the Eisenhower administration as opposed to the good fortune that the Soviet Union did not produce substantial numbers of long-range delivery systems. On a more basic level, there is disagreement over the extent to which U.S. strategic policies during this period satisfied the criteria of deterrence and stability.

It must be kept in mind that much of the conflict between the Eisenhower administration and its critics was fueled by domestic political factors, and that U.S. weapons decisions were therefore influenced by the need to compromise with the Congress. In addition, the character of the administration's strategic programs was often shaped less by logic than by the effects of interservice rivalry, a lack of strong civilian control over specific projects, and the imposition of budget ceilings on military spending. Nevertheless, central to the great strategic debate of the late 1950s was a fundamental *substantive* disagreement over the nature of deterrence in the nuclear age, involving differences of opinion about such vital questions as the stability of the strategic balance and the requirements for an effective retaliatory force—doctrinal issues that carried forward into the 1960s and continue to be debated today.

In setting guidelines for U.S. strategic programs, President Eisenhower operated on the premise that the "balance of terror" was not overly sensitive to variations in the levels or types of U.S. and Soviet nuclear forces. From the American standpoint, this meant that a large and diverse U.S. delivery force would be sufficient to dissuade Kremlin leaders from launching a nuclear attack—even if a major fraction of the force were to become vulnerable to Soviet ballistic missile strikes. Under this philosophy, unless Soviet policymakers felt certain of destroying virtually *all* U.S. systems before or after launch, they would avoid a nuclear exchange that could lead to great destruction in the USSR and would also exercise caution in taking actions that might escalate to large-scale conflicts. The President's concept of strategic adequacy was reflected first in his attempt to limit the size of B-52 procurements and later in his efforts to enhance the survivability of the U.S. bomber force and to acquire ballistic missiles through orderly plans rather than crash programs. He was willing to plan forces on the basis of probable rather than worst-case estimates and to permit particular imbalances or partial vulnerabilities to occur as long as the overall U.S. deterrent remained powerful.

Articulate opponents of the administration's nuclear programs and policies contended that considerably more stringent criteria and a greater degree of conservatism should be used in designing the U.S. strategic posture.[104] Arguing that deterrence was neither automatically assured nor easy to acquire and claiming that the strategic balance was "delicate," proponents of this view expressed concern that the USSR might be able to acquire the ability to negate much of America's nuclear capability unless actions were taken to build a highly survivable force capable of penetrating Soviet defenses and inflicting tens of millions of fatalities. They emphasized that U.S. systems should be structured so that Soviet military planners would be persuaded beyond

104. For significant criticisms of the Eisenhower approach, see Albert Wohlstetter, "The Delicate Balance of Terror," *Foreign Affairs*, vol. 37 (January 1959), pp. 211–34; and Herman Kahn, *On Thermonuclear War* (Princeton University Press, 1960).

all reasonable doubt of the impossibility of destroying a major portion of our nuclear force. Otherwise, it was feared, Kremlin leaders might be motivated either to launch a counterforce attack in the belief that they could cripple most of America's strategic power or to threaten such an action and expose Washington to nuclear blackmail. Vulnerable systems were regarded as doubly disadvantageous and dangerous; they not only increased the chances of a Soviet preemptive strike but also increased the possibility that American leaders might fire U.S. weapons prematurely in an effort to forestall Soviet attacks on these systems and therefore raised the risk of accidents or of war occurring from misunderstandings. Some experts also pointed out that the very ease with which one could perform calculations to demonstrate the potential threat posed to U.S. bombers by possible Soviet ICBM deployments was in itself a source of instability that could lead to a failure of deterrence. For these reasons, the administration was urged to expand all programs designed to decrease bomber vulnerability and to accelerate the development of invulnerable ballistic missile systems.

Thus, much of the nuclear policy debate during the late 1950s revolved around the practical question of whether appropriate U.S. ballistic missile projects were proceeding as rapidly as possible. Unfortunately, attempts to evaluate the relative success or failure of the strategic missile programs initiated and pursued during the Eisenhower years inevitably suffer from the distortions of hindsight. Virtually all observers agree that after Sputnik the success of the Polaris and Minuteman programs in particular represented a remarkable technological triumph and a major managerial feat that could not have been measurably improved either by greater expenditures or a higher policy status. Analyses of the pre-Sputnik period, however, are particularly uncertain and controversial. Some experts support the administration's claim that top priority was placed on ballistic missile efforts and that maximum feasible financial support was given to missile developments during the 1955–57 period. These experts agree that of necessity technology paced the speed of these programs, restricted the choice of systems to liquid-fueled missiles, made redundant projects necessary to ensure success, and precluded more rapid development of solid-fuel rockets. But other experts critical of the administration indicate that fiscal constraints and the momentum behind the Air Force bomber programs restricted missile priorities and initially limited the rate of missile development. These critics further suggest that multiple programs and bureaucratic rivalry inhibited progress in solving important scientific and engineering problems related to the development of advanced and survivable missile programs.

As events finally turned out, compromises between the contending viewpoints toward U.S. nuclear policies that characterized the Eisenhower years led to an American strategic posture with more strengths than weaknesses. Perhaps the specter of a Soviet first strike was overdrawn by administration critics, but their analysis was not without theoretical merit or practical significance. Indeed, the pressure of these countervailing views had a significant—perhaps even a decisive —effect in moving the administration toward the very position advocated by its severest critics. Partly as a consequence of the leak of the Gaither Report and the ensuing public debate over the adequacy of U.S. deterrent programs, for example, the administration requested funds to further decrease SAC's potential vulnerability and to initiate construction of the BMEWS system. More important, as a result of the domestic political furor caused by Sputnik, the President requested a supplementary budget authorization for Titan and Minuteman and for greater acceleration of the Polaris program.[105] In the absence of pressure, such technically feasible decisions might not have been made, primarily because of budgetary reasons but also because of the administration's fairly relaxed interpretation of the requirements for a sufficient deterrent.

Given the lack of large-scale Soviet strategic missile deployments, one could conclude in retrospect that there was no need for the Eisenhower administration to have developed survivable systems as rapidly as reflected in its final program decisions. But if the administration had not been pushed in this direction and the Soviet Union had gone forward with the construction of a sizable first-generation ICBM force —a decision that would have been technically possible, whatever its high costs or questionable deterrent value—the United States might have passed through a period in the early 1960s when the risk of a Soviet counterforce attack or the prospect of Soviet blackmail could have been serious. During those years, the BMEWS missile warning system would not have been operational to alert U.S. bombers, only soft U.S. ICBMs would have been deployed, and few Polaris submarines, if any, would have been on station.

105. Perry, "The Ballistic Missile Decision," p. 19. As Perry put it, Sputnik "cut the purse strings" on U.S. ballistic missile programs.

From this perspective, it is possible to argue that the President's policy preferences represented a calculated gamble in regard to projections of Soviet missile deployments and the reliability of the U.S. deterrent posture, which was never put to the test. Even after the administration's "compromise" programs were implemented, General Thomas S. Powers of SAC expressed concern in 1960 that a force of only 150 Soviet ICBMs, which could soon be available, together with an equal number of Soviet IRBMs, might be able to destroy the 100 soft U.S. bomber and missile bases in a first strike.[106]

On the other hand, without the tempering effect of President Eisenhower's policy outlook, the approach of his critics might have been fully followed, with the result that U.S. strategic programs would have been greatly expanded throughout the late 1950s and carried forward into the 1960s. While this might have given the United States more survivable forces at an earlier date, it would also have increased expenditures for strategic arms and stimulated the Soviet-American nuclear competition to a far greater degree than actually occurred. Moreover, many of those opposed to the Eisenhower administration's strategic policies offered proposals that were inconsistent with the criteria of survivability, stability, and cost-effectiveness.

Some Senate Democrats initially argued for U.S. superiority in bombers and later insisted that more funds be allocated for the construction of first-generation ICBMs. Even the Gaither Report, with its stress on invulnerable forces, contained a recommendation that the IRBM and Atlas programs be expanded. If the advice of certain critics had been accepted, therefore, the United States might have deployed a force of soft liquid-fueled missiles two or three times larger than that authorized by President Eisenhower—a wasteful and destabilizing procurement pattern. Many experts have therefore concluded that the Eisenhower administration pursued moderate and wise policies and that the succeeding administration escalated the arms race unnecessarily.

Nevertheless, despite the alleged restraint exercised by President Eisenhower, U.S. nuclear power grew dramatically during the years 1953–60. Furthermore, it seems fair to suggest that the Eisenhower administration's strategic policies were neither motivated by considera-

106. Speech before the Economic Club of New York, January 19, 1960. Kahn, in *On Thermonuclear War*, presented similar analyses and argued that Eisenhower's policies represented a "calculated gamble" (pp. 193–204).

tion of the consequences of U.S. decisions on Soviet forces and policies nor matched by meaningful attempts to negotiate realistic arms control agreements. Although the United States could not be blamed for the USSR's mischievous attitude or the many technical difficulties blocking progress in strategic arms control, U.S. defense policies made constructive negotiations difficult, if not impossible, and set no beneficial examples. The New Look was inherently incompatible with nuclear stability and arms control, owing to its stress on nuclear weaponry at the expense of conventional arms and its reliance on the threat of massive retaliation. Seen in this broader context, the administration's strategic programs had many provocative and destabilizing effects that clouded the international political climate, increased the risk of nuclear war, and contributed to subsequent Soviet efforts to redress the nuclear balance.

CHAPTER TWO

Assured Destruction and the Analytic Approach: 1961–1968

President John F. Kennedy entered office determined to correct what he and his advisers believed to be the two fundamental flaws in the nation's military posture: the inadequacy of both our strategic deterrent and our conventional capabilities. A "flexible response" doctrine providing substantial nonnuclear alternatives, they claimed, would improve the reliability of our deterrent capabilities, enhance the effectiveness of U.S. fighting forces, and provide dependable tools for managing crises. Administration leaders argued that greater reliance on conventional forces, combined with powerful and highly survivable strategic forces, would minimize the risk of inadvertent nuclear war, retard further nuclear weapon proliferation, and provide a foundation for negotiating arms control arrangements. As part of its attempt to revise U.S. military policy, the new administration made important changes in the process of defense planning. Under Defense Secretary Robert McNamara's direction, the Eisenhower approach of establishing a fixed budget ceiling, which left important weapon decisions to the military services, was replaced by a centralized attempt to evaluate defense needs functionally and on the basis of overall requirements, using cost-effectiveness criteria and systems analysis techniques.

Defense Doctrine

In its first major series of defense decisions, the Kennedy administration paid particular attention to the U.S. strategic posture. The President's supplementary budget of 1961 called for accelerating and expanding the Polaris and Minuteman missile programs, eliminating costly and potentially vulnerable missile and bomber systems, and improving U.S. command and control facilities. To support these decisions, additional funds of $1.2 billion for strategic forces were requested.[1] During the next five years, the United States acquired a highly effective and survivable strategic force consisting of 1,054 silo-based intercontinental ballistic missiles (ICBMs), 656 submarine-launched ballistic missiles (SLBMs), and 630 B-52 bombers. When the Johnson administration ended, programs were under way to improve these strategic capabilities—notably through the development of multiple independently targetable reentry vehicles (MIRVs). Annual spending for strategic arms during the Kennedy-Johnson years averaged $25 billion (in 1974 dollars), representing about 30 percent of the annual non-Vietnam defense budget.[2]

By the end of its first year in office, the Kennedy administration had made substantial progress toward improving U.S. conventional defense capabilities. Stimulated in part by the Berlin crisis of 1961, administration officials requested and received additional funds to increase military personnel, to procure nonnuclear ordnance and equipment for ground and air forces, and to expand U.S. air- and sea-lift capabilities. The Army was ordered to change its field organization from the so-called pentomic divisions trained and equipped for nuclear war to one emphasizing conventional weaponry and doctrine, and tactical aircraft from Air Force and Navy units were integrated into the war plans of the general purpose forces. To support this reorganization, the number of combat-ready Army divisions increased from 11 to 16, and total military manpower increased by 200,000 before the Vietnam expansion in 1965. As a consequence of these and other postwar force decisions, U.S. military capabilities were improved to the point where a variety of contingencies, including relatively large-scale attacks in Europe or Asia, could be handled without resort to nuclear weapons.[3]

1. *Recommendations Relating to Our Defense Budget: Message from the President of the United States*, H. Doc. 123, 87 Cong. 1 sess. (1961).

2. See Edward R. Fried and others, *Setting National Priorities: The 1974 Budget* (Brookings Institution, 1973), p. 296.

3. For budgets, divisions, etc., see *United States Defense Policies in 1961*, H. Doc. 502, 87 Cong. 2 sess. (1961), pp. 28, 81–83. For a general discussion of the buildup of U.S. conventional forces in the early sixties, see William W. Kaufman, *The McNamara Strategy* (Harper and Row, 1964); and Alain C. Enthoven and K. Wayne Smith, *How Much Is Enough? Shaping the Defense Program, 1961–1969* (Harper and Row, 1971).

The Kennedy-Johnson defense posture was not intended to rely on conventional strategy alone—just as the Eisenhower-Dulles policy had not relied solely on nuclear weapons. But the two approaches differed significantly in the degree of emphasis placed on nuclear and nonnuclear defense. The key objective of flexible response was to maintain forces capable of meeting conventional threats so that the United States would not be faced with the choice of either using nuclear weapons or forgoing vital interests abroad because it lacked nonnuclear options. Administration officials left open the possibility that they might decide to initiate tactical or even strategic nuclear strikes in certain circumstances, but viewed this as an undesirable option to be considered as a last resort.

Unlike many officials in the Eisenhower administration, Kennedy administration analysts considered tactical nuclear weapons to be dangerous and ineffective military instruments. Secretary McNamara explained that the use of these "extremely destructive devices" would lead to substantial damage in "such heavily populated areas as Europe" and would represent "a very definite threshold, beyond which we enter a vast unknown."[4] Defense Department planners generally were skeptical of the feasibility of fighting a limited war with tactical nuclear weapons and urged that the United States retain a "firebreak" between conventional conflict and *any* type of nuclear war. Accordingly, while the administration eventually increased U.S. tactical nuclear capabilities in Europe and Asia by 60 percent, it emphasized that these weapons were not a substitute for conventional forces but had been deployed primarily to deter the use of tactical nuclear weapons by the USSR and to strengthen deterrence by introducing the possibility that such weapons might be launched in response to large-scale aggression.

Although the administration never denied the importance of U.S. strategic and tactical nuclear forces in deterring large-scale Soviet conventional or nuclear aggression, it attempted to persuade America's European allies of the necessity of strengthening the conventional capabilities of the North Atlantic Treaty Organization (NATO). A similar effort had been made during the early 1950s, but Kennedy ad-

4. Statement of Secretary of Defense Robert S. McNamara in *Hearings on Military Posture*.... before the House Committee on Armed Services, 88 Cong. 1 sess. (1963), no. 4, p. 299.

ministration officials buttressed their case for increased allied force contributions by arguing that effective conventional defense was now feasible due to more realistic assessments of the conventional capabilities of the Warsaw Pact nations. Nevertheless, Western European leaders remained reluctant to build conventional defenses or to base NATO planning on fighting limited wars—whether conventional or nuclear—and continued to advocate a policy of automatic escalation based on the early use of nuclear weapons. Despite these objections, NATO's conventional strength gradually increased, and before the Johnson administration ended, the alliance officially adopted a flexible response strategy that retained a nuclear first-use option but reflected movement away from the earlier and more rigid "massive retaliation" doctrine. In Asia, the United States retained a tactical nuclear force, but conventional capabilities in the region were expanded even before the Vietnam escalation to permit a sustained nonnuclear response to Chinese aggression.

Responses to Crises

In policy statements as well as in defense posture decisions, the Kennedy-Johnson administrations sought to diminish the political importance of nuclear power and the military utility of nuclear force. Administration leaders were more prone to consider nonnuclear alternatives when faced with crises than were their counterparts in the Eisenhower administration. During the Kennedy-Johnson years, the United States faced overseas crises during the Bay of Pigs invasion, the revolt in the Dominican Republic, and Communist activities in Laos. Like the Vietnam war, these conflicts did not affect the U.S.-Soviet strategic balance and raised little prospect of nuclear escalation. On the other hand, the Berlin crisis and the Cuban missile crisis, both of which forced the Kennedy administration to early tests of its defense policy, did involve the strategic balance and revealed the practical limitations as well as the effectiveness of the flexible response doctrine.

BERLIN REPLAYED

Like the Eisenhower administration before it, the Kennedy administration responded with determination to Khrushchev's renewed demands concerning Berlin in the spring of 1961. Having rejected massive retaliation, however, the new administration attempted to apply its defense concept in reacting to the renewed Berlin crisis. In a major statement on Berlin, delivered on July 25 of that year, President Kennedy stressed that the United States intended to "have a wider choice than humiliation or all-out nuclear action."[5] To provide improved conventional capabilities, the President requested supplementary defense funds of nearly $3 billion for nonnuclear material, mobilized National Guard divisions, moved 40,000 men to Europe, and doubled draft calls. This was quite the opposite of Eisenhower's decision to emphasize *reductions* in conventional strength in the middle of the Berlin situation of 1959.

However, despite a preference for flexible response and the approval of the military budget supplement to carry out this policy, the Kennedy administration, still burdened with the previous administration's defense posture, lacked the operational nonnuclear capabilities needed to support its doctrine at the time of the Berlin crisis. For this reason, the President brought strategic power into the picture. In his July statement, for example, President Kennedy reminded Kremlin leaders that "an attack upon [Berlin] will be regarded as an attack upon us all," alluded to the possibility of nuclear war, requested additional funds for civil defense, and announced a delay in the planned deactivation of B-47 bombers.[6] These declarations and decisions could have been interpreted as prudential steps designed to deter Soviet military action without provocation and to place the United States in a position of readiness in the event of a major military clash. On the other hand, such moves might have represented a deliberate attempt to bring American nuclear capabilities to bear on the situation in Berlin.

It is important to recall that the Berlin crisis of 1961 occurred when the Kennedy administration was attempting to accurately assess the Soviet Union's strategic programs. By the early fall of 1961, fears of a possible "missile gap" had officially been put to rest, and the unsettled situation in Berlin provided a particularly timely reason for informing Soviet leaders that their missile claims were known to be false. If Khrushchev "were allowed to continue to assume that we still believed

5. "Radio and Television Report to the American People on the Berlin Crisis, July 25, 1961," *Public Papers of the Presidents of The United States: John F. Kennedy, 1961* (1962), p. 535.

6. Ibid., pp. 534–36.

in the missile gap," Roger Hilsman, then of the State Department, ex-plained, "he would very probably bring the world dangerously close to war."[7] During a meeting in early October, the President may have told Soviet Foreign Minister Andrei Gromyko that the United States was able to accurately assess Soviet missile deployments.[8] In any case, within a few weeks, Deputy Defense Secretary Roswell Gilpatric pub-licly exposed the myth of Soviet missile superiority. Before the end of the month, Khrushchev took the pressure off Berlin and by early 1962 the crisis had dissipated. Perhaps Kremlin leaders were intimidated by the West's generally firm stance and the activation of conventional forces in the United States or were simply content with having achieved the erection of the Berlin Wall. But U.S. strategic superiority and President Kennedy's allusions to nuclear war probably hastened Khrushchev's decision to end the crisis.[9]

The precise degree to which the Kennedy administration deliber-ately used its strategic advantage to affect the outcome in Berlin can-not be established. At one point in the crisis, President Kennedy acknowledged that a misjudgment on either side could unleash a thermonuclear holocaust, and in planning his responses the President sought to minimize the chance of a direct confrontation between U.S. and Soviet forces.[10] However, although the President sought to deal with the crisis through diplomatic means and limited military maneu-vers, he did not hesitate to stress U.S. strategic power in what seemed to be an attempt to influence Soviet actions.[11] To the extent that Kennedy administration officials appreciated the value of U.S. strategic power during the Berlin crisis, they also saw its risks and subsequently set out with increased energy to acquire the nonnuclear defense capa-bilities necessary to depart from Eisenhower's policy of nuclear em-phasis. One year later, however, a more serious crisis arose when it

7. Roger Hilsman, To Move a Nation: The Politics of Foreign Policy in the Administration of John F. Kennedy (Doubleday, 1964), p. 163.

8. Philip J. Klass, Secret Sentries in Space (Random House, 1971), pp. 107–8.

9. See Arnold L. Horelick and Myron Rush, Strategic Power and Soviet Foreign Policy (University of Chicago Press, 1966), pp. 85–88 and 125–26.

10. "Radio and Television Report on the Berlin Crisis," Public Papers, 1961, p. 536.

11. This interpretation of Kennedy's policies in the Cuban crisis is supported in Herbert S. Dinerstein, "The Soviet Outlook," in Robert E. Osgood and others, America and the World (Johns Hopkins Press, 1970), pp. 93–94; and Michael Brower, "Controlled Thermonuclear War," The New Republic, July 30, 1962, pp. 9–15.

became clear to the U.S. government that the Soviet Union had begun to install medium- and intermediate-range ballistic missiles (MR/IRBMs) in Cuba.

CUBAN MISSILE CRISIS

Concern over the possible effect of these Soviet deployments in Cuba on the relative strategic positions of the United States and the Soviet Union were among the factors motivating Kennedy administration leaders to take the actions necessary to force Khrushchev to remove the missiles. To some extent, the President and the secretary of defense may have feared that the United States could lose some of the political advantage it had recently acquired and that America's prestige might suffer a setback because of a rapid increase of Soviet nuclear power. On October 22, 1972, the President told the American people:

This secret, swift, and extraordinary buildup of Communist missiles . . . in violation of Soviet assurances, and in defiance of American hemispheric policy . . . is a deliberately provocative and unjustified change in the status quo which cannot be accepted by this country if our courage and our commitments are ever to be trusted again by either friend or foe.[12]

For these and other reasons, President Kennedy said that America's "unswerving objective" must be to "secure withdrawal or elimination" of the Soviet missiles in Cuba.[13] Efforts were made to deal with the crisis through the United Nations, the Organization of American States, and contacts with Soviet officials, but success appeared improbable. Moreover, for a variety of reasons the President was reluctant to immediately seek a purely diplomatic means of settling the crisis. The most notable example was his refusal to accept suggestions made at an early stage that he formally agree to "trade" U.S. IRBMs still based in Turkey and Italy as a quid pro quo for Soviet withdrawal of missiles from Cuba, although he eventually accepted this plan informally during the final resolution of the situation.

In short, the administration sought to remove the missiles through

---

12. "Radio and Television Report to the American People on the Soviet Arms Buildup in Cuba, October 22, 1962," *Public Papers of the Presidents of the United States: John F. Kennedy, 1962* (1963), p. 807.

13. Ibid. For comprehensive analyses of the Cuban missile crisis, see Graham T. Allison, *Essence of Decision: Explaining the Cuban Missile Crisis* (Little, Brown, 1971); and Jerome H. Kahan and Anne K. Long, "The Cuban Missile Crisis: A Study of Its Strategic Context," *Political Science Quarterly*, vol. 87 (December 1972), pp. 564–90.

military means, applying the principles of flexible response. All of the military options discussed by the Executive Committee of the National Security Council (Ex Comm)—naval blockade, air strikes against the sites, the invasion of the island—were nonnuclear and consistent with the plan to use a graduated series of military moves.[14] As an immediate reaction to the crisis, the United States had already arrayed massive conventional power for potential use against Cuba, establishing large naval forces in the area and redeploying tactical aircraft wings within striking range. Thus, unlike the earlier challenge in Berlin, the preponderance of U.S. nonnuclear capabilities in the area now made flexible response a credible, practical, and effective alternative.

In considering military options, President Kennedy at once rejected any first use of U.S. nuclear weapons, knowing that a strategic war would be catastrophic. The President also was extremely concerned that events might drift out of control, and he remained alert to the possibility that a strategic nuclear war could occur inadvertently by miscalculation or through an irreversible series of limited moves on each side. Despite cautious behavior designed to avoid nuclear war, however, President Kennedy seemed prepared to take an action—the launching of an air strike against Cuba—that could have had this result.

On October 27, 1962, the difficult decision had been made to respond to a letter from Khrushchev and to accept his solution of exchanging a U.S. pledge not to invade Cuba for the removal of the Soviet missiles. The crisis was then at a crucial point, for it was apparent from reconnaissance overflights that, despite the U.S. naval blockade, the missile sites would soon be operational. In an interview with Soviet Ambassador Anatoliy Dobrynin, Robert Kennedy explained that if the United States did not receive a Soviet commitment to remove the bases, the United States would remove them. He reminded Dobrynin that if the United States were forced to invade Cuba, and if the Soviet Union took retaliatory action, "there would be not only dead Americans but dead Russians as well."[15] In effect, this was an ultimatum, deliberately conveyed to Dobrynin by President Kennedy's

14. For a fuller discussion of the Kennedy administration's use of the flexible response strategy, see Albert and Roberta Wohlstetter, "Controlling the Risks in Cuba," *Adelphi Papers*, no. 17 (London: Institute for Strategic Studies, April 1965).

15. Robert F. Kennedy, *Thirteen Days: A Memoir of the Cuban Missile Crisis* (New American Library, 1969), p. 108.

order. That Robert Kennedy, in a belated gesture, also transmitted the President's offer to withdraw U.S. missiles from Turkey once the crisis was over does not alter the fact of the ultimatum.[16]

Two days after the meeting between Robert Kennedy and Dobrynin, Khrushchev accepted the U.S. terms and agreed to withdraw the missiles. There were several reasons for the withdrawal. For one thing, Washington's interests in Cuba were more dominant than Moscow's, and the Kremlin's deceitful behavior during the crisis had put the United States in a stronger diplomatic position than the USSR. Moreover, President Kennedy's pledge not to invade Cuba and his eleventh-hour offer to remove U.S. missiles from Turkey gave Khrushchev the opportunity to save face. But many experts contend that the most compelling reason of all for the withdrawal was the overwhelming superiority of U.S. military forces during the Cuban crisis. Secretary McNamara asserted that "Khrushchev knew . . . that he faced the full military power of the United States, including its nuclear weapons . . . that is the reason, and the only reason, why he withdrew those weapons."[17]

U.S. dominance in conventional arms was clearly a major factor in the USSR's decision to remove its missiles. But a case can be made that U.S. strategic superiority strengthened the President's resolve in dealing with Khrushchev. Although President Kennedy made no direct nuclear threats or specific references to the U.S. strategic advantage, he may well have concluded that the nation's nuclear power would have a restraining and possibly a coercive effect on the behavior of Soviet leaders. As the crisis progressed, the military position of U.S. strategic forces, which could at least limit damage from Soviet nuclear strikes, might have increased the propensity of administration officials to risk the possibility of nuclear war through their actions. Significantly, Defense Secretary McNamara later acknowledged that, while waiting for Khrushchev's

16. Alexander L. George, David K. Hall, and William E. Simons, in *The Limits of Coercive Diplomacy: Laos, Cuba, Vietnam* (Little, Brown, 1971), explained that Kennedy, in addition to demanding removal of the missiles, "had finally added the two missing elements of a classical ultimatum—a time limit for compliance and a credible threat of punishment for non-compliance" (p. 125). Allison, in *Essence of Decision*, noted that the Soviet Union attached great significance to the threat of an air strike (pp. 64–65).

17. *Department of Defense Appropriations for 1964*, Hearings before a Subcommittee of the House Committee on Appropriations, 88 Cong. 1 sess. (1963), pt. 1, p. 31.

reaction to the President's proposed settlement, the United States "faced ... the possibility of launching nuclear weapons" in the event the Soviet Union did not comply.[18] Robert Kennedy recalled that the consensus of Ex Comm was "that if the Russians were ready to go to nuclear war over Cuba . . . we might as well have the showdown [immediately] as six months later."[19]

President Kennedy's actions during the Cuban crisis have been both praised and criticized. Much of the controversy centered on two related questions: the importance of getting the missiles withdrawn and the degree of nuclear risk the United States should be prepared to take given the stakes involved. Many observers—and almost all participants in the government's decisions—maintain that the President exhibited great restraint in his efforts to obtain removal of the missiles. They emphasize the President's use of graduated responses, his obvious sensitivity to the danger of nuclear war, and the masterful way in which he gave Khrushchev room to maneuver. Others argue that he acted irresponsibly by bringing the world too close to nuclear war, refusing to seek a negotiated settlement early in the crisis, and taking a strong position for domestic political reasons.

Entirely apart from politics, it was, of course, essential for the administration to have the Soviet missiles removed from Cuba. The foreign policy consequences of a rapid increase in Soviet nuclear power and the way in which Moscow ignored our previous warnings could have raised serious security problems for the West and ultimately could have led to other crises, while the existence of soft Soviet missile sites close to the United States would have introduced a potential instability. Balanced against these possible but uncertain future prospects was the more immediate danger that, despite attempts to apply graduated options and to guard against escalation, U.S. actions designed to force removal of the missiles could have led to nuclear war. An earlier willingness to trade U.S. missiles stationed in Turkey— missiles already approved for deactivation—might have solved the problem with less risk of nuclear war by avoiding the need to present

18. Ibid. For a discussion of strategic balance and the Cuban missile crisis, see Kahan and Long, "The Cuban Missile Crisis"; and Walter Slocombe, "The Political Implications of Strategic Parity," *Adelphi Papers*, no. 77 (London: Institute for Strategic Studies, 1971).

19. Cited in Arthur Schlesinger, *A Thousand Days: John F. Kennedy in the White House* (Houghton Mifflin, 1965), pp. 829–30.

Khrushchev with an ultimatum and to seriously consider an air strike against Cuba.

According to Arthur Scheslinger, President Kennedy's "feelings underwent a qualitative change after Cuba: a world in which nations threatened each other with nuclear weapons now seemed to him . . . an intolerable and impossible world."[20] As a result of the Cuban experience, Khrushchev as well as Kennedy gained a clearer appreciation of the nuclear dangers inherent in a U.S.-Soviet confrontation, and the crisis gave immediate impetus to negotiations that led to the partial test ban and other limited agreements. On the other hand, the Cuban crisis had the destabilizing effect of stimulating Soviet programs to redress the intercontinental nuclear balance and of retarding progress in the field of strategic arms control.

Strategic Arms Policies

In his first budget message to Congress, President Kennedy observed that the adequacy of U.S. deterrent power should be measured by the ability of our strategic forces to survive a first strike and to inflict devastating retaliatory damage on any potential aggressor and not by simple comparisons of U.S.-Soviet missile and bomber deployments.[21] Strategic force decisions during the Kennedy-Johnson years were greatly influenced by Secretary McNamara's analytic approach to defense planning, which emphasized combat effectiveness over numerical comparisons. But U.S. strategic policies throughout this period were also influenced by a political interest in maintaining some degree of visible superiority and were not guided solely by cost-effectiveness criteria or the need to maintain a militarily adequate deterrent.

Reversing the Gap

In January 1961, President Kennedy instructed Secretary McNamara to undertake a broad reappraisal of defense strategy and capabilities, including a major study of the requirements for U.S. strategic forces during the decade ahead.[22] After he evaluated the preliminary results of this review, the President formulated a series of recommendations

20. Ibid., p. 893.
21. *Recommendations Relating to Our Defense Budget*, pp. 5–8.
22. See Enthoven and Smith, *How Much Is Enough?* p. 172.

relating to the U.S. defense posture and conveyed these proposals to Congress. The most important part of the President's request dealt with the Polaris and Minuteman missile programs. The initial plan called for a major acceleration of Polaris submarine construction. Ten additional boats were to be built by 1964, bringing the authorized force level to 29. Minuteman production would be doubled, which would increase the number of missiles to 800. President Kennedy justified these requests, particularly the Polaris expansion, on the grounds that such actions were needed to ensure the acquisition of a powerful and invulnerable strategic deterrent as soon as possible.

Many scholars and former officials have questioned the validity of the Kennedy administration's rationale for expanding U.S. strategic missile programs, arguing that the President was motivated, not by national security considerations, but by the need to support his campaign claims of a missile gap and to accommodate demands from the military services.[23] While the significance of these factors cannot be ignored, it should be recalled that, when the President made his special defense budget proposals in early 1961, there appeared to be real uncertainty within the administration about the Soviet Union's ICBM efforts. In all probability, a select group of incoming administration leaders were made aware of U-2 intelligence information, but the coverage of the U-2 flights had not been extensive. Moreover, no aircraft overflights had been undertaken since May 1960, and during the latter part of that year the USSR could have begun to deploy ICBMs without our knowledge. Although information was becoming available from reconnaissance satellites launched in late 1960, the evidence was either incomplete or inconclusive, and contradictory intelligence estimates compounded the problem of gaining accurate insights into the actual strategic situation.

At a background press briefing in February 1961, Secretary Mc-Namara remarked that at that time the Soviet Union probably had no more intercontinental ballistic missiles than the United States. Press Secretary Pierre Salinger and President Kennedy himself, however, immediately challenged McNamara's statement, claiming that it was premature to conclude that the missile gap had vanished, since administra-

23. See D. J. Ball, "The Strategic Missile Programme of the Kennedy Administration, 1961–1963" (Ph.D. dissertation, Australian National University, 1972). See also Graham T. Allison and Frederic A. Morris, "Armaments and Arms Control: Exploring the Determinants of Military Weapons," *Daedalus*, vol. 104 (Summer 1975), pp. 99–129.

86 SECURITY IN THE NUCLEAR AGE

tion studies of this issue had not yet been completed.[24] Despite McNamara's controversial slip, which suggested to some that the administration might be withholding information that could explode the missile gap myth, it seems plausible that the ambiguities characterizing Soviet missile programs during the early months of 1961 were sufficient to support President Kennedy's belief that the Polaris and Minuteman efforts should be increased in order to strengthen U.S. strategic deterrent capabilities.

Although it is difficult to reliably reconstruct the sequence of events, shifts in perceptions, and decision processes that influenced estimates and interpretations of Soviet missile programs throughout the Kennedy administration's first year, apparently it was not until the middle of September 1961 that the administration officially dismissed the possibility that the Kremlin was pursuing a substantial ICBM buildup.[25] Throughout the spring and summer of that year, unofficial reports and leaks suggested that estimates of Soviet ICBM levels had been lowered even further, but the USSR had a production potential, and intelligence information indicated that Soviet missile development had not slackened—thus strengthening the position of analysts who argued that substantial Soviet missile deployments might be under way. Satellite missions indicated, for example, that the USSR was developing a new generation SS-7 ICBM, and in August 1961 the Soviet Union tested an extended-range ICBM. By the fall, however, more detailed and comprehensive photographic data from satellite missions became available, covering all potential Soviet missile deployment sites. At last administration leaders generally agreed that the United States was *ahead* of the USSR in number of deployed strategic missiles, finally putting to rest the fear of a missile gap.

Pursuing a Strategic Buildup

But the lowered estimates associated with the demise of the missile gap did not result in a modification of the Kennedy administration's

24. See Harold W. Chase and Allen H. Lerman, eds., *Kennedy and the Press: The News Conferences* (Crowell, 1965), pp. 19–20; and "The Missile Gap Flap," *Time*, February 17, 1961, pp. 12–13.

25. This view is supported in Klass, *Secret Sentries in Space*, pp. 100–108; Hilsman, *To Move a Nation*, p. 163; and Ball, "The Strategic Missile Program." The latter concluded that "the whole Administration was apparently convinced of the disappearance of the 'missile gap' by the fall of 1961" (p. 166).

initial strategic force decisions. In fact, rather than slowing down the pace of U.S. procurement programs or reducing deployment goals, the administration subsequently raised the Minuteman and Polaris force levels to 1,000 missiles and 41 submarines. It is possible to justify the decision to continue enlarging U.S. strategic forces after it became clear that the USSR had only a token operational ICBM force on the basis of prudent defense planning. From the viewpoint of a conservative U.S. defense analyst, it might have seemed plausible that the Kremlin could initiate a major ICBM deployment effort in the near future. This was the very explanation later offered by Defense Secretary McNamara when he indicated that the USSR had only a "very small operational arsenal of intercontinental missiles" in 1961 but possessed the *capacity* to expand its forces substantially.[26] Since the United States could not be certain that the Soviet Union would not build a large force in the near future, McNamara explained, the administration had no choice but to continue its planned missile programs as a hedge against this eventuality.

Nevertheless, even if these premises are accepted, it is difficult to construct a persuasive case on *military grounds alone* that the United States, at that time, needed to go beyond the previous administration's plans for Minuteman and Polaris in order to guarantee a secure deterrent posture for the 1960s. The Kennedy administration had, of course, cut back or canceled a number of strategic programs contained in the Eisenhower administration's last defense budget, including additional liquid-fuel missile deployments, and had eliminated an approved project for three wings of land-mobile ICBMs. But the fully authorized Eisenhower program of 19 missile-firing submarines and 450 silo-based Minuteman missiles—approximately half the size of the final Kennedy programs—would have provided the United States with an extremely powerful deterrent capability. To take the argument one step further, if the USSR had moved toward a major missile buildup, U.S. intelligence systems could have detected such actions in time for necessary countermeasures to be instituted. Although defense studies in the early 1960s produced a range of military requirements for future U.S. force levels, they provided no unique quantitative solution, and there is

26. Robert S. McNamara, "The Dynamics of Nuclear Strategy," Address given at the annual convention of United Press International Editors and Publishers in San Francisco, September 18, 1967, *Department of State Bulletin*, vol. 57 (October 9, 1967), pp. 443–45.

evidence that certain White House advisers had concluded that the United States could accept significantly lower levels of strategic missiles than those being proposed by the Pentagon.[27]

POLITICAL PRESSURES

But a full appreciation of the administration's second series of missile decisions cannot be acquired through strict military considerations. For one thing, domestic politics, which played a role in the initial decision to expand U.S. strategic programs, continued to constrain the President's choices. When the missile gap was exposed, the administration apparently was reluctant to approach Congress and reverse its earlier budget requests. Secretary McNamara's concern over "getting murdered" on Capitol Hill was reported to have influenced his recommendation to President Kennedy that the number of Minuteman ICBMs be increased.[28] Equally important were the effects of the bureaucracy on the Kennedy administration's decisions on strategic force levels. It has been suggested, for instance, that the ultimate decision to build 1,000 Minuteman missiles may simply have represented a compromise between Air Force demands for at least 3,000 and alternative proposals for a minimum ICBM force, while the final number of 41 Polaris submarines may have reflected an arbitrary 10 percent cut in the official Navy request of 45 boats.[29] On the other hand, to attempt to explain the administration's missile programs in the years 1961–62 entirely on domestic political and bureaucratic grounds is to ignore the fact that President Kennedy's decisions to accelerate and then to sustain U.S. strategic programs were strongly motivated by foreign policy considerations.

FOREIGN POLICY CONSIDERATIONS

Notwithstanding official claims that military requirements should determine force levels, the Kennedy administration attached appreciable

27. See Schlesinger, *A Thousand Days*, pp. 499–500; and statement of Jerome B. Wiesner, Provost, Massachusetts Institute of Technology, in *ABM, MIRV, SALT and the Nuclear Arms Race,* Hearings before the Subcommittee on Arms Control, International Law and Organization of the Senate Foreign Relations Committee, 91 Cong. 2 sess. (1970), pp. 395–96.

28. David Halberstam, *The Best and the Brightest* (Random House, 1972), p. 72.

29. Air Force desires concerning ICBMs ranged widely during the bargaining process with McNamara, but former presidential science adviser Jerome Wiesner claimed that the Air Force wanted 3,000 ICBMs and that McNamara settled for 1,000. See Wiesner statement in *ABM, MIRV, SALT, and the Nuclear Arms Race,* p. 396. See also Allison and Morris, "Armaments and Arms Control."

importance to regaining America's position of strategic superiority. The President seemed to believe that the United States had been on the defensive since Sputnik and that it was imperative for the country to obtain a superior nuclear position that all nations could clearly recognize. Many administration leaders shared the view of Assistant Secretary of Defense Paul Nitze that U.S. superiority was "strategically important in the equation of deterrence and strategy" when dealing with the USSR.[30] They also judged it particularly important to acquire the image of superiority as a means of enhancing the credibility of the U.S. nuclear commitment while persuading our NATO allies to contribute to the conventional defense of Europe.

In the fall of 1961, therefore, the President decided to expose the myth of Soviet superiority while emphasizing the growing U.S. strategic advantage.[31] The Berlin situation presented the administration with a particularly timely reason for underscoring this point and informing Soviet leaders in early October that the United States was well aware of the USSR's weak strategic position. Over the next few months, the theme of U.S. superiority was hammered home in a series of coordinated public statements by administration officials, most notably by Deputy Defense Secretary Gilpatric who claimed in late October that the United States could now "penetrate" the secrecy surrounding the Soviet Union's military forces. On the basis of this knowledge, he asserted, America's strategic power was clearly superior to that of the Soviet Union. Gilpatric dramatized this conclusion by pointing out that the United States possessed a second-strike capability that was "at least as extensive as that the Soviets can deliver by striking first."[32]

The Kennedy administration's concern over the relative U.S.-Soviet balance of forces on the strategic level was demonstrated the following year during the Cuban missile crisis. It was difficult to ignore the fact that the USSR, with an increased capacity to deliver missile-launched nuclear warheads against the United States, would pose a greater threat to both the U.S. population and to our strategic forces. Further-

30. Cited in William Kaufmann, *The McNamara Strategy* (Harper and Row, 1964), p. 109.

31. See McGeorge Bundy, "The Presidency and the Peace," *Foreign Affairs*, vol. 42 (April 1964), pp. 353–65; Hilsman, *To Move a Nation*, p. 163; and Horelick and Rush, *Strategic Power and Soviet Foreign Policy*, p. 125.

32. Roswell L. Gilpatric, "Present Defense Policies and Program," Speech delivered before the Business Council at the Homestead, Hot Springs, Va., October 21, 1961, *Vital Speeches of the Day*, vol. 28 (December 1, 1961), p. 99.

more, because the missiles were at close range and could bypass the U.S. warning net, they endangered the survivability of many of our bombers, while their soft basing suggested to some officials that they could be used only in a first strike and could therefore introduce an unstable element into the strategic relationship. But the President and his advisers knew that the Soviet deployment could not seriously endanger the U.S. deterrent—if for no other reason than that our Polaris submarines and hardened ICBMs would remain secure. Moreover, they were aware that the USSR already had the ability to deliver nuclear weapons against the United States with a small force of intercontinental missiles. If the Soviet Union had increased its *long-range* missile force instead of emplacing short-range missiles in Cuba, the effect would have been essentially the same.

The potential foreign policy consequences of a perceived shift in the strategic balance were more significant in shaping the administration's response than either military considerations or domestic politics. During the crisis, for example, the President stated publicly that the USSR had never before stationed nuclear systems outside its borders and observed that any "sudden change" in nuclear deployments "may well be regarded as a definite threat to peace."[33] He later explained that he did not believe the Soviet Union would actually fire the missiles placed in Cuba, but that these deployments "would have politically changed the balance of power. It would have appeared to, and appearances contribute to reality."[34]

CONTROLLED RESPONSE

In addition to serving broad foreign policy objectives, a superior U.S. strategic position was a prerequisite of one of the most controversial aspects of the Kennedy administration's military policy—the doctrine of "controlled response." Many administration officials entered office believing that there was more to strategic planning than designing an invulnerable force that could withstand a Soviet nuclear attack and inflict retaliatory damage on the Soviet Union's population centers. In their view, the basic defense concept of flexible response, which emphasized the importance of conventional forces to provide nonnuclear options,

33. "Radio and Television Report on the Soviet Arms Buildup in Cuba," *Public Papers, 1962*, p. 807.
34. "Television and Radio Interview, 'After Two Years: A Conversation with the President,' December 17, 1962," *Public Papers, 1962*, pp. 897–98.

needed to be applied to strategic forces. Under the controlled response doctrine, the President would be given options permitting him to use strategic forces in limited ways rather than restricting his choice to destruction of the USSR through all-out massive retaliation.

The purpose of the controlled response doctrine was to introduce flexibility into the use of strategic forces in order to reduce damage to the United States and its allies in the event strategic weapons were ever used. As Secretary McNamara explained, such strategic flexibility would allow the United States to absorb a surprise attack and to use its remaining forces to limit damage by destroying Soviet nuclear systems before the USSR could launch a second salvo. Damage could also be limited by avoiding cities and by seeking to terminate a strategic exchange before it escalated to all-out destruction of population centers. Although command and control improvements were central to controlled response, the doctrine demanded a superior force that would enable U.S. leaders to launch counterforce attacks while holding a countercity deterrent in reserve. The controlled response doctrine received public prominence when Secretary McNamara described it in a speech delivered in Ann Arbor, Michigan, on June 16, 1962. In this speech, McNamara theorized that our large reserve of protected forces would give an opponent "the strongest imaginable incentive to refrain from striking our own cities," and thus the controlled response policy also became known as the "no-cities" doctrine.[35]

The Ann Arbor speech touched off a controversy in strategic circles within the United States. According to most official explanations, under the controlled response approach the United States would attempt to limit damage by means of *second-strike* counterforce attacks and, more important, by giving the USSR incentives to avoid targeting our cities in the event the Soviet Union launched its strategic weapons first. Critics, on the other hand, claimed that a second-strike counterforce capability was indistinguishable from a U.S. first-strike strategy and accused the administration of moving in destabilizing directions. Secretary McNamara expressed surprise that anyone could conclude that the United States was preparing a preemptive strike against the Soviet

35. Robert S. McNamara, "Defense Arrangements of the North Atlantic Community," Address given at the University of Michigan, June 16, 1962, *Department of State Bulletin*, vol. 47 (July 9, 1962), p. 67. For a detailed discussion of the origin and evolution of the controlled response, or no-cities, concept see Kaufmann, *The McNamara Strategy.*

Union, emphasizing that there was no reason for such a plan because America's nuclear forces were strong and survivable.

Throughout this debate, however, no administration official ever denied that the United States *might* use its controlled response capabilities to initiate a strategic nuclear attack in response to conventional aggression against its allies. Official policy had stopped short of a "no-first-use" declaration, keeping open the option of using strategic as well as tactical nuclear weapons if necessary to counter conventional aggression by the USSR. Even before Ann Arbor, McNamara had said that the first requirement of U.S. military policy was to maintain our strategic power as a "realistic, effective deterrent against Soviet initiation of major wars"—clearly encompassing a massive Soviet ground attack against our NATO allies.[36]

Kennedy administration officials saw the controlled response doctrine as a potentially useful political strategy for dealing with practical alliance difficulties, quite apart from its perceived military value. The Ann Arbor speech, it should be noted, was specifically tailored to European issues and had been drawn from closed-session remarks made by Secretary McNamara at an earlier meeting of the NATO Council in Athens. The new doctrine affirmed that the United States was prepared to use nuclear forces to defend Western Europe and implied that it might be possible to "fight" a strategic war without necessarily sustaining catastrophic damage—points, it was believed, that would enhance the credibility of our nuclear commitments, decrease the motivations for independent nuclear forces, and provide our allies with greater incentives to expand their conventional forces. The administration's policy did not serve its intended NATO objectives, however; overseas reactions to controlled response were largely negative due to concern that Western Europe might become a nuclear battlefield in the event of war, the long-standing NATO fear that limited nuclear war doctrines would weaken deterrence by reducing the risk of escalation, and the basic opposition in Europe to a conventional defense strategy.

In any case, U.S. strategic doctrine quickly began to place less emphasis on controlled response as a consequence of further analyses and changes in the nuclear balance. During 1963, for example, Pentagon officials spoke of the many uncertainties associated with attempts to

36. Department of Defense News Release 239-62, February 17, 1962, p. 5.

find means to control any U.S.-USSR strategic exchange that might occur and to prevent escalation into all-out nuclear war. Secretary McNamara explained to Congress that, as the USSR deployed large numbers of hardened ICBMs and sea-based ballistic missiles, "it will become increasingly difficult . . . to preclude major damage to the United States regardless of how large or what kind of strategic forces we build."[37] Toward the end of the year, in an important speech before the Economic Club in New York, McNamara suggested that it would be technically and financially impossible to prevent the Soviet Union from acquiring the capability to inflict severe damage on the United States and concluded that strategic nuclear war would be "highly destructive to both sides" under "all foreseeable circumstances."[38]

Despite the departure from the controlled response doctrine, the Kennedy administration continued to justify expenditures for offensive forces, above the level necessary to provide a countercity deterrent, as a means of providing damage-limitation options and contributing to a margin of U.S. superiority. The strategic plan of January 1963, for example, called for U.S. retaliatory forces to maintain the ability to destroy soft and semihard missile sites in the Soviet Union, and, even in his Economic Club speech, McNamara claimed that the "damage-limiting capability of our numerically superior forces is . . . well worth its incremental cost."[39] During the early 1960s, defense officials apparently believed that a U.S. counterforce capability was needed as a temporary measure to support commitments in Europe until NATO conventional force goals could be satisfied. Assistant Defense Secretary Alain Enthoven told a congressional committee:

We did not have adequate alternatives to threatening the use of nuclear force. And also we foresaw a period when our ballistic missile force would increase and advance very rapidly, and the Soviet forces would be quite vulnerable. So at that time and under those circumstances, damage limiting appeared to be a potentially usable strategy.[40]

By late 1963, the United States had an ambiguous strategic policy.

37. Statement of Secretary of Defense Robert S. McNamara in Hearings on Military Posture, p. 309.

38. Department of Defense News Release 1486-63, November 18, 1963, p. 8.

39. Ibid., p. 7.

40. Status of U.S. Strategic Power, Hearings before the Preparedness Investigating Subcommittee of the Senate Committee on Armed Services, 90 Cong. 2 sess. (1968), p. 138.

The Kennedy administration, like the Eisenhower administration in its second term, decided to steer between the strategies of pure deterrence and all-out superiority, and Secretary McNamara portrayed the administration's approach in those very terms, explicitly referring to the two extremes. On one side, explained the secretary, were the advocates of a full first-strike objective. But McNamara dismissed this goal as unattainable, regardless of the amount of effort put into either offensive or defensive damage-limiting programs. On the other side were those who advocated a "minimum deterrent" posture of survivable forces, sufficient only to retaliate against Soviet cities. McNamara rejected this approach as well, arguing that the nation needed a force "considerably larger" than that required for deterrence, since it was both desirable and possible to use our strategic forces to substantially reduce damage to the United States and Western Europe. Thus, he concluded, a policy that supplemented our basic offensive retaliatory deterrent force with a damage-limitation capability "appears to be the most practical and effective course."[41]

The Move to Assured Destruction

By the time President Johnson entered office, Secretary McNamara and his staff had formulated a highly structured approach to making specific weapon decisions and shaping the characteristics of our strategic posture. Within this framework, the direction of U.S. nuclear arms policies was to become clearer and the dominant features of the McNamara strategy were to be formed.

Secretary McNamara posited two strategic objectives: (1) "to deter a deliberate nuclear attack upon the United States and its allies by maintaining a clear and convincing capability to inflict unacceptable damage on an attacker"; and (2) in the event of war, "to limit damage to our population and industrial capacities."[42] The first objective was called "assured destruction" and the second "damage limitation." Since the early days of the Kennedy administration, these basic goals had

41. "Statement of Secretary of Defense Robert S. McNamara before the House Armed Services Committee on the Fiscal Year 1965–69 Defense Program and 1965 Defense Budget" (January 27, 1964; processed), pp. 30–31.

42. "Statement of Secretary of Defense Robert S. McNamara before the House Armed Services Committee on the Fiscal Year 1966–70 Defense Program and 1966 Defense Budget" (February 18, 1965; processed), p. 38.

been publicly discussed and used to guide U.S. weapon decisions, and virtually identical terms had been used by Defense Secretary Thomas Gates and others during the latter years of the Eisenhower administration.[43] Even though these strategic objectives were not new, however, they had never before been presented so comprehensively or applied so systematically to force planning.

In evaluating the forces needed to satisfy U.S. strategic objectives, defense planners tended to concentrate on the effectiveness of weapons and not on the number of delivery systems or the size of warheads. Again, this seemed to reflect the earlier Eisenhower administration concept of "adequacy," which called for the U.S. deterrent to satisfy performance requirements and not be guided by the simple balance of forces. But McNamara applied the effectiveness approach far more rigorously, turning it into an operational tool for managing our strategic posture. The Defense Department used techniques of systems analysis to compare the capabilities of both sides' strategic forces to inflict damage, taking into account such factors as survivability, reliability, and penetrability. Calculations covered a variety of assumed strategic war scenarios and possible Soviet threats. Within this framework, alternative annual force and budget decisions as well as five-year program plans were analyzed in an attempt to find the most effective way of meeting U.S. strategic objectives at the least cost. Weapon systems that were not needed to support these requirements or that provided only marginal contributions at great expense were viewed with disfavor.[44]

Under the formalized McNamara approach, assured destruction was given top priority, receiving first call on resources, and damage limitation was assigned a secondary role. Secretary McNamara succinctly expressed the reason for these priorities when he explained that "it is our ability to destroy an attacker . . . that provides the deterrent, not

43. In January 1960, for example, Defense Secretary Gates explained that the United States must establish and maintain an "assured retaliatory capability" through such techniques as "improved warning against both missile and aircraft attack, reduction of reaction time, dispersal, protective hardening, concealment, and mobility for our weapons systems." (*Department of Defense Appropriations for 1961*, Hearings before the Subcommittee of the House Committee on Appropriations, 88 Cong. 2 sess. [1960], pt. 1, p. 7.)

44. For a fuller discussion of McNamara's systems analysis approach to strategic planning, see Enthoven and Smith, *How Much Is Enough?* pp. 170–210; and Samuel A. Tucker, ed., *A Modern Design for Defense Decision: A McNamara-Hitch-Enthoven Anthology* (Industrial College of the Armed Forces, 1966).

our ability to partially limit damage to ourselves."[45] Left to be resolved, however, was the issue of how our assured destruction capability was to be measured and defined. It was obviously impossible to establish scientifically the necessary degree of destruction to deter the Soviet Union from launching a strategic attack or making moves that ran a high risk of escalating into nuclear war. Secretary McNamara judged, however, that a potential to destroy at least 25–30 percent of the USSR's population and two-thirds of its industrial capacity should serve as an effective deterrent. These requirements certainly seemed high enough, since they represented over twice the number of Russian lives lost in the Second World War. In any case, because of the rule of diminishing returns, substantially higher damage levels would have required a significant expansion in U.S. strategic forces and a sizable increase in defense spending. The precise figures were, of course, rather arbitrary, and McNamara later lowered the assured destruction levels to 20–25 percent population fatalities and one-half the Soviet Union's industrial capacity. As evidence of Chinese missile efforts mounted, the ability to destroy fifty urban centers (over 50 million people and half the industry) was set as an assured destruction level for the People's Republic of China.

ACHIEVING A CONFIDENT DETERRENT

Aside from damage levels, the concept of deterrence formulated by Secretary McNamara had another characteristic—that of assurance. McNamara argued that U.S. strategic forces must be able to perform their retaliatory mission with a high degree of confidence under all foreseeable conditions of deliberate nuclear attack. This would not only satisfy the requirement for maintaining a strong strategic posture, but in McNamara's judgment it would also improve the credibility of U.S. forces as seen by Soviet leaders and thus help ensure that deterrence would operate effectively. Because of the importance attached to designing a confident U.S. deterrent, the Pentagon devised procedures for evaluating force requirements that ultimately influenced the size and composition of the U.S. strategic force structure far more than the criteria for levels of destruction.

To begin with, defense analysts instituted systematic procedures for

45. "Statement of Secretary of Defense Robert S. McNamara before the House Armed Services Committee on the Fiscal Year 1968–72 Defense Program and 1968 Defense Budget" (January 23, 1967; processed), p. 39.

assessing U.S. strategic force requirements on a "worst-case" basis. Because of the long lead time between weapon development and deployment and the difficulty of predicting future Soviet nuclear capabilities, two sets of intelligence estimates were designed to guide U.S. weapon and budget decisions. One projected Soviet strategic posture was based on a so-called expected threat, which was plausible but biased toward the worst-case end of the spectrum. This estimate was used to determine procurement and deployment decisions necessary to satisfy the assured destruction requirement. The second estimate was based on an extremely unlikely "greater-than-expected" Soviet threat. Defense planners often used this projection to justify research and development programs needed to protect the U.S. deterrent against unexpected dangers.

As a related procedure, in analyses of hypothetical strategic exchanges devised as a means of evaluating current capabilities and estimating future needs, the USSR's weapons were assumed to operate relatively reliably, while U.S. systems were given less optimistic performance characteristics. U.S. strategic forces were then required to withstand an all-out Soviet counterforce strike and to inflict at least 25 percent fatalities in retaliation—analysts recognized that long-term casualties could be substantially greater but considered only the immediate effects of blast damage.

Finally, additional confidence was gained by maintaining a posture comprising three different systems—land-based ICBMs, sea-based missiles, and bombers—each of which could inflict considerable damage, approaching, if not always reaching, the assured destruction figure. Such diversification, it was claimed, would strengthen the U.S. deterrent by making a Soviet counterforce attack more complicated, offering insurance in the event of a catastrophic failure of one of the U.S. systems, and guarding against a possible Soviet technological breakthrough that might endanger the survivability of one particular type of weapon.

By the mid-1960s, the strategic plans instituted under the Kennedy administration were nearing completion. Deployment of ICBMs had leveled off at 1,000 Minuteman and 54 Titan II silo-based missiles, and the Polaris force was about to reach its full strength of 41 submarines. At the same time, earlier-model Atlas and Titan I ICBMs had been eliminated, and U.S. IRBMs had been withdrawn from Western Europe. The B-70 bomber program had been abandoned and the medium-range B-47 fleet was almost entirely deactivated, but the force of over 600 long-range B-52 aircraft remained a powerful component of the U.S. deterrent. In his annual posture statements and other public forums, Secretary McNamara sought to demonstrate that this force structure was more than adequate to satisfy the assured destruction objective. Calculations were presented to show that U.S. strategic forces could absorb a Soviet attack and inflict over 40 percent fatality damage—well above the minimum. A typical assessment indicated that more than half the total U.S. force would survive and remain effective if the Soviet Union were to launch all its available missiles in a counterforce attack.

Well before the Minuteman and Polaris deployment programs reached fruition, however, the prospect that the Soviet Union might field a large-scale antiballistic missile (ABM) system had created serious concern in the Pentagon over the ability of U.S. strategic forces to maintain an assured destruction capability through the late 1960s and early 1970s. As early as 1961, U.S. intelligence information suggested that the USSR might be installing an ABM defense near Leningrad, but this activity did not evolve into an operational deployment. In 1964, the Galosh ABM interceptor was displayed, and earlier evidence had already shown that the Soviet Union was constructing ABM defenses around Moscow. Compounding the problem were fears that the USSR's expanding Tallinn air-defense system, which was initially thought to be an ABM system itself, might have the capability of being upgraded to achieve a missile defense mission. These intelligence indicators, together with the stream of public statements by Soviet spokesmen favoring ABM deployments and claiming that the USSR had developed missile defense technology, put pressure on the United States to improve its strategic deterrent forces. By the logic of the McNamara approach, Soviet city-defense deployments would represent an attempt to prevent the United States from maintaining a reliable retaliatory capability, and "an increase in [Soviet] damage-limiting capability would require [the United States] to make greater investments in assured destruction."[46] In particular, uncertainty over Soviet ABMs gave impetus to a major strategic program—the multiple independently targetable reentry vehicle (MIRV).

46. Ibid.

MIRV DEVELOPMENT

The origins of MIRV and the factors that shaped its evolution into an operational weapon are extremely complicated questions involving a changing mixture of doctrinal logic, technical momentum, and bureaucratic politics.[47] In the early 1960s, the technology of multiple, or clustered, warheads had been developed as a means of increasing the destructive efficiency of U.S. missile payloads against urban targets and as a device for countering early-model short-range Soviet ABM systems. For these reasons, the United States had decided to install the multiple warhead A-3 SLBM on its late-model Polaris submarines. MIRV was essentially an extension of the simple multiple warhead approach, made feasible by improvements in guidance systems and the "space-bus" used by NASA. Although some signs of advanced Soviet ABM activities were seen, the initial interest in pursuing MIRV developments, according to John S. Foster, Jr., director of defense research and engineering at the Pentagon, stemmed largely if not entirely from the desire to "increase our targeting capability rather than to penetrate ABM defenses."[48] By subdividing the payload of a single missile and giving individual warheads the ability to be independently targeted, the number of "aim-points" in the USSR capable of being covered by a fixed number of U.S. launchers would be greatly increased. Such strategic requirements were consistent with the Kennedy administration's early stress on controlled response options.

By the mid-1960s, however, the notion that MIRVs should be viewed as a response to the anticipated construction of an extensive ABM network in the Soviet Union took hold as the dominant official rationale for stepping up efforts to acquire MIRV-carrying missiles. To be sure, the United States was developing and deploying a variety of penetration aids to enable its strategic missiles to offset Soviet ABMs, but studies such as the PEN-X Project demonstrated that MIRVs would offer a far more reliable technique for countering Soviet missile

47. For the single most comprehensive analysis of the U.S. MIRV program, see Ted Greenwood, "Qualitative Improvements in Offensive Strategic Arms: The Case of MIRV" (Ph.D. dissertation, Center for International Studies, Massachusetts Institute of Technology, August 1973).

48. Cited in James R. Kurth, "Why We Buy the Weapons We Do," *Foreign Policy*, no. 11 (Summer 1973), p. 48.

defenses than decoys, electronic jamming, or multiple warheads.[49] It was shown that, with MIRVs, the United States could retain a confident retaliatory capability for Minuteman and Polaris, regardless of the size and character of future Soviet ABMs, simply through the technique of "exhausting" the supply of missile defense interceptors. From a cost-effectiveness standpoint, MIRVs were much more attractive to civilian planners in the Pentagon than the alternative of building additional missile launchers to offset Soviet defensive systems.

"Of all the stimuli that led to the development of MIRV," arms expert Herbert York said, "the most important was the perceived need to penetrate ABM systems."[50] Whatever the precise mixture of reasons, the development of MIRVs was officially authorized in 1964, and within two years the MIRV-carrying Minuteman III and Poseidon missiles were approved as replacements for the early-model Minuteman ICBM and Polaris SLBMs.

As the Minuteman III and Poseidon programs were gaining momentum through increased funding and procurement decisions, the prospect of large-scale Soviet ABM deployments began to diminish. Throughout 1967 and 1968, there were no indications that the Moscow-type Galosh system was being installed in other parts of the Soviet Union, and mounting evidence suggested that the widely deployed Tallinn system was primarily for bomber defense. However, the Johnson administration's MIRV programs went ahead on schedule. In an attempt to explain the continued requests for funds to support MIRV efforts, Secretary McNamara acknowledged that "the majority of our intelligence community no longer believes that the so-called Tallinn system . . . has any significant ABM capability" but noted that, although no effort had been made to expand the Galosh ABM system beyond Moscow, it was necessary to "plan our forces on the assumption that [the Kremlin leaders] will have deployed some sort of an ABM system around their major cities by the early 1970s."[51]

49. The PEN-X Project did the technical design work for MIRVs, supported the Mark 100 warhead for multiple use on Polaris and Minuteman, and studied shielding problems of reentry vehicles. See Greenwood, "Qualitative Improvements in Offensive Strategic Arms," p. 168.

50. Herbert T. York, "Multiple-Warhead Missiles," *Scientific American*, November 1973, p. 27.

51. "Statement of Secretary of Defense Robert S. McNamara before the Senate Armed Services Committee on the Fiscal Year 1969–73 Defense Program and 1969 Defense Budget" (January 22, 1968; processed), pp. 55–56.

A persuasive case can be made that prudent planning justified the continuation of U.S. MIRV programs. Given the uncertainties regarding the meaning of ongoing Soviet test activities and the numerous statements issued by Kremlin leaders stressing the virtues of missile defenses, the possibility that the USSR would soon initiate a substantial ABM construction program could not be dismissed. Because MIRVs were scheduled for installation well before the USSR could mount such a massive ABM effort, even the most pessimistic calculations showed that with MIRVs the United States could retain a highly reliable and credible assured destruction capability. The MIRV-equipped Poseidon sea-based force would be especially effective, since it provided insurance against the *combined* greater-than-expected threat—that is, a large Soviet ABM capability coupled with a Soviet ICBM counterforce capability that could destroy American land-based missiles.

On the other hand, it can be argued that the decision to proceed with MIRVs represented an extreme application of worst-case planning.[52] Had the United States halted progress on Minuteman III and Poseidon MIRVs, for example, many experts claim that there would have been ample time to move ahead with these programs in response to Soviet ABM deployments if this proved necessary, and that penetration aids could have provided reasonable assurance of offsetting any initial defensive expansion in the USSR while more reliable countermeasures were being pursued to meet a full ABM threat. In any event, it is misleading to discuss the MIRV issue only in the context of assured destruction and the need to deal with Soviet ABMs. MIRV programs in the late 1960s shifted away from this orientation to include other strategic policy objectives reminiscent of those that had influenced the earliest development of these systems.

THE ABM BATTLE

Before turning to strategic offensive force issues during the final years of the Johnson administration, it would be appropriate to examine the question that dominated American nuclear strategy during the last half of the 1960s—the deployment of an ABM network in the United States. By 1965, a growing number of American officials had begun to share Secretary McNamara's view that the United States could not realistically hope to prevent the USSR from acquiring an invulnerable strategic pos-

52. See George W. Rathjens, *The Future of the Strategic Arms Race: Options for the 1970's* (Carnegie Endowment for International Peace, 1969).

ture and that the goal of achieving a major damage limitation capability through the development of improved offensive forces was becoming impractical. At about that time, however, the development of the advanced Nike-X ABM system had progressed to the point where many military and civilian leaders, believing that *defensive* damage limitation was now feasible, were advocating ABM deployment more intensely than they had supported the original Nike-Zeus system of the late 1950s and early 1960s. In addition to arguing that meaningful protection against Soviet missile attacks could be purchased at reasonable cost, Nike-X supporters strengthened their position by claiming that the United States should construct an ABM in order to match the USSR's apparent program to deploy missile defenses.

Although Secretary McNamara had approved ABM research and civil defense programs in the early 1960s, he later fought a sustained battle against the mounting pressure to field a large-scale U.S. ABM system.[53] Central to McNamara's position was the argument that the appropriate strategic response to a Soviet ABM deployment was *not* to build a matching system but to increase the ability of U.S. offensive forces to penetrate the USSR's defenses and maintain our assured destruction capability. Moreover, the secretary claimed, the deployment of an extensive ABM network at a cost of tens of billions of dollars could not be relied on to substantially reduce damage. The system itself would probably not work with perfect reliability, and it could be confused and overwhelmed by the size and tactics of an offensive attack. If the USSR increased its offensive capabilities, it could negate the benefits of our ABMs, since the cost advantage in an offense-defense race lay heavily with the offense. Surmising that the Soviet Union probably followed a strategy similar to ours, McNamara maintained that the USSR would almost certainly react to such a large U.S. damage-limiting program in order to preserve its deterrent. In any case, it would be useless to deploy an ABM without spending additional billions to build balanced defenses against bombers and to provide widespread civil defense protection. McNamara eventually went beyond the notion that ABM deployments would simply waste money and bring no security benefits, suggesting that mutual deployments of ABMs could stimulate the arms race and increase the danger of nuclear war.

53. Enthoven and Smith in *How Much Is Enough?* discussed McNamara's ABM battle. For McNamara's views, see his annual defense posture statements before the Senate Armed Services Committee for fiscal years 1965–69.

McNamara mustered persuasive analytic data to support the position that even an ABM costing tens of billions of dollars could not provide meaningful protection against Soviet attacks. In his annual posture statements, he presented tables showing the results of calculations assessing the implications of possible U.S. ABM deployments. Typically, two levels of ABMs were postulated—the so-called Posture A and Posture B configurations costing $15 billion and $25 billion respectively. The damage-limiting effectiveness of each system was then evaluated against two Soviet offensive threats—one developed from nominal intelligence projections and the other representing a "reactive threat" based on the assumption that the Soviet Union would act to counter our ABMs. The results were dramatic. With the larger ABM system installed, and under conditions favorable to America, U.S. fatalities would not drop below 20 million, even against the nominal threat. At far less cost than our ABM system, the Soviet Union could respond and raise U.S. fatalities to 90 million.

Despite McNamara's success in avoiding the deployment of a massive ABM system designed to limit damage from Soviet attacks, a decision was made in 1967 to construct the Sentinel system—a "light" ABM with nationwide coverage. In his annual posture statements during the previous few years, McNamara had referred to two types of ABM configurations other than the large-scale city defenses that were under consideration. The first was the so-called Thin-X option, which ultimately became Sentinel, and the second was a "hard-point" defense system designed to protect ICBM sites rather than population centers. Unlike the full Nike-X deployment or the Thin-X variation, both of which had damage limitation goals, hard-point defenses fulfilled the assured destruction objective of strengthening the survivability of offensive missile sites. Early research programs had indicated that effective site-defense systems required the development of special radars and interceptors optimized for this mission. Primarily owing to lack of support from the military services, however, only the Nike-X city-defense components were developed. Nevertheless, some Pentagon analysts advocated this form of missile-defense deployment in the months leading up to the ABM decision in 1967 as a prudent action to take in anticipation of possible Soviet threats to the survivability of the Minuteman force.[54]

When faced with the need to approve some form of ABM deploy-

54. See John Newhouse, *Cold Dawn: The Story of SALT* (Holt, Rinehart, and Winston, 1973), p. 86; and Allison and Morris, "Armaments and Arms Control."

ment in response to intense pressure from President Johnson and the Joint Chiefs of Staff, McNamara selected the Thin-X, or Sentinel, option. Some observers contend that both the timing of the ABM announcement and the type of system chosen were made inevitable by domestic political and military factors influencing the President.[55] Further delay, it is argued, was simply not possible, and the selection of a hard-point deployment pattern—even if preferred by McNamara— would have been inconsistent with "guidelines" allegedly given by President Johnson to the secretary of defense that required constructing a system with population protection capabilities in order to satisfy Congress and the Joint Chiefs. The question of Sentinel's "inevitability" will be explored below. Suffice it to say at this point that, in explaining the decision, Secretary McNamara and other U.S. officials argued that Sentinel would improve the reliability of our deterrent in crises, strengthen U.S. nonproliferation policies by enhancing the credibility of our nuclear guarantees in Asia, limit fatalities from Chinese ICBM attacks, and preclude major damage to the United States in the event of a small-scale missile attack from any source.[56]

It has been suggested that the rationale for Sentinel, particularly its anti-Chinese orientation, was essentially fabricated to justify a thin ABM configuration, which was the minimum system necessary to satisfy domestic demands. But many officials actually saw substantive merit in deploying a thin defense as a prudent response to China's anticipated deployment of a small ICBM force—despite the fact that most sinologists opposed a China-oriented system as unnecessary and potentially disadvantageous, while nongovernmental scientists questioned the technical effectiveness of an area ABM.[57]

Secretary McNamara made a determined effort to draw a distinction between a thin system and the Nike-X anti-Soviet ABM system and to minimize the possible destabilizing impact of Sentinel. What-

55. See Morton Halperin, "The Decision to Deploy the ABM: Bureaucratic and Domestic Politics in the Johnson Administration," *World Politics*, vol. 25 (October 1972), pp. 62–95 (Brookings Reprint 265).

56. For the administration's position, see Richard B. Stolley, "Defense Fantasy Now Come True," an interview with Robert McNamara, *Life*, September 29, 1967, pp. 28a–28c; and "Address by Assistant Secretary of Defense [Paul] Warnke to the Detroit Advocates Club (Extract), October 6, 1967," *Documents on Disarmament: 1967* (U.S. Arms Control and Disarmament Agency, 1968), pp. 454–59.

57. See J. I. Coffey, "The Anti-Ballistic Missile Debate," *Foreign Affairs*, vol. 45 (April 1967), pp. 403–13; and Richard L. Garwin and Hans A. Bethe, "Anti-Ballistic-Missile Systems," *Scientific American*, March 1968, pp. 21–31.

ever might be said regarding the validity of this distinction and the necessity for or desirability of the Sentinel decision itself, Sentinel fell far short of a full missile defense deployment and reflected Secretary McNamara's conviction that the United States should refrain from investing in major damage-limiting programs.

OFFENSIVE DAMAGE LIMITATION

On the offensive as well as on the defensive side, U.S. strategic arms decisions in the late 1960s demonstrated a lively interest in acquiring modest damage limitation capabilities. Because of the USSR's relatively invulnerable strategic force, military planners knew that the United States could not count on substantial damage limitation, but they argued that it was still possible to reduce damage to the United States and its allies by developing some capability to destroy Soviet land-based missiles. It was particularly significant that the Pentagon, throughout the rise of the assured destruction policy, still retained a counterforce option in its strategic plans and that U.S. forces were geared for this mission. As late as 1968, U.S. officials acknowledged that our targeting policy had never changed from that of the controlled response doctrine of 1962.

Renewed interest in counterforce options was reflected in arms programs, particularly in regard to MIRVs. While reaffirming that these weapons were being procured primarily for assured destruction purposes, administration spokesmen were quite candid in publicly admitting that in their opinion MIRVs were also a means of eventually obtaining damage-limiting capabilities.[58] The question of whether MIRVs were sought deliberately to satisfy this secondary objective was often avoided by officials who readily admitted that these and other offensive weapons acquired as a consequence of conservative planning were "in excess" of assured destruction needs, but they argued that it made economic as well as strategic sense to use such weapons for damage limitation and to develop the characteristics needed to support this mission—including improved accuracy and command and control capabilities. Although McNamara canceled a counterforce MIRV package for Poseidon consisting of three large

58. See, for example, the statement of Deputy Defense Secretary Paul Nitze in *Scope, Magnitude, and Implications of the United States Antiballistic Missile Program*, Hearings before the Subcommittee on Military Applications of the Joint Committee on Atomic Energy, 90 Cong. 1 sess. (1968), pp. 48–49.

warheads and stressed the need to install large numbers of small-yield warheads on U.S. land- and sea-based missiles, he nonetheless supported programs designed to improve accuracies.[59]

Renewed Emphasis on Superiority

The drive behind MIRV during the final phase of the Johnson administration raises the broader question of the degree to which strategic programs were related to a policy of nuclear superiority. In examining this issue, it is important to recall that throughout the last half of the 1960s, Secretary McNamara and other prominent spokesmen stressed the theme that strategic superiority was of limited significance and often described the concept itself as misleading. Once a nation had the capability for assured destruction, they argued, comparisons of missiles, megatonnage, and warheads had little meaning. Despite our strategic superiority, McNamara explained, "the blunt, inescapable fact remains that the Soviet Union could still effectively destroy the United States, even after absorbing the full weight of an American first strike."[60] The defense secretary presented a more sweeping conclusion when he stated that thermonuclear power "has proven to be a limited diplomatic instrument" and observed that America's substantial superiority "does not effectively translate into political control or diplomatic leverage."[61]

McNamara attempted to keep the quest for superiority in check by limiting the number of Minuteman and Polaris missiles and rejecting military requests for new strategic procurements, such as a follow-on bomber, an improved ICBM, and an advanced sea-based system—proposals that were gaining supporters as a result of major Defense Department studies undertaken in 1966, particularly the extensive STRAT-X study of future strategic requirements and alternative responses to the Soviet buildup of ICBMs and ABMs. In this sense, MIRV might well have represented a necessary concession in order to avoid going forward with the large-scale production of entirely new weapon systems. According to one observer, "MIRV was put to the

59. See Greenwood, "Qualitative Improvements in Offensive Strategic Arms," pp. 75–78, 110–21.

60. "Statement . . . on Fiscal Years 1969–73 Defense Program and 1969 Defense Budget," p. 52.

61. McNamara, "The Dynamics of Nuclear Strategy," p. 446.

service of restraint, and became a strong bureaucratic instrument for discouraging other new systems and high numbers of systems."[62] More generally, in his efforts to temper the size and character of offensive weapon programs, as in his fight against the ABM, Secretary Mc-Namara recognized the dynamics and dangers of the U.S.-Soviet strategic competition. This concern over the "action-reaction" cycle led McNamara first to seek to exert a restraining influence on Pentagon programs as a means of stabilizing the balance through unilateral actions and later to play an instrumental role in developing plans for the initiation of strategic arms control negotiations with the Soviet Union.

But even as they sought to downgrade the value of nuclear superiority and to highlight the concept of mutual stability, Johnson administration leaders did not hesitate to demonstrate that the United States was superior to the USSR and would remain so. Assistant Defense Secretary Enthoven supported McNamara's views on the limits of superiority but explained in 1968 that "we do not intend to allow our policy of basing the size of our forces on assured destruction to result in the Soviets overtaking us or even matching our strategic nuclear capability."[63] At the same time, however, Enthoven denied that U.S. strategic superiority was destabilizing and emphasized that the USSR would acquire a survivable strategic retaliatory force regardless of what the United States did.[64] U.S. officials buttressed their claims of superiority by focusing on simple numerical comparisons of power—an approach that contradicted the calculations of military effectiveness involved in the analytic approach to strategic planning. When presenting data on the relative U.S.-Soviet strategic balance, for example, Secretary McNamara would emphasize that the United States possessed a three-to-one to four-to-one superiority over the Soviet Union in separately deliverable warheads—a measure described as the most meaningful numerical, or "static," comparison of nuclear capabilities. Since the number of U.S. missile launchers remained constant and the size of the USSR's missile forces increased, America's large lead in warheads during the late 1960s was primarily based on an advantage in *bomber* capabilities. Owing to the planned introduction of MIRV, however, projections for the early 1970s showed a substantial U.S. edge in missile warheads.

62. Newhouse, *Cold Dawn*, p. 76.
63. *Status of U.S. Strategic Power*, Hearings, pt. 1, p. 118.
64. Ibid., p. 145.

During the last year of the Johnson administration, Defense Secretary Clark Clifford stressed superiority with considerably more vigor than his predecessor. Clifford took office when the USSR was approaching parity in ICBMs, and he therefore was under greater pressure than McNamara to defend U.S. strategic programs, but he seemed to have an especially strong belief in the value of superiority in deterring and dealing with the Soviet Union.[65] In particular, Secretary Clifford supported a continuation of MIRV and other U.S. programs in order to provide America with a strengthened negotiating position at the strategic arms talks that were scheduled to begin in the fall of 1968. Finally, Clifford as well as McNamara may have viewed the procurement of MIRVs as a means of regaining a European damage-limiting option and of generally minimizing NATO fears that U.S. nuclear guarantees would lose further credibility as the USSR approached parity in number of ICBMs.

Thus, it becomes apparent that the move toward superiority through MIRVs in the late 1960s cannot be dismissed as either an "accident" of conservative military planning or a result of technological momentum combined with the inability of civilian policymakers to control the Pentagon bureaucracy. Nor can the arms decisions and doctrinal statements made by officials of the Johnson administration simply be explained away by the domestic need to calm congressional and public concern over the nature of the strategic balance. During Senate hearings in 1968, Assistant Secretary of Defense Enthoven suggested that earlier testimony that upgraded the significance of U.S. nuclear superiority might have been misconstrued because of the way in which committee members put their questions.[66] Despite attempts like this one to blame the Senate for drawing certain public statements out of U.S. officials in hearings and elsewhere, Enthoven and others went beyond a mere response to congressional questioning and emphasized their strong belief in the value of counterforce options, improving U.S. MIRV accuracies, and maintaining U.S. superiority. In short, much of the motivation for the MIRV program seemed to reflect a deliberate desire on the part of President Johnson and his advisers to secure a U.S. nuclear advantage for foreign policy purposes—much as President Kennedy had done in the early 1960s. This policy should not

65. See Newhouse, *Cold Dawn*, p. 134.
66. *Status of U.S. Strategic Power*, Hearings, pt. 1, p. 159.

seem surprising; McGeorge Bundy, national security adviser to both men, observed that all U.S. presidents since the nuclear age began

have measured our strength against that of the Soviet Union and have aimed at strategic superiority; that superiority has had different meanings at different stages, but seen from the White House its value for peace has never been small.[67]

Soviet Strategic Policies

As noted earlier, the USSR found itself in an extremely unfavorable strategic position in the early 1960s. The lack of large-scale Soviet ICBM deployments and the sizable and expanding U.S. strategic arsenal had led to a reversal of the missile gap. Moreover, the dramatic disclosure in mid-1961 that the United States was able not only to count but to locate and target the USSR's small missile force and its bomber bases caused some Kremlin leaders to fear, as in 1954, that the United States was moving toward a first-strike doctrine. Public pronouncements of American superiority added to Soviet concern. Defense Minister Rodion Malinovsky, for example, reacting to Gilpatric's speech in late 1961, accused the United States of preparing a surprise nuclear attack, and a statement attributed to President Kennedy in early 1962, suggesting that the United States would be prepared to use nuclear weapons first in certain circumstances, was apparently interpreted by Khrushchev as an effort to intimidate the Soviet Union. Finally, when Secretary McNamara articulated the no-cities doctrine in June 1962, Soviet fears that the United States was pursuing a counterforce strategy were exacerbated.[68]

Redressing the Strategic Imbalance

Most Kremlinologists claim that, aside from the potential threat to Soviet deterrent forces, the nature of the nuclear balance raised serious foreign policy problems for Moscow. The crisis over Berlin in late 1961, which coincided with U.S. exposure of the missile gap myth,

67. McGeorge Bundy, "The Presidency and the Peace," *Foreign Affairs*, vol. 42 (April 1964), p. 355.

68. For a discussion of Soviet reactions to early Kennedy administration strategic policies, see Horelick and Rush, *Strategic Power*, pp. 85–105; and Thomas W. Wolfe, *Soviet Power and Europe, 1945–1970* (Johns Hopkins Press, 1970), pp. 85–95.

seemed to demonstrate to many Soviet officials that it was no longer possible to sustain the image of superiority and underscored the danger as well as the futility of attempting to obtain political benefits through Sputnik diplomacy. The Kennedy administration's behavior during the Berlin crisis and the accelerated U.S. strategic buildup may have been viewed by the Kremlin as a systematic strategy to use nuclear power for diplomatic purposes. With the strategic balance shifted against them, Soviet leaders apparently feared that they might be unable to protect their vital interests in diplomatic dealings with the West and to maintain their image as leader of the Communist bloc. In addition, planned improvements in U.S. *nonnuclear* capabilities threatened to deprive the Soviet Union of its conventional superiority in Europe and thus negate what the Kremlin considered to be a crucial counterweight to Washington's nuclear advantage.

By mid-1962, therefore, the prospect of overwhelming U.S. military superiority gave the Soviet Union a strong political as well as military incentive to redress the balance of intercontinental strategic forces. It was not enough for the USSR to rely on its large medium-range missile and bomber capability targeted against Western Europe, since long-range strategic missiles had become the most relevant measure of nuclear strength. Ironically, Khrushchev's "rocket-rattling" policy of the late 1950s had actually enhanced the value of these systems as political currency. But attempts to overtake the United States in number of intercontinental systems would have entailed a massive Soviet effort, for the United States had a considerable lead in ICBMs and SLBMs— apart from its established superiority in long-range bombers. Furthermore, the existing Soviet technology of soft and slow-reacting missiles would have made a crash ICBM program particularly costly while yielding marginal security benefits. In any event, the Soviet leader remained unwilling to commit his nation to an enormously expensive strategic program that would detract from his ability to meet domestic requirements. Thus, Khrushchev was faced with the need to increase the USSR's strategic strength rapidly while holding expenditures in check.

THE CUBAN FIASCO

Cuba offered a solution to Khrushchev's dilemma. The Soviet Union had a foothold on this island and had been supplying Castro with arms of all types, including surface-to-air missiles. By installing MR/IRBMs within range of the United States, Kremlin officials apparently concluded that they could obtain many of the benefits of an ICBM construction program more quickly and at less cost. Although a number of important ancillary objectives were served by emplacing missiles in Cuba—and these considerations undoubtedly contributed to Moscow's decision—the desire to redress the strategic balance, in the opinion of most analysts, was the primary motivation behind the Kremlin's decision to install missiles on the island.[69] Even Khrushchev later acknowledged that Soviet missiles "would have equalized what the West likes to call the balance of power," although he claimed that the main Soviet goal was to defend Cuba.[70]

When the U.S. blockade was imposed, the USSR had already delivered seventy-five MR/IRBMs—almost twice the number of ICBMs in their inventory—and there is no evidence that they intended to stop at that point. Missiles located in Cuba would have been vulnerable to our nuclear and conventional strikes, but they would have made an attack by the United States more difficult, thereby strengthening the USSR's deterrent until a survivable intercontinental force became available. At a minimum, Soviet officials may have felt that the deployment of a few hundred MR/IRBMs would have the political payoff of blunting the U.S. strategic advantage, possibly permitting Moscow to regain the strategic initiative.

As it turned out, the Cuban experience highlighted problems associated with the USSR's inferior strategic position. Because of America's recognized preponderance of strategic power during the crisis, the USSR was at a disadvantage, psychologically as well as militarily.[71] As the crisis intensified, Soviet officials feared that U.S. leaders, buttressed by strategic superiority, would be apt to initiate conventional military action on the assumption that the Soviet Union would be reluctant to respond with a nuclear strike. Soviet anxieties were heightened by

69. This point is made forcefully by Allison in *The Essence of Decision*. See also Michael Tatu, *Power in the Kremlin* (Viking, 1970), p. 231; Horelick and Rush, *Strategic Power*, pp. 127–38, 141; and Elie Abel, *The Missile Crisis* (Lippincott, 1966), p. 28.

70. Strobe Talbott, ed. and trans., *Khrushchev Remembers* (Little, Brown, 1970), p. 494.

71. For a discussion of the "psychological edge" thesis, see Slocombe, "The Political Implications of Strategic Parity," p. 32. Also see Zbigniew Brzezinski, "U.S.-Soviet Relations," in Henry Owen, ed., *The Next Phase in Foreign Policy* (Brookings Institution, 1973), pp. 113–32.

President Kennedy's reference to our full retaliatory response policy in his statement of October 22, which the Kremlin may have perceived as a threat to launch a preemptive nuclear attack against the USSR if it did not remove the missiles. Through nonnuclear means, the Soviet Union could not have prevented the United States from invading Cuba or from destroying the missile sites with conventional air attacks. This failure would have resulted in adverse political consequences for the USSR. Yet, since U.S. strategic power more than neutralized that of the USSR, Soviet nuclear retaliation to U.S. air attacks or invasion would have been irrational.

In the end, Khrushchev was not prepared to run a serious risk of nuclear war over the missiles in Cuba. The American ultimatum had been received and could not be dismissed lightly. Thus Soviet officials may well have been persuaded that the U.S. nuclear advantage enabled the Kennedy administration to practice coercive diplomacy and to force Khrushchev to withdraw the missiles. Indeed, the U.S. "victory" in Cuba both vindicated Moscow's view that strategic strength conferred political power and raised the prospect of other circumstances in which U.S. strategic preponderance would again become decisive. To Kremlin leaders, the acquisition of a minimum military deterrent posture would not be sufficient to satisfy the USSR's future security needs. Thus, the Soviet Union came away from Cuba with an even greater desire to rectify the nuclear balance. As one expert said, "The American strategic superiority was doubly confirmed," since the failure to emplace missiles in Cuba not only denied Khrushchev a means to redress the balance, "but bore impressive witness to the American superiority that compelled him to capitulate."[72] In subsequent years, Soviet officials acknowledged that they felt "humiliated" by the Cuban episode, and First Deputy Foreign Minister Vasily Kuznetsov was quoted as stating "you Americans will never be able to do this to us again."[73]

After Cuba, Khrushchev could not avoid drawing the conclusion that the balance must be corrected in a straightforward way, without seeking instant or inexpensive alternatives. Accordingly, he decided to increase the SS-7 ICBM construction rate and to press ahead with

72. Raymond L. Garthoff, "Military Power in Soviet Policy," in John Erickson, ed., *The Military-Technical Revolution: Its Impact on Strategy and Foreign Policy* (Praeger, 1966), p. 255.

73. Cited in the *New York Times*, May 9, 1972.

the development of the more advanced SS-9 and SS-11 hardened ICBMs, a Polaris-type missile-launching submarine, and the Galosh ABM interceptor. But he still refused to authorize the massive missile *production* program being advocated by other Kremlin officials.[74] Over the long term, Khrushchev may have planned a gradual buildup of Soviet strategic strength aimed toward achieving parity or perhaps even superiority. More immediately, however, as in the days of Sputnik, Khrushchev turned to diplomacy to provide a substitute for weaponry—but this time the course was one of restraint, not of rocket rattling, involving a policy of détente, a nonbelligerent stance when discussing the nuclear balance, and a readiness to negotiate with the West. To be sure, Khrushchev remained interested in keeping defense spending from spiraling upward and, particularly after the Cuban crisis, in finding ways to reduce the risk of nuclear war. But the Kremlin's post-Cuban policy may also have been designed to buy time for Soviet missile deployments, while slowing down U.S. programs, minimizing the possibility of another nuclear-related confrontation, and generally blunting the embarrassing effect of the Cuban experience. In any case, Khrushchev's turn toward détente coincided with President Kennedy's "strategy for peace" policy, and within a few years agreement had been reached on the limited test ban treaty and the hot line communications link.[75] Of course, fundamental U.S.-Soviet differences remained, and despite progress in many areas of arms control the movement toward strategic arms limitations was slow and uncertain.

STRATEGIC ARMS EXPANSION

After Khrushchev's departure in late 1964, the Soviet Union launched a major effort to redress the nuclear balance. Evidence suggests that Leonid Brezhnev and Alexei Kosygin were more motivated than Khrushchev to accomplish this objective and were willing to allocate greater resources to improve the Soviet Union's defense posture. In early 1965,

74. The details of Soviet missile decisions during this period cannot be determined with confidence. The summary of programs and policies in this chapter draws heavily from Wolfe, *Soviet Power and Europe*.

75. Treaty Banning Nuclear Weapon Tests in the Atmosphere, in Outer Space and under Water, signed at Moscow, August 15, 1963; and Memorandum of Understanding between the United States and the Union of Soviet Socialist Republics Regarding the Establishment of a Direct Communications Link, signed at Geneva, June 20, 1963.

drawing on the research and development programs initiated under Khrushchev, the new Kremlin leaders decided to substantially upgrade and enlarge the Soviet Union's strategic force. The decisions to deploy the SS-9 and SS-11 ICBMs were apparently made at that time, as well as the commitment to acquire a Polaris-type system to supplement the small and relatively ineffective Soviet missile-firing submarine fleet. The Soviet force increased from a level of about 200 ICBMs in late 1964— which represented a four-to-one inferiority in this category alone—to 340 in 1966 and to 730 in 1967. By the end of 1968, the USSR was approaching parity with the United States in number of hardened ICBMs and had begun to deploy operational missile-firing submarines. As it turned out, the USSR built a substantially larger strategic force during the years 1966–69 than even worst-case U.S. estimates had predicted.

Soviet decisions to pass the United States in number of ICBMs, develop simple multiple warheads, and construct a large SLBM fleet were obviously influenced by a variety of factors. Some USSR officials may have seen these programs as an opportunity to gain numerical superiority and an eventual counterforce capability against U.S. ICBMs; and bureaucratic considerations, technological momentum, and the desire to negotiate from strength undoubtedly contributed to the Soviet arms buildup. Nevertheless, one of the most important reasons for the sustained Soviet buildup may have been the USSR's basic need to maintain a confident deterrent posture—for, as the Soviet Union began to close the gap in the late 1960s, the United States had moved the arms competition into a new phase. Although the number of U.S. strategic missiles and bombers had remained constant, a conservative Soviet analyst projecting ahead to the early 1970s could easily have demonstrated that the combination of accurate U.S. MIRVs and the completed Sentinel ABM deployment would endanger the USSR's nuclear retaliatory capability, unless additional systems, particularly sea-based forces, were produced.

Any reconstruction of the precise reasons for the specific size and character of the USSR's offensive force buildup must be conjectural and incomplete, but Soviet actions on the defensive side are even less explicable. As early as 1961, Defense Minister Malinovsky claimed that "the problem of destroying missiles in flight has been successfully solved."[76] Within a few years, as noted, after what appeared to be an abortive attempt to deploy an ABM defense near Leningrad, the Soviet

76. Cited by John W. Finney, *New York Times*, October 24, 1961.

Union began to install the Galosh missile defense system around Moscow. Throughout most of the decade, moreover, Soviet writers, spokesmen, and government officials, in direct contrast to those in the United States, expressed little understanding of the concept that defenses could be destabilizing and actually stressed the benefits of ABMs. As late as 1967, after the Kremlin had agreed in principle to hold arms limitation talks, Kosygin publicly proclaimed that ABMs were desirable and reportedly argued at the Glassboro meeting with President Johnson that attention should be given to limiting offensive weapons.[77]

Despite these policy pronouncements and preferences, the Soviets *did not* deploy the large ABM network predicted by U.S. planners. The lack of widespread Soviet ABM deployments may simply have reflected the Kremlin's reluctance to invest billions in a system that might not be effective, since the USSR apparently experienced technical difficulties and cost escalations while building the small Moscow ABM. The prospect of U.S. MIRVs could have forced Soviet defense planners to question the feasibility of constructing meaningful defenses against future U.S. weapons. In addition, the Soviet leaders may have feared that resources invested in ABMs would detract from the more important goal of acquiring a powerful strategic offensive force. Finally, in conjunction with these factors, it is possible that Kremlin leaders might have begun to question their traditional belief in the strategic value of ABMs—a hypothesis that helps explain the position Soviet negotiators later took at the U.S.-USSR arms talks.[78]

While adopting a tougher foreign policy, Brezhnev and Kosygin continued Khrushchev's post-Cuban policy of pursuing arms control possibilities and avoiding direct East-West confrontations. Successful agreements were reached on a number of issues, notably the outer space and the nuclear nonproliferation treaties.[79] These measures were

---

77. See "Joint Communiqué by Premier Kosygin and Prime Minister Wilson (Extract), February 13, 1967," *Documents on Disarmament: 1967*, publication 46 (U.S. Arms Control and Disarmament Agency, 1968), pp. 66–68. For a report of the Glassboro meeting in June 1967, see Newhouse, *Cold Dawn*, pp. 94–95.

78. Possible Soviet motivation for agreeing to enter into strategic arms limitation talks in the late 1960s is analyzed in Wolfe, *Soviet Power and Europe*, pp. 501–10.

79. Treaty on Principles Governing the Activities of States on the Exploration and Use of Outer Space, signed at Washington, London, and Moscow, January 27, 1967; and Treaty on the Non-Proliferation of Nuclear Weapons, signed at Washington, London, and Moscow, July 1, 1968.

obviously in the interest of the Soviet Union's security, but following in Khrushchev's footsteps, the new leaders may also have sought to stabilize relations as a means of minimizing conflict while the USSR continued to expand its strategic forces. Most important, in 1967 the Soviet Union accepted in principle President Johnson's proposal to hold strategic arms limitations talks (SALT). In responding to the offer to initiate arms talks—and in eventually agreeing to a summit meeting as a means of starting the SALT process—the Soviet Union was undoubtedly pursuing a complex set of policies shaped by many considerations. It was of major significance, however, that the USSR had reached a strategic position that gave it a secure foundation for attempting to obtain military, political, and economic benefits from bargaining with the United States over arms limitations. Indeed, it appears that in the late 1960s Kremlin political leaders viewed SALT as a way of codifying a parity relationship and limiting future strategic expenditures. Military officials, on the other hand, were highly suspicious of SALT and probably hoped that the talks would fail or would possibly permit the USSR to gain strategic superiority through diplomatic means.

The Soviet Union did not slacken its offensive missile buildup during the final years of the Johnson administration and launched its first multiple warhead test in late August 1968, approximately one week after the first U.S. MIRV flight test. Although the Soviet test had no direct relationship to MIRV technology, U.S. officials were concerned that America's qualitative lead might soon be challenged—a concern that reached great intensity when the Nixon administration entered office.

In many respects, the Soviet strategic posture that evolved during the last few years of the decade showed signs of paralleling that of the United States during the mid-1960s. With the deployment of a large silo-based ICBM force, the start of a Polaris-type SLBM program, and the absence of more than a token ABM network, the USSR seemed to be emphasizing a retaliatory deterrent force—although counterforce and warfighting traditions remained part of the Kremlin doctrine. It is difficult to determine whether this strategic pattern resulted from a desire to emulate the U.S. posture, from sheer technological momentum, or from a deliberate policy decision influenced by McNamara's explanation of the requirements of deterrence and the action-reaction cycle. In any case, the Soviet Union may not have been able to consider any form of an assured destruction doctrine until its technology permitted the construction of highly survivable offensive missiles, notably advanced missile-firing submarines. Whatever the explanation, Kremlin leaders paid a price for not moving in this direction earlier or changing the thrust of their policy statements, since the USSR's advocacy of a doctrine emphasizing defense and the installation of Soviet ABM sites triggered the U.S. MIRV program, put further pressure on Moscow to build additional forces, and delayed progress in strategic arms control.

The Seeds of SALT

The potential dangers of the strategic arms race and its internal dynamics were cogently described by Secretary McNamara in a speech in San Francisco on September 18, 1967.

What is essential to understand here is that the Soviet Union and the United States mutually influence one another's strategic plans. Whatever be their intentions, whatever be our intentions, actions . . . on either side relating to the buildup of nuclear forces . . . necessarily trigger reactions on the other side.

He then observed that "it is precisely this action-reaction phenomenon that fuels an arms race," but argued that the United States would prefer to avoid such a race and enter into an agreement with the USSR.[80]

Self-restraint versus Negotiated Limitations

Similar concepts of arms interactions and related issues had been expressed five years earlier by Kennedy administration officials, many of whom played important roles in developing the theories of modern arms control. One concept basic to the Kennedy administration's policy, however, was that arms control was an integral part of defense planning in the nuclear age and need not necessarily involve formal agreements. This approach was perhaps best outlined by Assistant Secretary of Defense John McNaughton in an address in 1962 at the University of Michigan. While slowing down the arms race was important, McNaughton argued, the purpose of arms control was not simply to

80. McNamara, "The Dynamics of Nuclear Strategy," p. 446.

reduce weapon levels but to lower the risk that nuclear war might occur and to reduce damage in the event of a nuclear war. Moreover, nonnegotiated techniques and unilateral actions could be used to achieve these objectives by weaving the strategy of arms control into defense policy decisions and by pursuing control as a means of enhancing U.S. security. Accordingly, McNaughton concluded that "we must, in every decision we make, concern ourselves with the factors of stability and of the dynamic effect on the arms race."[81]

As McNaughton pointed out in his Michigan speech, the Kennedy administration had already made many unilateral arms control decisions. A plan to phase out unnecessary systems, such as the huge fleet of B-47 medium bombers, represented arms restraints, and the elimination of soft strategic missiles reduced the likelihood of a Soviet attack and diminished the danger of premature or inappropriate use of U.S. forces. Furthermore, improvements in command, control, and communication procedures guarded against accidental firings and provided the President with options that could help keep damage levels low in the event of a nuclear exchange. Even the controlled response doctrine was characterized as a form of tacit arms control that could minimize damage by giving the Soviet Union an incentive to avoid targeting U.S. cities. But U.S. doctrinal, command and control, and survivability decisions in the early 1960s were not matched by arms restraint in *force levels*. Although the number of Minuteman ICBMs and Polaris submarines was eventually frozen at levels lower than those requested by the Joint Chiefs, the Kennedy administration not only expanded U.S. strategic programs in 1961 and 1962 but seemed to display a lack of sensitivity to possible Soviet reactions.

Whatever one might conclude about the Kennedy administration's policy of unilateral restraint, it seems clear that the administration progressed slowly toward seeking *negotiated* arms arrangements that might satisfy the objective of strategic stability. To be sure, President Kennedy sought and achieved two important arms control agreements —the partial nuclear test ban treaty and the Washington-Moscow hot line. But there is little doubt that military and congressional opposition to negotiating with the USSR inhibited the President from taking early initiatives in the field of strategic arms control. In addition, two fea-

81. John T. McNaughton, "Arms Restraint in Military Decisions," *Journal of Conflict Resolution*, vol. 7 (September 1963), p. 234.

tures of the President's approach to arms control policy may have contributed to his reluctance to enter into serious negotiations.

First, President Kennedy and his advisers favored a policy of negotiating from strength and believed that a superior U.S. strategic position would increase the possibility of achieving arms limitations. This viewpoint was expressed in the President's first budget message and was later reflected in Secretary McNamara's claim that the partial test ban treaty would permit the United States to retain superiority in low-yield weapons, to maintain an overall numerical advantage in strategic delivery systems, and to improve missile accuracies.[82]

Second, statements in the President's first budget message suggest that he apparently believed that arms buildups were primarily a result of disagreement between nations, not a cause. While this attitude did not preclude constructive negotiations on nuclear weapons testing, the President may have been unwilling to discuss strategic delivery systems—which affected U.S. security more directly—until the foreign policy atmosphere had improved substantially.

THE "FREEZE" PROPOSAL

By 1963, however, President Kennedy had apparently decided that the political climate and the nuclear balance made it possible to at least offer to discuss strategic arms control with the Soviet Union. For two years, the administration had been investigating so-called collateral arms control measures—partial and more practical plans than the complete disarmament treaties tabled by the USSR and the United States at meetings of the Eighteen Nation Disarmament Committee (ENDC), which had carried forward the multination disarmament efforts of the late 1950s in Geneva under United Nations auspices. One such measure called for 30 percent reductions in strategic nuclear delivery vehicles (SNDVs), without placing limits on other categories of arms, such as conventional forces or tactical nuclear weapons. After considering various SNDV schemes, President Kennedy decided against arms reductions and requested that a "freeze" proposal be developed for possible presentation to the ENDC in 1963.

After assuming office, President Johnson agreed to go forward with the SNDV plan, and in his statement to the ENDC in January 1964,

82. See testimony of Secretary of Defense Robert S. McNamara in *Nuclear Test Ban Treaty*, Hearings before the Senate Committee on Foreign Relations, 88 Cong. 1 sess. (1963), pp. 97–203.

he proposed exploration of this measure. The U.S. proposal called for a freeze on the "number and characteristics of strategic nuclear offensive and defensive vehicles," and covered ABM systems as well as long-range missiles and bombers.[83] Force deployments would be limited to existing levels, and no significant new types of vehicles could be installed, although the proposal contained some replacement provisions. Verification requirements were less extensive than in previous U.S. proposals but still encompassed on-site inspection at declared fabrication plants, spot checks of facilities suspected of clandestine production, and agreed procedures to guard against prohibited missile test activities.

Not surprisingly, the Soviet Union immediately rejected the SNDV freeze proposal. Soviet spokesmen stressed the plan's obtrusive inspection provisions, but behind Moscow's opposition was the concern that the U.S. proposal would have frozen the USSR into a permanent position of inferiority. A series of futile debates began over the freeze and other strategic arms proposals, such as the USSR's "nuclear umbrella" and the American "bomber bonfire" plans. The Soviet proposal, also known as the Gromyko plan, called for the two nations to reduce their offensive missile forces to extremely low levels under an ABM screen that would protect populations and forces. The United States objected to the absence of inspection provisions for the nuclear umbrella plan, and, more important, found the premise of permitting defense incompatible with its strategic doctrine. Soviet spokesmen were equally negative toward the U.S. bomber proposal, which entailed the destruction of B-47 aircraft on the American side matched by the destruction of Badger medium-range bombers by the USSR. In addition to the fact that Badgers were vital to the Soviet Union in providing a deterrent against Western Europe, Soviet leaders had little incentive to negotiate, since it was widely known that the United States had decided to eliminate its B-47s unilaterally.

Efforts to negotiate strategic weapons controls foundered, although the United States continued its attempts to exercise restraint in its arms decisions and to highlight the need for mutual stability. In fact, Secretary McNamara had dramatized the need for mutual stability in late 1963 when he observed that, once the USSR acquired a survivable force, the

83. "Message from President Johnson to the Eighteen Nation Disarmament Committee, January 21, 1964," *Documents on Disarmament: 1964* (U.S. Arms Control and Disarmament Agency, 1965), p. 8.

probability of a Soviet preemptive strike against the United States during a crisis would decrease, and that this would be "to our advantage."[84] Thus, well before his later efforts to publicize arms race problems, the secretary of defense had not merely acknowledged that mutual deterrence was inevitable but had taken the controversial, albeit correct, position that a survivable Soviet deterrent could actually *improve* U.S. security.

ABMS AND ARMS CONTROL

In attempting to counter demands for ABMs in subsequent years, McNamara stressed that the resultant cycle of U.S.-Soviet arms build-ups would result in wasted resources with no gain in security for either side and argued further that "it would actually increase the risk to both of the parties were they to deploy antiballistic missile systems."[85] Despite the decision to develop MIRVs, McNamara continued to oppose major U.S. damage-limiting programs, offensive as well as defensive, for reasons of cost and effectiveness and also because he desired to avoid stimulating the strategic arms race.

By 1966, however, it became clear that unilateral restraint, to the degree it had been applied, had its limitations. Intense pressure was being generated by the Joint Chiefs to persuade President Johnson to approve an anti-Soviet ABM deployment, and it was also proving increasingly difficult to hold the line against advocates of a wide range of U.S. strategic offensive programs. McNamara may well have feared that, if the Kremlin began to expand its ABM network as predicted, the administration would be forced to engage in a massive round of strategic procurements. Thus, the negotiation of a bilateral agreement with the USSR—perhaps only a moratorium—that would ban or restrict ABMs seemed to be the most effective way of curbing both the Soviet threat and *our own* programs.

Toward the end of 1966, when McNamara approached President Johnson about the possibility of pursuing an ABM pact, the President approved a plan to delay any firm decision on missile defenses until the possibility of holding arms limitation talks had been explored with Soviet officials. The President, although under domestic political pres-

84. Testimony in *Military Procurement Authorization Fiscal Year 1964*, Hearings before the Senate Committee on Armed Services, 88 Cong. 1 sess. (1963), p. 330.

85. "Secretary McNamara Comments on Risks of Anti-Ballistic-Missile System," *Department of State Bulletin*, vol. 56 (March 20, 1967), p. 442.

sure to deploy an ABM system, was apparently strongly motivated to pursue nuclear arms negotiations with the Soviet Union for foreign policy reasons and probably saw the benefits of initiating such negotiations in the election year of 1968.[86]

As a consequence of McNamara's initiative, and with the assistance of Llewellyn Thompson who had been assigned as ambassador to Moscow, the United States initiated informal diplomatic contacts with Soviet leaders to interest them in talks about the problem of missile limitations, paying special attention to ABM controls. After President Johnson wrote to Premier Kosygin in January 1967, the Kremlin expressed a willingness to discuss "means of limiting the arms race in offensive and defensive nuclear missiles."[87] But this was still only an agreement in principle to begin talks. At the Glassboro meeting in June 1967, Johnson and McNamara, arguing the urgency of ABM controls to an unresponsive audience, unsuccessfully sought to persuade Kosygin to agree to a specific time and place for negotiations.

While waiting for the Kremlin's reply to the U.S. proposal to initiate talks on ABM limitations, demands for U.S. ABM deployment increased, and administration officials attempted to use the prospect of arms limitation talks as a means of blunting these forces. In early 1967, President Johnson officially announced that he was delaying an ABM decision pending the initiation and outcome of arms limitation talks.[88] By September, the USSR had not yet agreed to begin arms talks. Responding to mounting domestic pressure to deploy ABMs, President Johnson decided to go forward with the Sentinel program, and this was announced publicly by Secretary McNamara in his San Francisco speech.

It is likely that McNamara was aware of the inconsistency between his analysis of U.S. overreactions to the early signs of a small Soviet ABM deployment and his assertion that Soviet leaders would not react

86. A meeting at the LBJ ranch in November 1966 between McNamara and the President apparently triggered the decision to pursue SALT seriously. See Newhouse, *Cold Dawn*, pp. 83–99; Chalmers M. Roberts, *The Nuclear Years: The Arms Race and Arms Control, 1945–70* (Praeger, 1970), pp. 80–88; and Lyndon Baines Johnson, *The Vantage Point: Perspectives of the Presidency 1963–1969* (Holt, Rinehart, and Winston, 1971), pp. 474–80.

87. "The President's News Conference of March 2, 1967," *Public Papers of the Presidents of the United States: Lyndon B. Johnson 1967*, bk. 1 (1968), p. 259.

88. "Annual Budget Message to the Congress, Fiscal Year 1968, January 24, 1967," *Public Papers, 1967*, p. 48.

to Sentinel—a nationwide ABM system more advanced than the Moscow ABM system.[89] To make matters worse, U.S. military leaders were quick to explain to Congress that Sentinel had anti-Soviet capabilities and was viewed by the Joint Chiefs as a first step toward a heavy ABM deployment.[90] Nevertheless, in his San Francisco speech and in an interview published in *Life*, McNamara attempted to minimize the potentially destabilizing consequences of the ABM decision by explaining that Sentinel was a limited system directed against China and by expressing the hope that the Soviet Union would be able to distinguish between such a "thin" missile defense network and a "thick" U.S. ABM deployment that could threaten the USSR's deterrent. Indeed, the secretary explicitly warned that the "mad momentum" associated with all new weapons could create pressures to expand the Sentinel system into a heavy ABM deployment.[91]

Although a hard-point ABM configuration had not been approved, McNamara also sought to mitigate any adverse consequences of the Sentinel decision by observing that the proposed system provided a foundation for the United States to defend its ICBMs with ABMs. Such a defense system would be stabilizing, McNamara suggested, since it offered an alternative to deploying additional offensive forces and represented the option "least likely to force the Soviets into a counter-reaction."[92]

It is unclear whether the secretary was contemplating a last-minute policy shift to modify Sentinel for missile-site protection. Any change in the deployment plan along these lines would have been inconsistent with the presidential guidelines for population defense and would also have complicated our relations with our NATO allies. Reports suggest that McNamara's tentative attempts to emphasize the hard-point potential of Sentinel evoked strongly negative reactions from Western European officials at a NATO meeting in late September.[93] This reaction undoubtedly was due to the fact that our allies regarded the defense of America's ICBM sites against Soviet missile attack as an

89. See Enthoven and Smith, *How Much Is Enough?* p. 193.
90. See statement of General Earle G. Wheeler in *Status of U.S. Strategic Power*, p. 11.
91. Stolley, "Defense Fantasy Now Come True," p. 28c; and McNamara, "The Dynamics of Nuclear Strategy," p. 450.
92. Stolley, "Defense Fantasy Now Come True," p. 28c.
93. See *New York Times*, September 29, 1967; and Newhouse, *Cold Dawn*, pp. 78–102.

issue requiring careful consultation within NATO, while in their view, the deployment of an anti-Chinese ABM network throughout the United States had no direct bearing on Western European security. In any event, Sentinel remained a nationwide area defense configuration, and the plan contained merely the option to deploy hard-point ABMs.

Throughout late 1967 and early 1968, the administration went out of its way to assure the American people, U.S. allies, and the Kremlin that the Sentinel decision did not signify a slackening of the United States' desire to enter into arms limitations discussions. In his posture statements and major speeches, Secretary McNamara stressed that each side had achieved a secure second-strike capability, that additional arms would not improve either nation's security, and that both sides would be better off if agreements were reached limiting strategic nuclear forces. McNamara emphasized how arms control agreements could help prevent the United States and the USSR from acquiring "strategic nuclear arsenals greatly in excess of a credible assured destruction capability . . . because we each wanted to be able to cope with the 'worst possible case.' "[94] McNamara's successor, Defense Secretary Clifford, also expressed support for strategic arms negotiations, stating in 1968 that "an appropriately designed and safeguarded arms limitation agreement can . . . enhance the stability of the strategic balance."[95]

It has been suggested that the Kremlin was slow in responding to the U.S. initiative, partly because of delays caused by bureaucratic battles, but also because the USSR had not yet reached a sufficient level of nuclear strength. Whatever the reasons, it was not until the spring of 1968 that the Soviet government actually agreed to exchange opinions on arms control, and in July, at the signing of the nonproliferation treaty—which committed the United States and the USSR to seek limitations on their own arms—the two superpowers jointly announced that strategic talks would be held in the immediate future.

Developing a U.S. Position

After the Soviet Union finally agreed to begin talks, the United States undertook an intense effort to forge a negotiating position. The

94. *Scope, Magnitude, and Implications of the U.S. Antiballistic Missile Program,* Hearings, app. 4, p. 109.

95. "Statement of Secretary of Defense Clark M. Clifford: The Fiscal Year 1970-74 Defense Program and 1970 Defense Budget" (January 1969; processed), p. 49.

goal of these preparations was to present President Johnson with a proposal he could submit at a meeting in Moscow scheduled for early October. The U.S. attitude toward SALT was now far more serious than it had been when the SNDV freeze had been proposed, and attempts were made to formulate a realistic plan. The imperative of developing a position in time for the summit created substantial momentum within the U.S. government toward SALT, and substantive shifts in the direction of a less negative outlook on strategic arms limitations could be discerned. As a result, many officials throughout the executive branch saw improved Soviet-American relations, financial savings, and reduced nuclear risks as potential benefits to be derived from arms talks. In addition, SALT advocates believed that the USSR had attained a sufficiently powerful strategic position vis-à-vis the United States for an equitable agreement to be negotiated.

In making SALT possible, it was particularly significant that the United States could design an agreement that would limit the strategic competition without requiring intrusive inspection. For many years, studies had been made of the utility of national means of verification in monitoring certain categories of strategic arms limitations. These studies showed that, by using remote radar detectors and photoreconnaissance systems, the United States could verify the number of operational Soviet offensive and defensive missile launchers within reasonable tolerances—although certain qualitative restrictions could require supplementary inspection provisions. Accordingly, arms control specialists concentrated on *deployment* limitations and rejected earlier plans, such as the 1964 SNDV proposal, that had emphasized *production* controls demanding rather comprehensive on-site inspection arrangements.

The Johnson administration's willingness to rely primarily on national means of verification may have been privately conveyed to Soviet leaders when the SALT initiative was taken in the hope that the logjam over inspection would be broken, and the USSR's willingness to enter into talks could have been influenced by such hints. In the fall of 1967, it might be noted, Assistant Defense Secretary Paul Warnke explicitly signaled the new approach to verification by referring publicly to the possibility that a strategic limitation accord might be verified by unilateral capabilities.[96] Earlier that year, President Johnson had dropped informal hints to this effect when he remarked

96. "Address by Assistant Secretary of Defense Warnke," pp. 454–59.

to a group of educators that advances in "space photography" made it possible to "know how many missiles the enemy has."[97]

The desire to limit ABMs was the major motive behind the administration's interest in arms control discussions, and in private contacts with Soviet leaders as well as in public statements U.S. officials stressed this point. Even before Ambassador Thompson got in touch with the Kremlin, this basic American premise had been made clear. For example, in Geneva on August 16, 1966, U.S. delegate Adrian Fisher had reminded all the participating nations at the ENDC that the earlier U.S. freeze proposal included ABM limitations and had gone on to explain that an agreement constraining only offensive weapons "would create undesirable tensions and uncertainties and threaten to destroy the existing stability."[98] On the other hand, the Glassboro meeting, as well as Soviet literature and statements by Kremlin leaders, left no doubt that the USSR did not share the U.S. desire to limit ABMs. But U.S. leaders were prepared to consider limiting the growth of offensive forces in concert with an ABM accord and readily accepted the Soviet Union's request to discuss both categories of weapons in SALT. The U.S. SALT preparations in 1968 therefore covered offensive and defensive options.

NATURE OF THE U.S. PROPOSAL

After considerable analytic effort and bureaucratic maneuvering, a SALT proposal was agreed upon by the relevant organizations, including the Joint Chiefs, and was transmitted to the President in late August 1968 by the Committee of Principals—the Cabinet-level group officially responsible for developing arms control positions.[99] The SALT proposal, approved in principle by President Johnson, called for the number of strategic missiles deployed on each side to be limited to existing levels and for a ceiling to be placed on ABM launchers, based on a set and equivalent number for each nation. The ABM level the administration preferred was not fixed, but it ranged from 100 launchers to the 1,000-

97. Cited in Philip J. Klass, "Keeping the Nuclear Peace: Spies in the Sky," *New York Times Magazine*, September 3, 1972, p. 7.

98. "Statement by ACDA Deputy Director Fisher to the Eighteen Nation Disarmament Committee, August 16, 1966," *Documents on Disarmament: 1966*, publication 43 (U.S. Arms Control and Disarmament Agency, 1967), p. 556.

99. See Newhouse, *Cold Dawn*, pp. 127–30; John W. Finney, *New York Times*, November 11, 1969; and William Beecher, *New York Times*, December 30, 1969, for discussions of the Johnson administration's SALT position.

launcher Sentinel system, and a total ban was also a possibility. Land-mobile missiles were banned, and constraints were placed on the external configuration of missile silos to preclude the replacement of small ICBMs with larger systems. But the proposal lacked qualitative controls over strategic arms, most notably reflected in the absence of restrictions on MIRV testing or accuracy improvements. As a final point, both sides were to rely principally on national means of verification, but some possibilities for providing additional assurances were left open—primarily related to the problem of eliminating uncertainty about the potential ABM capability of the Tallinn air defense network.

The administration's SALT proposal was limited in scope, obviously reflecting a series of compromises necessary to ensure the approval of the Joint Chiefs, specifically the absence of MIRV controls and a fixed low ABM limit. Considering the state of the strategic balance at that time, moreover, the measure decidedly favored the United States and placed minimal constraints on the arms race. Officials advocating a more equitable and comprehensive measure, particularly one that included both a MIRV and an ABM ban, apparently hoped to move the administration in this direction once the negotiations began. Whether efforts to modify the U.S. position would have succeeded is unknown, but the chances of success were small.

It is perhaps significant to recall that belated but serious efforts were made by civilian Pentagon officials during the SALT preparations in 1968 to persuade Defense Secretary Clifford to delay the start of U.S. MIRV tests because of SALT. Clifford reportedly rejected this proposal, and the Poseidon and Minuteman MIRV testing programs began as scheduled on August 16, 1968—approximately six weeks before the planned SALT summit.[100] Secretary Clifford's reluctance to delay the MIRV tests may have been motivated by the realization that there would soon be an opportunity to discuss a mutual MIRV ban and that it was preferable to deal with this matter at the negotiating table. Indeed, Clifford expressed confidence that the initiation of U.S. MIRV tests would not prejudice SALT.[101] On the other hand, it is equally plausible that MIRV testing proceeded because the secretary of defense and other officials were simply uninterested in MIRV limita-

100. See Greenwood, "Qualitative Improvements in Offensive Strategic Arms," pp. 205–20.

101. See William Beecher, *New York Times*, January 19, 1969; and *Washington Post*, October 5, 9, and 28, 1968.

128 SECURITY IN THE NUCLEAR AGE

tions or believed that technical difficulties, coupled with the Joint
Chiefs' opposition, made such a position impracticable.

More generally, it can be argued that the decisions to initiate
MIRV testing and to deploy Sentinel were influenced in part by the
perceived need to persuade the Soviet Union to enter into discussions
and to strengthen the hand of U.S. negotiators once SALT began. It
has been claimed, for example, that Senate approval of the administration's Sentinel request on June 24, 1968, induced the Kremlin to finally
announce a readiness to begin talks, although the Soviet decision was
actually transmitted privately to the United States shortly before the
favorable Senate note. In any event, Secretary Clifford, in the months
before the scheduled SALT negotiations, was fairly direct in stating
that Sentinel and MIRVs were necessary "bargaining chips."[102]

ROADBLOCKS TO SALT

As it turned out, the Johnson administration was not given the
opportunity to conduct negotiations and thus did not face the prospect
of modifying its position on MIRVs or of solidifying its stance on ABM
launcher levels. On August 20, 1968, the day before the announcement
of the President's scheduled visit to Moscow, the Soviet Union invaded
Czechoslovakia. The domestic and international political implications of
this move persuaded President Johnson that it would be neither wise nor
appropriate to go to Moscow, and he ordered the announcement with-
held.

Undoubtedly driven by the desire to mitigate the effect of the invasion, Kremlin leaders showed increased interest in SALT during the
fall of 1968—the time of the U.S. presidential election. As it happened,
U.S. officials had held open the option of rescheduling SALT in the
months following the invasion of Czechoslovakia, and immediately
after the November elections President Johnson decided to mount a
last-minute effort to set the talks in motion. Informal contacts were
made with Soviet officials on this question, and the two sides appeared
to have reached a common understanding of the basic objectives and
principles that might guide arms talks. Nevertheless, before proceeding further, President Johnson judged it essential to gain the support
of President-elect Richard Nixon. But Nixon and his advisers responded
negatively to the Johnson administration's plan; they were unwilling to

102. Address given at the National Press Club, Washington, D.C., September 5,
1968.

assume responsibility for such negotiations before they had had an opportunity to study SALT in detail. At the same time, representatives of the President-elect reportedly sought to dissuade the Soviet Union from reacting favorably to the outgoing administration's attempts to establish a time and place for the talks.[103] When the Johnson administration left office, therefore, the precedent of preliminary SALT preparations and commitments existed, but strategic arms negotiations had not begun, and each nation was continuing to expand its strategic arsenals. The problem of handling this complex and contradictory situation was left to President Nixon.

Policy Paradoxes

By the time the Johnson administration ended, many of the defense policy goals outlined by President Kennedy in January 1961 had been achieved. Great strides had been made in reversing Eisenhower's defense approach and in reducing the prominence of nuclear weapons in dealings with our adversaries and allies. Although the United States never eschewed the first use of nuclear weapons, our overall defense posture was designed to provide credible conventional options. Moreover, the United States had adopted the position that nuclear power had only limited political and military value, and after the early Berlin and Cuban crises had ended, the strategic balance played no direct role in the management of conflicts. Progress in negotiating important arms control measures—the hot line, the limited test ban, and the nonproliferation treaty—could largely be attributed to initiatives taken by the Kennedy and Johnson administrations.

Throughout the Kennedy-Johnson years substantial progress was made toward stabilizing the nuclear balance. By the late 1960s, U.S. strategic forces were highly survivable, reliable, and designed primarily for retaliatory deterrence. The number of deployed delivery systems had been limited, and procurement of new-generation offensive weapons had been rejected in favor of continued research. Perhaps

103. This episode and other aspects of the attempt to salvage SALT are discussed in Johnson, *The Vantage Point*, pp. 487–91; and in Newhouse, *Cold Dawn*, pp. 136–38. In a television interview in 1969, Hubert Humphrey claimed that President Nixon blocked the SALT summit planned for 1968. (See *Washington Post*, September 16, 1969.)

most significant was the administration's success in rejecting large-scale ABM construction, establishing the position that mutual deterrence was inevitable, and attempting to initiate arms talks with the USSR in order to control the strategic competition.

On the other hand, strategic nuclear policies under both President Kennedy and President Johnson contained significant elements that contradicted and countered these stability gains. The decisions to accelerate U.S. strategic programs and to stress superiority were inconsistent with President Kennedy's dismissal of numerical comparisons and his premise that the utility of nuclear power was limited. Furthermore, despite the rejection of a full first-strike doctrine and the later emphasis given to assured destruction, this early interest in numerical superiority and counterforce options continued to influence subsequent strategic plans. Finally, the Johnson administration procured MIRVs and approved Sentinel—two decisions that many experts believe were unnecessary as well as destabilizing. In short, strategic policies during the Kennedy-Johnson years contained policy paradoxes that were reflected in weapon programs and underlying doctrinal attitudes.

McNamara's Analytic Approach

Without doubt, McNamara's approach to strategic force planning contributed much to the unilateral restraint and mutual stability that did emerge under the Kennedy-Johnson administrations. The emphasis placed on the assured destruction objective, combined with the use of a precise methodology for establishing force requirements, exposed the futility of major damage-limiting policies and provided a management tool for warding off many bureaucratic and domestic political pressures to deploy weapon systems. To highlight this point, two related features of the so-called systems approach might be examined: worst-case planning and cost-effectiveness.

WORST-CASE PLANNING

From a number of standpoints, the argument for worst-case planning was both substantively and bureaucratically sound. Because the U.S. deterrent was designed to cope with greater-than-expected threats and to handle postulated attacks weighted heavily in the USSR's favor, U.S. leaders could act more confidently during crises, allies found U.S. commitments more credible, and Soviet policymakers were able to assess

America's strategic deterrent power quite clearly. Moreover, designing U.S. strategic forces to satisfy assured destruction under worst-case assumptions became a useful technique that the secretary of defense employed to counter requests for increased arms levels or new-generation weapons. Once a sufficiently high level of retaliatory capability was attained, expenditures for additional weapons were shown to bring diminishing returns in the ability to inflict damage. Accordingly, this approach to defense planning provided many stabilizing features to Secretary McNamara's strategic policies.

Yet the analytic approach had weaknesses that contributed to the many imperfections and inconsistencies in the strategic policy and weapons decisions made under the Kennedy-Johnson administrations. For one thing, defense planning under worst-case assumptions raised U.S. strategic arms levels to the point where prudence seemed to have been replaced by a somewhat unrealistic concern over remote possibilities. In the fall of 1961, for example, when satellite information finally showed no evidence of major Soviet ICBM deployment activities, it became difficult to support the view that prudent planning demanded a continuation and expansion of the original series of Kennedy administration strategic procurement decisions. Secretary McNamara subsequently acknowledged that these decisions, which were based on "conservative" calculations, led to a larger force than the United States actually required because uncertainty over Soviet intentions and the USSR's substantial technical-industrial capacity left the United States no choice but to hedge "against what was then only a theoretically possible Soviet buildup."[104] As discussed earlier, however, the absence of accurate data regarding the Soviet Union's future force plans would not seem to have necessitated a further expansion of the Minuteman and Polaris deployment programs. American strategic superiority, our ability to detect the start of any massive Soviet missile construction program, and our potential for procuring additional weapons would have given the United States sufficient insurance for its nuclear deterrent posture.

A similar pattern was to be repeated when worst-case logic was applied to resolving uncertainties regarding Soviet ABMs and resulted in an intensive drive toward MIRVs. Assuredly, the arguments for MIRV as a reliable counter to ABMs lent credence to initial efforts to

104. McNamara, "The Dynamics of Nuclear Strategy," p. 446.

develop independent warheads. But when subsequent evidence indicated that the USSR was not expanding its missile defenses, the United States could have relaxed the stringency of the assured destruction criteria and delayed MIRV flight-test and procurement decisions until signs of a large-scale Soviet ABM deployment emerged. Putting more weight on policy actions than on procedures, in the case of both the missile deployment and MIRV development decisions it is possible to argue that worst-case planning in the context of an assured destruction approach was not an analytic "trap" that automatically resulted in larger forces but a deliberate attempt to use military logic to rationalize decisions made for other reasons—whether attributed to bureaucratic politics involving concessions to the Joint Chiefs or to the desire to acquire a superior position relative to the USSR. But even under this interpretation, the calculus of conservative planning was often inconsistent with the objectives of mutual stability and arms control.

COST-EFFECTIVENESS

Secretary McNamara was particularly successful in using cost-effectiveness calculations in his fight against large-scale damage limitation programs, especially large ABM systems. Once the assured destruction objective was met, further spending an offensive and defensive forces for damage-limiting purposes was expected to yield a reasonable return in U.S. lives saved. As the Soviet Union's strategic posture grew larger and more invulnerable, this condition could not be satisfied. Thus, the administration was able to argue that it was simply not possible to build an ABM system or to develop offensive forces that could meaningfully reduce damage from Soviet attacks. Even after spending tens of billions of dollars, America would be no better off, for the Soviet Union could negate our efforts at considerably less cost. By emphasizing these technical and economic factors and downplaying the more controversial notion that damage limitation programs were destabilizing, sensitive issues were avoided. After all, it was politically and bureaucratically preferable to claim that mutual deterrence was *unavoidable* rather than desirable—as McNamara would suggest on occasion.

The administration's stress on cost-effectiveness as a central criterion for evaluating weapon options created problems, however. Though valuable as a tool for opposing expensive strategic programs, cost-effectiveness was an inappropriate measure for dealing with relatively inexpensive programs that had potentially significant policy impact.

During the mid-1960s, many U.S. officials supported the concept of deploying a so-called thin ABM network in the belief that such defenses could be highly effective against low-level ICBM attacks at a cost of only $5 billion—far less than the $50 billion required for a full missile defense program. For instance, McNamara often pointed to Sentinel's effectiveness against limited attacks and confirmed that the decision to deploy a thin ABM system involved technical and economic factors different from those of large ABM systems. MIRVs were also attractive on cost-effective grounds. These systems were not merely efficient assured destruction weapons whose cost was substantially less than that of building additional missiles, but with minimal supplementary funding, warhead accuracies could be improved and MIRVs could satisfy damage-limiting objectives as well. Consequently, the Johnson administration found itself powerfully drawn toward MIRVs for economic reasons because this system could serve these multiple military missions—while providing the United States with a numerical advantage in warheads to support foreign policy objectives.

Throughout the Sentinel and MIRV decisionmaking process, some members of the Johnson administration and eventually critics from nongovernmental quarters contended that these programs were contrary to mutual stability. Many of their arguments went beyond analyses of military requirements into questions of Soviet reactions and arms negotiations. The limits of the analytic approach were identified by Pentagon planners, who acknowledged that assured destruction determined only the gross size of U.S. strategic forces, and by Secretary McNamara, who personally admitted that the degree to which America hedges against uncertainties is primarily a question of judgment rather than of quantitative techniques or mechanical rules.[105] An important issue to explore, however, is whether crucial qualitative judgments on such issues as Soviet reactions and arms control were in fact given priority within the system of U.S. defense planning.

Strategic Stability and Soviet Reactions

The stated policy of Presidents Kennedy and Johnson was to consider the effect of U.S. strategic weapon decisions on the Soviet

105. See "Statement of Secretary of Defense Robert S. McNamara on Fiscal Year 1967–71 Defense Program and 1967 Defense Budget" (January 1966; processed), pp. 55–56.

Union's programs and the overall stability of the balance. This was explained by Assistant Defense Secretary John McNaughton as early as 1962 and later formalized by Secretary McNamara in his description of the action-reaction phenomenon. The decisions to eliminate vulnerable systems, limit the number of U.S. strategic vehicles to the levels of the mid-1960s, and emphasize assured destruction rather than damage limitation were influenced by a desire to avoid stimulating Soviet reactions or disrupting the stability of the balance, and the fight against the deployment of a large U.S. ABM system was increasingly motivated by arms race concerns. On the other hand, in a number of important cases, neither the policy judgments brought to bear by administration officials nor their use of the analytic system seemed to reflect full awareness of potential Soviet reactions.

One series of events concerning the question of Soviet reactions revolved around the U.S. strategic buildup of the early 1960s. Many experts claim that these U.S. programs influenced the USSR's strategic arms buildup of later years, and in retrospect Secretary McNamara lent his support to this view. In explaining this line of reasoning, McNamara observed that, while U.S. program decisions were designed to improve future deterrent capabilities, the USSR could not read U.S. intentions and "undoubtedly reasoned that if our buildup were to continue at its accelerated pace, we might conceivably reach, in time, a credible first-strike capability against the Soviet Union."[106] It should not have been surprising that an emphasis on superiority would induce Soviet responses, considering the strategic advantage enjoyed by the United States at that time. Significantly, shortly before President Kennedy assumed office, V. V. Kuznetsov of the Soviet Foreign Office actually warned representatives of the incoming administration that if the United States expanded its strategic weapons arsenal, the USSR could not be expected to stand still.[107]

Yet the Kennedy administration chose to ignore this warning, partly because of an apparent insensitivity to the likelihood of a Soviet reaction and to the implications of such a reaction, but also because of the belief that a superior U.S. position was needed to provide the USSR with the incentive to accept arms limitations.[108] The resultant expan-

106. McNamara, "The Dynamics of Nuclear Strategy," p. 446.

107. Schlesinger, A Thousand Days, p. 301.

108. See ibid., for a discussion of the Kennedy administration's policy of "arming to disarm" (pp. 494–500).

sion of U.S. strategic programs and public exposure of the missile gap, followed by the Kremlin's abortive attempt to install missiles in Cuba, ultimately led to a Soviet buildup that stimulated the nuclear arms race and restricted progress in strategic arms control—two results with adverse consequences for U.S. security. If U.S. officials had given greater weight to the Soviet desire for nuclear equality—in both political and military terms—and had been more sensitive to the possible backlash effect of their strategic policies, they might have minimized the pressure on Kremlin leaders to redress the nuclear balance by reducing the size and pace of U.S. strategic programs, avoiding public claims of superiority, and rejecting the controlled response doctrine. Although success could not have been assured, such a strategy might have made it possible for the United States to avoid the immediate nuclear risks associated with the Cuban missile crisis and the longer-term strategic disadvantages that followed.[109]

During the Johnson years, the United States still seemed to downgrade Moscow's desire for numerical parity or even military sufficiency. For one thing, it was premature for McNamara to herald the arrival of mutual deterrence in 1963 merely because the USSR had acquired a minimal retaliatory force.[110] The USSR remained in a decidedly inferior security position throughout the mid-1960s. But McNamara's model of the arms race did not deal with *political* action-reaction—that is, Soviet interest in matching U.S. strength and attaining a visible as well as actual position of comparability. As late as 1965, McNamara claimed that "there is no indication that the Soviets are seeking to develop a strategic force as large as ours," and going beyond factual assessments of the existing situation, he suggested that the Soviet leaders had apparently concluded that they had "lost the quantitative race."[111]

It is significant that, while professing to examine U.S. programs from the Soviet point of view, Pentagon planners did not accurately

109. Roger Hilsman, as if foreshadowing what was to come, suggested that there were risks involved in the Kennedy administration's decision to inform the Soviet Union about the "reverse missile gap" in October 1961 and argued that "the Soviets would undoubtedly speed up their ICBM program" with more urgency than would otherwise have been the case. (*To Move a Nation*, pp. 163–64.)

110. McNamara made the point in his speech before the Economic Club in New York. See Department of Defense News Release 1486-63, November 18, 1963, p. 8.

111. "Interview with Robert S. McNamara, Defense Secretary: Is Russia Slowing Down the Arms Race?" *U.S. News and World Report*, April 12, 1965, p. 52.

evaluate the effect of our strategic programs on the USSR's deterrent. Annual defense statements, to be sure, did contain quantitative estimates of possible Soviet reactions to U.S. defense programs, but the figures presented were for U.S. damage limitation, *not* Soviet assured destruction.[112] The difference between these two calculations—U.S. damage limitation and Soviet assured destruction—is crucial. The purpose of the first is to see if U.S. damage-limiting programs can save American lives, and the assumptions are therefore conservative from *our* point of view. For this calculation, programmed U.S. forces are assumed to perform relatively unreliably against greater-than-expected Soviet forces performing relatively well. The purpose of the second, however, is to assess the USSR's ability to maintain assured destruction against the United States. Accordingly, the assumptions behind these calculations are conservative from the *Soviet* perspective, since they impute a high level of effectiveness to U.S. forces and a low level to those of the USSR.

Soviet assured destruction computations had been performed for many years by analysts in the Arms Control and Disarmament Agency and were finally undertaken by the Pentagon during the course of the SALT preparations in 1968. But it seems strange that these calculations were not done earlier on a systematic basis by the Defense Department. After all, the United States reacted to worst-case USSR threats on the offensive side and was extremely conservative in its response to signs of Soviet ABMs. Since administration leaders thought they had educated the USSR to our way of making strategic analyses, it is difficult to see how U.S. planners could have avoided concluding that Kremlin analysts would be likely to evaluate programs in these terms and respond as called for by *our own* system. Such calculations would have shown, for example, that conservative military planners in Moscow, examining the implications of ongoing U.S. strategic development programs, might well have feared that the combination of Sentinel and MIRV deployments would pose a serious threat to the USSR's projected retaliatory capability. Quantitative analyses are not always needed to demonstrate the possible effects of weapon decisions, but

112. Ibid. In *How Much Is Enough?* Alain Enthoven and K. Wayne Smith, Pentagon officials under Secretary McNamara, displayed a "typical" table from an annual defense posture statement that *included* the results of Soviet assured destruction calculations (p. 189). But such figures *did not* appear in any official posture statement—or indeed in any public statement by officials of the Kennedy-Johnson administrations.

the lack of early systematic Pentagon studies of Soviet reactions to MIRVs and Sentinel might have made it more difficult for top policy-makers to see the potential consequences of these decisions for the future strategic balance.

THE SENTINEL AND MIRV DECISIONS

In the case of Sentinel, there is evidence that Soviet reactions were considered. Two of McNamara's associates claim that he saw and weighed the risk of a Soviet reaction to Sentinel before approving the program.[113] If this is correct, then even greater sensitivity to the desta-bilizing effects of such a defensive system might have enabled U.S. officials to persuade President Johnson to maintain an anti-ABM posi-tion. In addition to mounting political and bureaucratic insistence on ABMs, however, the pro-Sentinel group within the administration obviously presented national security arguments for approving a thin ABM system. Nonetheless, many experts had questioned both the tech-nical effectiveness and the doctrinal utility of a China-oriented system, and, if U.S.-Soviet stability had received more emphasis, it is certainly conceivable that the prospect of a mutual ABM ban and the potential political payoff of negotiating an early nuclear arms agreement with the USSR might have given the President sufficient incentive to override the Joint Chiefs and to contend with negative congressional attitudes. At a minimum, such a policy might have resulted in the authorization of the hard-point deployment preferred by some arms control analysts and perhaps by McNamara himself.

The issues involved in the connection between MIRVs and the Johnson administration's concern over Soviet reactions are more com-plicated than in the case of ABMs. To begin with, the Johnson admin-istration's MIRV decision could be seen as a less destabilizing alterna-tive than the procurement of entirely new strategic systems or the expansion of existing forces. Furthermore, there are ambiguities regard-ing the question of whether MIRV technology itself is destabilizing, as the majority of arms control experts contend. Although accurate MIRVs can endanger the survivability of fixed ICBMs, they do not threaten sea-based missiles. Moreover, the MIRV technique offers a confident counter to nationwide ABMs by preserving deterrence and discouraging an adversary from deploying large-scale missile defenses. Indeed, it should be recalled that Secretary McNamara canceled a

113. Enthoven and Smith, *How Much Is Enough?* p. 193.

project to develop a MIRV package containing a small number of large warheads with obvious counterforce capabilities in favor of packages containing large numbers of small warheads that were optimized for penetration and assured destruction. Some analysts suggest that Kremlin leaders may have been dissuaded from continuing the Soviet ABM program because they deemed U.S. MIRVs capable of negating such a system at far less cost; thus one analyst concluded that MIRVs may actually have benefited "the cause of arms control."[114]

On balance, however, in a situation where area ABM deployments are either nonexistent or limited to a few hundred interceptors, it can be argued that MIRVs introduce instabilities into the strategic balance by increasing the incentives for a counterforce strike, by creating pressures to procure new systems to replace potentially vulnerable ICBMs, and by raising uncertainties regarding the relative capabilities of U.S. and Soviet nuclear forces.[115] But the prospect that U.S. MIRV programs might ultimately bring destabilizing consequences apparently was not a central element in the Johnson administration's decision.

Many Pentagon analysts analyzed MIRVs primarily as assured destruction weapons for offsetting Soviet ABMs. To the degree that internal calculations did cover the use of MIRV as a damage-limiting device, there is little indication that evaluations of Soviet responses were given weight. If, through widespread discussions of this issue, U.S. officials had realized that the acquisition of MIRVs with counterforce capabilities would not only stimulate Soviet reactions in general but would probably induce the USSR to develop MIRVs with a potential to destroy our own ICBMs—a problem facing the United States in the 1970s—it is possible that the decision to procure or flight-test MIRVs might have been deferred pending the start of SALT. Perhaps McNamara might have decided to reject MIRV procurement and to compromise with the Joint Chiefs by agreeing to develop new sea-based systems or an advanced bomber—programs that were more costly but in a number of respects less destabilizing.

It is ironic that McNamara did not seem to apply the analysis of U.S.-USSR action-reaction to MIRVs as well as to ABMs. Perhaps the energy devoted to opposing the ABM decision and the bureaucratic difficulty of fighting more than one major system may explain this anomaly. Whatever the reasons, it was not until the SALT prepara-

114. York, "Multiple Warhead-Missiles," p. 26.
115. See, for example, Herbert Scoville, Jr., *Toward a Strategic Arms Limitation Agreement* (Carnegie Endowment for International Peace, 1970).

tions in 1968 that the effect of MIRVs on the strategic balance was systematically considered at high levels, but by that time the momentum behind MIRVs proved too great for these systems to be controlled through either unilateral restraint or negotiated agreements.

U.S. Strategic Policy as an Impediment to SALT

Notwithstanding the successful negotiation of the partial test ban and hot line agreements, during the early 1960s the United States simply was not ready to take serious steps toward controlling strategic systems. By the middle of the decade, there is no doubt that many U.S. officials believed that a SALT agreement could serve U.S. security interests. In their initial consideration of strategic limitation possibilities, however, many administration policymakers demanded that American superiority be guaranteed under an agreement, and the Joint Chiefs pressed for virtually foolproof verification arrangements with on-site inspection. American SALT proposals in 1968 reflected a substantial softening of these strict conditions but as a whole maximized the U.S. position and probably had little chance of being accepted by the Soviet Union. Commenting on U.S. strategic arms policies during the 1960s, former presidential adviser Jerome Wiesner claimed that the United States had "tried to have it both ways" by attempting "to maintain a superior nuclear force and to get the Soviet Union to enter into an agreement which would preserve our superiority."[116]

Of course, if SALT negotiations had begun as planned, the United States might have modified its position to permit the USSR to gain a more equitable force-level relationship. Yet it is far from clear that the Johnson administration would have been prepared to bargain away MIRVs or to accept low ABM limits under an agreement. At a minimum, the anti-Chinese rationale of Sentinel and the momentum behind the ABM program generally would have made it difficult for the administration to forgo these systems under a U.S.-Soviet arrangement. In fact, there is evidence that the United States might have been prepared to propose to the USSR that both sides retain thin area ABM defenses under a negotiated arrangement.[117]

There is little evidence, moreover, to suggest that the gains of a mutual MIRV ban were weighed against the perceived need to install

116. See Wiesner statement in *ABM, MIRV, SALT, and the Nuclear Arms Race,* pp. 395–96.

117. See John W. Finney, *New York Times,* November 11, 1969.

these systems as a means of strengthening America's strategic capabilities. This failure, combined with uncertainty about the verification of MIRV limitations and the internal drive behind the Minuteman III and Poseidon programs, made it unlikely that MIRVs would have been controlled even if SALT had been initiated in 1968. Even if the United States had proposed a MIRV ban, the USSR would have been reluctant to accept an accord that gave America a technological lead in missilery. Unfortunately, this period—when U.S. testing had only recently been initiated and the USSR had not yet tested a comparable system— might well have represented the last realistic chance to prevent MIRVs from entering the strategic arsenals of both sides.

On the other hand, if arms control had been assigned higher priority as a U.S. policy objective, the need for prudent hedges against possible future threats to our retaliatory capability and additional weapons to provide a certain amount of damage limitation might have been more fairly balanced against the security benefits that could come from an effective agreement. Significantly, in evaluating U.S. strategic force requirements, Pentagon planners gave little attention to the implications of possible limitation agreements in which postures on both sides were constrained. If the United States had faced lower-than-expected Soviet threats because of such an agreement, it would have been logical to assume that a less powerful U.S. posture would satisfy our objectives as effectively as a larger U.S. force facing a Soviet force unconstrained by limitations. The idea of attempting to assess relative risks and gains by evaluating U.S. security under arms control agreements and comparing this situation with that of an uncontrolled arms race was late in taking hold. Stimulated by the urgent need to prepare for SALT, the Defense Department apparently did this kind of analysis in 1968 but not during the early and mid-1960s when the lack of such relative risk analyses might have made it more difficult for administration officials to appreciate the potential value of strategic arms control.[118]

Although some observers contend that it might have been necessary to pay the price of a small ABM deployment to defeat a large one and to purchase multiple warheads in lieu of entirely new offensive missile systems, civilian policymakers did not institute the MIRV and Sentinel

118. Calculations of this kind were undertaken by analysts in the Arms Control and Disarmament Agency as early as 1965 but had little effect on U.S. weapons decisions or strategic arms limitations policies.

programs simply to placate military demands. Many U.S. officials gave credence to the notion that a thin ABM could improve deterrence against China, guard against accidental launchings, and strengthen U.S. nonproliferation policies. Similarly, Pentagon planners saw a real requirement for proceeding with MIRVs as a means of preserving our assured destruction capability, contributing to damage limitation, and helping the United States maintain superiority. Greater awareness of the potential instabilities of Sentinel and MIRVs could have resulted in less weight being assigned to the possible benefits of these systems and could have strengthened the ability of administration leaders to cope with countervailing domestic and bureaucratic pressures. Perhaps the United States would then have been able to delay these programs and to prepare a more comprehensive SALT proposal.

NATO COMPLICATIONS

As a final point, the relation between U.S. strategic arms policies and NATO might be mentioned, since America's ties to Western Europe impelled administration leaders during the 1960s to make strategic force and policy decisions that often conflicted with the goals of U.S.-Soviet stability and strategic arms control. The no-cities doctrine of 1962, for example, was designed to assuage NATO's concern about the credibility of U.S. guarantees and to diminish European interest in independent nuclear forces. Although officially hailed as an arms control move, this doctrine not only contradicted the administration's goal of reducing reliance on nuclear weapons but also tended to destabilize the U.S.-Soviet strategic balance by creating fears in the Kremlin of a U.S. first strike. Throughout the Kennedy and Johnson administrations, moreover, spokesmen stated quite explicitly that American superiority was necessary to convince our allies that the United States would in fact use its nuclear power in the event of an attack on Europe. The continuing interest in counterforce options was strongly motivated by a desire to limit damage to NATO by targeting Soviet medium-range missiles in addition to ICBMs directed against the United States. America's security commitments to Western Europe often raise the dilemma of choosing between alliance solidarity and superpower stability. In the cases cited above, it can be argued that officials of the Kennedy-Johnson administration may not have assigned sufficient priority to U.S.-USSR stability in making tradeoffs between opposing objectives.

CHAPTER THREE

Parity, Sufficiency, and SALT: 1969–1974

When President Nixon entered office, he was faced with a difficult and dynamic strategic arms environment. The substantial size and uncertain direction of the USSR's strategic force buildup had already raised crucial questions regarding the political as well as the military implications of the shifting nuclear balance. For the first time in the nuclear age, the United States was confronted with the reality of strategic parity and the prospect of Soviet numerical superiority in missile launchers. What effect would the loss of America's strategic preponderance have on Moscow's behavior and on relations with our allies? Was the growth of Soviet nuclear power threatening the reliability of U.S. deterrent capabilities? Soon after entering office, President Nixon was forced to make operational decisions in response to the new strategic issues of the 1970s.

It was of particular concern to the President and his advisers that the Johnson administration had left a legacy of weapon programs that were gathering momentum. Flight testing of multiple independently targetable reentry vehicles (MIRVs) was already under way, for example, and funds for the procurement of the Minuteman III and Poseidon missile systems were included in the outgoing administration's proposed defense budget for fiscal year 1970. As for defensive weapons, the Sentinel antiballistic missile (ABM) program had been approved, and funds for initial site construction had been allocated. Driven by technological, budgetary, and bureaucratic demands, President Nixon had to decide almost immediately whether to continue, curtail, or expand these and other major strategic programs. The unresolved issue of the strategic arms limitation talks (SALT) was an added complication, but it also provided opportunities for strengthening U.S. security. Negotiations had not been rescheduled after the

Soviet move into Czechoslovakia, partly because the Nixon administration had requested that it be permitted to develop its own position on this matter. The new President had to appraise the SALT proposal prepared by the Johnson administration, decide whether to initiate SALT, and, if so, when to hold the talks and what agreements to consider.

The Nixon Defense Doctrine

It is important to remember that the Nixon administration's defense decisions were made within a changing domestic framework. The movement to reverse national priorities had prompted demands to lower the level of defense spending, and the Vietnam experience had given rise to a growing body of opinion that held that the United States was overextended and should reduce its role in the world. It is ironic that Richard Nixon, Eisenhower's vice president, was faced with the two domestic constraints that were salient when President Eisenhower took office in 1953—pressure to decrease defense spending and a reaction against land wars in Asia. In 1969, however, key members of Congress not only were taking an active interest in defense matters but were arguing for reduced military spending and arms control. Moreover, defense experts, many of whom had recently left government service, were contributing to the congressional and public debates. These activities had helped to create a widespread awareness of security issues unparalleled in postwar years. For example, both the public outcry against Sentinel deployments and the anti-ABM hearings in the Senate were in sharp contrast to the public apathy and strong Senate support for the ABM in earlier years.

As one of its first major efforts, the Nixon administration undertook a review of U.S. defense programs and policies. The Department of Defense immediately launched a survey of weapon projects in order to identify costly programs that might be cut back or eliminated. On a broader level, an interagency study was organized to examine the cost, feasibility, and foreign policy implications of a wide range of possible U.S. military force postures.[1] But even before this study was com-

---

1. National Security Study Memorandum-3 (known as NSSM-3), was the third in a series of National Security Council studies undertaken by the administration. For a discussion of the strategic forces portion of this study, see *New York Times*, January 22, 1969; May 1, 1969; and May 2, 1969.

pleted, the outlines of the administration's defense policy began to emerge.

Turning Point in Policy

During the presidential campaign in 1968, Richard Nixon strongly advocated a policy of nuclear superiority, and it was widely believed that this goal would guide his strategic arms decisions.[2] One week after assuming office, however, President Nixon returned to the concept introduced in 1956 under President Eisenhower and indicated his preference for strategic "sufficiency." Within a few months, the administration had formally rejected superiority in favor of sufficiency.[3]

Many observers claimed that the Nixon strategy either had no meaning or was merely a semantic disguise for a policy of superiority through technological progress, and even Deputy Secretary of Defense David Packard dismissed strategic sufficiency as a speechwriter's phrase.[4] However, by proclaiming a doctrine of sufficiency in 1969, President Nixon officially accepted nuclear parity between the United States and the USSR as a fact of life for the 1970s, established specific criteria for guiding strategic arms decisions in this new era, and informed our adversaries, our allies, and the American people that the years of U.S. superiority had ended. For these reasons, the strategy of sufficiency had real political and military significance for the Nixon administration, and the decision to adopt this doctrine marked a turning point in America's strategic policies.

The Nixon administration's decision to follow a policy of sufficiency rather than superiority can be attributed to at least three important factors.

• Because of the rapidly increasing Soviet strategic forces, superiority proved to be an economically impractical policy. In addition,

2. In his CBS radio-TV address, "Defense Dialogue," on October 27, 1968, Nixon stated his intention "to restore our objective of clear-cut military superiority."

3. "The President's News Conference of January 27, 1969," *Public Papers of the Presidents of the United States: Richard Nixon, 1969* (1971), p. 19. The President supported Henry Kissinger's earlier use of the term. Defense Secretary Laird, referring to the use of this phrase by Secretary of the Air Force Donald Quarles in 1956, accepted sufficiency in a news conference three days later.

4. Packard reportedly added that, beyond its use in speeches, sufficiency "doesn't mean a God-damned thing." Cited in Chalmers Roberts, *The Nuclear Years: The Arms Race and Arms Control* (Praeger, 1970), p. 98.

domestic demands made decreases, not increases, in defense spending imperative.

• President Nixon considered nuclear superiority to be unattainable. Administration studies showed that the United States would be unable to recapture its former strategic advantage; in all probability, the Soviet Union would offset our moves. The President further acknowledged that each superpower had acquired the ability to inflict unacceptable damage on the other, regardless of which side might strike first, and indicated that there was no feasible alternative to this situation of mutual deterrence. In rejecting the deployment of large-scale U.S. ABM defenses early in 1969, President Nixon admitted that even the heaviest system could not prevent the Soviet Union from maintaining the capacity to inflict catastrophic damage on the United States.[5]

• President Nixon explained that attempts to achieve superiority would trigger an arms race, increase the risk of nuclear war, and harm U.S.-Soviet relations, thus reducing the prospects for reaching an agreement on strategic arms and for moving toward an "era of negotiation."[6]

On the other hand, although the President rejected superiority in favor of sufficiency, he argued that the United States must not permit its strategic power to become inferior to that of any other nation. He claimed that sharp cutbacks in U.S. strategic forces would call into question the reliability of our nuclear deterrent, arouse the concern of our allies, and decrease Soviet incentives for arms negotiations. President Nixon recognized that small changes in the strategic relationship were insignificant and that neither side could easily obtain a first-strike capability, but he emphasized that the United States would respond to any Soviet effort to substantially alter the balance.[7]

DEFENSE GOALS AT HOME AND ABROAD

U.S. strategic forces under President Nixon continued to form the backbone of America's security, providing a deterrent to nuclear attacks against the United States or its allies and aiding in the deterrence of less

5. "Statement on Deployment of the Antiballistic Missile System, March 14, 1969," *Public Papers, 1969*, p. 218.

6. *U.S. Foreign Policy for the 1970's: A New Strategy for Peace*, A Report to the Congress by Richard Nixon, President of the United States (February 18, 1970), p. 123.

7. The President underscored this point in ibid., and one year later in *U.S. Foreign Policy for the 1970's: Building for Peace*, A Report to the Congress by Richard Nixon, President of the United States (February 25, 1971), p. 129.

than all-out attacks. The President stated that, beyond these military objectives, our strategic forces were "essential to the maintenance of a stable political environment within which the threat of aggression or coercion against the United States and its allies is minimized."[8]

The Nixon administration also continued the previous policy of relying on U.S. strategic forces to help prevent the further spread of nuclear weapons by providing a "nuclear umbrella" to allied nations lacking such weapons.[9] Together with strategic forces, tactical nuclear forces were to remain integral components of U.S. military strategy and were to serve as a deterrent to full-scale Soviet or Chinese aggression. Like the previous administrations, the Nixon administration never excluded the possibility that the United States might use its nuclear forces first to counter conventional aggression in Europe or Asia. The President declared that coordinated nonnuclear attacks in Europe and Asia should not be met "primarily by U.S. conventional forces."[10]

Nevertheless, both the President and the secretary of defense stated quite clearly that sole reliance on nuclear forces to inhibit or deter aggression was undesirable. They believed that a credible and effective U.S. defense posture required the capacity to deal with a broad spectrum of military aggression and with the possibility of coercion. This called for strong conventional forces, which, together with tactical nuclear forces and strategic forces, could provide a reinforcing deterrent with a full range of options. President Nixon and Defense Secretary Melvin Laird continually pointed out that, because of strategic parity, there was an *even greater* need for nonnuclear options than during the previous decade. The determination of the administration to counter congressional demands to lower U.S. conventional force levels in Western Europe was particularly significant. The President announced that he would reduce our forces only through "reciprocal reductions negotiated with the Warsaw Pact."[11]

The size and composition of the total defense budget reflected the Nixon administration's serious interest in maintaining conventional force options. Allocations for general purpose forces (excluding Vietnam) approached and then surpassed allocations of the mid-1960s; over 90 percent of these funds were used for nonnuclear capabilities.

8. *Building for Peace*, p. 167.
9. Ibid., p. 13.
10. *A New Strategy for Peace*, p. 129.
11. *U.S. Foreign Policy for the 1970's: The Emerging Structure of Peace*, A Report to the Congress by Richard Nixon, President of the United States (February 9, 1972), p. 44.

Expenditures for strategic nuclear forces during the years 1969–73 accounted for slightly more than 20 percent of the total defense outlay. Measured in constant dollars to account for inflation, the Nixon administration's average annual strategic budget of $18 billion for this period was lower than typical budgets under the Kennedy-Johnson administrations.[12]

In many respects, the Nixon administration's defense policy was similar to the "flexible response" strategy of the Kennedy-Johnson years. Despite these similarities, however, the role played by nuclear power in the Nixon defense policy was different in part from that under the previous administration. For one thing, even taking inflation into account, comparisons of budget levels can be misleading. Because actual equipment costs during the early 1970s were substantially higher than during the early 1960s, U.S. conventional forces under Nixon were comparable in cost but not equivalent in effectiveness to the forces available under Kennedy and Johnson. Furthermore, because of the Nixon doctrine's redefinition of America's overseas commitments and congressional insistence to keep defense spending in check, administration officials concluded that the general purpose forces, particularly ground forces for Asian requirements, could be reduced below the levels developed under President Johnson. In theory, under Johnson these forces had been designed to handle a so-called 2½ war—that is, to fight the initial stages of simultaneous major wars in both Europe and Asia as well as a smaller conflict elsewhere. The Nixon strategy, on the other hand, was based on the assumption that simultaneous conventional attacks against Europe and Asia were unlikely, that our principal long-term interests lay in Northeast Asia, that our Asian allies could and would improve their conventional defense capabilities, and that U.S. air and sea power would remain in the Western Pacific.

The Nixon administration's defense policy in Asia was somewhat reminiscent of Eisenhower's New Look program. In words similar to those of Secretary of State John Foster Dulles during the mid-1950s, administration officials urged U.S. allies in Japan and Korea to provide manpower for local defense; the United States would provide its "special assets" of air and sea power. But U.S. policymakers in the early 1970s still did not foresee substantial allied contributions to conventional defense capabilities. Like the policy a decade earlier, Nixon's

12. See Edward R. Fried and others, *Setting National Priorities: The 1974 Budget* (Brookings Institution, 1973), p. 296.

Asian defense policy showed signs of placing greater reliance on U.S. tactical and strategic nuclear forces in Asia as an alternative to manpower. Secretary Laird, for example, indicated that our nuclear superiority over China would enable U.S. forces to "contribute significantly to deterrence of Chinese nuclear attacks or conventional attacks on our Asian allies."[13] The importance attached to strategic power in dealing with China was manifested in the Nixon administration's efforts to obtain a nationwide ABM system on the grounds that this system was essential to the credibility of American diplomacy and the effectiveness of the U.S. deterrent in Asia.

After the President's visit to Peking and the signing of the Moscow SALT accord that banned ABMs directed against China, the administration's tendency to increase its reliance on nuclear weapons in Asia seemed to diminish. Nevertheless, continued evidence of Pentagon programs to develop improved tactical nuclear weapons systems for use in Europe as well as in Asia, suggests that a more nuclear-oriented strategy remained in favor.[14] On the the strategic level, the administration's interest in limited-strike options and "warfighting" doctrines seemed to parallel trends to modernize U.S. battlefield nuclear forces. In short, despite the interest in strengthening conventional forces, the role of nuclear weapons in U.S. security policies was ambiguous.

The President's response to crises did little to clear up this ambiguity. For example, in the fall of 1970 President Nixon successfully thwarted a Soviet attempt to install a submarine base in Cuba by avoiding military actions and applying firm diplomatic pressure on the USSR. During the Middle East crisis of 1973, however, some experts contend that the administration seemed to be delivering a nuclear threat to the USSR by putting all U.S. forces around the world on strategic alert.[15] Administration officials denied this and claimed that the alert represented a prudential measure to ensure the readiness of

13. *Statement of Secretary of Defense Melvin R. Laird before the House Armed Services Committee on the FY 1972–1976 Defense Program and the 1972 Defense Budget* (March 9, 1971), p. 19.

14. See William Beecher, " 'Clean' Tactical Nuclear Weapons for Europe: Over the Threshold," *Army*, July 1972, pp. 17–20; Dennis M. Gromley, "NATO's Tactical Nuclear Option: Past, Present, and Future," *Military Review*, vol. 53 (September 1973), pp. 3–17; and *U.S. Security Issues in Europe: Burden Sharing and Offset, MBFR and Nuclear Weapons*, A staff report prepared for the Subcommittee on U.S. Security Agreements and Commitments Abroad of the Senate Foreign Relations Committee, 93 Cong. 1 sess. (1973).

15. Barry Blechman, *Washington Star*, December 2, 1973.

our forces. Secretary of State Henry Kissinger, recognizing that the situation in the Middle East could possibly set off a U.S.-Soviet nuclear conflict, observed that both superpowers had "a special duty to see to it that confrontations are kept within bounds that do not threaten civilized life."[16] But this observation left open the question of whether, in certain circumstances, the United States would be prepared to use the threat of limited nuclear war to counter Soviet political pressures or military actions.

The Strategy of Sufficiency

President Nixon's pronouncement that sufficiency would become the official U.S. strategic policy had important consequences at home and abroad but the policy itself provided only a general framework for the management of America's nuclear programs. Accordingly, the administration adopted a series of planning factors, or criteria, that were used to define the substance of sufficiency and to guide strategic weapon decisions. These criteria for sufficiency can be summarized as follows:

• Maintaining an effective strategic retaliatory capability to deter a surprise attack by any nation against the United States.

• Preserving stability by reducing the vulnerability of U.S. strategic forces and thereby minimizing the Soviet Union's incentive to strike first in a crisis.

• Preventing the Soviet Union from being able to inflict considerably more damage on America's population and industry than U.S. forces could inflict on the USSR.

• Defending the United States against small-scale nuclear attacks or accidental launches.

• Developing flexible options permitting U.S. strategic forces to be used in controlled and limited ways.

• Ensuring that the overall numerical balance between U.S. and Soviet strategic forces does not become disadvantageous to the United States.[17]

16. *Washington Post*, October 26, 1973.

17. The first four sufficiency criteria were described by Defense Secretary Laird in *Statement . . . on the FY 1972–1976 Defense Program and the 1972 Defense Budget*, p. 62. The last two factors, while never officially designated as criteria, were crucial considerations in the administration's doctrinal statements and arms programs.

The precise meaning and relative priority of each sufficiency criterion changed with evolving technical, military, and political circumstances. Taken together, however, all six exerted a substantial and sustained influence on the Nixon administration's strategic arms policy decisions.

Retaliatory Deterrent Capability: The Essential Criterion

The maintenance of an effective retaliatory capability was the most crucial criterion, since it represented the essence of America's strategic deterrent. While never designating a precise minimum acceptable "assured destruction" level or using this phrase to describe its policy, the Nixon administration followed the McNamara approach in designing U.S. strategic forces to provide a powerful and credible retaliatory capability for inflicting decisive damage on the USSR under all foreseeable conditions. Defense experts continued to plan U.S. forces by using conservative assumptions regarding future Soviet strategic threats. Moreover, the President and Secretary Laird both strongly supported the previous administration's policy of preserving a diversified deterrent consisting of land-based missiles, sea-based missiles, and manned bombers. This triad, they believed, would offer insurance against surprise Soviet technological breakthroughs or unforeseen operational failures of U.S. systems and would complicate the USSR's task of planning attacks on the United States.

When the Nixon administration took office, the Soviet Union's strategic buildup showed signs of eventually being able to endanger the survivability of U.S. strategic forces. Secretary Laird claimed that continued increases in the SS-9 intercontinental ballistic missile (ICBM) force and the development of accurate MIRVs for these missiles would enable the Soviet Union to destroy the bulk of the U.S. Minuteman ICBMs in a counterforce strike. At the same time, the secretary stressed that, because of the growing Soviet Polaris-type submarine force, our B-52 bombers could become vulnerable to submarine-launched ballistic missiles (SLBMs) launched from close range. To a lesser extent, administration officials expressed concern that possible Soviet progress in antisubmarine warfare (ASW) might threaten our sea-based deterrent. These threats were greatly overdrawn at first. Secretary Laird declared to the Senate Foreign Relations Committee in March 1969 that the Soviet Union was "going for a first-strike capability. There is no question about it."[18] Pentagon spokesmen suggested that the USSR might deploy as many as 2,500 ICBMs by the end of the decade. Many of these predictions, such as the Soviet SLBM threat to U.S. bombers, never materialized, while other projected Soviet programs were either curtailed by agreement or were slow in developing, as in the case of MIRVs. In any event, early concern about the future direction of the USSR's nuclear arms buildup led the Nixon administration to make a series of weapon decisions designed to preserve the invulnerability of U.S. deterrent systems.

THE RISE AND FALL OF SAFEGUARD

One of the administration's most significant actions was to modify the Sentinel ABM and turn it into the Safeguard system. President Nixon announced this decision on March 14, 1969.[19] As noted in chapter 2, Sentinel had been initiated by the Johnson administration to provide a thin area defense of the United States against small-scale missile attacks and to defend our ICBMs if necessary. The Safeguard program, on the other hand, called for ABM sites to be deployed at Minuteman ICBM fields in the first stage and for nationwide coverage to be installed in a second stage. It has been suggested that the Safeguard decision was shaped by domestic pressures to move ABM sites away from cities, by bureaucratic struggles within the executive branch, and by the President's desire to cut defense spending.[20] Obviously, these issues were influential. But the shift to Safeguard was in line with the administration's policy and responsive to the prevailing strategic situation. By 1969, intelligence analyses indicated that China's ICBM efforts were not proceeding as rapidly as predicted. At the same time, there was reason to believe that the Soviet Union was developing a MIRV capability that

18. *Strategic and Foreign Policy Implications of ABM Systems,* Hearings before the Subcommittee on International Organization and Disarmament Affairs of the Senate Committee on Foreign Relations, 91 Cong. 1 sess. (1969), pt. 1, p. 196.

19. *New York Times,* March 15, 1969. For additional information on Safeguard, see *Statement of Secretary of Defense Melvin R. Laird before a Joint Session of the Senate Armed Services Committee and the Senate Subcommittee on Department of Defense Appropriations on the Fiscal Year 1971 Defense Program and Budget* (February 20, 1970).

20. For a discussion of this issue, see Michael Brenner, "Strategy in the Nixon Administration," *Stanford Journal of International Studies,* vol. 7 (Spring 1972), pp. 109–31; and Aaron Wildavsky, "The Politics of ABM," *Commentary,* November 1969, pp. 55–63.

could endanger the survivability of the Minuteman force. Thus, the decision to modify the Sentinel ABM program and direct it toward early protection of U.S. ICBM sites, with a subsequent phase for a thin nation-wide defense, was a logical one.

In justifying the ABM decision, administration officials claimed that Safeguard would prevent U.S. land-based forces from becoming vulnerable without posing a threat to the USSR's deterrent. Therefore, they maintained, the Safeguard program was completely consistent with strategic stability and the goal of negotiating a meaningful SALT accord. Nongovernmental experts questioned these propositions. Many distinguished scientists presented persuasive analyses demonstrating that Safeguard could not be relied on to defend U.S. ICBMs against the anticipated Soviet offensive buildup. In their opinion, whatever marginal protection might be obtained would be short-lived, and billions of dollars would be wasted on an ineffective system. Some arms control experts disagreed with the premise that Safeguard was stabilizing; they contended that Kremlin leaders would regard the area defense portion of the system—and possibly even the phase-one Minuteman ABM sites—as direct threats to their deterrent.[21]

As early as 1970, the Nixon administration's enthusiasm for Safeguard had begun to wane. For one thing, it became apparent that the Safeguard components available from Sentinel and built for city defenses were incapable of providing an effective defense of ICBM sites. Defense Secretary Laird finally acknowledged that the system could not protect American ICBMs against a sophisticated Soviet MIRV capability, which might well materialize within five years, and proposed the development of more cost-effective missile-site ABM components.[22] Furthermore, Congress denied the President funds to begin construction of area ABM sites and actively sought to cut back the number of ICBM defense sites.[23] In any case, the Moscow treaty negotiated in the spring of 1972 restricted the United States to a single ABM site for ICBM defense and

21. For a particularly effective and responsible criticism of Safeguard, see the statement of W. K. H. Panofsky in *ABM, MIRV, SALT, and the Nuclear Arms Race*, pp. 186–90.

22. *Statement . . . on the Fiscal Year 1971 Defense Program and Budget*, pp. 48–49. The lack of specialized hard-point defenses plagued Secretary McNamara in 1967 when the Sentinel decision was made.

23. See *Authorizing Appropriations for Fiscal Year 1971 for Military Procurements, Research and Development. . . . *S. Rept. 91–1016, 91 Cong. 2 sess. (1970), p. 19.

one site to defend Washington, D.C.[24] It is possible to argue, therefore, that this SALT agreement saved the administration from the dilemma of either being forced by Congress to halt Safeguard, with no guarantee that the Soviet Union would refrain from expanding its ABM system, or having to complete an expensive program of dubious value simply to match the USSR's program.

The SALT accords did not eliminate the potential threat to Minuteman, since MIRVs were not banned and Soviet ICBM levels were not reduced. Even before the Moscow treaty was signed, however, President Nixon explained that the United States was "willing to forgo extensive ABM protection in return for greater stability offered by an equitable limit on both offensive and defensive strategic forces."[25] In advocating support of the agreement, SALT negotiator Gerard Smith amplified this view by arguing that the benefits of limiting Soviet ABMs in terms of improving the U.S. deterrent were worth the loss of the Safeguard program.[26] As permitted under the accords, however, the administration continued to request research funds for missile-site defense systems and completed the silo-hardening program in an attempt to improve Minuteman survivability. The flight-testing of MIRVs by the Soviet Union in August 1973, during what Defense Secretary James Schlesinger characterized as an aggressive Soviet missile development program, gave impetus to these efforts and also created greater interest in investigating other programs, such as airborne or land-mobile ICBMs, which might offer alternatives to fixed land-based missiles at some future time.[27]

MIRV PROGRAMS

The MIRV program pursued by the Nixon administration was also tied to the question of Minuteman vulnerability and the first criterion of sufficiency. Although the Soviet Union showed no clear signs of constructing a large-scale ABM network, the President and Secretary Laird claimed that MIRVs were essential for sufficiency—not only to offset possible future Soviet ABM expansion or the upgrading of surface-to-air missile defenses but to provide a greater number of surviving Minute-

24. Treaty between the United States of America and the Union of Soviet Socialist Republics on the Limitation of Anti-Ballistic Missile Systems, signed at Moscow, May 26, 1972.

25. *The Emerging Structure of Peace*, p. 162.

26. Statement before the Senate Armed Services Committee, June 28, 1972; and address before the National Security Industrial Association, September 17, 1972.

27. *Washington Post*, August 18, 1973.

man warheads if a portion of the U.S. force were destroyed by a counter-force strike. At the same time, it was argued, installing MIRVs on submarine-launched missiles would give U.S. sea-based forces greater deterrent power as a hedge against the potential reduction of U.S. ICBM retaliatory capabilities. In spite of demands by Congress and the public to halt MIRV programs, the administration continued to test these systems throughout 1969 and early 1970. By mid-1970, both the Minute-man and Poseidon MIRV testing programs were completed and deploy-ment had begun. During the SALT negotiations, the MIRV installation program went forward as planned and remained unaffected by the Moscow agreements in 1972.

The Nixon administration's MIRV decisions aroused a debate inside and outside the U.S. government second only in significance and inten-sity to the Safeguard debate.[28] In addition to contending that U.S. MIRV programs were destabilizing, critics claimed that the continued lack of evidence of widespread Soviet ABM construction made it unnecessary to proceed with Minuteman III or Poseidon missile procurements. This position was obviously strengthened after Soviet ABMs were limited by the Moscow treaty. But Nixon officials, like those in the Johnson admin-istration, saw MIRVs as a multipurpose system serving many strategic policy objectives and negotiating needs within the broad scope of suf-ficiency. The sum total of these perceived security requirements made the deployment of Poseidon and Minuteman III virtually inevitable—quite apart from the institutional momentum in the Pentagon that, ac-cording to some experts, has been responsible for the continued commit-ment to MIRVs.[29]

TRIDENT AND THE B-1 BOMBER

Although U.S. officials did not express serious concern about main-taining the invulnerability of the Polaris submarine fleet, they attached high priority to the Navy's program to develop the Trident submarine. Defense Secretary Laird and other Pentagon leaders claimed that Tri-

28. For a comprehensive discussion of executive branch policies on this issue and the way Congress attempted to influence the administration's MIRV decisions, see Ted Greenwood, "Qualitative Improvements in Offensive Strategic Arms: The Case of MIRV" (Ph.D. dissertation, Massachusetts Institute of Technology, 1973), pp. 155–244.

29. See Graham T. Allison and Frederic A. Morris, "Armaments and Arms Con-trol: Exploring the Determinants of Military Weapons," Daedalus, vol. 104 (Sum-mer 1975), pp. 99–129.

dent would ensure the security of America's sea-based deterrent through the 1980s and argued that deploying more powerful missile-firing submarines would be particularly crucial in the event Soviet MIRV developments endangered the survivability of U.S. land-based forces. Congressional and scientific critics, on the other hand, claimed that the Trident program was costly, unnecessary, and inappropriate as a means of strengthening America's sea-based deterrent. They also contended that Trident was being pursued because of bureaucratic pressure from the Navy. Although military justifications were presented by proponents of the program, the administration's decision to accelerate the Trident program in late 1971—and to reverse an earlier plan to develop a longer-range missile to replace Poseidon before constructing new boats—was primarily based on perceived negotiating needs and other policy requirements having little to do with fears of Soviet ASW breakthroughs. These considerations will be detailed later when the "force matching" and "bargaining chip" concepts are discussed.[30]

In addition to weapon decisions affecting ICBMs and SLBMs, the Nixon administration took actions to improve the effectiveness of the third element of the triad—strategic bombers. It instituted programs to disperse bombers and decrease their takeoff time, installed radars to provide better warning against SLBM attacks, and developed and deployed advanced air-to-surface missiles. Of more long-term significance was the decision to develop the B-1 bomber as a replacement for the B-52. Many congressmen and nongovernmental experts questioned the B-1 effort, as they had Trident, claiming that the system was excessively costly, that it would not provide significant improvements in deterrent capabilities over the B-52 weapon, and that other bomber configurations could satisfy the requirements for a follow-on strategic bomber more efficiently and at less cost. But the administration pressed the program before and after the SALT accords were signed, on the grounds that the B-1 was essential for maintaining a viable strategic bomber deterrent and that the existence of an ongoing bomber program would strengthen America's bargaining position in SALT. Entirely apart from these considerations, some studies suggest that the drive toward the B-1 and the lack of bomber alternatives might well have been influenced largely by

30. For a full treatment of the factors that influenced the Trident decisions, see John Steinbruner and Barry Carter, "Organizational and Political Dimensions of the Strategic Posture: Problems of Reform," *Daedalus*, vol. 104 (Summer 1975), pp. 131–54.

the Air Force's bureaucratic desires to retain a manned bomber mission.[31]

Preserving Stability in Crises

Notwithstanding the emphasis given to maintaining an effective retaliatory deterrent capability, President Nixon claimed that it would be inconsistent with the meaning of sufficiency for the United States to base its force planning "solely on some finite—and theoretical—capacity to inflict casualties presumed to be unacceptable to the other side."[32] The President and administration spokesmen, including Henry Kissinger and Melvin Laird, argued that a retaliatory capability would deter a large-scale premeditated Soviet attack but would not necessarily meet the requirement of preserving stability in a crisis. They explained their position by outlining a hypothetical situation in which the USSR might be able to destroy almost all of America's land-based strategic forces in a time of tension. Even though Soviet leaders would realize that our remaining sea-based missile forces might be able to inflict large-scale damage on the USSR in retaliation, it was argued, they might launch a preemptive counterforce strike nonetheless in the hope of limiting damage to their society. Although such a move would be risky, proponents of the crisis stability criterion claimed that Soviet leaders might conclude that the President, fearing a full countercity reprisal, would be inhibited from launching a retaliatory strike against the USSR in response to an attack on our ICBMs.[33]

The issue of crisis stability was attacked by nongovernmental experts as an artificial one that could lead to a needless escalation of strategic arms by creating demands for new systems and for programs to protect existing land-based forces. Critics maintained, for instance, that Soviet leaders would be inhibited from launching an attack against U.S. ICBMs that would cause millions of American fatalities through collateral effects as long as our sea-based deterrent remained viable. But Nixon officials continued to claim that it would be unwise to provide Moscow with the

31. See Peter J. Ognibene, "Did Someone Mention Arms Control? The B-1 Ballyhoo," *New Republic*, June 17, 1972, pp. 17–20; and Berkeley Rice, "The B-1 Bomber: The Very Model of a Modern Major Misconception," *Saturday Review*, December 11, 1971, p. 20.

32. *Building for Peace*, pp. 170–71.

33. See ibid., pp. 172–73; and William Beecher, *New York Times*, October 19, 1970.

option of being able to destroy a significant fraction of U.S. land-based forces. However unlikely counterforce scenarios might seem, administration leaders argued, prudence dictated taking measures to minimize the likelihood of a nuclear exchange occurring inadvertently because of a Soviet miscalculation. While the United States could always rely on a launch-on-warning firing doctrine for its ICBMs, the administration considered this a dangerous and inflexible substitute for protecting our forces. The criterion of crisis stability thus provided a further rationale for the Safeguard ABM and silo-hardening programs.

Relative Levels of Destruction

The basic assured destruction concept developed by Secretary of Defense McNamara called for U.S. strategic forces to maintain a minimum level of retaliatory damage-inflicting potential, independent of the level of damage the USSR could inflict on the United States. The Nixon administration accepted this basic deterrence principle as a fundamental element of its strategic policy. After reviewing U.S. strategic policies, however, Nixon officials feared that the risk of nuclear war might increase if Kremlin leaders came to view the outcome of a strategic exchange as "favorable" to the USSR. They decided, therefore, that the degree of destruction the United States should be able to achieve during a retaliatory strike against the USSR would be meaesured on a *relative* scale, taking into account the Soviet Union's capacity to damage the United States.[34]

The meaning of the relative destruction criterion was not spelled out in detail. In particular, neither the maximum tolerable damage differential nor the relationship between the degree of acceptable asymmetry and the absolute levels of destruction were specified by Nixon administration officials. For example, if the United States possessed a retaliatory force capable of destroying 25 percent of the Soviet Union's population, it was not clear whether a Soviet potential to destroy 30–40 percent of the U.S. population in a retaliatory strike would require countermeasures on our part. Furthermore, fatality ratios vary widely as a function of attack and targeting assumptions, but the situations that were to form the basis for damage comparisons were not described. Finally,

34. In reporting the results of the Nixon administration's strategic doctrine review, William Beecher noted that the United States had increased its "assured destruction requirement" to ensure that no unfavorable fatality ratio would occur. (*New York Times*, October 19, 1969.)

this criterion seemed to have no obvious weapon implications. The administration did not attempt to justify new offensive weapons by citing the need to increase the capacity to inflict damage on the Soviet Union and did not press major defensive programs, such as large-scale ABM deployments, which could have been built in an effort to substantially lower the USSR's destructive potential. To the extent that the Nixon administration developed offensive counterforce capabilities, these programs were tied to the sufficiency criterion dealing with the flexible use of strategic forces.

Defense against Small Attacks

The criterion of defending the United States against damage from small-scale ICBM attacks or accidental missile launches was, of course, closely related to the nationwide ABM plan associated with phase two of the Safeguard ABM program. In attempting to justify the area ABM proposal, President Nixon and his spokesmen emphasized the prudential value of protecting the United States with a thin missile defense network. Since a small nuclear attack from any source would be a catastrophe, the President stated that "no administration with the responsibility for the lives and security of the American people could fail to provide every possible protection against such eventualities."[35] As in the case of the earlier Sentinel program, however, the primary reason for the Nixon administration's early interest in area ABMs was the prospect that China might soon acquire a small ICBM force. Indeed, shortly after assuming office, the President stated that an ABM directed against China was "essential" for a "credible foreign policy in the Pacific."[36] During 1969 and 1970, Defense Secretary Laird questioned whether the nation could rely on the rational calculus of deterrence to dissuade Chinese leaders from using or threatening to use nuclear weapons and suggested that, once U.S. cities became "hostages" to China, Peking might use nuclear blackmail to threaten our Asian allies.

But, as noted earlier, the administration's Safeguard area ABM plans were blocked by congressional action. At Senate hearings and elsewhere, severe criticisms were leveled against the cost and effectiveness of such a system—criticisms that applied to the Johnson administration's Sentinel program but that had not been made with force in 1967 and 1968.

35. *A New Strategy for Peace*, p. 125.
36. "The President's News Conference of January 30, 1970," *Public Papers of the Presidents of the United States: Richard Nixon, 1970* (1971), p. 42.

In addition to technical onslaughts against Safeguard, experts argued that a thin ABM deployment was not necessary for deterring China and claimed that the deployment of a nationwide missile defense network would pose a direct threat to the Soviet Union's deterrent and would endanger the SALT negotiations. After Congress rejected the President's request for funds to initiate the construction of area ABM sites, President Nixon did not request funds for this program in the 1972 budget. It is, of course, difficult to judge whether the administration would have eventually succeeded in obtaining congressional approval of the complete Safeguard program if it had not had to forgo its nationwide ABM plans because of the SALT treaty.

The Moscow agreements did not affect China's ICBM potential, but Henry Kissinger, then presidential adviser, suggested that the President's visit to Peking had improved Sino-American understanding and obviated the need for a nationwide ABM.[37] Perhaps this accounted for our willingness to forgo an area ABM. But it is more likely that the stability benefits of the negotiated *mutual* ABM limitations in 1972 outweighed the advantages of constructing nationwide defenses. In the absence of area defenses, neither the United States nor the USSR have any direct protection against accidental missile launchings, but Washington and Moscow have taken other negotiated actions to minimize the risks and consequences of accidental nuclear war. Nevertheless, even after the ABM treaty was signed, limiting damage from small-scale attacks remained one of the official criteria for sufficiency and the Nixon administration continued research and development efforts on an improved area interceptor—perhaps for eventual installation at permitted sites or possibly to provide the option for nationwide defense in the event the agreements were abrogated.

Flexible Options

Providing U.S. strategic forces with the ability to respond at a variety of levels was a particularly controversial component of the sufficiency strategy. In his first foreign policy message, President Nixon questioned

37. Questions and answers after congressional briefing on the Moscow SALT Agreements, June 15, 1972, in *Strategic Arms Limitation Agreements*, Hearings before the Senate Committee on Foreign Relations, 92 Cong. 1 sess. (1972), p. 405. In his press conference, January 30, 1970, President Nixon did relate the necessity of going forward with an anti-Chinese ABM system to relations with China, implying that the United States might conceivably reverse its policy if relations between Washington and Peking improved. (*Public Papers, 1970,* p. 40.)

whether, in the event of a nuclear attack, a U.S. president should be left "with the single option of ordering the mass destruction of enemy civilians in the face of certainty that it would be followed by the mass slaughter of Americans."[38] The President subsequently suggested that acquiring such flexibility would require changes in strategic plans as well as in command and control capabilities and explained that studies of this issue were being undertaken. Although the flexible option criterion was not discussed in detail, it seems clear that during the administration's first term officials found U.S. strategic war plans too rigid and desired to develop operational plans for using strategic forces selectively —not unlike the "controlled response" doctrine advocated by Secretary McNamara in the early 1960s but subsequently downgraded.

Nixon administration officials offered three reasons for acquiring flexible strategic options: (1) to deter the Soviet Union from launching limited strikes by being in a position to respond in kind; (2) to provide the United States with the capacity to initiate limited strikes in certain circumstances, such as a massive Soviet conventional attack in Western Europe; and (3) to institute a prudential measure for minimizing damage if deterrence failed. But President Nixon's plea for flexibility also included the goal of developing a "hard-target kill" capability to destroy Soviet silo-based ICBMs. Throughout the administration's first term, spokesmen explained that the purpose of acquiring such an option was to deter the Soviet Union from launching an attack against our land-based forces by giving the United States the ability to respond with a counterforce second-strike blow against Soviet systems. Officials expressed concern that, in the absence of this capability and in the event the survivability of U.S. land-based forces could not be ensured, Soviet leaders might launch such an attack in the belief that the President might yield rather than risk mutual destruction.

The administration's interest in flexible options created yet another intense strategic policy controversy between the executive branch, on the one hand, and congressional and nongovernmental experts on the other hand. Some administration opponents questioned the necessity as well as the desirability of placing excessive emphasis on programs designed to give U.S. forces the alleged capacity to wage "limited" strategic war, but most critics attacked one particular aspect of flexibility—the question of hard-target kill capabilities. Opponents of this program

38. *A New Strategy for Peace*, p. 122.

argued that the development of counterforce weapons would be destabilizing and would harm prospects for reaching a productive SALT accord. They claimed that the prudent response to Soviet counterforce programs, failing attempts to remove this danger through negotiated agreements, would be to seek ways of reducing the potential vulnerability of U.S. land-based missiles. As a consequence of pressure exerted by Senator Edward Brooke and others in late 1969, the administration canceled an advanced development program to improve Poseidon warhead accuracies, and in response to Brooke's questions, President Nixon denied that there was an ongoing U.S. program "to develop a so-called hard-target MIRV capabilitiy."[39]

But the hard-target issue was far from being resolved. Notwithstanding the President's statement, Defense Secretary Laird and other military officials implied that the United States would seek to develop counterforce capabilities, although they affirmed that the nation would not continue these activities to the point of posing a first-strike threat to the Soviet Union. Indications that the administration was continuing to pursue improved missile accuracy programs led the Senate Armed Services Committee to reduce requested funds for the advanced warhead development programs in the 1971 budget on the grounds that there is no technical distinction between a first-strike and second-strike counterforce weapon.

After the Moscow SALT agreements, the administration attempted to reinstitute a specific hard-target warhead project, which was again denied by congressional action. During 1973, a number of research programs indirectly related to developing improved accuracy continued to be conducted. Finally, in August of that year, the new defense secretary, James Schlesinger, stated that, while rejecting policies designed to achieve the capacity to destroy Soviet forces by launching a first strike, the administration had not forsworn efforts to acquire "precision instruments that would be used in a limited counterforce role."[40] Later Schlesinger reported that the United States was modifying its strategic plans to place greater emphasis on striking military targets and that there had been requests for direct funds to support accuracy improvements. Thus, the question of hard-target capabilities triggered a major debate—a debate that is still in progress and that can affect America's future strategic posture and the future of the arms limitation talks.

39. *Congressional Record* (daily ed., April 23, 1970), p. 12699.
40. News conference, August 17, 1973.

Keeping a Numerical Balance

President Nixon's view of strategic forces extended beyond military considerations, and the administration's interpretation of sufficiency specifically reflected this outlook. In his foreign policy report in 1971, the President was quite explicit in stating that

sufficiency has two meanings. In its narrow military sense, it means enough force to inflict a level of damage on a potential aggressor sufficient to deter him from attacking. . . . In its broader political sense, sufficiency means the maintenance of forces adequate to prevent us and our allies from being coerced.[41]

Concern about the political side of sufficiency influenced the formulation and interpretation of military planning criteria. For example, administration officials indicated that the criteria of crisis stability and flexible options served the *political* purpose of deterring possible Soviet nuclear blackmail threats that might be made if U.S. ICBMs became vulnerable or if the President had no flexibility in targeting U.S. strategic forces. But the most direct connection made between political requirements and strategic force policy was the emphasis placed on the criterion of ensuring that the United States would not become inferior to the Soviet Union in the numerical balance of forces.

Shortly after entering office, President Nixon raised the possibility that the Soviet leaders might be tempted into "bolder challenges" in the mistaken belief that they could successfully exploit their newly acquired strategic strength for political or limited military purposes to the detriment of the United States or its allies.[42] Administration officials contrasted the U.S.-Soviet nuclear balance at the time of the Cuban missile crisis with the existing situation of parity. They claimed that President Kennedy was able to act with assurance in 1962 because the nuclear balance was four-to-one in his favor, and that the Soviet Union, appreciating the situation, was forced to back down. In future crises, they said, the loss of U.S. numerical superiority could lead Moscow to underestimate our resolve and take risky actions. President Nixon stated that he did not wish to see an American president "have his diplomatic credibility be so impaired because the United States was in a second-class or inferior position."[43] Throughout 1969, the administration suggested

41. *Building for Peace*, p. 170.
42. Ibid., p. 159.
43. "The President's News Conference of April 18, 1969," *Public Papers, 1969,* p. 303.

that Moscow might already be attempting to translate its strategic power into political leverage and pointed to the pattern of "irresponsible" Soviet actions in the Middle East. The Soviet Union's attempt to install a submarine base in Cuba in the fall of 1970 seemed to confirm these fears by raising the specter of a repeat of the earlier Cuban missile crisis.

Although the Middle East and Cuban situations did not erupt into major confrontations, officials continued to stress the importance of maintaining a U.S. strategic posture designed to minimize the likelihood that the Soviet Union might underestimate U.S. resolve or miscalculate the danger of certain courses of action. Admiral Thomas Moorer, chairman of the Joint Chiefs of Staff, summed up the Nixon administration's position by stating that "the mere appearance of Soviet strategic superiority could have a debilitating effect on our foreign policy and our negotiating posture . . . even if that superiority would have no practical effect on the outcome of an all-out nuclear exchange."[44]

The administration's interest in the numerical balance provided a force-matching rationale for many strategic weapon decisions. In recommending acceleration of the Trident submarine program early in 1972, for example, Secretary Laird was rather direct in stating that "it would be diplomatically and politically unacceptable for the United States to allow the Soviets to achieve a large numerical superiority in both land-based and sea-based strategic missiles."[45] To highlight their concern over the numerical balance, administration officials often alluded to the USSR's numerical superiority in ICBMs, while downgrading our advantage in force quality, number of warheads, and long-range bombers. Analyses of the existing and projected U.S.-Soviet strategic relationship often ignored capabilities and stressed numerical comparisons of missile launchers. Although the commitment to MIRV deployment was obviously influenced by the need to offset the USSR's buildup of missile launchers, it was not until 1972 that spokesmen began to systematically emphasize America's qualitative superiority and the U.S. lead in MIRV and strategic bomber forces.

Opponents of the Nixon administration's strategic policies, represent-

44. *United States Military Posture for FY 1973*, Hearings before the Senate Armed Services Committee, 92 Cong. 2 sess. (February 15, 1972), pp. 505–6.

45. *Statement of Secretary of Defense Melvin R. Laird before the Senate Armed Services Committee on the FY 1973 Defense Budget and FY 1973–1977 Program* (February 15, 1972), p. 69.

ing a coalition of liberal congressmen and nongovernmental experts, were particularly hostile to the force-matching policy, arguing that even major shifts in the U.S.-Soviet strategic balance would have little military or political significance. Although official U.S. policy did not change as a result of these domestic pressures, it is ironic to note that the administration eventually accepted a five-year interim agreement that conceded to the USSR almost a 50 percent numerical advantage in ICBM and SLBM launchers.[46] Indeed, during the summer of 1972 administration spokesmen found themselves forced to defend SALT against *conservative* critics by de-emphasizing the importance of missile launchers and stressing U.S. superiority in number of bombers and nuclear warheads and in overall technological capacity. But administration leaders judged the numerical balance under the Interim Agreement to be no worse and possibly better than it would have been otherwise. On a more general level, the climate of détente that began to take hold in 1971 and that culminated in President Nixon's summit meeting in Moscow undoubtedly helped blunt the earlier extreme sensitivity to the potential dangers of a shifting strategic nuclear balance.

After the Interim Agreement, the Nixon administration planned its future strategic policies and formulated its objectives for subsequent SALT negotiations with apparent determination to maintain, in the President's words, an "essential equivalency" between U.S. and Soviet strategic forces.[47] Defense Secretary Schlesinger was even more explicit after announcing the initiation of Soviet MIRV flight-testing when he explained that America's qualitative advantages were "waning" and concluded that "as the Soviets close the technological gap . . . the United States is not in a position to tolerate the numerical . . . advantages [in ICBM launchers] presently possessed by the Soviet Union."[48] Later, when the Senate passed a resolution calling for the United States to seek numerical equality in intercontinental-range strategic delivery vehicles under a permanent offensive arms treaty, Congress, despite opposition to force matching in some quarters, seemed prepared to support the administration's approach.

46. Interim Agreement between the United States of America and the Union of Soviet Socialist Republics on Certain Measures with Respect to the Limitation of Strategic Offensive Arms, signed at Moscow, May 26, 1972.

47. *U.S. Foreign Policy for the 1970s: Shaping a Durable Peace*, A Report to the Congress by Richard Nixon, President of the United States (May 3, 1973), p. 202.

48. News conference, August 17, 1973.

Soviet Strategic Policies

When the Nixon administration assumed office in 1969, it encountered a substantial strategic buildup by the Soviet Union. From a force of 200 relatively vulnerable ICBMs in 1964, the USSR reached parity in ICBMs in early 1969 with a force of 1,060 land-based missiles, including a total of 800 hardened SS-11 and SS-9 systems. As the Soviet Union enlarged its offensive forces, however, it refrained from extending its ABM network beyond the nominal system deployed at Moscow and later accepted ABM limitations under the SALT treaty.

During the next few years, the Soviet Union further expanded its ICBM force, reaching a total of over 1,600 missiles at the end of 1972. After the Interim Agreement was negotiated, U.S. intelligence estimates showed that the USSR was pursuing a vigorous test program involving at least three improved land-based missile systems, successors to the SS-9 and SS-11. Of more significance was the initiation of Soviet MIRV flight-tests in mid-1973; U.S. officials predicted that operational MIRV payloads could begin to be deployed on the new generation of Soviet ICBMs within four or five years. At the time the SALT accords were signed, the number of Soviet SLBM systems at sea and under construction surpassed the U.S. Polaris fleet of 41 missile-firing submarines, the Soviet Union was about to deploy an advanced Y-class boat carrying an SLBM of substantially increased range, and an entirely new-generation strategic submarine was apparently under development. Finally, throughout the early 1970s, the USSR evidently continued its efforts to develop land-mobile ICBM systems.[49]

It is possible that the Kremlin's strategic programs in the years 1969–73 represented a sustained reaction to America's nuclear arms activities—following the same stream of responses stimulated by the outcome of the Cuban missile crisis in 1962 and carried forward by the strategic arms decisions of the Kennedy and Johnson administrations. Early in the Nixon administration, the completion of U.S. MIRV tests and

49. For Soviet strategic programs during this period, see Alton H. Quanbeck and Barry M. Blechman, *Strategic Forces: Issues for the Mid-Seventies* (Brookings Institution, 1973); statements by the secretaries of defense on programs and budgets for fiscal years 1970–74; and John Ericson, *Soviet Military Power* (London: Royal United Services Institute, 1971).

the start of Minuteman III and Poseidon missile deployments dramatized the fact that the United States would have 10,000 warheads deployed on its strategic missile forces by the mid-1970s. Measured by this
all-important criterion, the USSR would find itself in an *inferior* position,
despite its substantial gains in deploying missile launchers, since it was
well behind the United States in MIRV technology. Continued indications that the United States had not halted efforts to acquire a hard-
target kill capability could have led Kremlin leaders to conclude that
their ICBM force would lose its deterrent value. Because of their further
concern that Safeguard would become the first step to a large-scale defense system, Soviet planners had reason to fear that America might be
moving toward a first-strike capability. The problem was further compounded by the U.S. lead in long-range bombers and the stepped-up
development of Trident and the B-1, which meant that the United States
would have two major advanced strategic systems available in considerable strength by the early 1980s.

Moscow may have had no alternative but to continue deploying
land-based missiles as a way of countering the potential military and
political dangers posed by the United States. Despite the possible future
vulnerability of ICBM systems, Soviet planners might have concluded
that additional numbers, with some improved hardening of silos, would
contribute to deterrence—until qualitative improvements, such as
MIRVs, became available and until a sufficiently powerful SLBM capability was assured. The USSR has severe geographic disadvantages
that reduce the on-station rates and increase the vulnerability of its submarines, and Soviet SLBMs are qualitatively inferior to the U.S. MIRV-
carrying Poseidon system. These factors not only help explain why the
USSR felt it necessary to eventually build a numerically superior sea-
based missile force as well as a large ICBM force but could have motivated the apparent Soviet attempt to establish a submarine base in Cuba
in 1970.

It seems even more likely that the Soviet Union structured its strategic
programs to preserve a reliable retaliatory force if an attempt is made to
discern the doctrinal basis for Kremlin arms decisions. This is a difficult
task at best, but the emphasis on survivable submarine-launched missiles
and hardened ICBMs in Soviet weapon deployments during the early
1970s appeared to reflect a shift away from a preference for defense and
toward a doctrine of deterrence. This hypothesis is supported by the re-

markable reversal of the USSR's long-standing policy of favoring ABMs, which will be discussed later.

Although Soviet spokesmen refrained from using such terms as "assured destruction" or "mutual deterrence," many Soviet writings and public statements during the 1969–73 period reflected changes in strategic thinking.[50] Kremlin leaders now argued for mutual deterrence, described the action-reaction cycle of the arms race, and stressed the critical importance of limiting ABMs. In addition, there were statements to the effect that neither side could achieve a first-strike capability and that both superpowers should recognize the need to reduce the costs and risks of nuclear war and to stabilize the strategic relationship at a point of parity. Going still further, some Soviet spokesmen claimed that superiority had become unattainable and that nuclear weapons were useless as political instruments, while Kremlin leaders argued the need for strategic arms negotiations. Public statements do not necessarily convey a nation's actual position, but the USSR's strategic posture—as a reflection of policy—seemed to signify a greater convergence of positions on nuclear matters between Washington and Moscow than had been the case in the past.

From an opposite perspective, however, it is possible that the Soviet Union was not responding to U.S. nuclear programs or seeking to stabilize the balance on the basis of parity and mutual assured destruction but was actively expanding its strategic capabilities to support the objective of nuclear superiority. Although Nixon administration analyses of the Soviet threat were at times overstated, the possible motivations behind the USSR's strategic program gave legitimate cause for concern. With its large payload capacity, for example, the SS-9 ICBM seemed more suited for a counterforce mission than a countercity retaliatory role, and there is evidence in statements by Soviet military leaders that the USSR had not reversed its belief in the need to pursue such a strategy.

In regard to the Soviet SALT position on limiting missile defense, it is possible that Kremlin leaders, finding the USSR's ABM program costly

50. See, for example, "Between Helsinki and Vienna," *Ekonomika, Politika, and Ideologiya,* January 1970 (Foreign Broadcast Information Service, *Daily Report: Soviet Union,* February 19, 1970), pp. F1–F5; "An Important Problem," *Pravda,* March 7, 1970 (ibid., March 9, 1970), pp. F1–F5; and O. Grinev and V. Pavlov, "An Important Step toward Curbing the Arms Race," *Pravda,* June 22, 1972 (ibid., June 23, 1972), pp. H1–H5.

or ineffective, decided to curb their effort for reasons unrelated to acceptance of the assured destruction concept. Moscow's concern that the Safeguard program might expand to a full area defense may have been real, but Soviet officials may also have sought to secure severe restrictions on U.S. ABMs as a means of ensuring that Russian offensive missiles would be able to achieve a counterforce capability against the Minuteman force.

In line with traditional Soviet political attitudes, moreover, Kremlin leaders could have concluded that numerical superiority in ICBMs would bring greater diplomatic opportunity and increased leverage in crises. The pattern of increasing Soviet military strength on all levels during the late 1960s and early 1970s suggested an expansionist policy and lent credence to the view that Moscow might be seeking some form of superiority on the strategic level—particularly at a time when the United States was under domestic pressure to reduce its defense spending. It is even possible to conclude that the repeated Soviet accusations that the United States was escalating the arms race were ploys to place the Nixon administration on the defensive and to cripple U.S. weapon programs by stimulating congressional opposition to Pentagon arms proposals.

An examination of the USSR's basic attitude toward SALT reinforces the conclusion that Moscow's strategic policies during the early 1970s were ambivalent. The USSR's motives for entering the SALT talks and signing the accords were unquestionably mixed.[51] Evidently the Kremlin did regard SALT as a means of furthering détente—out of an interest in reducing the risk of nuclear war, stimulating economic cooperation, and blunting progress in U.S.-Chinese relations. The positive side of the Soviet Union's attitude toward SALT was underscored by the acceptance of the ban on nationwide ABMs under the SALT treaty, which suggested to many that the Kremlin had at least acknowledged mutual deterrence as the basis for a U.S.-Soviet nuclear relationship. At the same time, the Soviet government was clearly not prepared to accept a comprehensive SALT agreement, and the Soviet Union's effort to legitimize its overall lead in strategic missile levels through agreement casts doubt on its

51. See Roman Kolkowicz and others, *The Soviet Union and Arms Control: A Superpower Dilemma* (Johns Hopkins Press, 1970); Thomas Wolfe, "Soviet Interests in SALT: Political, Economic, Bureaucratic, and Strategic Contributions and Impediments to Arms Control," in William Kintner and Robert Pfaltzgraff, eds., *SALT: Implications for Arms Control in the 1970's* (University of Pittsburgh Press, 1973); and Lawrence T. Caldwell, "Soviet Attitude to SALT," *Adelphi Papers*, no. 75 (London: International Institute for Strategic Studies, February 1971).

stated goal of equal security and on the sincerity of its interest in stability. When the Moscow agreements were finally reached, Kremlin leaders were enthusiastic in their support and officially ordered the Soviet military to comply with the terms, but after the accords were in effect the Kremlin continued an active program to develop new and improved strategic systems and announced that the USSR intended to take the actions necessary to maintain a strong strategic position.

In sum, the major elements of Soviet strategic policies in the early 1970s were neither consistent nor constant. Part of the explanation may be that, as in the United States, bureaucratic pressures had to be accommodated that often led to contradictory and rationally inexplicable policy decisions and weapon programs. But Soviet leaders were also experiencing difficulties in formulating a logical course of action for the 1970s because of uncertainties over the evolution of SALT, the direction of future U.S. strategic policies, and the development of Chinese nuclear forces.

Nevertheless, it can be said with some confidence that the common denominator of Soviet strategic policy was the decision to accept nothing less than parity, with or without SALT, and that Moscow's strategy seemed to reflect an awareness of the need to walk the line between furthering the USSR's strategic position and risking both an expansion of the nuclear arms race and an unfavorable SALT outcome. In this sense, the Soviet Union's apparent policy of maintaining a retaliatory deterrent while seeking warfighting options and a numerically favorable force balance resembled the Nixon administration's sufficiency doctrine. But the degree to which Kremlin leaders—and their U.S. counterparts—were prepared to place priority on the goal of mutual stability in future strategic arms policy decisions remained unclear at the end of 1973. The agreement on strategic arms control guidelines at Vladivostok in November 1974 reflected concern about mutual stability but did not end the uncertainty.[52]

Strategic Arms Limitations

Immediately after President Nixon assumed office, Soviet leaders urged him to arrange a specific date for the initiation of SALT, originally scheduled to begin in the fall of 1968 but delayed because of the

52. Joint Soviet-American Statement on Strategic Arms Limitation, November 24, 1974.

Czechoslovakian incursion. But the new administration was reluctant to agree to hold arms talks without first examining the Johnson administration's proposal and formulating its own ideas on the purposes and parameters of SALT. Nixon officials did not turn to a detailed analysis of SALT, however, until the initial study of U.S. defense policies was well under way. At that point, in March 1969, a major interagency review of strategic arms control issues was instituted, and in June the Nixon administration informed the Soviet government that the United States was prepared to begin the talks.[53] For a variety of reasons, the Soviet Union then delayed its acceptance until October, and negotiations did not commence until November 1969.

The Nixon Approach to SALT

The premise of the Nixon administration's approach to SALT was that arms control must fit into the broader framework of defense policy and U.S. foreign policy objectives—an outlook shared by officials of the Kennedy administration a decade earlier. It was considered essential to first establish a national security strategy and then structure arms control policies and proposals. This accounted in large part for the six-month period of review before an official decision was made to proceed with arms negotiations, although critics accused the President of deliberately attempting to undermine or downgrade SALT in favor of Pentagon demands for continued weapon deployments.

In addition to the time needed to prepare a position and consult with allies, the delay in the decision may also have been influenced by the administration's concept of "linkage" between SALT and other aspects of the U.S.-Soviet relationship. Early in 1969, President Nixon indicated that SALT should be geared to promote settlement in such areas as the Middle East and Vietnam, suggesting to some that the administration might have attempted to use the Soviet Union's interest in arms limitations as a lever to influence Moscow's behavior in these and other areas, such as Berlin. The administration shortly clarified its position, claiming that SALT would not be conditional on progress elsewhere, but the President observed that the interrelationship between strategic and political issues was a "fact of life"—implying that severely negative Soviet

53. This review was NSSM-28, one of the many National Security Council studies undertaken during Nixon's first years in office. For a description of the Nixon administration's SALT preparations and the subsequent negotiations, see John Newhouse, *Cold Dawn: The Story of SALT* (Holt, Rinehart, and Winston, 1973).

behavior could not help but affect the U.S. attitude toward SALT.[54] Once talks began, however, both sides successfully sought to isolate SALT from other questions and to minimize confrontations that might endanger the negotiations.

In announcing the decision to engage in SALT, President Nixon not only maintained that the arms competition absorbed resources but noted that the intensity of the competition and of technological change tended to increase uncertainties. This, in turn, stimulated still higher force levels; as a result, the risks and consequences of nuclear war would increase. Although self-restraint was sensible, the President observed, neither side seemed willing to concede the advantage, and in the absence of a negotiated arrangement, one side might mistakenly seek to acquire a tactical advantage in a crisis or marginal superiority in arms. Through SALT, both sides would have a unique opportunity to establish a stable relationship that could provide each with greater security at less cost.

President Nixon particularly stressed that mutual arms limitations offered the possibility of enhancing U.S. security more effectively than unilateral arms policies. Indeed, he stated that the United States had defined its security requirements "in terms that facilitate arms control."[55] The administration seemed especially interested in ensuring that planning for weapons systems and planning for arms control were closely integrated. To this end, the National Security Council created a formal framework for the Defense Department to contribute to the development of SALT proposals as well as a mechanism for officials of the Arms Control and Disarmament Agency (ACDA) to participate in decisions on weapons, budgets, and doctrine. The U.S. SALT delegation, led by the director of ACDA, included representatives of the office of the secretary of defense and of the Joint Chiefs of Staff.

PROCEDURAL PATTERNS AND DOMESTIC DIFFICULTIES

The administration's extensive and systematic approach to SALT preparations reflected a serious interest in obtaining the benefits of arms limitation agreements. Interagency groups designed a series of alterna-

54. The President initially referred to this linkage during his press conference on January 27, 1969. In a news conference on October 25, 1969, Secretary of State Rogers stated that the forthcoming SALT talks were "not conditional in any sense of the word" in terms of overall East-West relations. ("Secretary Rogers Discusses Forthcoming U.S.-USSR Talks on Curbing Strategic Arms," *Department of State Bulletin*, vol. 61 [November 10, 1969], p. 393.)

55. *Building for Peace*, p. 198.

tive agreements, ranging from partial to comprehensive agreements. Among the options were measures limiting the number of offensive systems, agreements banning MIRVs, and arrangements calling for mutual reductions in ICBMs. For each set of offensive limitations, a variety of ABM restrictions were postulated—a total ban, protection of Washington and Moscow, agreed defenses of ICBM sites, and nationwide ABM deployments. Taking into account the use of national means of verification as well as possible supplementary on-site inspection procedures, the interagency group weighed the options against the criteria for sufficiency and compared them to the projected situation without agreed arms constraints. As a result of this process, the administration developed a number of agreements that were potentially acceptable to the United States and that seemed negotiable when Soviet preferences were considered.

Rather than presenting a specific proposal at the outset of the talks, however, the Nixon administration preferred to follow a three-step approach.[56] Initially, there would be discussions of strategic issues and the objectives of arms control, permitting each side to better understand the other's strategic outlook, concerns, and weapon rationales. Administration officials believed that a dialogue that probed opposing views and permitted an exchange of ideas could be useful in its own right in reducing uncertainties and misapprehensions; if successful, it would establish a common foundation for agreement. The second phase would follow a "building-block" procedure, by which the two sides could discuss issues and problems associated with limiting particular weapon systems. Model agreements would be developed by both sides as a means of facilitating understanding of crucial issues, such as verification requirements for specific systems and the equitability between U.S. and Soviet weapons. Finally, there would be detailed negotiations of specific proposals that might result from the preliminary talks, and, it was hoped, that would lead to a limitation agreement, either in the form of a treaty or some other arrangement.

During the opening round of SALT I negotiations in late 1969 and early 1970, many observers believed that the President's approach to SALT was less a logical U.S.-USSR negotiating strategy and more a technique to avoid facing difficult choices within the U.S. government, possibly to delay consideration of specific limitation possibilities to the point where a mutual agreement would no longer be feasible. Moreover,

56. *A New Strategy for Peace*, pp. 143–45.

some experts contended that discussing concepts and options with the Soviet Union would be less productive than giving the Kremlin a specific U.S. proposal to consider. They maintained, for example, that it was unnecessary for Washington and Moscow to explore basic questions in depth before bargaining over specifics, that Soviet negotiators would not reciprocate in holding generalized talks, and that broad discussions of the issues would allow both sides to progress further in weapon programs, thereby narrowing the range of negotiable agreements. One arms control expert stated that the administration's exploratory approach "would only serve to strengthen the arguments of those in the Soviet Union who have been arguing that SALT has from the start been a fishing expedition designed by the United States to gain intelligence information about Soviet programs and to stall Soviet strategic programs until [the United States] could again step up its own strategic spending."[57]

These differences of opinion over negotiating procedures were of less significance than the specific controversy over the relationship between unilateral U.S. defense programs and SALT. This issue arose during the six-month preparatory period before the start of negotiations when a number of congressmen and nongovernmental experts, as well as members of the executive branch, urged President Nixon to halt U.S. MIRV tests in order to retain the option of discussing with the USSR the possibility of arranging a mutual ban on MIRV flight tests once official talks began. The President, however, rejected suggestions of a unilateral moratorium, or even the idea of a joint moratorium with the Soviet Union, and adhered to the scheduled MIRV testing program. After talks began, MIRV tests were continued to completion, and MIRV deployments were initiated in the midst of the negotiations in June 1970. Similarly, both during the preparatory phase and while SALT was in progress, the administration requested funds for the continuation of the Safeguard program and other major weapon programs, such as Trident and the B-1, even though limitations on ABMs and all categories of strategic offensive weapons were included within the range of arms control options under consideration.

Pointing to the continued efforts to improve and expand U.S. strategic forces after negotiations were under way, critics and commentators

57. Morton H. Halperin, cited by John Finney, *New York Times*, November 11, 1969. See also Alton Frye, "U.S. Decision-Making for SALT: Executive and Legislative Dimensions," in Mason Willrich and John B. Rhinelander, eds., *SALT: The Moscow Agreements and Beyond* (Free Press, 1974).

charged the administration with a lack of serious interest in reaching an arms limitation accord. The official policy, they argued, was unnecessary and destabilizing, particularly since there was no clear evidence that the Soviet Union was enlarging its ABM network or testing a MIRV—the two potential threats given as the principal reasons for proceeding with *our* MIRV and ABM programs. Nevertheless, the Nixon administration saw no inconsistency in maintaining strategic force programs while seeking to negotiate an agreement and offered three explanations for its actions.

First, since there was no guarantee that an agreement would be reached, U.S. officials claimed they had to maintain programs considered essential to sufficiency and to the preservation of the flexibility required to respond to future threats. The Soviet Union was not slackening its quantitative missile buildup or its developmental programs. Unless SALT constrained this threat, America would be forced to take actions to maintain the survivability and reliability of the U.S. deterrent. Even if an agreement were negotiated, the United States would need to procure additional systems, because likely SALT outcomes would not necessarily remove qualitative threats to the U.S. deterrent.

Second, administration spokesmen claimed that a temporary moratorium on one system could stand in the way of designing a durable permanent agreement. By this reasoning, it was preferable to consider a mutual MIRV ban during actual negotiations when related restrictions could be explored. For instance, since a MIRV ban would require associated ABM limitations, officials thought it undesirable to initiate the former without being assured of the latter. Later in the negotiations, the administration refused to accept an agreement limiting ABMs without associated offensive limitations. In any event, rather than attempt to induce de facto arrangements of any kind, the administration seemed more interested in reaching an explicit agreement with the USSR.

Third, administration officials advocated a strategy of negotiating from strength, arguing that U.S. weapon programs would be useful as bargaining chips at the SALT table. Unilateral restraint, they claimed, would reduce Soviet incentives to negotiate and make it difficult to persuade the USSR to accept controls that the United States might consider crucial for the achievement of a stable and equitable agreement.[58]

58. On July 13, 1971, for example, Deputy Defense Secretary Packard told a Senate committee that the United States must extend its ABM systems as a bargaining chip with the Soviet Union. (*Arms Control Implications of Current Defense Budget*, Hearings before the Subcommittee on Arms Control, International Law and

Initially, this rationale was used to justify continuation of the Safeguard program, on the grounds that the development of Safeguard would persuade the USSR to accept limits on its SS-9 ICBMs. In later years, the desire to pressure the Soviet Union to agree to accept SLBM limits in SALT was in large part responsible for the administration's decision to undertake "a major new strategic initiative" through a substantial acceleration of the Trident submarine program in early 1972.[59]

THE BARGAINING CHIP POLICY

The bargaining chip issue became perhaps the most prominent element of the Nixon administration's strategic arms policy, often overshadowing questions of whether U.S. strategic programs were stabilizing, technically sound, or economically viable. Many congressmen and scholars intensely criticized the administration's SALT negotiating tactics throughout the years 1969–73. They argued, for example, that a policy of negotiating from strength would simply force the USSR to continue its own strategic buildup and would foreclose opportunities for concluding comprehensive agreements by irreversibly committing both sides to major arms programs. One expert on Soviet policy explained that Kremlin leaders would feel "obliged to match each step with comparable measures" in order to avoid being "pressured into agreement," and for this reason he concluded that bargaining chip diplomacy in the strategic weapon field "provides dynamism for the arms race."[60] It was also claimed that bargaining needs were being used by the administration to gain approval of a range of strategic weapon programs that might otherwise have been rejected.

Without attempting to assess the motives behind such activities, it is a matter of record that administration officials sought to persuade a number of key senators that continuation of the Safeguard ABM program for the defense of U.S. ICBM sites was vital to the success of the negotiations.[61] Congressional approval of the phase-one Safeguard program in

---

Organization of the Senate Committee on Foreign Relations, 92 Cong. 1 sess. [1971], p. 170.)

59. *Statement . . . on the FY 1973 Defense Budget and FY 1973–1977 Program*, p. 69.

60. Statement of Marshall Shulman in *Arms Control Implications of Current Defense Budget*, p. 251. In these same hearings former Assistant Defense Secretary Paul Warnke also criticized the administration's bargaining chip tactic (p. 212).

61. See, for example, the *Newsweek* reports of Kissinger's talks with congressmen and the bargaining chip arguments attributed to the U.S. chief SALT negotiator, Gerard Smith. (August 10, 1970, p. 18; and August 24, 1970, p. 31.)

1970 and 1971 was undoubtedly influenced by this connection to SALT —although subsequent requests for initiating the phase-two area ABM sites were denied. Negotiating considerations also influenced congressional support for the B-1 bomber and the Trident submarine, and senators interested in arms control found themselves in the paradoxical position of voting in favor of weapon projects for fear of harming prospects at SALT. Even congressmen who questioned the technical viability or strategic necessity of certain proposed programs were motivated to modify their views by the logic of strengthening America's bargaining power. One notable instance of this phenomenon was the administration's success in persuading Senator John Stennis in 1972 to reverse his position and support the Trident acceleration.[62]

The intermittent but nonetheless intensive Soviet program of missile deployment and development lent credence to the administration's bargaining stance. After the SALT agreements were reached in 1972, Nixon administration officials defended their approach and pursued it further as the agreements awaited formal approval. Defense Secretary Laird actually stated that he could not support the agreements if Congress failed to approve the administration's strategic force requests.[63] While President Nixon denied that the administration was seeking to *condition* SALT on the approval of defense requests, he stressed the need to move forward with U.S. military programs, stating that Kremlin leaders had informed him that the USSR would continue with weapon efforts not prohibited by the agreements.[64]

The administration also maintained that the military requirements for sufficiency demanded the continuation of U.S. programs permitted by the Moscow agreements and the initiation of research and development programs in order to maintain a secure deterrent and a hedge against the possibility of Soviet abrogation or a failure in future negotiations. Accordingly, the Joint Chiefs suggested that strategic planning under SALT should be guided by three "assurances": improved U.S. intelli-

62. Stennis acknowledged the impact of the bargaining chip argument on June 15, 1972. See *Strategic Arms Limitation Agreements*, p. 404.

63. "I could not support the SALT agreements," Laird said, "if the Congress fails to act on the movement forward of the Trident system, on the B-1 bomber and on the other programs that we have outlined to improve our strategic offensive systems during this five-year period." (Cited by George Wilson, *Washington Post*, June 8, 1972.)

64. "President's News Conference on June 22, 1972," *Public Papers of the Presidents of the United States: Richard Nixon, 1972* (1974), p. 692.

gence capabilities, continued modernization programs, and vigorous research and development to maintain technical superiority.[65] The Pentagon's proposed post-SALT weapon program included (1) continued
acceleration of Trident; (2) stepped-up development of the B-1 bomber;
(3) research on a new strategic cruise-missile, a maneuvering warhead,
and more accurate missile warheads; (4) studies of air- and land-mobile
missile-launching possibilities; and (5) development of improved hard-
point defenses.

Despite executive branch pressure, Congress refused to establish any
formal linkage between U.S. weapon programs and approval of the
SALT accords and either canceled or cut back a number of proposed
strategic programs—including the hard-target warhead program; the
President's request to construct an ABM site at Washington, D.C., as
permitted by the treaty; hard-site defense; and the new cruise missile.
But the close votes in favor of certain systems suggest that the bargaining chip and assurance concepts combined to help win congressional
endorsement of many strategic weapon requests in the defense budget
appropriations of late 1972. Moreover, it seems certain that future strategic arms programs will invariably remain closely tied to the evolution
of U.S.-Soviet strategic arms limitation talks and that Congress will come
under increasing pressure to approve the administration's strategic
budget requests as a means of supporting SALT and hedging against a
failure of the negotiations. Indeed, as the defense program for 1974 was
being developed, Defense Secretary Schlesinger pointed out that the
United States needed to sustain its negotiating strength and to remain
"prepared to be in a position to have an adequate deterrent which is fully
equal to that of the Soviet Union" should the next phases of SALT prove
unsuccessful.[66] After the Vladivostok agreement of November 1974,
administration spokesmen stressed the need to maintain U.S. forces at
agreed ceilings.

The Stages of SALT

From the outset of SALT I, which opened officially on November 17,
1969, in Helsinki, both sides dealt with strategic arms issues construc-
tively and in a businesslike manner. The American delegates were

65. *Statement by Admiral Thomas H. Moorer, USN, Chairman, Joint Chiefs of
Staff, before the Senate Armed Services Committee* (June 20, 1972).
66. News conference, November 30, 1973.

favorably impressed by the skill, seriousness, and knowledge of the Soviet team but were struck by the team's apparent lack of technical expertise and by the unwillingness of Kremlin leaders to permit their negotiators to discuss in depth certain strategic issues, such as qualitative limitations or precise force levels. Evidently Soviet delegates were less informed about the size and characteristics of the USSR's strategic posture than the U.S. delegates were. The ensuing exchange of views on strategic matters thus fell short of expectations. Many reports suggested that little was learned about the Soviet Union's nuclear objectives or military doctrine. One American expert claimed that the talks "were less a dialogue . . . than a U.S. monologue."[67] Concepts of particular interest to U.S. strategists, such as stability and vulnerability, apparently were not appreciated by the Soviet representatives. Yet there is evidence that the first round of SALT I was successful in exposing each side to the other's basic outlook on strategic questions and in identifying topics for further discussion. Even more important in shaping the subsequent course of SALT were the positions expressed by the USSR in the preliminary talks on two issues—ABMs and forward-based systems (FBS).

PRELIMINARY PROGRESS AND PROBLEMS

The Soviet position on ABM limitations not only was the surprise event of the first round of SALT but was undoubtedly the most significant event of the entire series of negotiations. America's interest in mutual ABM limitations, it should be recalled, was the driving force behind the Johnson administration's efforts to initiate strategic arms talks with the Kremlin. Although the Nixon administration had not reached a decision on the type of ABM agreement it might be prepared to accept when it entered the preliminary SALT talks, its attitude toward ABM restrictions was based on the view that large-scale population defenses were destabilizing. Because of the U.S. commitment to Safeguard, however, one option considered was to permit both sides to deploy missile-site defenses and thin area defenses, although other options, including a total ban on ABMs, were also considered.

Because Soviet leaders had traditionally claimed that missile defenses were desirable and nonprovocative, U.S. officials expected that negotiating ABM limitations would present the single most difficult problem at

67. W. Van Cleave, *International Negotiation*, Hearings before the Subcommittee on National Security and International Operations of the Senate Committee on Government Operations, 92 Cong. 2 sess. (July 25, 1972), pt. 7, p. 201.

SALT. Early in the talks, however, the Soviet delegation took a position *opposing* large ABM deployments and expressed a preference for either a total ban or limited coverage under a SALT agreement. The final accord contained the USSR's sweeping proposal committing both sides to refrain from deploying nationwide ABMs or even constructing the bases for such systems.

The Soviet interest in limiting ABMs to very low levels could have been based on a genuine appreciation of the destabilizing consequences of these systems. Alternatively, Soviet leaders may have found their present-generation ABM technology too costly to pursue and may have decided to accept an ABM treaty as a means of preventing the United States from gaining a defensive advantage.[68] However, if the ABM treaty represented only a reluctant concession or short-term tactic on the part of Kremlin leaders rather than a fundamental decision, it is difficult to understand why the USSR favored such stringent defensive restrictions and did not seek a temporary agreement banning offensive missile deployments. The Soviet stand on the question of defensive weapons was so strong that it almost seemed that the United States and the Soviet Union had reversed their attitudes on ABMs. Although it took several years to negotiate a final agreement, the initial meeting in Helsinki created the foundation for the substantive negotiations that culminated in the ABM treaty, which most observers believe was the most significant outcome of SALT.

Unfortunately, at the preliminary discussion, the Soviet Union's position on another vital question affecting the types of *offensive* systems to be covered caused a major disagreement between the two nations. This pernicious issue involved the definition of the term "strategic." In an unexpected move at an early stage in round one, Soviet representatives argued that all nuclear delivery systems capable of being launched against the homeland of either nation fell into this category. According to the USSR's interpretation, U.S. forward-based fighters in Europe and on aircraft carriers would be subject to limitations, but Soviet intermediate- and medium-range ballistic missiles (IR/MRBMs) and medium-range bombers targeted against Western Europe would be uncontrolled. This definition of strategic arms was a logical one, considering Soviet concern over the proximity of U.S. overseas bases. At the same time, Soviet negotiators might have pursued the FBS issue as a negotiat-

68. See in particular the analysis by Thomas W. Wolfe, *Worldwide Soviet Military Strategy and Policy*, Rand Report p-5008 (April 1973).

ing tactic designed to disrupt the North Atlantic Treaty Organization (NATO) or to obtain concessions from the United States during SALT.

The American delegation found the Soviet plan unacceptable. U.S. forward-based systems were considered to be theater weapons, and on a political level, FBS limitations would affect America's NATO allies and were therefore an unsuitable topic for bilateral negotiations between the superpowers. The FBS issue proved impossible to resolve, created complicated negotiating difficulties, and ultimately forced the United States to accept an offensive arms agreement reflecting a marked change from its official position.

After a recess of four months, the talks were resumed on April 15, 1970, in Vienna. The second round of SALT was devoted to consideration of a series of optional U.S. arms control packages covering a variety of limitations. The purpose of these model proposals was to provide the framework for a detailed exploration of substantive issues associated with negotiating an actual accord. On the defensive side, some proposals called for ABMs to be totally banned, while others limited ABMs to the local defense of Washington and Moscow. Most proposals permitted both sides to convert offensive land-based missiles to sea-based missiles but limited long-range missiles to 1,710—a figure equal to the sum of the U.S. Minuteman and Polaris forces—and froze intercontinental bombers at the current levels of 450 on the U.S. side and 200 on the Soviet side. Certain proposals required reductions in ICBMs, while others included restrictions on MIRVs. A series of "collateral constraints" were suggested as a means of strengthening these quantitative limits with additional controls, including a special subceiling on large ICBMs, such as the Soviet SS-9, and technical restrictions on ABM-related radar systems.

The decision to include a MIRV ban in the model proposals during the second round of SALT was the product of sustained bureaucratic battling and complicated analyses. Although President Nixon had dismissed a unilateral moratorium on MIRV testing, administration planning involved detailed studies on possible mutual MIRV limitations as elements in a number of SALT proposals. A high-level decision on MIRVs was made difficult by intense disagreement among major agencies and among officials regarding the feasibility of adequately verifying a MIRV ban through national monitoring of Soviet missile tests. Equally important was the split over whether a MIRV ban was desirable—even if it could be adequately verified. Advocates of a MIRV ban claimed that it would enhance U.S. security by removing the counterforce threat posed by Soviet SS-9 ICBMs, while opponents argued that MIRVs provided a technological advantage needed to counter the USSR's position of numerical parity and to provide a hedge against future uncertainty in the strategic balance. Finally, Senate pressure for a MIRV ban was undoubtedly weighed against countervailing conservative domestic political forces supporting the military establishment's desire to deploy MIRV under any circumstance.

In a last-minute move, President Nixon reportedly decided to instruct the American delegation to surface the idea of a ban on MIRV testing, which would be verified through national means, but to couple this measure with a ban on MIRV deployment, which would require on-site inspections to assure compliance. Given the long-standing negative Soviet attitude toward on-site inspection and the apparent understanding between the United States and the USSR that SALT agreements should be based primarily, if not solely, on national means of verification, this proposal seemed certain to be rejected. Perhaps the United States was simply pursuing a negotiating tactic and would have been prepared to remove its inspection demand, but some observers have suggested that the MIRV ban proposal was presented in the full knowledge that the Soviet Union would reject it out of hand. This view is supported by the fact that on-site inspection schemes to monitor MIRV deployments are considered by most experts to be technically unsound and unacceptable *even to the United States.*

The Soviet Union rejected the U.S. MIRV proposal and offered instead a ban on MIRV production to be verified without on-site inspection—an unacceptable proposal from the viewpoint of the United States and one that made little if any practical sense in the opinion of arms control experts. Moscow's position can be explained partly as traditional rebellion against the inspection provisions associated with the U.S. proposal to ban MIRV deployment and partly as understandable reluctance to freeze the USSR in an inferior position by accepting a test ban on multiple warheads. On the other hand, the USSR's apparent unwillingness to discuss the technical problems of MIRV verification in an effort to reach a compromise and the unrealistic counterproposal of a production ban without inspection strongly suggest that the USSR was simply not interested in such an agreement. It might have desired to regain the option of exploiting its advantage in missile throw-weight and to eventually install large quantities of multiple warheads on its ICBM force. As it turned out, both sides dropped the question of banning MIRVs.

Two months after the second round of negotiations started, the United States completed MIRV flight-testing and began to install MIRVs on its Minuteman missiles. From the Soviet Union's standpoint, a ban on MIRVs was now surely out of the question. In short, the most significant result to emerge from the second stage of SALT I was the realization that MIRV restrictions—or other serious qualitative controls leading to a comprehensive offensive arms limitation agreement—were unlikely to be negotiated as part of any initial accord.

SERIOUS NEGOTIATIONS BEGIN

A few weeks before the second round of talks was scheduled to end, the United States formally presented a strategic arms limitation agreement based on the results of the discussions of the model proposals. Under this so-called August 4 plan, the total number of land- and sea-based missiles and strategic bombers on both sides was to be limited to a specified level of some 1,900 delivery systems. The USSR had earlier dismissed the prospect of ICBM reductions, but the proposed U.S. agreement retained provisions for freedom to mix land and sea missiles within the agreed ceiling. On the defensive side, the proposal called for either a total ban on ABMs or the restriction of antimissile systems to the low level of 100 launchers each deployed at Moscow and Washington. Although the United States was to temporarily reverse field on the question of ABM limits at a later stage, the August 4 proposal reflected the administration's willingness to forgo its Safeguard ABM program in return for low limitations on Soviet ABMs and restrictions on the number of SS-9 ICBMs.

The third round of SALT began in early November 1970 in Helsinki and lasted through the third week in December. The Soviet delegation responded to the August 4 proposal by explicitly applying the USSR's definition of "strategic," insisting that American forward-based systems be included in the total U.S. offensive weapons quota. The United States refused to give ground, and a serious deadlock occurred. Henry Kissinger explained that an acceptance of the Soviet approach "would have prejudiced our alliance commitments and raised a distinction between our own security and that of our European allies."[69]

In an apparently unexpected move toward the end of the third round, the Soviet Union suggested that the two nations set aside discussions of

69. Cited in Newhouse, *Cold Dawn,* p. 195.

offensive weapons and focus on the problem of ABM limitations. The USSR then presented a formal proposal for a treaty covering defensive systems and limiting ABMs to 100 interceptors at each nation's capital. Perhaps the Kremlin suggested the separation of offensive and defensive arms agreements in order to temporarily bypass the more difficult negotiating problems and to reach early agreement on the crucial question of ABMs. On the other hand, it is also possible that the USSR proposed an agreement to limit only ABMs in an attempt to prevent the United States from gaining an advantage in ABMs while the USSR increased its ICBM lead, acquired an edge in the number of SLBMs, and preserved the option of mobile missiles.

The United States responded negatively to the plan, but the USSR's proposal quickly found its way into the American press and became a prominent issue during early 1971. Nongovernmental experts, congressmen, and the news media urged the administration to accept the Soviet Union's proposal for a separate ABM treaty, on the grounds that this accord would in fact curb the most important part of the arms race. Nevertheless, the President remained committed to the position that limits on offensive as well as defensive weapons were necessary, arguing that limits on only one side of the equation "could rechannel the arms competition rather than effectively curtail it.[70] The discovery that the USSR was constructing sites for what appeared to be a new-generation ICBM led Defense Secretary Laird to conclude that it was unreasonable to expect the United States to forgo ABM protection of its land-based missiles if the USSR accepted no restraints on its large ICBMs—the threat Safeguard was designed to counter.

The Soviet Union's ABM proposal, together with the upsurge in the USSR's offensive missile program and the recognition that a MIRV ban was out of reach, focused the attention of Pentagon planners on the fact that the August 4 proposal, which contained no provision for the defense of Minuteman ICBMs, did not adequately relate ABM controls to the USSR's offensive missiles. The American delegation therefore introduced another variation into its defensive arms proposal—the so-called four-to-one option, which would permit the United States to complete its four Safeguard sites at ICBM fields but would grant the USSR only one site near Moscow. The Soviet Union naturally rejected the new ABM option

70. *Building for Peace*, p. 194.

as unbalanced, and the fourth round of SALT, which ran from March through May of 1971 in Vienna, showed little signs of progress.

BREAKING THE DEADLOCK

Attempts to break the SALT impasse, however, were going on behind the scenes by way of the so-called back-channel, involving private contacts between Henry Kissinger and Soviet Ambassador Anatoliy Dobrynin that had begun in January. During these meetings, the two men reached a compromise. The USSR agreed to defer its demand that FBS be included and to accept the principle of simultaneous limits on offensive and defensive arms. The United States modified its proposal for numerical equality in delivery systems to permit the Soviet Union to preserve an edge in ICBM launchers and agreed to reduce the comprehensiveness of earlier American plans. As a consequence of the Kissinger-Dobrynin discussions, President Nixon and Chairman Leonid Brezhnev issued simultaneous announcements on May 20, 1971, stating that the two governments had agreed to "concentrate" on negotiating an ABM accord during the coming year, but that certain measures regarding the limitation of offensive strategic weapons would be agreed upon together with the ABM limitation.[71]

U.S. and Soviet negotiators met in Helsinki for the fifth round of talks in July, hoping that the broad understanding between their leaders would facilitate progress on specific measures. Early in this SALT session, the United States proposed a modified version of the plan it had offered the previous year. On the offensive side, the new plan removed all restrictions on strategic bombers but called for SLBMs as well as ICBMs to be frozen at existing force levels. In response to Soviet objections, the full freedom-to-mix option was no longer part of the U.S. plan. On the defensive side, the United States removed its strict four-to-one formula and introduced still another variation that would permit each nation to select either an ABM configuration composed of 300 launchers deployed at ICBM fields or a 100-launcher defense of its capital city.

The Soviet Union reacted unfavorably to the revised American proposal. A major problem arose over the optional ABM concept—which either would force the USSR to dismantle its Moscow defenses and initiate an entirely new program to protect its ICBM sites or would result

71. *Washington Post*, May 21, 1971.

in an inequitable agreement if the United States chose the 300-launcher system to protect Minuteman while the Kremlin retained its existing 100-launcher system. In addition, the USSR raised a serious objection to the proposed SLBM limitations, first claiming that submarine-launched missiles were not covered in the Kissinger-Dobrynin compromise and then returning to the FBS issue by insisting that SLBMs could be controlled only if limits were also placed on American forward-based systems. Despite the promise of the Nixon-Brezhnev communiqué, the year ended with SALT still stalemated, although an important pair of collateral agreements were signed in the fall of 1971: (1) a plan to modernize the hot line by using satellites to ensure rapid and reliable communication in crises, and (2) an understanding on procedures to be followed in the event of an accidental or unauthorized missile launch.[72]

After returning from Peking, President Nixon made an effort to break the SALT impasse by announcing on October 12 that he would fly to Moscow in May 1972 for discussions with Kremlin leaders. The President expressed hope that a SALT agreement would be reached before that time but indicated that the scheduled talks would include the subject of arms limitations—whether aimed at finalizing an initial accord or paving the way for follow-on negotiations.[73]

FORGING AN AGREEMENT

The prospect of a summit meeting had the effect of stimulating movement toward an agreement. During the sixth round of SALT I negotiations, which began on November 15, 1971, in Vienna, the USSR finally accepted a ceiling on large ICBMs and agreed to the U.S. proposal to impose restrictions on "exotic" ABM systems. But the two delegations remained divided on ABM limitations—interceptor levels, site locations, and radar restrictions—and the question of controls over SLBMs, since the Soviet Union now began to insist on a numerical advantage in sea-based missiles as the price for agreement. Nevertheless, sufficient progress had been made in Vienna through the late months of 1971 and the

---

72. Agreement between the United States of America and the Union of Soviet Socialist Republics on Measures to Improve the USA-USSR Direct Communications Link; and Agreement on Measures to Reduce the Risk of Outbreak of Nuclear War between the United States of America and the Union of Soviet Socialist Republics— both signed at Washington, September 30, 1971. For texts of agreements, see *New York Times*, October 1, 1971.

73. *Washington Post*, October 13, 1971.

early months of the following year to enable the delegations to start the
process of drafting an agreement.

The months leading up to the signing of the SALT accords in Moscow
on May 26, 1972, probably represented one of the most intensive, complex, and crucial periods of diplomatic activity ever recorded. In Washington, the Nixon administration was attempting to hammer out a consensus on a final U.S. position, while the U.S. and Soviet delegations were
attempting to narrow the negotiating differences at the seventh round of
talks taking place in Helsinki. Once again, however, the back-channel
was operating in an attempt to work out an accommodation before the
summit meeting. Henry Kissinger flew to Moscow in April, when he and
Soviet leaders made a number of key decisions. In essence, as a consequence of this visit, Kissinger and the President agreed to a Soviet proposal for a two-site ABM limit on each side and accepted the USSR's
demand for a greater number of SLBMs. This soon became the official
position in Washington after military support had been assured on the
issue of a Soviet SLBM advantage—a decision apparently not easily
accepted by the chief U.S. SALT negotiator or the secretary of state.[74]

At this stage, other important details, notably defensive limits, were
dealt with successfully in the formal Helsinki talks, but a few key issues,
including agreement on submarine replacement modalities, remained
unresolved when the President arrived in the USSR early in May. At the
summit meeting, where SALT was a major topic, U.S. and Soviet leaders
reached a last-minute compromise on the SLBM issue and disposed of
other unsettled issues. After a rapid drafting session to bring the written
accords carried by the two delegations from Helsinki in line with the
agreements reached in Moscow, a signing ceremony was held signifying
the successful conclusion of the first series of SALT negotiations, and
both sides committed themselves to continue these negotiations in
search of more comprehensive agreements.

The ABM treaty signed in Moscow restricted both sides to a total of
200 ABM interceptors to be deployed at two separate sites of 100 launchers each, one at each nation's capital and one at an ICBM facility. Of
more significance than the limitations themselves was the commitment
of both nations "not to deploy ABM systems for a defense of the territory
of its country and not to provide a base for such a [nationwide] de-

---

74. Newhouse discussed this unusual reversal of positions between military and
civilian officials in *Cold Dawn*, p. 246.

fense."[75] The five-year Interim Agreement, affecting offensive weapons, limited land-based missiles to existing levels, placed special constraints on the number of large ICBMs, set a ceiling on sea-based missile systems, and provided for replacing older-model ICBMs with additional SLBMs. Under the Interim Agreement, the USSR could retain 1,618 ICBMs, compared with 1,054 for the United States. The Soviet Union would be permitted to deploy a maximum sea-based force of 950 SLBMs and 62 submarines, while the United States could deploy no more than 710 SLBMs and 44 submarines. No restrictions were placed on MIRVs, bombers, forward-based systems, or land-mobile ICBMs, although it was understood that these would be among the issues addressed in a later series of negotiations.

IMPACT OF THE MOSCOW ACCORDS

The ABM treaty received widespread support in the United States, but conservatives opposed the Interim Agreement on the grounds that it placed the nation in a militarily inferior and politically disadvantageous position. Defending the agreement, administration officials argued that the Soviet Union's numerical advantage in strategic offensive missiles was more than offset by our advantage in number of warheads and strategic bombers and in the quality of our forces. President Nixon and Henry Kissinger also pointed out that the offensive arms agreement would curb the USSR's buildup without preventing the United States from continuing with its planned strategic programs.[76] Some arms control advocates contended that the Interim Agreement was not sufficiently comprehensive and that it could become an excuse for expanding strategic programs in uncontrolled areas and accelerating the qualitative arms competition.

In August 1972, the Senate quickly ratified the ABM treaty, although action on the offensive arms accord was complicated by a lengthy debate over a controversial resolution introduced by Senator Henry Jackson that called for the President to ensure that future agreements would maintain stability without placing the United States in a numerically inferior strategic position.[77] The administration reportedly supported the Jack-

75. "Treaty Between the United States of America and the Union of Soviet Socialist Republics on the Limitation of Anti-Ballistic Missile Systems," *Weekly Compilation of Presidential Documents*, vol. 8 (June 19, 1972), p. 1035.

76. *Shaping a Durable Peace*, p. 197.

77. S.J. Res. 241, 92 Cong. 2 sess. (September 13, 1972).

son resolution, which upheld the belief of the executive branch that negotiations must be continued to turn the Interim Agreement into a more complete, stabilizing, equitable, and permanent accord.[78]

Finally, in October 1972, almost three years after the SALT negotiations began, the United States and the USSR formally implemented the strategic arms limitation agreements. The successful agreements, together with a broad declaration of principles on U.S.-Soviet relations drawn up during the Moscow summit,[79] represented an unprecedented step in the attempt to control the nuclear arms race. Apart from the technical content of the accords, the overarching political significance of a U.S.-Soviet agreement on strategic arms and the mutual commitment to continue efforts to minimize nuclear risks may represent the real successes of SALT.

The next series of negotiations, known as SALT II, which began in November 1972 in Geneva, must bear the burden of solving the many problems deferred by U.S. and Soviet negotiators in SALT I. During Brezhnev's visit to the United States in June 1973, the two governments issued a second statement on "basic principles"—these to guide future SALT negotiations. The principles reaffirmed the proposition that subsequent accords must recognize the "equal security interests" of both sides, acknowledged that national means of verification would continue to be utilized, and committed both nations to negotiate a more comprehensive and permanent offensive arms agreement in 1974.[80]

The Nixon-Brezhnev statement was undoubtedly aimed at speeding up the SALT talks, but by the end of 1973 there was serious doubt about whether the 1974 deadline would be met. After the Soviet Union's initial MIRV test in August 1973, administration spokesmen expressed with renewed energy their concern that Moscow would close the qualitative gap by the end of the decade and continued to hammer home the position that quantitative equality must be achieved in a permanent accord. This interest in equality was not tied solely to the USSR's MIRV capability but was related to the Soviet advantage in missile throw-weight,

78. See John W. Finney, *New York Times*, September 14, 1972. Alton Frye, in "U.S. Decision-Making for SALT," discussed the administration's support for Jackson's proposal and the legislative maneuvering associated with the amendment.

79. Basic Principles of Relations between the United States of America and the Union of Soviet Socialist Republics, signed at Moscow, May 29, 1972.

80. Basic Principles of Negotiations on the Further Limitation of Strategic Offensive Arms, signed at Washington, June 21, 1973. See text of U.S.-Soviet accords in the *New York Times*, June 22, 1973.

which, it was feared, would ultimately enable the Kremlin to obtain a superior counterforce capability. Yet it seemed evident to many observers that the USSR would attempt to preserve its numerical advantage in any permanent offensive arms treaty.

Nevertheless, Secretary of State Henry Kissinger, in a press conference toward the end of 1973, stated with apparent optimism that the United States and the USSR "have a chance" of meeting the deadline for negotiating a new offensive arms agreement in 1974.[81] Articles in the Soviet press appearing at about the same time suggested that Kremlin leaders might be more serious in negotiating an accord than the formal USSR proposal implied.[82] In Vladivostok in late 1974, the Soviet Union and the United States reached an agreement in principle to preserve parity at the approximate level of programmed offensive forces they had at that time and to hold subsequent discussions to seek reductions. Whether or not a permanent accord based on the Vladivostok guidelines is reached, the process of strategic arms negotiations is likely to last throughout the remainder of the decade.

Lessons and Legacies

President Nixon maintained that the doctrine of sufficiency was fully compatible with arms limitations and indicated that, independent of SALT, the United States would attempt to avoid strategic programs that might be misconstrued by Kremlin leaders as posing a danger to the USSR's basic deterrent posture. Therefore, one approach to analyzing the lessons of the Nixon administration's nuclear arms policies is to focus on two fundamental strategic objectives set forth by the President himself—maintaining a stable U.S.-Soviet nuclear relationship and negotiating an effective strategic arms limitation accord.

Inconsistent Moves toward Mutual Stability

The administration's interest in mutual stability influenced a number of strategic force decisions. As noted earlier, the President rejected the deployment of a large anti-Soviet ABM system partly on the grounds that it might threaten the USSR's deterrent, and U.S. officials stressed the

81. *New York Times*, December 23, 1973.
82. See Robert O. Kaiser, *Washington Post*, December 15, 1973.

stabilizing value of defending our ICBM sites with Safeguard, arguing that this was preferable to increasing our strength through additional offensive missile deployments that could threaten USSR forces. In regard to offensive weapons, while criticisms of the pace and character of major strategic arms programs such as Trident and the B-1 may have been justified on cost-effectiveness grounds, these programs were shaped in part by the decision to improve the long-term survivability and retaliatory capability of the strategic triad. Whatever else might be said about them, it is difficult to argue that new-generation missile-firing submarines or strategic bombers are "bad" in the sense of threatening the USSR's deterrent posture—although many experts claim they are wasteful.[83] Other programs, including Minuteman silo hardening and a variety of measures geared to enhance B-52 survivability, were pursued vigorously to ensure that destabilizing force vulnerabilities would not occur in the short term.

Some of the sufficiency criteria followed by the Nixon administration can be considered stabilizing in both the military and political sense. For example, flexible response options contribute to stability to the extent that they deter the USSR from initiating limited nuclear strikes. Similarly, maintaining a relatively comparable numerical balance of forces with the Soviet Union may well prevent the USSR from miscalculating the power of America's strategic arms posture and from attempting to exploit the Soviet strategic position for diplomatic purposes against the United States or its allies.

Finally, despite the tendency of administration spokesmen to overstate potential strategic dangers, from the viewpoint of responsible policymakers entering office in 1969, the prospect of Soviet MIRV-equipped SS-9 and depressed-trajectory SLBMs endangering the invulnerability of America's land-based deterrent forces seemed to demand that immediate action be taken. Although these and other Soviet threats did not materialize or were late in coming, the massive missile development programs pursued by Moscow during the early 1970s strengthened the credibility of conservative Pentagon defense planners. In any case, whether or not the Nixon administration's strategic arms programs will turn out to have been excessive, it can be argued that many Soviet strategic programs during the 1969–70 period were triggered by factors other than the need to respond to U.S. weapon decisions. Even if the United

83. See Morton H. Halperin, "The Good, the Bad, and the Wasteful," *Foreign Policy*, no. 6 (Spring 1972), pp. 69–83 (Brookings Reprint 227).

States had halted its MIRV program, for example, it is doubtful that the USSR would have sharply curtailed its missile buildup or halted its development of multiple warheads.

On the other hand, both the sufficiency criteria and actual weapon decisions reflected strategic policies that seemed incompatible with the President's proclaimed interest in mutual stability. Under certain conditions, for instance, the relative damage criterion requires strategic forces well above those needed for high levels of assured destruction, and, when combined with the criteria of flexible options and limiting damage from small-scale attacks, could be construed as a warfighting or counterforce doctrine that may have forced the USSR to improve its forces. A more persuasive case can be made that the Nixon administration's strategic policies, when applied to two weapons programs—area ABMs and accuracy improvements—were inconsistent with its objective of mutual stability.

Although the Safeguard program, with its emphasis on ICBM protection, was a major improvement over the Johnson administration's ABM program when measured against stability criteria, phase two of Safeguard was largely indistinguishable from the Sentinel area defense. To most experts, the potentially destabilizing consequences of such a nationwide ABM system are magnitudes greater than the possible indirect effects of phase-one defenses located at ICBM fields. Yet, even as the Nixon administration emphasized stability as its goal and worried about Soviet ABM expansion, officials continued to argue the necessity of a thin ABM deployment throughout the first few years of the President's term in office and to include limiting damage from small-scale attacks in the list of sufficiency criteria. In the final analysis, it took congressional action to defuse the area ABM program and the SALT negotiations to finally persuade the administration to agree to forgo nationwide defenses.

Nixon policies on developing hard-target kill capabilities for U.S. missile warheads raised serious questions regarding the administration's interest in mutual stability. To be sure, soon after entering office the administration announced the cancellation of an accuracy improvement program for Poseidon, and both President Nixon and Defense Secretary Laird declared that it was U.S. policy to eschew systems that could be viewed as threatening the USSR's deterrent. But both these actions, it should be emphasized, represented reluctant responses to congressional opposition rather than executive branch initiatives. Throughout 1970 and 1971, there were indications that research on improved missile accuracy was proceeding, and after the Moscow agreements were signed in mid-1972 the administration requested funds to develop warheads with hard-target kill capabilities. This time, direct congressional action denied the administration its request, but official spokesmen continued to discuss the concept of improved accuracy and toward the end of 1973 indicated that the forthcoming budget would again contain a request for financing development programs in this field. If Congress had not acted, it is likely that the Nixon administration would have acquired accurate MIRVs to support its flexible response doctrine and to fulfill its desire to match USSR capabilities.

The SALT negotiations were an important influence on the Nixon administration's unilateral strategic policies. This in itself was not surprising, for both President Nixon and Secretary Laird had indicated that the sufficiency criteria would be reviewed in the light of new technology, changing strategic circumstances, and the evolution of SALT.[84] The effect of SALT on stability, however, was mixed. To the extent that the negotiating process may have stimulated U.S. strategic programs for bargaining purposes and to the degree that the Moscow accords did not prevent the administration from pressing ahead with accurate MIRVs, the stabilizing benefits of SALT can be questioned. On the other hand, the SALT agreements denied the administration an area ABM and softened the significance of maintaining numerical equality with the Soviet Union in all categories of strategic weapons. These modifications of the sufficiency criteria tended to strengthen the stabilizing elements of the administration's doctrine.

An Assessment of the SALT Accords

The Nixon administration's initial cautious attitude toward such a crucial and complicated issue as SALT was understandable. Adopting the previous administration's position before establishing an independent set of nuclear objectives and arms control policies would have been as strategically unsound as it was politically inappropriate. As it turned out, only nine months passed before negotiations actually began—and part of this delay was due to the Soviet Union's last-minute hesitancy in reacting to the administration's proposal to arrange talks.

84. *Statement . . . on the Fiscal Year 1972–1976 Defense Program and Defense Budget*, pp. 61–62; and *Building for Peace*, p. 172.

As expected, the conduct of the actual negotiations—the unexpected Soviet views, the shifting U.S. positions, and the use of a high-level back-channel to bypass the formal talks—differed from initial administration plans. This caused some critics to claim that the United States did not follow a strict negotiating strategy designed to obtain Soviet concessions but made the mistake of viewing SALT as a cooperative rather than a competitive process and of readily compromising its position as a result of internal bargaining and the strong desire to negotiate an agreement with the USSR dictated by the timetable of the 1972 elections. On the other hand, many important issues—including subceilings on heavy missiles, restrictions on SLBMs, and the link between defense and offense—were negotiated in favor of the United States. In addition, the United States succeeded in gaining Soviet acceptance of a number of technical controls that improved the effectiveness of the final accords—notably the limits on ABM radars and the question of dealing with exotic missile defense systems that might be developed.

It is ironic to note that, while conservative critics claimed that the Nixon administration was allowing itself to be weakened and manipulated by the USSR in SALT, liberal critics argued that the United States was perverting the purposes and principles of arms control by pushing the bargaining chip approach to the point where unnecessary or potentially destabilizing U.S. strategic systems were procured and options for comprehensive agreements were undercut. It is claimed that the specific use of U.S. MIRV and Safeguard programs as negotiating leverage foreclosed prospects for a ban on multiple warheads and a total prohibition of ABMs. The USSR, however, seemed to be pursuing a negotiating-from-strength policy of its own, and Soviet representatives were reluctant to accept U.S. proposals and limitations. Many Soviet positions, moreover, were undoubtedly motivated as much by bargaining tactics designed to maximize the Soviet Union's side of any accord as by the proclaimed Kremlin goal of acquiring equal security. From this perspective, it is difficult to discount Henry Kissinger's observation that "our experience to date has been that an on-going program is no obstacle to an agreement, and, on the contrary, may accelerate it."[85]

One issue that has continued to receive considerable attention is the lack of MIRV restrictions in the Interim Agreement. Even the Vladivostok agreement approached the MIRV issue only indirectly. Many arms

85. *New York Times,* June 23, 1972.

control experts, reviewing SALT agreements, have contended that U.S. MIRV testing could have been safely halted, that verification of a test ban would have been possible, and that the benefits of banning Soviet MIRVs in removing the threat to Minuteman would have far outweighed any disadvantages of forgoing U.S. MIRVs and would have improved national security more than limiting the number of Soviet SS-9 launchers. It is fair, however, to conclude that the verification and negotiation problems associated with a MIRV ban were far more complicated when the Nixon administration faced these issues than during the final years of the Johnson administration—before U.S. MIRV testing had been initiated and when the opportunity to attempt to negotiate controls over this weapon was ripe. Furthermore, the momentum behind MIRV in 1969 and 1970 made U.S. acceptance of limitations on this system extremely difficult as a practical matter within the executive branch. Whether the Nixon administration's on-site inspection proposal reflected a lack of interest in banning MIRVs or an initial attempt to draw a Soviet response cannot be determined. In any case, the USSR showed no interest in discussing the MIRV ban—either in response to this U.S. proposal or during the preliminary talks when many U.S. experts believed that the Kremlin would press intensely for such a ban. By the time the Vladivostok guidelines were under negotiation, programs on both sides had progressed too far for MIRV prohibitions to be devised.

Beyond the question of MIRVs, the SALT accords can be considered a success in curbing the arms competition and serving U.S. security interests. The ABM treaty by itself greatly contributed to reducing the risks and costs of the nuclear arms race and removed the most serious potential threat to the U.S. deterrent—the prospect of large Soviet city-defense deployments. Indeed, this treaty marked the successful attainment of a goal sought by arms control experts for over a decade and the culmination of U.S. policy activities begun by Defense Secretary Robert McNamara in 1966. The price paid to obtain an area ABM limitation was to forgo the option of protecting U.S. ICBM sites with hard-point defenses, but the high cost and inefficiency of such systems, coupled with the problem of designing site defenses that do not "overlap" with populated areas, suggests that the negotiated outcome was sensible.

In concluding the Interim Agreement, the administration compromised its strict force-matching criterion. But under its unilateral strategic plans, the United States could not in any case have maintained an equal missile-launcher balance with the Soviet Union during the five-year span of the accord, nor could it have prevented the USSR from crossing the MIRV testing threshold and starting to narrow America's warhead advantage. More generally, the Moscow accords had political value as unprecedented steps signifying a move toward détente and promoted long-term stability by establishing procedures for continuing discussions in the strategic nuclear field between the two superpowers. If nothing else, the Interim Agreement reflected a decision by both the United States and the USSR to place temporary curbs on the strategic offensive competition while attempting to secure more comprehensive controls.

At the same time, the need for an improved agreement was evident after SALT I. There were imperfections and inadequacies in the Interim Agreement that made it unacceptable to the United States as a permanent pact unless modified. For example, the lack of controls over MIRVs would eventually permit the Soviet Union to match the U.S. capability in this field and to pose a threat to the survivability of our Minuteman ICBM force. As a permanent accord, the Interim Agreement may also have been unsatisfactory to the Soviet Union, since limitations were not placed on U.S. forward-based systems or strategic bombers, nor were the Trident and B-1 programs affected. Therefore, it seemed reasonable to expect that Soviet leaders might be motivated during subsequent phases of SALT II to accommodate the United States in order to negotiate stricter controls over American programs. Failure to meet America's security needs, moreover, could induce an intensified arms race that Kremlin leaders would be unlikely to welcome. These considerations may have contributed to the Soviet decision to sign the 1974 Vladivostok agreement.

At Vladivostok, the United States and the USSR established guidelines to govern negotiations for a new ten-year agreement covering offensive strategic weapons to replace the Interim Agreement, which expires in 1977. Under these guidelines, which call for an indefinite extension of the treaty limiting antiballistic missiles, each side would be limited to 2,400 delivery systems, covering strategic bombers as well as land- and sea-based missiles. Within this limit, up to 1,320 missiles could be equipped with MIRVs, and each side could decide its own mix of different kinds of missiles, including land-mobile missiles.

In mid-1975 the two sides were negotiating to try to translate these guidelines into a detailed agreement. If they are successful, they presumably would begin negotiations for a follow-on agreement that might involve reductions in the totals fixed at Vladivostok. Thus the question of what constitutes acceptable strategic arms control agreements will remain very much on the U.S. agenda for the coming decade.

In the final analysis, America's own strategic arms decisions and approach to SALT will determine the direction of future negotiations at least as much as Soviet policies will. A debate on basic nuclear policies and the details of an American position on SALT was initiated within the administration at the end of 1973 and continued with increased intensity into 1974. In a speech on the Senate floor, Senator Jackson joined the debate by offering a SALT plan that involved reductions in strategic systems based on a concern for stability and "the principle of equivalence."[86] During these attempts to carve out a U.S. policy on arms limitations, the Pentagon in its proposed budget requested a new series of strategic weapon development programs to support the objectives of matching Soviet arms buildups and providing hedges in the event SALT failed.[87] On a more basic level, the issues of SALT and strategic doctrine were taking on political overtones. Domestically, "missile gap" alarms were beginning to sound again, thus placing a burden on SALT to maintain détente and to satisfy American security interests under a durable agreement or risk a repeat of the over-responses in U.S. strategic programs and the ensuing disruption of U.S.-Soviet political relations that occurred in the past.[88] It was in this context that in 1974 the Vladivostok agreement was reached and that in 1975 its merits were being debated and negotiations to translate it into a formal accord were being carried forward.

86. "SALT: An Analysis and a Proposal," statement of Senator Jackson to the Senate, December 4, 1973 (press release, December 4, 1973).

87. John W. Finney, *New York Times*, December 1, 1973.

88. As he had in the late 1950s, columnist Joseph Alsop wrote of a possible "missile gap" in the *Washington Post*, November 28, 1973.

PART TWO

The Search for Stability

US	SOVIET

Do anything you like, as long as I can nuke you out of existence.

Build up enough to nuke you?

Fine, as long as you dont defend yourself too well.

Why are you confident.

I wont start it without hell of a reason, so I'm not worried

~~break~~ down here.

CHAPTER FOUR

Future Strategic Policy Issues

Despite the spirit of détente that has entered East-West relations and the initial success of the strategic arms limitation talks (SALT), the USSR will in all probability remain America's principal adversary during the next decade. Completely apart from any judgments regarding Soviet intentions or from attempts to evaluate the propensity of Kremlin leaders to take risks to support their foreign policy, it is obvious that the sheer size and power of the USSR's strategic nuclear forces constitute a threat to the survival of the United States. A fraction of the Soviet Union's strategic nuclear arsenal launched against U.S. population centers would bring catastrophic consequences, and any nuclear strike, however limited, would not only be highly destructive in itself but could escalate into an all-out strategic conflict between the United States and the Soviet Union. Under these circumstances, U.S. policymakers have no choice but to view the central purpose of America's strategic nuclear forces as the deterrence of a Soviet nuclear attack. Once Peking acquires an intercontinental-range nuclear delivery capability to supplement its medium-range nuclear forces, the United States must also add the deterrence of Chinese nuclear attacks against the American homeland to its list of essential security concerns.

Notwithstanding the broad consensus on basic strategic policy in the United States, opinions differ over the precise weapons mixture and defense doctrine required to maintain a dependable strategic posture in an era of nuclear parity. In addition to the issue of what constitutes an effective second-strike strategic force, questions are being asked about the degree to which U.S. strategic forces should be given added capabilities—besides those required for assured destruction—in order to strengthen deterrence and to limit damage to the United States should deterrence fail. A further crucial question is what broad political and security purposes America's strategic forces should serve beyond nuclear deterrence and how these objectives are affected by the U.S.-USSR strategic balance. There is disagreement over the degree to which U.S. strategic forces are effective in containing and countering possible Soviet attempts at political coercion, in supporting the United States in its peacetime diplomatic pursuits, and in enhancing the ability of American leaders to manage international crises. Experts are also looking more carefully at the utility of America's strategic "umbrella" in deterring Soviet or Chinese nuclear attacks or threats against U.S. allies and in contributing to the deterrence of large-scale conventional aggression in Europe or Asia. Finally, and perhaps most fundamentally, some analysts are attempting to find alternative strategies for the longer term that might permit the United States and the USSR to eventually eliminate the necessity of relying on assured destruction as the foundation of their nuclear policies.

Retaliation vs Destruction?

Requirements for Assured Retaliation

Regardless of any variations that might be introduced into U.S. strategic arms policy, the need to preserve a retaliatory strike capability will undoubtedly remain the chief determinant of America's nuclear posture during the coming decade. Therefore, before exploring the questions of supplementing deterrence, extending the purposes of strategic forces, and shifting away from counterpopulation retaliatory policies altogether, it is important to consider the elements of a strategic posture designed for assured destruction.

Damage Levels and Confidence

The assured destruction approach rests on the premise that Soviet leaders will refrain from launching a nuclear attack against the United States if they remain convinced that sufficient American strategic forces would remain intact to be capable of a retaliatory strike that would inflict unacceptable damage on the USSR's centers of population and industry. Kremlin leaders for well over a decade have appreciated the destructive potential of nuclear weapons and have placed top priority on avoiding a nuclear war with the United States. But American policymakers have been unable to decide what level of damage U.S. strategic forces must be able to inflict in a retaliatory strike in order to deter a Soviet attack.

Defense Secretary Robert McNamara's well-known assured destruction figure of 20–25 percent Soviet fatalities was somewhat arbitrarily developed on the grounds that substantially higher levels were not easily attainable, while substantially lower levels might weaken the U.S. deterrent. Few experts, if any, currently contend that damage levels for nuclear deterrence must be raised, although some express concern over maintaining an appropriate U.S.-Soviet ratio of damage-inflicting capabilities. During the past few years, however, an increasing number of observers have argued that nuclear damage levels have been set needlessly high, and they have suggested that deterrence could operate with equal reliability if a prospective attacker faced a significantly less intense counterstrike. Former presidential security adviser McGeorge Bundy, for example, in a widely quoted article published in late 1969, maintained that "there is an enormous gulf between what political leaders really think about nuclear weapons and what is assumed in complex calculations ... in simulated strategic warfare."[1] Although American think-tank analysts may set the required destruction level of retaliatory deterrence in the tens of millions of lives, Bundy claimed that Soviet leaders would be deterred from launching a strategic attack by the risk of having ten, or even one or two, of their major cities destroyed in a nuclear war. Scientists have also been critical of the tendency toward nuclear overkill, pointing out that U.S. military planners traditionally understate the destructive consequences of nuclear strikes against urban areas and that retaliatory forces could be designed to deliver substantially fewer warheads while still retaining a satisfactory counterstrike threat.[2]

The calculations involved in determining the damage-inflicting capabilities of nuclear strikes against the Soviet Union can often become quite complex, but simple and accurate estimates have been derived.[3]

1. McGeorge Bundy, "To Cap the Volcano," Foreign Affairs, vol. 48 (October 1969), pp. 9–10.

2. See W. K. H. Panofsky, "Roots of the Strategic Arms Race," Science and Public Affairs, July 1971, p. 18.

3. For a table of nuclear damage estimates, see Alain C. Enthoven and K. Wayne Smith, How Much Is Enough? Shaping the Defense Program, 1961–1969 (Harper and Row, 1971), p. 207.

The delivery of 100 1-megaton-equivalent warheads in a so-called countervalue attack, for example, would destroy 15 percent of the Soviet Union's population and 60 percent of the USSR's industrial capacity through immediate blast and prompt radiation effects; the delivery of 200 1-megaton equivalents would destroy 20 percent of the population and over 70 percent of the industrial capacity; and 400 1-megaton equivalent warheads would destroy 30 percent of the population and 75 percent of the industrial base. Increments in damage-inflicting capability gained from delivering additional weapons would be extremely marginal as the "saturation" effect set in—that is, few populated areas in the Soviet Union would remain free from destruction.

It should be noted that the actual casualty rate could run close to twice the population fatality figures cited, owing to fallout, long-term radiation effects, and indirect deaths resulting from societal disruptions of an unprecedented degree. When fatalities are combined with damage to industry, cities, and transportation, it is no exaggeration to conclude that, after a U.S. assured destruction attack, the Soviet Union would cease to exist as a modern nation for an indeterminate period of time. In principle, it is possible to argue the relative merits of emphasizing population fatalities or industrial damage as the more effective deterrent threat. In practice, however, the co-location of Soviet industry and urban centers indicated by the foregoing figures suggests that assured destruction requirements and capabilities cannot be realistically formulated on the basis of such a distinction. Massive attacks designed to destroy Soviet cities would be largely indistinguishable in terms of total population fatalities and industrial damage from massive attacks optimized to destroy Soviet civilian manufacturing, military production, or major transportation assets.

Clearly, the assured destruction concept does not simply involve the total nuclear power available to a nation but stresses the ability of strategic forces to deliver nuclear weapons against urban-industrial targets *after* absorbing an attack aimed at negating these forces. The United States should easily be able to satisfy the condition of inflicting unacceptable damage on the USSR, given present strategic force inventories and ongoing programs. U.S. strategic forces—intercontinental ballistic missiles (ICBMs), submarine-launched ballistic missiles (SLBMs), and long-range bombers—currently carry a total of more than 5,000 warheads, and within a few years this figure will rise to 10,000 under present plans.[4] U.S. bomber warheads run approximately 1 megaton, but missile yields are substantially smaller, falling in the 50–200-kiloton range. Taking into account the relationship between small and large warheads, the capacity of existing U.S. missile forces alone translates into approximately 2,000 equivalent megatons—five times that needed to cause 30 percent fatalities in the Soviet Union and to destroy three-quarters of its industrial base. To this force must be added the thousands of equivalent megatons potentially deliverable by bomber systems. Without considering bombers, however, a small fraction of the U.S. strategic missile force surviving an attack would be capable of launching warheads with the power to inflict tens of millions of fatalities, and, facing only the small Soviet ABM system near Moscow, the bulk of these warheads would be virtually certain to land on target. Indeed, if only 10 percent of the warheads scheduled to be available to our strategic forces by the late 1970s were to survive an attack and were to be launched in retaliation against Soviet urban centers, immediate damage to the USSR would run well above any reasonable assured destruction requirement.

It is difficult to refute the argument that Soviet leaders should not even consider launching a nuclear attack out of the blue against the United States unless they could be absolutely certain that they would succeed in negating our retaliatory capability. The Moscow treaty in 1972 banned nationwide antiballistic missiles (ABMs) in both the United States and the USSR;[5] thus Kremlin officials would have to be confident of launching an effective counterforce strike with offensive missiles coordinated to destroy virtually all the U.S. land-based missiles, bombers, and sea-based forces simultaneously and with little advance warning. It is extremely doubtful that any Soviet leader would stake the survival of his nation on such an expectation. Even if the USSR acquired the capability to inflict greater urban-industrial damage on the United States than the latter could inflict on the Soviet Union, Kremlin leaders would almost certainly be deterred from engaging in actions that ran a high risk of leading to all-out nuclear war and the virtual destruction of their nation as an industrial state.

4. For estimates of future U.S. warhead inventories and other features of the strategic arms balance, see Alton H. Quanbeck and Barry M. Blechman, *Strategic Forces: Issues for the Mid-Seventies* (Brookings Institution, 1973), p. 26.

5. Treaty between the United States of America and the Union of Soviet Socialist Republics on the Limitation of Anti-Ballistic Missile Systems, signed at Moscow, May 26, 1972.

Nevertheless, deterrence of a premeditated Soviet first strike is *not* the central strategic issue of the future or the most critical problem facing U.S. policymakers. It is more important to consider possible Soviet behavior during crises and to explore the range of diplomatic and military circumstances in which the USSR might be tempted to initiate strategic war or political actions that could increase the risk of nuclear war. During a tense U.S.-Soviet confrontation involving major stakes, for instance, the USSR's leaders might conclude that escalation to nuclear war was preferable to either inaction or waiting for a possible U.S. strategic attack. In any crisis, the burden would of course be placed on those Soviet military or political decisionmakers advocating a nuclear attack to demonstrate that such an action could successfully eliminate or severely cripple our ability to retaliate. Accordingly, as one analyst recently observed, the U.S. deterrent posture should make it impossible for a "clever briefer" in the USSR to develop a credible situation in which a Soviet first strike could mean a potential victory—with little or no damage to the Soviet Union—while retaliation against a potential U.S. nuclear attack might well mean defeat.[6] Furthermore, the U.S. strategic posture should be designed to minimize the chance that Soviet leaders might misjudge our capabilities or intentions and either decide to launch limited nuclear strikes against a component of our nuclear forces or seek to extract political concessions through nuclear coercion or threats against the United States or its allies. Our strategic posture must also serve to persuade *American* leaders of the reliability of U.S. deterrent capabilities so that they can respond confidently to difficult international situations. Finally, our posture must help strengthen the credibility of our overseas nuclear guarantees in the eyes of our allies and friends.

The preceding discussion leads to the conclusion that meeting the requirements of strategic deterrence, broadly defined, can be a complicated and difficult task demanding constant attention. It suggests that the U.S.-Soviet strategic balance may indeed be more delicate than critics of past and present strategic policies seem prepared to acknowl-

6. Morton H. Halperin, "Clever Briefers, Crazy Leaders and Myopic Analysts," *The Washington Monthly*, September 1974, pp. 42–49. Significantly, in 1960 Herman Kahn, a prominent strategist, argued that the U.S. deterrent capability must "provide an objective basis for a Soviet calculation that would persuade [Soviet leaders] that, no matter how skillful or igenious they were, an attack on the United States would lead to a very high risk if not certainty of large-scale destruction to Soviet civil society and military forces." (*On Thermonuclear War* [Princeton University Press, 1960], p. 557.)

edge. The inference to be drawn is that *the key to nuclear deterrence through assured destruction lies less in the degree of destruction involved than it does in the amount of assurance or confidence built into a deterrent posture.* The question of confidence, in turn, leads to specific issues regarding force structure that involve weapon characteristics and the composition of America's strategic deterrent.

Before examining further these and other issues involved in designing a U.S. strategic deterrent against the Soviet Union, however, the question of China should be mentioned briefly. As noted, two of the purposes of U.S. strategic forces vis-à-vis China are (1) to deter the Chinese from using or threatening to use their growing nuclear capability against American overseas forces or our Asian allies, and (2) eventually to deter Peking from launching nuclear attacks against the United States itself. Because of the concentration of Chinese urban-industrial areas, only a small fraction of the U.S. strategic force—less than 10 percent—need be allocated to the assured destruction mission against China. A few hundred warheads delivered in a countervalue strike would not cause 25 percent population fatalities, but it would destroy the bulk of China's industrial capacity and government institutions. Most Sinologists believe that such a threat would be adequate to deter China, and considering the overall military power of the United States, they expect Peking to continue its cautious policy and to refrain from undertaking either nuclear or large-scale conventional aggression.[7] Without detracting from their ability to deter the USSR, therefore, U.S. strategic offensive forces could easily provide such deterrent capabilities against China. Thus, the following discussion will deal with the requirements for an anti-Soviet deterrent on the assumption that the anti-Chinese deterrent would automatically be satisfied.

Characteristics of an Assured Destruction Force

In an evaluation of assured destruction requirements, the important questions center on the penetrability, reliability, and survivability of America's strategic systems—that is, what fraction of our deployed forces could actually be expected to deliver weapons against the Soviet Union in a retaliatory strike.

7. See, for example, A. Doak Barnett, "A Nuclear China and U.S. Arms Policy," *Foreign Affairs*, vol. 48 (April 1970), pp. 427–42.

PENETRABILITY

With the ABM treaty in effect, penetration is no longer the serious problem it was in the 1960s when Pentagon planners feared that the USSR would deploy extensive ballistic missile defenses. In the unlikely event that the Soviet Union abrogated the agreement, U.S. strategic missile forces would be able to maintain the capability to overwhelm ABM defenses ten times as large as the present Soviet deployments. This excess capability, which exists because currently deployed Poseidon and Minuteman systems carrying multiple independently targetable reentry vehicles (MIRVs) were originally developed to offset Soviet nationwide missile defenses, provides a cushion against ABM treaty violations. By the end of 1977, for example, the total number of warheads available on U.S. land- and sea-based missiles, as programmed at present, will exceed 6,000. If a greater strategic missile capability is desired, more extensive MIRV procurements could easily bring this figure to over 8,000. For the longer term, the United States is developing Trident, the new submarine-based missile system, which could carry a larger MIRV payload, and research is being conducted on a maneuvering reentry vehicle, which could provide greater penetration flexibility for the strategic missile force if needed.

The strategic bomber force, while less prominent in recent years than the missile forces, is an important arm of America's deterrent capability. Although Soviet bomber defenses may well remain at high levels and could be improved, with the deployment of the short-range attack air-to-surface missile, for example, U.S. bomber penetration capabilities are also improving. Bomber penetration calculations are complicated and uncertain, but it is reasonable to assume that half of the U.S. incoming bombers might penetrate to target. This would represent a substantial damage-inflicting potential. Indeed, if a force of 100 bombers survived a Soviet attack and if only 30 percent of this force penetrated Soviet defenses, over 200 megatons could be delivered against Soviet urban-industrial areas.[8] New strategic bomber systems currently under development, such as the B-1, and the possible procurement of an air-to-surface cruise missile, will ensure that U.S. strategic bombers maintain an effective penetration capability.

8. Quanbeck and Blechman analyzed U.S. bomber capabilities in *Strategic Forces*, pp. 43–50 and app. D.

RELIABILITY

The reliability of strategic systems can be divided into two categories —the technical reliability of the forces themselves and the reliability of the command and control network associated with these systems. Bomber reliability is excellent, and the reliability of a fully tested missile system generally runs about 80 percent. Among other techniques, development and proof tests help U.S. military officials gain confidence in the reliability of strategic systems and, as in the case of a series of unsuccessful Poseidon SLBM firings in 1973, to identify problems that require attention. In the past, the United States has not tested its ICBMs from operational silos, since missile trajectories would pass over populated areas, but such tests are now scheduled to take place. Some experts, however, question whether inland tests from Minuteman fields add substantially more "realism" to a simulated firing than the traditional use of special silos for this purpose at West Coast military bases.[9]

The dependability of command and control systems is difficult to evaluate, given the lack of public information on this subject. The chain of command for U.S. nuclear forces, however, apparently runs from the President through the military command centers to the bomber crews or missile commanders. Technical and procedural arrangements, such as the "two-key" system, positive release codes, and secure channels of communication, help guard against unauthorized or accidental launches and are designed to ensure that a firing signal is issued and implemented only when authorized. The Washington-Moscow hot line complements the rapid and reliable communication networks within our own command structure. Finally, through improvements in command arrangements and targeting, U.S. offensive forces are being given selective options to permit limited use of these weapons under close control. The policy implications of such flexibility for strategic forces are discussed below.

The U.S. strategic posture includes a variety of warning, control, and surveillance systems. These programs affect the ability of American deterrent forces to survive attacks, influence the way U.S. retaliatory forces can be used, and increase the information available to our decisionmakers regarding the nature of the Soviet threat. Warning systems,

9. See Alton H. Quanbeck and Barry M. Blechman, *New York Times*, January 30, 1974.

[Handwritten margin notes: How does always when authorized? Recent Alert syst. failure.]

[Handwritten note at bottom: Designs to keep accidental fire from occurring only tested by time — never fired. What about a block in arteries not being discovered until actual desire to fire? Assumption of fire only under obvious retaliatory conditions?]

such as the ballistic missile early warning system (BMEWS), alert U.S. forces to actual or impending strategic attack, and the Spacetrack system monitors USSR satellite launchings and maintains an inventory of Soviet objects in orbit. Surveillance systems, such as the Strategic Satellite System, can provide real-time data on military activities—information that is useful in managing crises. Because they can identify the size and source of nuclear attacks on the United States, reconnaissance and warning systems can help decisionmakers take appropriate action in the event of nuclear war.

Concern is occasionally expressed over whether U.S. land-based systems and sea-based systems can remain secure and under proper control. Bombers, of course, can be tightly managed while remaining airborne and can be recalled from an attack route hours after a commitment to target. Unlike bombers, ballistic missiles cannot be recalled, although it would be technically possible to disarm or destroy ICBMs or SLBMs during the early minutes of flight. Land-based missile forces in silos have extremely dependable control systems with two-way communication links between launch sites and command centers. Submarine-based missile forces can remain in a highly invulnerable submerged state and receive information, but they must approach the surface to transmit data to central authorities.[10] This disadvantage, which can be alleviated by new communications systems, is not serious for the operation of a credible and controllable strategic deterrent. More generally, a broad array of programs is being pursued to improve the effectiveness, responsiveness, and survivability of the U.S. military command and control system, including the presidential chain of command. One important effort is the program to institute a more sophisticated airborne command post to decrease the danger that the National Command Authority (NCA) could be crippled by a Soviet strike.

Planned improvements will permit U.S. strategic forces to remain reliable in a technical as well as a command sense, to preserve an effective deterrent capability, and to keep risks at a minimum. Some experts have even questioned whether U.S. strategic systems might be over-designed and thus might *fail* to fire when ordered to do so. In any case, it is doubtful that Soviet leaders would be able to conclude with confidence that the reliability of U.S. strategic retaliatory forces was in-

reliance on satellites?

10. See Herbert Scoville, Jr., "Missile Submarines and National Security," *Scientific American*, June 1972, pp. 15–27.

herently weak or could be sufficiently degraded to permit the USSR to launch a nuclear attack without fearing a catastrophically damaging counterstrike.

SURVIVABILITY

The most significant link in the deterrence chain, of course, is prelaunch survivability, or the ability of U.S. strategic forces to remain invulnerable to a Soviet first strike. Survivability became an important issue during the Kennedy administration, when Secretary McNamara stressed that it would be risky to retain U.S. strategic systems that could be easily destroyed by Soviet attacks and to rely solely on a launch-on-warning strategy to save our strategic forces. A launch-on-warning policy, most experts have concluded, would involve serious risks by making a Soviet first strike seem less implausible to Kremlin leaders who might find ways of destroying or bypassing U.S. warning systems —or who might believe they had discovered such techniques. An equally important risk is that the President, concerned about vulnerable U.S. strategic systems, might decide to launch all our forces at once in a preemptive move before the reality, size, and nature of a Soviet nuclear attack could be assessed and an appropriate response determined.

Survivability can be obtained in a variety of ways; one way, for example, is to simply increase both the number of vehicles capable of delivering warheads and the number of warheads deployed on individual systems. The size of the U.S. strategic force—1,050 ICBMs, 650 SLBMs, and over 400 long-range bombers, together with the installation of MIRVs on our missile systems—reflects this approach to a degree. For the past decade, however, U.S. administrations have not emphasized this "brute force" approach as the most desirable technique for ensuring that sufficient retaliatory power would remain after a Soviet attack. Reliance on the sheer proliferation of delivery systems or weapons is not a dependable option, since it could easily be offset by corresponding increases in Soviet offensive systems. Moreover, it is generally not a costeffective approach and can be destabilizing in the sense that it could lead to an increase in U.S. strategic force levels that could trigger Soviet reactions.

For these and other reasons, the United States has emphasized other survivability techniques, particularly hardening and mobility, which permit high survivability with a limited number of delivery systems. In the early 1960s, the United States built the hardened Minuteman ICBM system and phased out the soft Atlas and early Titan-model ICBMs. Even though the Minuteman force *can* be launched rapidly on warning, it *need not* be launched if the bulk of the force is strong enough to withstand a Soviet countermilitary attack. The Polaris submarine was developed enthusiastically in the late 1950s because mobility and undetectability under the sea made Polaris highly survivable. These survivability features of ICBMs and SLBMs remain valid in the current strategic environment. Bombers, on the other hand, continue to obtain survivability through warning combined with dispersion, although units on airborne alert cannot be targeted.

Maintaining a diversified deterrent composed of varying types of strategic delivery systems also strengthens the overall survivability of a strategic posture. To begin with, a diverse U.S. deterrent force complicates the planning and execution of a successful Soviet counterforce strike. Systems with different basing modes are threatened by different weapons and attack strategy. Fixed ICBM systems, for example, would become more vulnerable if the USSR improved the number and kill capability of Soviet offensive missiles. The potential danger to submarine survivability, however, is in the totally different field of antisubmarine warfare improvements, and bombers could be endangered by so-called depressed-trajectory, or short-time-of-flight, missiles, which need not be highly accurate and would not necessarily threaten ICBMs. Success in developing the capability to threaten one or two components of the U.S. strategic posture therefore would not provide the Soviet Union with a full first-strike potential, since the remaining U.S. forces could mount a devastating retaliatory response. Thus, a diversified deterrent can guard against unforeseen technological breakthroughs or a catastrophic failure that might endanger one type of deterrent force. In addition, the USSR would find it difficult to launch a coordinated attack against a diverse U.S. posture because strikes directed against one type of system could alert the others, and, once launched, systems with differing penetration characteristics pose far more complicated problems for defensive systems than do identical weapons.

It should be emphasized that no serious participant in the present U.S. strategic debate questions the principle of survivability on the *aggregate* level. However, when considering the specific mix and characteristics of our strategic posture, there are substantial differences of opinion about the potential danger of permitting partial vulnerabilities to occur and about whether the nation should maintain and modernize its present triad of strategic forces—ICBMs, SLBMs, and bombers. Some experts have even raised the issue of why the United States should continue to sustain a diversified deterrent into the 1980s. The various views expressed on these and other issues affecting major weapons programs are often influenced by the proponent's institutional position or bureaucratic bias, but real differences of opinion exist on such substantive strategic policy issues as the degree of confidence needed for a reliable assured destruction force, the severity of future Soviet military threats, the comparative cost-effectiveness of weapons options, and the budget to be committed for strategic forces.

Partial Vulnerabilities

Two categories of potential strategic force vulnerabilities can be identified. First, the survivability of one or more force types could be endangered. Second, the survivability of all force components could be substantially degraded beyond their present levels. In either case, the question is whether the U.S. deterrent would be unacceptably weakened by such partial vulnerabilities if our basic assured retaliatory capability remained unaltered.

To some degree, the second type of partial vulnerability already exists, since each element of our strategic posture is not fully survivable under all conditions. For instance, under typical circumstances a substantial fraction of the U.S. strategic bomber force does not remain on active alert, and as much as 60 percent of the bomber force might not survive an all-out surprise Soviet counterforce missile attack. In addition, about 30 percent of the U.S. SLBM force remains in home port under normal conditions and could be attacked by Soviet offensive missile strikes, and nearly 20 percent of our ICBM force could be destroyed, given present Soviet capabilities, if the USSR launched a massive countersilo strike. But these partial vulnerabilities have been accepted as unavoidable for many years; they have been taken into account in strategic planning, and our overall strategic posture has been seen as exhibiting high survivability nonetheless. Future trends, however, indicate that the first type of vulnerability—affecting one particular category of weapons—poses the greater danger. Submarine-launched ballistic missile systems in all probability will remain survivable, while bombers will retain a reasonable degree of invulnerability. Ironically, it appears that by the end of the decade ICBMs will shift from being the most survivable force component in the U.S. inventory to the least. A closer examination of survivability issues will expose the details supporting such generalities.

SUBMARINES

Most experts agree that Soviet progress in antisubmarine warfare (ASW) is not likely to endanger the survivability of the Polaris-Poseidon fleet for some time to come. Nuclear-powered submarines, operating in the vast expanse of the ocean, are extremely difficult to detect and identify with acoustic or other devices. Even if units were located and tracked by attack submarines, it would be virtually impossible for an adversary to mount the coordinated attack needed to destroy all on-station submarines simultaneously. In the event ASW improvements occur, a variety of countermeasures could be instituted, such as quieting the propulsion system; installing longer-range missiles that would permit submarines to move in wider ocean areas; and jamming, deception, or other evasive actions. Major breakthroughs in ASW systems—the use of high-energy transmitters deployed in huge ocean arrays, for example —are not only technically difficult and expensive but could be detected in time to take countermeasures.[11]

Ten Trident submarines are scheduled for procurement and operation by 1978. They will be somewhat quieter than the Polaris systems and will carry 24 missiles—initially a 4,000-mile-range SLBM and eventually a 6,000-mile intercontinental-range missile. Many experts claim that the premature commitment to production will considerably increase both the cost of the Trident and the risk that the United States might not design the system efficiently enough to counter future Soviet ASW threats. Some argue persuasively that smaller submarines carrying fewer SLBMs would provide a more secure sea-based deterrent by offering fewer targets. The Nixon Administration, in early 1973, requested preliminary funds to develop such a system—the Narwhal—which apparently would be designed as an improved version of the Polaris, but Congress did not approve the program.[12]

11. For a discussion of ASW possibilities, see *Strategic Survey 1970* (London: Institute for Strategic Studies, 1970), pp. 12–17; Richard L. Garwin, "Antisubmarine Warfare and National Security," *Scientific American*, July 1972, pp. 14–25; and V. C. Anderson, "Ocean Technology," in Bernard T. Feld and others, eds., *Impact of New Technologies on the Arms Race* (MIT Press, 1971), pp. 201–26.

12. The Narwhal submarine and other proposed strategic arms development programs are discussed in "Arming to Disarm in the Age of Détente," *Time*, February 11, 1974, pp. 15–24. For a critical analysis of the Trident system, see George W.

BOMBERS

The effectiveness of strategic bomber forces is often forgotten, given the emphasis placed on missiles during the past fifteen years. The survivability of bombers can be maintained reasonably well. A substantial portion of the aircraft of the Strategic Air Command (SAC) usually remains on fifteen-minute alert, and new surveillance systems will increase warning time from ICBM attacks to as much as thirty minutes. To guard against possible Soviet development of depressed-trajectory SLBMs or large-scale deployment of the fractional orbital bombardment system (FOBS), the United States has established a higher ground-alert rate, has developed a rapid start capability for its bomber systems, has begun to base its aircraft in the interior of the country, and has deployed new radar and satellite systems. Furthermore, in a time of tension, or if large numbers of Soviet sea-based missiles were detected in waters close to the United States, a fraction of the U.S. bomber force could be put on airborne alert. These countermeasures, many analysts believe, make a destructive Soviet attack against our bomber force more difficult to execute than launching a successful counterforce attack against U.S. ICBMs with MIRV-carrying SS-9 missiles.

An important future problem facing U.S. officials concerns the decision to procure a replacement for the B-52 systems. These aircraft have been in the inventory for well over a decade, and, while modifications could keep the force viable until at least 1980, at some stage a new bomber will be needed. The only candidate currently under consideration as a replacement for the B-52 is the B-1 bomber; research has been undertaken and prototypes are being constructed. If the B-1 is procured, it could become operational by 1980. Some experts claim that the B-1 may not be the preferred alternative to the B-52. Apart from its high cost, the system provides only marginal improvements over the B-52 in speed, low-altitude capability, and prelaunch survivability. One proposal for an alternative follow-on bomber capable of meeting these requirements is to utilize a large subsonic aircraft similar to the C-5.[13] The system would not be designed to penetrate near the Soviet Union but would operate far from the USSR's borders and carry a large array of standoff missiles.

Rathjens and Jack P. Ruina, "Trident," in Kosta Tsipis, Anne H. Kahn, and Bernard T. Feld, eds., *The Future of the Sea-Based Deterrent* (MIT Press, 1973), pp. 54–75.

13. Quanbeck and Blechman presented the relative cost-effectiveness of a "standoff" bomber and the B-1 in *Strategic Forces*, pp. 48–50.

[handwritten note: not the worst of both planes & missiles again? No recall & too slow.]

It would also be given improved ground alert capabilities and the ability to remain airborne for long periods of time without tanker support.

ICBMS

The most serious problem in maintaining survivable U.S. deterrent forces is the preservation of a viable ICBM force. The Soviet Union has flight-tested a MIRV system and will undoubtedly deploy this warhead package on its large and small land-based missile force beginning in the mid-1970s. In all probability, effective controls to eliminate the threat posed by accurate multiple warheads to fixed ICBM forces will not be negotiated in SALT, and, with accuracy improvements tied to the substantial throw-weight of its ICBMs, the USSR could acquire a fully installed multiple warhead capability by the early 1980s.[14] Thus, the USSR could use a smaller number of attacking missiles to destroy the bulk of our force of 1,054 ICBMs. This efficient counterforce potential would be possible because MIRVs alter the exchange ratio of the number of attacking missiles needed to destroy a silo-based ICBM from more than one to less than one.

The United States is strengthening its existing ICBM silos and could place MIRVs on the entire Minuteman force. These measures will marginally improve ICBM survivability and the retaliatory power of each missile. Over the long term, however, there may be no reliable or cost-effective solution for preventing fixed ICBMs from eventually becoming vulnerable to attacks from offensive missiles carrying large numbers of accurate warheads in MIRV packages. The ABM treaty bars the United States from deploying more than a token ABM system to defend its missiles, but it is doubtful that even extensive ABM installations—based on existing technology or the new hard-site concept—could guarantee the invulnerability of American ICBMs.

Apart from the fact that deploying larger numbers of ICBMs is prohibited under the Interim Agreement and the Vladivostok agreement,[15] this would not be an effective response to a Soviet MIRV threat; additional missiles could be negated by improvements in Soviet MIRV ca-

14. Defense Secretary Schlesinger estimated that the Soviet Union could complete MIRV deployments by the early 1980s. (News conference, November 30, 1973.)

15. Interim Agreement between the United States of America and the Union of Soviet Socialist Republics on Certain Measures with Respect to the Limitation of Strategic Offensive Arms, signed at Moscow, May 26, 1972; and Joint Soviet-American Statement on Strategic Arms Limitation, November 24, 1974.

pabilities or the construction of additional Soviet offensive systems. As another alternative, the United States could install ICBMs in superhard silos built into bedrock. But major alterations in the deployment mode of fixed ICBMs are also prohibited under these agreements, and the United States has already rejected this solution as a technically difficult and costly option that could be offset by Soviet accuracy improvements. Another possibility would be to replace fixed ICBMs with land-mobile missiles. This would be permissible under both agreements, although the United States had once expressed an interest in negotiating a mutual ban on land-mobile ICBMs. Research is being carried out on land-mobile missile concepts, but implementation is far from certain. Many defense planners are inclined to dismiss the option of deploying land-mobile missiles in the United States, largely because of domestic problems but also because of the difficult logistics associated with such systems, their high cost, and the prospect that they could become vulnerable to attack. Finally, the possibility of air-launching ICBMs from modified jumbo-jets is being studied.[16] But, whatever its technical or policy merits, this option would be so far removed from the concept of land-based missiles that it would represent an entirely new system rather than a technique for "saving" Minuteman.

DOCTRINAL ISSUES

The prospect that U.S. ICBMs will become vulnerable within the decade has stimulated a debate that has implications for broader doctrinal questions concerning partially vulnerable strategic forces. A number of experts now claim, for example, that it would be beneficial to retain land-based missiles, even though the missiles had become vulnerable to attack, on the grounds that such ICBMs would continue to complicate Soviet attack plans and could inhibit Kremlin leaders from launching counterforce strikes against U.S. land-based systems.[17] More specifically, these experts emphasize that bombers and missiles mutu-

16. See *Department of Defense Appropriations for 1974*, Hearings before the Defense Subcommittee of the House Committee on Appropriations, 93 Cong. 1 sess. (1973), pt. 7, pp. 1028–38.

17. See statement of Carl Kaysen, Director, Institute for Advanced Study, Princeton University, in *Arms Control Implications of Current Defense Budget*, Hearings before the Subcommittee on Arms Control, International Law and Organization of the Senate Committee on Foreign Relations, 92 Cong. 1 sess. (1971), pp. 57–76. Dr. Kaysen identified the problem of ICBM vulnerability but stated that it did not warrant serious concern if the submarines and bombers remained survivable.

ally reinforce each other's survivability. While U.S. bombers could be threatened if Soviet submarines fired SLBMs at close range in an attempt to reduce the warning time for our aircraft to as little as five minutes, the Soviet threat to American ICBMs would take the form of land-based missiles launched from the Soviet Union. If the USSR attempted to design its strike for simultaneous impact on U.S. bomber bases and Minuteman sites, therefore, the Soviet ICBM launchings could be detected, and SAC aircraft could have almost thirty minutes to become airborne, since that is how long it would take for missiles launched from the Soviet Union to reach the United States. Alternatively, simultaneous launchings of Soviet ICBMs and SLBMs in an attempt to negate *both* components of our land-based force would result in our ICBMs being attacked about twenty-five minutes after our bomber bases were destroyed, thus giving the President additional time to fire Minuteman missiles before they could be destroyed by incoming Soviet MIRV warheads.

no MIRVed
SLBMs?

A series of additional arguments have been presented by analysts who question the concern over ICBM vulnerability. Some experts suggest that the mere prospect of a launch on warning will continue to inhibit Soviet attacks, thereby maintaining the deterrent effect of ICBMs, and argue that the operational difficulties facing a Soviet planner in executing a coordinated strike aimed at destroying over 90 percent of U.S. ICBMs are often ignored by those determined to demonstrate that Minuteman will inevitably lose its invulnerability. Because statistics show that a small number of ICBMs will undoubtedly survive any attack, it is claimed that there will always be a residual deterrent capability in the land-based missile force that could be increased further by installing MIRVs in all the Minuteman systems and eventually by building a larger ICBM force, capable of carrying many more warheads, to replace Minuteman. A few observers even note that vulnerable ICBMs can contribute to damage limitation since they draw fire from Soviet offensive missiles away from U.S. population centers. Finally, a number of experts have taken the fairly relaxed position that as long as sea-based missiles and bombers remain reasonably survivable, it makes little difference whether fixed ICBMs are retained or removed.

But the potential risks and instabilities associated with vulnerable force components, on balance, appear to outweigh the possible marginal gain of retaining them and also argue against a neutral stance. If U.S. fixed ICBMs became vulnerable, for example, there might be an incentive for the Soviet Union to launch its offensive missiles in an attempt to destroy our force, notwithstanding the existence of secure U.S. sea-based and bomber forces. Fearing that the United States might be about to launch its missiles during a severe crisis, Soviet leaders could decide on such an action in the hope of at least limiting damage to their society. This would pose grave dangers for the Kremlin, for an attack against U.S. ICBMs would inevitably cause collateral damage to the American population measured in millions of fatalities, and U.S. decisionmakers would be likely to order retaliation against Soviet population centers. Nonetheless, by withholding their sea-based systems and bombers as a threat to our population, Soviet leaders might believe that American leaders would be inhibited from mounting a retaliatory response with our surviving SLBMs and bombers—in order to preclude a massive Soviet counterstrike aimed *directly* against U.S. cities. The probability of such "crisis instability" occurring as long as the United States has a minimum assured destruction capability is admittedly very low, but there is some risk that Soviet leaders might misinterpret the effectiveness of the U.S. deterrent and take actions that could heighten the danger of nuclear war. The existence of lucrative U.S. missile targets that can be shown to be vulnerable through simple calculations would increase the chance that a Soviet clever briefer could make his case for a first use of nuclear weapons more persuasively than if such targets were not present.

WHAT? NO CHANCE!

However risky and difficult an attack might seem, many experts have argued that the incentive for a first strike in a crisis increases in proportion to the difference in potential fatalities to the attacking nation between launching a first strike or waiting to respond in a second strike. In commenting on future strategic arms issues, Secretary of State Henry Kissinger expressed concern over the possibility "of a gap between the first strike and the second strike capability" of both sides "which would put a premium on striking first and, therefore, contribute to the danger of the outbreak of nuclear war."[18] Highly survivable forces deployed on both sides narrow this gap and diminish the danger that Kremlin leaders might contemplate initiating a nuclear attack.

No way to end a nuke war short of annihilation

Once our ICBMs became vulnerable, the President would have to launch them if he wished to preserve this component of the U.S. deterrent, since our land-based missiles could not "ride out" an attack—an uncomfortable and potentially risky situation. Under such time pressure,

This is crazy.

18. Press conference, January 22, 1974.

destruction still assured!

it is difficult to visualize effective use of the control and flexibility features of land-based missiles. Perhaps the benefits of being able to withhold the release of U.S. ICBMs for hours or perhaps days cannot be fully appreciated, given the imponderables associated with nuclear war. But it is apparent that the shorter the time needed to launch a system, the greater the danger that a false alarm or inadequately informed decision might lead to an inadvertent, unauthorized, or inappropriate missile firing. Furthermore, whatever deterrent advantages might remain from Kremlin fears of a U.S. launch on warning would seem to be outweighed by the disadvantages and disutilities of keeping vulnerable ICBMs in the U.S. strategic posture. It is unreliable for deterrent purposes to base missile survivability on warning, for the USSR would then have the option of negating U.S. warning systems. Because accurate MIRVs will eventually make hard silos soft, it would be wasteful as well as futile to build a new-generation ICBM or even to install MIRVs on the complete force of 1,000 Minuteman units. Indeed, such actions could actually make a Soviet counterforce strike more attractive by increasing the payoff of successfully destroying U.S. land-based missile sites in a preemptive attack.

Finally, it might be borne in mind that military posture characteristics can have political implications. If the United States were to retain an obviously vulnerable strategic component in its inventory, the Soviet leadership might simply threaten to knock out a large portion of these forces in a counterforce attack. American leaders might then lose confidence in the power of our deterrent, feel compelled to make concessions or counterthreats, or even consider instituting a preemptive attack. In the absence of visibly vulnerable U.S. forces, on the other hand, such contingencies, however illogical or remote, would be far less likely. Even a reduction in Minuteman force levels would lower the likelihood of threats or actual attacks against U.S. ICBMs. Obviously, the USSR would find it easier to destroy a small number of Minuteman sites than the existing force of 1,000 missiles. But if ICBMs represented only a minor fraction of the overall U.S. deterrent, the Soviet Union's incentive to preempt would be greatly diminished. Ultimately, if the United States eliminated all its land-based missiles, the problem of Minuteman vulnerability would be solved, for the Soviet Union would have no time-urgent targets to threaten with their MIRV-carrying ICBMs.

On a more fundamental level, the deliberate retention of vulnerable ICBMs could set a precedent that could adversely affect basic U.S.

strategic policy. For example, this precedent could be used to argue that U.S. leaders need not be concerned if either our bomber or submarine forces become substantially vulnerable. Persuasive analyses could probably be performed to highlight the difficulty of mounting coordinated counterforce attacks against such systems and to demonstrate the inhibiting effect of launch-on-warning options for strategic aircraft and SLBMs. Within limits, these arguments might be constructive in supporting the goal of maintaining a reliable deterrent. On the other hand, reliance on sheer size and warning as a substitute for securing survivability through more confident, durable, and stabilizing means would be risky and would reverse a fundamental precept that has shaped U.S. strategic nuclear policy for over fifteen years.

Diversified Deterrent

A number of analysts note that technological momentum, interservice rivalry, and domestic political considerations had more to do with the evolution of the triad of U.S. strategic forces than doctrine had. The doctrinal justification for the triad, it is claimed, was simply invented as a policy rationalization after the fact. In the future, it is argued, the United States should reevaluate the diversity dogma.[19] Some of these experts suggest that the United States might simply eliminate its land-based missile and bomber forces, since these systems will become difficult to maintain, will be costly to modernize, and will contribute less to the effectiveness of the nation's deterrent posture as they become increasingly less survivable. Submarine-based systems, on the other hand, will remain highly survivable and will provide more than enough retaliatory power to support U.S. strategic deterrent policies. It is often shown that, when the current conversion program is completed and the MIRV-equipped Poseidon missile is fully installed, the U.S. fleet of 41 submarines could deliver at least 2,500 warheads against the Soviet homeland, after taking reliability and other operational factors into account.

SEA-BASED DETERRENT POSTURE

The views expressed by proponents of a sea-based deterrent are backed by considerable logic and technical validity. Nevertheless, there

19. Dr. Herbert York, for example, argued that the triad derived from technological capabilities, interservice rivalry, and other "accidental" factors that have never been directly relevant to official strategic doctrine. (See *Arms Control Implications*, p. 98.)

is some concern that a unilateral elimination of U.S. land-based forces that resulted in a marked shift of the numerical strategic nuclear balance to the disadvantage of the United States might be inadvisable for diplomatic and foreign policy reasons. But strictly on the basis of the military requirements for a confident strategic deterrent, it would be unwise for the United States to rely exclusively on a single deterrent system. For one thing, if American planners were to retain submarine-based deterrent systems—the most survivable type of strategic system currently in the inventory—as our only force, uncertainty over the future relative safety of U.S. submarines could nonetheless introduce instabilities into the strategic relationship. If all U.S. nuclear forces were at sea, the Soviet Union could apply appreciably greater resources to antisubmarine technology and programs. Although it is difficult to conceive of Soviet planners reaching the conclusion that they could completely negate our sea-based force, it is certainly plausible that Kremlin analysts could produce credible computations suggesting that the USSR could negate a significant fraction of the American sea-based deterrent. These perceptions might not completely reflect reality, nor would they automatically make the Soviet Union willing to initiate a strategic exchange, but they could diminish the reliability of our deterrent and increase the chance that Soviet actions would lead to a breakdown in deterrence.

In addition, if America were to rely solely on submarine-based forces, uncertainties and doubts about the reliability of our deterrent might begin to plague U.S. leaders. After all, the prospect of substantial Soviet progress in ASW before the end of the decade cannot be completely ruled out, and even if technically appropriate counteractions were taken, American policymakers might begin to question the viability of our sea-based deterrent. Furthermore, submarine-based systems have less reliable command, control, and communication characteristics than land-based systems, and the accidental loss of a single American submarine or selective Soviet attacks against U.S. sea-based deterrent forces could have serious consequences if the United States relied completely on a submarine-based deterrent. Some analysts have also contended that a deterrent force limited to submarines only—the so-called blue water option—would permit "clean" counterforce wars to be fought at sea without collateral damage to populations. But this feature of submarine warfare may be undesirable, since it could weaken deterrence by making a nuclear conflict more likely.

RECONSIDERING THE TRIAD

Thus, there are substantive arguments in favor of diversity as a means of building a dependable deterrent posture; they are historically sound and remain justified for the design of a future U.S. strategic posture. Obviously, however, nothing is sacred about the triad—neither the number of different force types required nor the nature of each particular type. In principle, at least, by retaining a flexible interpretation of what constitutes a diversified deterrent, it might be possible to develop strategic force structures that would maintain the benefits of diversity without necessarily perpetuating the present triad. For example, the introduction of a new generation of submarines, such as the Trident, as a supplement to the Polaris-Poseidon fleet constitutes a form of diversity, since the characteristics of the two systems are somewhat different in range, speed, and quietness. Attempts to diversify a submarine-only posture could include locating groups of submarines in unusual areas to create a "mixed" force—such as operating Trident close to shore or possibly in the Great Lakes. Even so, such efforts would not be as effective or reliable in providing diversity as more traditional approaches that rely on totally different classes of systems. Other alternatives for maintaining diversity that depart from the traditional triad could include developing land-mobile or air-mobile ICBMs to supplement or replace fixed ICBMs, basing ballistic missiles on surface ships, or developing an ICBM-range cruise missile capable of being launched from submarines or surface ships. Interesting as some of these options may seem, when their survivability, cost-effectiveness, reliability, and contributions to overall strategic stability are examined more closely, none appear to be serious candidates for replacing or supplementing the three prongs of the present U.S. strategic posture.

Some analysts claim that the forward-based system maintained by the United States in the form of nuclear-capable tactical aircraft deployed in Western Europe and Asia and on aircraft carriers already represents a fourth arm of the U.S. deterrent. Many of these systems can reach targets in the Soviet Union, which is why the USSR demanded at the SALT I negotiations that such systems be considered "strategic." Nevertheless, apart from the alliance-related difficulties of accepting the Soviet argument, the low survivability of these forward-based systems, as well as their primary tactical and regional functions, suggests that they should not become an alternative to maintaining multiple long-range delivery systems—although they are useful as a backstop to the central U.S. strategic deterrent forces.

The preceding discussion suggests that the triad may still represent the most desirable approach to diversifying the U.S. strategic posture. Greater diversification than a triad, although possible, appears to be unnecessary at this time and could have undesirable cost and stability implications. As a practical matter, however, it will be neither technically simple nor inexpensive to retain a diversified and survivable triad during the coming decade. If this proves to be the case, a double deterrent, or diad, of invulnerable forces could suffice.

THE DIAD

The contention that a survivable diad would be preferable to a triad containing one highly vulnerable component is not self-evident and involves close choices between competing considerations. If applied literally, it would lead to the controversial proposal to phase out our ICBMs as they become vulnerable and to rely on a deterrent posture composed of SLBMs and bombers.[20] This posture would be more diverse and therefore more reliable than a dual deterrent composed of SLBMs and ICBMs, for example, since bombers would provide a unique hedge against what still remains the single most dangerous strategic threat to the United States—the possibility that the USSR might someday abrogate the ABM treaty and build a nationwide missile defense network that, together with Soviet ASW improvements, could render our sea-based ballistic missile force ineffective. By relying on SLBMs and bombers, the United States would eliminate the many dangers and disadvantages of maintaining vulnerable ICBMs—the increased risk of a Soviet counterforce MIRV strike, the possibility of launch-on-warning plans, and generally heightened instabilities in times of tension.

Yet it cannot be denied that the elimination of ICBMs would diminish the benefits of full diversity and, in some respects, weaken the credibility of our deterrent. The Soviet Union could, for example, focus its energies on finding offensive or defensive countermeasures to U.S. submarines and bombers. Moreover, if the United States unilaterally removed its ICBMs, Moscow might be motivated politically to attempt to exploit its

20. Quanbeck and Blechman concluded that "strategic stability would seem to require that land-based missiles be eliminated from the [U.S.] strategic force over the long term." (*Strategic Forces*, p. 68.)

monopoly in land-based missiles and its marked numerical advantage in ballistic missiles—an issue that raises a policy conflict to be discussed further below. One possible solution to this dilemma would be the negotiation of an agreement with the USSR to reduce and eventually eliminate fixed ICBMs on both sides. What makes ICBM bad is the others

In sum, the purpose of diversity is not simply to acquire overkill but ICBM to ensure a sufficient retaliatory capability against a wide variety of Soviet threats and attack strategies by giving each U.S. deterrent system a separate retaliatory capability and capitalizing on the connection among the various forces. A basic strategy of preserving a multiple and survivable strategic posture with redundant and reinforcing characteristics would enable the United States to preserve a confident deterrent in the face of technological changes, diplomatic demands, and crises. U.S. leaders would feel more secure regarding the credibility of America's deterrent, knowing that its viability was apparent to Moscow. This posture would also minimize the chance that Soviet officials might misperceive the reliability of our strategic forces or discern weaknesses in our capabilities that might permit the launching of attacks against certain components of our forces.

Flexible Strategic Options

As a result of the debate over what constitutes an assured retaliatory capability, American policymakers and experts alike are paying increased attention to the more basic issue of whether an assured destruction capability, however defined, is itself sufficient to satisfy U.S. policy objectives. This question is an old one and comes up periodically. During the Eisenhower years, the Air Force argued for counterforce and warfighting programs to supplement the massive retaliation doctrine, and in 1962 Defense Secretary McNamara flirted briefly with the controlled response doctrine. More recently, the Nixon administration sought to acquire greater flexibility for U.S. strategic forces.

Flexibility Defined

Strategic flexibility has many meanings but can be said to encompass those doctrines, plans, and force capabilities that permit strategic armaments to be employed in a variety of ways besides massive strikes against urban areas. This set of employment options runs the gamut from the

"surgical" application of one or two weapons against a selected target—
whether a single city or a nonurban target, such as nuclear storage sites,
military bases, or industrial facilities—to heavy counterforce attacks
against all of an opponent's deployed delivery systems. The doctrinal
justifications for flexibility are as varied as the options themselves, but,
in general, two major reasons are given in favor of such strategies—to
strengthen deterrence and to limit damage.

STRENGTHENING DETERRENCE

The arguments for flexibility as a means of enhancing nuclear deterrence center on the conviction that the capability to retaliate massively
against population centers does not represent a sufficiently reliable or
credible deterrent. Because the USSR has achieved a powerful and invulnerable strategic force at least comparable to that of the United
States in military effectiveness and political credibility, an American
countercity strike against the Soviet homeland would be virtually certain to bring a comparable response against the United States. Therefore, exercising the assured destruction option would be equivalent to
risking national suicide.

Most observers believe that the threat of assured destruction, supported by adequate retaliatory capabilities, will undoubtedly continue
to prevent a *massive* Soviet strategic attack against the United States
and, to a lesser extent, against our allies. But the effectiveness of an assured destruction strategy in deterring the USSR from launching *limited*
nuclear attacks against the United States or its allies—or threatening to
launch such attacks—has been seriously questioned. It is feared that
Kremlin leaders might decide that the United States would refrain from
responding to a limited attack with an assured destruction strike, because this would be certain to bring a Soviet countercity strike in return.
Accordingly, it is argued, there is a need to develop the ability to respond
in kind to limited nuclear attacks in order to dissuade the USSR from
initiating them. In this sense, the use of limited strategic force options
could enhance stability in crises.

Flexible strategic options are also justified as a means of giving greater
credence to the U.S. extended deterrence policy—that is, the American
commitment, notably, but not exclusively, to our allies in the North
Atlantic Treaty Organization (NATO), to initiate nuclear strikes if
needed to counter Soviet conventional aggression abroad. It is unlikely
in this era of nuclear parity and mutual assured destruction that the

United States would initiate a massive strategic strike in response to Soviet nonnuclear attacks in Western Europe. The limited and selective use of strategic forces, perhaps in conjunction with tactical nuclear strikes in the European theater, would be more believable. But this action in response to conventional aggression would inevitably introduce the risk of escalation to all-out strategic war in some future stage of the conflict if the Soviet Union did not cease its aggressive actions. Thus, it is claimed, Kremlin leaders would face both the prospect of continuing a limited strategic war with the United States and the possibility that the latter might choose to escalate the conflict to an all-out level (or that this might happen inadvertently), bringing devastation to the Soviet Union.

A final connection between strategic flexibility and deterrence is related to the development of counterforce, or warfighting, capabilities—an issue that raises the most extreme and controversial element of this entire matter. Proponents of flexibility suggest that an absolute level of assured destruction may not be sufficient to deter the Soviet Union and argue that the United States must also ensure that no unfavorable balance develops in the relative capability of both sides either to wage strategic warfare against each other's military forces or to inflict damage against urban-industrial targets. They claim that maintaining a superior, or at least comparable, warfighting capability vis-à-vis the Soviet Union would enhance strategic deterrence. The USSR would not be able to visualize gaining any military advantages by launching countermilitary strikes against the United States with the goal of reaching a position to dictate settlements or perhaps to "win" a nuclear exchange. Defense Secretary Schlesinger officially introduced such a concept in late 1973 when he argued that, in addition to maintaining a secure countercity retaliatory capability, the United States should seek "symmetry" with the USSR in the ability to launch selective strikes against military targets and avoid being placed in a relative position of inferiority "with regard to the ability to inflict major damage" on "military components."[21]

DAMAGE LIMITATION

The second reason for considering flexible strategic options is the desire to limit damage to the United States if strategic deterrence should fail. Because there is no guarantee that deterrence will operate successfully in all situations, particularly in the event of an irrational decision

21. News conference, November 30, 1973.

or accidental launching, it is argued that sheer prudence demands taking action to minimize nuclear damage in such circumstances. There are four ways of doing so: (1) sharply reducing the capabilities of both sides to inflict damage on each other, (2) constructing ABM defenses limited to either thin protection against small attacks or larger-scale defenses against major attacks, (3) attempting to obtain a counterforce capability that could reduce the Soviet Union's capability to inflict damage on the United States; and (4) developing flexible options for strategic forces that can limit the size and scope of a nuclear conflict.

The first approach is an impractical one at present, since neither side is likely to agree to major strategic arms reductions on its own, and SALT thus far shows no signs of leading to agreements involving major reductions. The second is forbidden by the ABM treaty, and for a variety of reasons ABMs provide no effective solution to the damage limitation problem. As for the third, it is virtually impossible for the United States to be able to substantially reduce the USSR's capability to inflict large-scale damage on the United States, given the relative invulnerability of Soviet submarine-based forces and the enormous destructive potential of even a small number of warheads delivered against cities. Consequently, acquiring flexible options for strategic forces may offer the most practical approach to damage limitation in the near term.

If the USSR restricted the size of any attack it might launch against the United States—either an initial attack or a response to a U.S. strike —the damage to our nation could be greatly reduced. The ability of the United States to limit its strategic attacks against the Soviet Union, while retaining in reserve an assured destruction capability, would help persuade Soviet leaders to exercise restraint or else risk escalation to all-out strategic war. Developing flexible strategic capabilities for U.S. forces would also, in principle, allow time for intrawar communication to take place between Washington and Moscow in order to limit or terminate a bilateral nuclear exchange before full escalation to attacks against cities occurred. This could be especially valuable in the case of an inadvertent or accidental nuclear strike by a third party against either the United States or the USSR.

TARGETING AND OTHER CONSIDERATIONS

In order to put the question of flexible options in perspective, a number of important points related to U.S. strategic capabilities and doctrines should be borne in mind. To begin with, it is incorrect to claim that U.S. strategic forces are now targeted only against urban areas.

During the 1960s, even as Secretary McNamara moved toward an assured destruction policy, a countercity damage requirement was not the sole basis for determining the size, nature, and use of U.S. strategic forces. There was a secondary interest in acquiring weapons for damage-limiting purposes as well. Totally apart from weapons levels, many non-city employment options were included in the Single Integrated Operations Plan (SIOP), which prescribes precise patterns for the timing and character of actual nuclear attacks involving all U.S. forces.[22] These targeting options were developed partly because conservative planning for assured destruction tended to yield excess forces, which could then be used for damage-limiting purposes, and partly because of deliberate decisions to provide city-avoidance choices. Under the Nixon administration, flexible strategic options were further refined and incorporated into U.S. targeting plans. In early 1974, for example, Defense Secretary Schlesinger announced that, through approved changes in targeting plans, the United States was acquiring options to launch its strategic weapons "against different sets of targets" with silos as well as other military targets "among the possibilities."[23]

Second, improvements in command, control, and communication, as well as in targeting procedures, are crucial in the development of flexible strategic capabilities. The United States, for example, has upgraded the retargeting capability of its ICBM force through the Command Data Buffer program, thereby permitting a larger number of preselected targets to be stored in an ICBM system and facilitating rapid changing of targets.[24] In addition, the United States is improving the reliability of the National Command Authority system and related reconnaissance and communications capabilities in order to quickly provide the President with reliable information on the cause and consequences of nuclear attacks against the United States, to provide him effective control over U.S. strategic forces in such a situation, and to enable him to communicate with Soviet leaders during crises. Among the programs being pur-

22. For a discussion of the SIOP and revisions in targeting made during the early 1960s, see Seymour M. Hersh, "The President and the Plumbers: A Look at Two Security Questions," *New York Times Magazine*, December 9, 1973, p. 1.

23. Remarks made at the Overseas Writers Association Luncheon, Washington, D.C., January 10, 1974.

24. For information on the Command Data Buffer, see *Department of Defense Appropriations for 1972*, Hearings before the Defense Subcommittee of the House Committee on Appropriations, 92 Cong. 1 sess. (1971), pt. 5, p. 1139; and "Statement of Secretary of Defense Elliot L. Richardson before the House Armed Services Committee on the FY 1974 Defense Budget and FY 1974–1978 Program" (1973, processed).

sued are the satellite warning system and the airborne command post. Some command and control programs are of course essential for the maintenance of a dependable assured destruction capability and need not be undertaken in specific support of flexibility.

Third, certain characteristics of specific strategic weapons systems, as well as the overall size and nature of our deterrent posture, can have an important bearing on the ability of U.S. strategic forces to operate flexibly. For the past fifteen years, U.S. strategic forces have been structured to avoid the necessity for rapid firing, to be able to withstand attacks, and to delay responses. Submarines contribute to the objective of delaying responses, ICBMs are particularly suited for close control, and aircraft can be placed on high alert as warranted by crisis situations. In many respects, these features of strategic systems support most flexibility objectives better than the number of delivery systems does. On the question of the implications of flexible options for future procurement decisions and force-level goals, Secretary Schlesinger stressed the need "to distinguish between [targeting] doctrine . . . and the sizing of our forces" and stated that the United States would be able to "introduce greater flexibility and selectivity without major hard-ware acquisition."[25] Yet increases in the number of deliverable warheads and the upgrading of payload capabilities of systems, if not increases in the number of launch vehicles themselves, could be required to cover the target system associated with a comprehensive flexibility policy.

Finally, it should be emphasized that flexible options and counterforce capabilities are unrelated strategic concepts. Qualitative improvements in the accuracies and yields of missile warheads, for example, could be justified as contributing to a greater capability for carrying out limited and selective strikes with strategic forces. However, given the wide spectrum of potential targets, situations, and options, a policy of flexibility *need not* include programs and strategies specifically designed to improve missile accuracies or yields in order to provide either a kill capability against hardened ICBM sites or any forces aimed at destroying an opponent's strategic systems.

Feasibility and Desirability of Flexible Options

Planned improvements will continue to broaden the range of flexible capabilities of U.S. strategic forces. The relevant policy question, therefore, is whether flexibility should be furthered and, if so, whether the

25. News conference, January 24, 1974.

United States has gone far enough—or perhaps too far—in acquiring flexible strategic options.

MAJOR COUNTERMILITARY STRIKES

In deciding on the degree and kind of flexibility to build into our strategic forces, it should be recognized at the outset that it is difficult to design weapon systems or to develop targeting doctrines that, as a practical matter, are highly reliable in avoiding substantial civilian fatalities in the event strategic nuclear weapons are used.[26] Extensive nuclear attacks of the type geared to destroy land-based missile or bomber forces, for instance, would inevitably cause between 5 million and 15 million population fatalities—so-called collateral damage. Even optimistic projections based on missile accuracy improvements and the acquisition of "clean" nuclear bombs for "surgical" strikes would not significantly diminish this figure, because thousands of equivalent megatons of warheads would have to impact on each side's land-based systems in any serious counterforce strike, and major consequences due to fallout could not be avoided. Although substantially fewer fatalities would result from heavy counterforce strikes than from those associated with direct attacks against cities, their projected level is high enough to cast doubt on the rationale that the use of such targeting options could provide realistic damage limitation.

Apart from the fatalities caused by mutual counterforce exchanges, the side receiving such attacks might misperceive the intent of the attacker, believe that an antipopulation strike had been launched, and retaliate against cities. Indeed, uncertainties regarding any nuclear exchange and the extent of collateral population damage raise serious doubts about whether either side would have the incentive or the ability to continue launching counterforce strikes during a strategic war. Within hours after the United States and the USSR initiated attacks aimed at destroying military forces, few attractive targets would remain. If the United States acquires a hard-target kill potential, there would be little reason for the USSR to refrain from launching ICBMs that might soon be destroyed in a retaliatory strike. After absorbing a Soviet counterforce strike, therefore, the United States might find itself mounting responsive attacks against empty silos whose missiles had either been fired in an initial strike or been launched on warning in response to the U.S.

26. See Wolfgang K. H. Panofsky, "The Mutual Hostage Relationship between America and Russia," *Foreign Affairs*, vol. 52 (October 1973), pp. 109–18.

retaliatory attack. Bombers on both sides that had not been destroyed on the ground in a first wave of strikes would be airborne and obviously invulnerable to subsequent counterforce attacks. If strategic air bases were put out of commission, airborne bombers could attempt to find alternative basing; if this approach failed or were dismissed on a policy level, bombers would undoubtedly fly toward targets in the opponent's homeland and inflict a high level of damage. Missile-firing submarines in port and submarine support facilities themselves could obviously be destroyed by counterforce attacks. Yet all Soviet and American submarines at sea with their substantial SLBM inventories would survive and remain free to deliver retaliatory strikes for a considerable period. While it is possible to visualize long strategic wars of attrition at sea, no persuasive analyses have yet been produced to demonstrate the purpose, progression, or outcome of extended counterforce exchanges at sea or on land.

Whether or not it might prove possible through countermilitary strikes to diminish the USSR's ability to use certain deployed strategic forces in antipopulation strikes against the United States, the question is whether an attempt to develop warfighting capabilities for this purpose is necessary. As indicated earlier, it is doubtful whether relative differences in damage-inflicting capabilities have any bearing on the propensity of the Soviet Union to run nuclear risks as long as the United States maintains an absolute assured destruction capability that is extremely high—for example, 20–25 percent immediate population fatalities, the figure traditionally used. If U.S. forces are capable of inflicting this degree of retaliation, no danger should attend incremental imbalances in damage-inflicting potential. In any case, even this issue may be moot, since conservatively designed retaliatory forces provide a U.S. assured destruction capability well above the "minimum" level. As a final observation, it may be significant to note that the more invulnerable each side's forces become as the United States and the USSR seek to retain highly survivable strategic weapons—a sensible course of action to pursue under *any* targeting doctrine—the less possible it will be for either nation to launch effective counterforce strikes for damage-limiting purposes.

LIMITED NUCLEAR EXCHANGES

Although it is virtually impossible to attempt to prevent large-scale counterforce attacks from causing substantial population damage, it would be possible in a technical sense to develop new warheads and control mechanisms that would permit *limited* strategic strikes to be launched against isolated nonurban targets without necessarily causing major civilian casualties. The major difficulty in this case, however, would be the uncertain progression of such attacks and not the collateral damage of the initial attacks themselves. Once the nuclear threshold is passed, both countries enter the unknown realm of strategic war. In this situation, it would be unwise to assume that leaders would receive the proper information and would take action in theoretically preferable ways. It is doubtful that either U.S. or Soviet leaders would find it easy to exercise restraint while nuclear weapons were landing in their respective countries or even to sustain a strategy of logical tit-for-tat strikes. Compounding the problem is the questionable utility of continuing to strike at nonurban targets during a strategic war for such vague reasons as attempting to coerce the other side, demonstrating resolve, or seeking to gain the upper hand psychologically. Even if one side attempted to follow a restrained strategy, the target systems in each nation would not be identical nor would the capabilities for launching limited strikes be comparable. Thus, if one side raised the stakes—whether through a deliberate policy decision, sheer miscalculation, or inadequate options —a process of escalation would begin that could lead to an all-out nuclear exchange. Finally, the prospect of warheads inadvertently landing on unintended urban targets might well threaten the entire effort to keep a nuclear war under control.

Of particular concern in deciding whether the United States should stress a policy of limited nuclear strike options is the question of Soviet doctrine and forces. As implied, if the Soviet Union is either unwilling or unable to adopt a comparable policy, the ability of the United States to follow a successful limited strategic escalation approach would be undercut. Although official Soviet doctrine calls for fighting nuclear wars and prevailing in a strategic exchange in the event deterrence fails, Kremlin spokesmen have traditionally eschewed the concept of keeping a nuclear war limited. This was reflected over a decade ago in Moscow's reactions to McNamara's "no-cities" speech when the Soviet Union accused the United States of attempting to legitimize nuclear war and of pursuing a provocative strategy. Recent Soviet articles responded to Secretary Schlesinger's discussions of flexible targeting by harking back to 1962 and questioning the feasibility of limited nuclear war as well as the compatibility of the "new" U.S. policy with the allegedly shared goal of mutual deterrence.[27] In addition, the relatively large size of Soviet warheads, the lag in Soviet accuracy improvements compared with U.S. capabilities in this field, and other qualitative features of Soviet strategic forces suggest that the USSR's technical capacity for flexibility may remain inferior to that of the United States.

In any of the possible strategic war situations along the flexibility scale, both the United States and the USSR would retain an assured destruction potential, and escalation to this level would be highly likely if not inevitable—whatever policy the United States pursues. Although the fear of escalation might create conditions for restraint, it is improbable that announced targeting changes or doctrinal decisions could fully persuade one side that the other side actually intended to exercise restraint. Perhaps the fear of escalation will be so strong that leaders in Moscow and Washington will simply refrain from launching limited strikes—although there is no guarantee that this will in fact be the case. In any event, the low probability that limited exchanges will occur, combined with the practical problems involved in executing such strategic options to achieve meaningful objectives, certainly leads to serious skepticism concerning the feasibility of acquiring greater flexibility or of even preserving current capabilities.

DETERRENCE AND STABILITY

Although one of the major arguments for flexibility is that it can strengthen deterrence by providing the ability to respond in kind, an equally persuasive case can be made that flexibility could weaken deterrence. By making limited strategic wars seem possible, flexibility might make the use of strategic nuclear weapons more likely. If Soviet leaders believed that the United States would simply respond to their limited strategic attacks with limited retaliatory attacks, it might seem less dangerous for the Soviet Union to initiate such limited attacks. But if U.S. doctrine made it probable that limited attacks could lead to massive retaliatory strikes, Soviet leaders might be inhibited from initiating limited strikes—even though there would be the possibility that the United States might take no retaliatory actions at all.

Similarly, if American leaders are given options for the use of strategic

27. G. A. Trofimenko, "The USSR and the U.S.: Peaceful Coexistence as the Norm of Mutual Relations," *Ekonomika, Politika, and Ideologiya*, January 11, 1974 (Foreign Broadcast Information Service, *Daily Report: Soviet Union*, February 12, 1974), pp. B1–B13.

forces in limited ways and come to believe that such efforts would not lead to all-out nuclear exchanges and massive damage to the United States, they might be more prone to use our strategic nuclear forces for such purposes. Bureaucratic pressures would operate more effectively for the use of strategic forces if flexible options were available, while a restricted list of strategic alternatives that would inevitably lead to total escalation would strengthen inhibitions against *any* use of nuclear force. Moreover, if flexible options resulted in the limited use of nuclear weapons, there would be no assurance of keeping the strategic war limited. Thus, the availability of flexible strategic options not only might contribute to a breakdown in deterrence but might fail to contribute to damage limitation in the event of a nuclear exchange.

The foregoing analysis has dealt with certain problems associated with flexibility in general, but, to the extent that *counterforce* strategies leading to the acquisition of hard-target kill capabilities are involved, particularly serious problems could arise. The potentially adverse consequences for mutual stability and arms limitations of acquiring a hard-target kill capability have been touched on earlier and will be dealt with in some detail in chapter 6. Suffice it to say at this point that direct threats to the survivability of an opponent's fixed ICBM force can increase the likelihood of a strategic exchange during a tense situation, stimulate the strategic arms competition, and complicate efforts to negotiate further SALT accords as the United States and the USSR seek to maintain a viable retaliatory capability.

The potentially destabilizing effects of a counterforce strategy cannot be eliminated either by announcing a doctrine that denies any intention of acquiring capabilities to destroy the bulk of an adversary's strategic forces or by asserting that it is impossible to obtain an effective first-strike capability. From an opponent's perspective, for example, there is no distinction between a retaliatory hard-target kill capability for second-strike purposes and the ability to *initiate* an attack against ICBMs. Even though an attack against ICBMs could not prevent a retaliatory strike with surviving sea-based missiles, policymakers have a propensity for "worst-case" planning that makes it doubtful that either nation would ignore attempts by the other to obtain improved counterforce capabilities—for fear that more meaningful military advantages might follow or simply to deter any attempt to exploit partial force vulnerabilities for political if not military purposes. The United States has expressed serious concern over the potential counterforce threat of Soviet MIRV-equipped missiles, and there is no reason to assume that Kremlin leaders would ignore a comparable American threat. For the United States to dismiss as "the Kremlin's problem" any threat to the USSR's deterrent that might be caused by an American counterforce strategy is to ignore the validity of mutual stability as a vital element of our strategic arms policy approach.

The adoption of a policy involving flexible options can have undesirable effects on the management of strategic weapons procurements and budgets. Once any form of flexibility begins to receive prominence, it will be difficult for policymakers to prevent this strategy from leading to increased force levels or more accurate systems. Efforts to draw the line between limited response and counterforce requirements may, as suggested, prove to be extremely difficult in practice, given the many detailed technical dimensions of military development programs that are unknown to, or cannot be controlled by, policy-level officials. The assured destruction policy also creates justifications for additional force procurements, but it has a built-in self-limitation due to the saturation effect of attacks against cities. Flexibility requirements, on the other hand, are far less precise and can remain rather open-ended. This is apparently one of the reasons why Secretary McNamara reversed the emphasis placed on the controlled response option in the early 1960s.[28]

As a final point, America's NATO allies are obviously uncomfortable with a pure assured destruction strategy in an era of parity and have welcomed flexible options that permit the United States to credibly threaten to initiate strategic nuclear strikes in response to conventional aggression in Europe. But most West European leaders apparently still believe that an assured retaliatory policy should remain the basis of the U.S. commitment. Indeed, some NATO analysts fear that an undue emphasis on flexible strategic options could disassociate U.S. strategic forces from the defense of Europe and ultimately weaken the deterrent effect of America's nuclear arsenal.[29]

With respect to the People's Republic of China, it seems neither necessary nor desirable for the United States to deliberately decide to acquire

28. See chapter 2 for reference to assured destruction as a management tool. Today, as in the early 1960s, many experts fear that an emphasis on flexibility will provide the military with a blank check for new weapons.

29. For a useful discussion of Western European views on U.S. nuclear strategy in the present era of parity, see Walter Slocombe, "The Political Implications of Strategic Parity," Adelphi Papers no. 77 (London: Institute for Strategic Studies, 1971).

counterforce options of any kind against the small Chinese strategic force, although some flexible options could be useful. The threat of assured destruction, as noted, would be more than sufficient to deter the Chinese from taking any provocative action with their nuclear forces and to inhibit them from mounting major conventional aggression beyond their borders. Of course, since the Chinese nuclear forces are small and deployed in relatively vulnerable modes, the United States may not be able to avoid maintaining some offensive counterforce capability against China for many years. But the active pursuit of such capabilities could increase the danger of nuclear war and the risk of a breakdown in the gradual improvement of U.S.-Chinese relations.

Policy Directions

It would seem unwise to totally reject the concept of flexibility, despite its complexities and inherent dangers. The possible benefits of flexible strategic options in enhancing deterrence and in potentially limiting damage if deterrence fails must be balanced against such possible disadvantages as an increased risk that strategic weapons might be used and the creation of instabilities in the nuclear balance with no guarantee that damage could be limited.

One way to rectify these countervailing tendencies would be to accept the proposition that our deterrent strategy rests on the threat of assured destruction and to recognize that the United States cannot remove the Soviet Union's assured destruction capability against us. Thus, flexibility could be seen simply and solely as providing prudent supplements to the assured destruction doctrine and could be pursued only as a means of providing a range of options that might have some insurance value in a deterrence or damaging-limiting sense but would not jeopardize deterrence itself. This would require further command and control improvements, greater reliability in weapons and communications systems, and changes in targeting plans and programs. It would not necessitate increased force levels or major changes in current strategic programs.

As part of this policy, the United States should forestall the potential instabilities of a counterforce strategy by refraining from pursuing projects that, through a combination of yield and accuracy improvements, could provide our missile warheads with a hard-target kill capability. It must be recognized that the Soviet Union might acquire a hard-target kill capability with its ICBM force, which could give the USSR a unilateral advantage in terms of strikes against these military targets. This is a crucial issue, and many observers believe that any American policy that deliberately eschewed a comparable U.S. program would be highly questionable. But it should be emphasized that the United States *need not respond in kind* to such a Soviet capability, should it materialize, in order to maintain a reliable deterrent posture. In structuring a response to a potential Soviet counterforce threat, the United States need only be guided by the goal of maintaining an adequate retaliatory force and, as a result, protect its fixed ICBMs, replace them with mobile systems, or eliminate them entirely, which might eventually prove to be the best course. Elimination of the targets most seriously threatened by Soviet counterforce improvements would in turn remove the fear of this threat, the necessity for a comparable U.S. capability, and the instability of a situation in which both sides have vulnerable ICBMs. Indeed, it can be argued that the deployment of American ICBMs with a hard-target kill capability, as called for under a counterforce symmetry strategy, would make the least sense on stability grounds—since it would increase the Soviet Union's incentive to launch a preemptive strike against our land-based missiles.

Moreover, there would be an adequate range of flexible strategic options available under the proposed policy, even without a hard-target kill capability. The President would not be forced to launch a massive anti-population response to a selective Soviet strike, but would be in a position to reply with strikes against a variety of soft military installations and could also destroy a small number of hard Soviet targets with existing U.S. warheads. Even the reduction or removal of fixed ICBMs would not substantially diminish the flexibility of U.S. forces, since the reliability and controllability of SLBM systems will be greatly improved by the time our land-based missiles become seriously endangered. Although the proposed approach might not close all loopholes, any marginal losses in deterrence that might be associated with a lack of perfect symmetry would probably be heavily outweighed by the gains in strategic stability and nuclear deterrence itself if a national decision to reject counterforce options were made.

Finally, in discussing strategic posture decisions publicly and within the executive branch itself, U.S. leaders should be wary of overstating the importance or the feasibility of flexibility. They should allude to this option as a prudent addition to our assured destruction capability and doctrine, stressing defensive and deterrent benefits. Defense Secretary Schlesinger did so, for example, when he told the House Armed Services Committee that assured destruction was "an essential ingredient" of U.S. deterrent strategy and that the purpose of improved flexibility was to "strengthen deterrence" by offering options to respond to less-than-massive Soviet attacks.[30]

The Numerical Balance of Forces

Over the years, much attention has been given to the relative numerical strength of U.S. and Soviet strategic forces. Numerical parameters, or so-called static measures, may or may not be related to the military effectiveness of strategic forces, but they can nevertheless influence the political and psychological dimensions of strategic deterrence and the effect of strategic power on international affairs. The question of the relevance of numerical comparisons is a central element in the present U.S. nuclear policy debate.

Significance of Static Comparisons

Strategic parity is an elusive concept, difficult to define and uncertain in its implications. But the Soviet Union's attainment of nuclear equality with the United States and the codification of this strategic relationship under the SALT accords of 1972 and the Vladivostok guidelines of 1974 are unprecedented political events with potential significance for U.S. security that must be carefully considered. In particular, the United States must decide what weight to give to the numerical balance of forces in planning its strategic posture over the coming years, particularly if the USSR gains a significant numerical advantage.

Any discussion of this question should begin by making a distinction between "rational" strategic analysis and what actually motivates the policy decisions of U.S. and Soviet leaders, influences weapon and budget choices within each nation, and affects the perceptions, attitudes, and reactions of other countries regarding the superpower strategic relationship. Clearly, as long as both the United States and the USSR maintain their assured destruction capabilities, and regardless of addi-

30. Cited by Michael Getler, *Washington Post*, February 2, 1974.

tional military options judged necessary for either deterrence or damage-limiting purposes, variations in the numerical balance *ought* to have no significance. As Paul Warnke, former assistant defense secretary, said, "Where a numerical advantage . . . is without military meaning, it should have no political potential."[31]

As a practical matter, for over two decades the numerical balance between the United States and the Soviet Union has shaped strategic force decisions on both sides. Historical analyses demonstrate that the relative balance has actually affected diplomatic relations and behavior in crises, but generalizations to guide future U.S. decisions cannot be derived easily, given all the variables involved. On a theoretical level, many analysts argue rather persuasively that the strategic balance is not sensitive to numerical variations and that even significant alterations that would be to our disadvantage could not be translated by the USSR into military or political gains. One expert has observed that "mutual deterrence has deprived nuclear weapons of any coercive utility, rendered strategic 'superiority' both a worthless instrument of foreign policy and a false guarantee of national security, and, in the process, made numerical comparisons of forces altogether useless as a means of measuring relative strategic power."[32]

Many writers emphasize that the state of the strategic balance is only one factor influencing the behavior of nations. At best, the strategic balance is a factor simply because the mere possession of nuclear weapons and the risk that these weapons might be used influence the behavior of leaders. But this fear of nuclear war, it is contended, is essentially unaffected by estimates of fatality levels or by detailed assessments of the numerical balance. Interests, commitments, conventional capabilities, and the overall international political climate, they claim, dominate events. Thus, in a climate of détente, strategic weapons issues and U.S.-Soviet nuclear force comparisons are less significant for peacetime diplomacy or crisis management than in a situation of intense and open political, economic, or conventional military conflict. Similarly, the at-

31. Statement of Paul C. Warnke, former assistant secretary of defense for international security affairs, *National Security Policy and the Changing World Power Alignment*, Hearing-Symposium before the Subcommittee on National Security Policy and Scientific Developments of the House Committee on Foreign Affairs, 92 Cong. 2 sess. (1972), p. 75.

32. Benjamin S. Lambeth, "Deterrence in the MIRV Era," *World Politics*, vol. 24 (January 1972), p. 240. See also Joseph I. Coffey, *Strategic Power and National Security* (University of Pittsburgh Press, 1972).

titudes of Western European nations toward U.S. nuclear guarantees and the effect of the U.S.-Soviet balance on these guarantees, it is argued, often are determined more by the character of our overall political and economic relations with Western Europe than by narrow analyses of the strategic balance itself.

Without entirely discounting the merits of the foregoing position, however, it may be unrealistic to dismiss the significance of numerical comparisons in designing U.S. strategic forces. Even if American leaders were to believe that such comparisons were meaningless, the Soviet attitude toward this question suggests that it would be unwise to completely reject these comparisons. After all, the United States must attempt to deter and to deal with the USSR in terms that the Kremlin understands and finds meaningful. It is difficult to imagine any rational Soviet leader deliberately risking the destruction of even a few major Russian cities by directly testing our deterrent, regardless of a numerical nuclear advantage. Furthermore, few if any Kremlinologists suggest that the USSR might be prone to take risky military actions against the West as a result of Moscow's attainment of nuclear parity or possibly of marginal superiority. Some experts contend that Soviet leaders might be more inclined to pursue a policy of détente *because* the USSR has reached a secure strategic position.

On the other hand, there is a chance that the USSR might see the changed nuclear balance as enabling it to pursue an aggressive foreign policy. The Soviet Union traditionally has viewed military power more politically than the United States, and throughout the fifties and sixties Kremlin leaders feared our overwhelmingly superior force—a fear that seemed justified in Soviet eyes by the experience of the Cuban missile crisis in 1962. It is possible, therefore, that the loss of U.S. strategic superiority, measured in numerical terms, could have unsettling effects on our ability to bargain with the Soviet Union during a major crisis and could increase the propensity of Soviet leaders to take political initiatives counter to American interests. Momentum is on Moscow's side, and the Soviet Union's international stature has already risen with its attainment of strategic parity. Regardless of the initial motivation behind Moscow's missile buildup, Soviet leaders might see psychological and political leverage to be derived from the new strategic relationship. As one prominent analyst warned, "Bargaining . . . in the setting of relative parity would test to a far greater extent than ever before the psychological and political staying power of the two systems [and] the erosion of American superiority . . . could have the effect of widening the margins of Soviet initiatives."[33]

If a superpower confrontation occurred, U.S. leaders might be more reluctant to act with certainty if they believed that Kremlin officials saw the strategic balance as favoring the Soviet Union. Even if American leaders were confident that Soviet efforts to exploit the nuclear balance would ultimately fail, it would still be in the interest of the United States to deter Soviet actions that might trigger a severe crisis between the two nations involving the risk of nuclear escalation. It is also possible that any weakening of U.S. resolve because of the current strategic balance could strengthen Moscow's ability to achieve its objectives diplomatically. Among other results, such trends could lead to excessive concessions at the negotiating table—whether involving SALT, mutual and balanced force reductions, or even trade and economic questions.

Finally, how other nations regard the international prestige, political power, and military might of the United States in the years ahead will undoubtedly continue to be affected to a considerable degree by our strategic nuclear position and, more particularly, by the numerical force balance between the United States and the Soviet Union. The loss of U.S. strategic superiority, while accepted as an inevitable and not necessarily damaging state of affairs, has already caused our allies concern over the reliability of our deterrent in protecting their interests. An obvious shift to U.S. inferiority would only exacerbate these fears and might ultimately increase the likelihood of independent allied security policies leading to further nuclear weapons proliferation.

Guidelines for Decisions

Any attempt to draw precise conclusions regarding the role of the numerical balance in formulating U.S. strategic arms policies is admittedly difficult. On the one hand, to deny the importance of static measures in the world of international politics is to refuse to recognize reality and to ignore the importance of political and subjective factors in the effective operation of nuclear deterrence and strategic forces. On the other hand, it would be imprudent and unprofitable for the United States to overemphasize the significance of numerical factors. The United

33. Zbigniew Brzezinski, "How the Cold War Was Played," *Foreign Affairs,* vol. 51 (October 1972), p. 206.

States cannot as a practical matter regain overall strategic superiority, given the size of the Soviet Union's strategic forces and its apparent determination never again to take second place, and attempting to do so would be both costly and potentially destabilizing.

As a middle course, the United States might seek to maintain overall numerical equality with the USSR. Whether preserved through unilateral actions or within the framework of arms limitation accords, basic parity is probably the most stable situation attainable in terms of bilateral relations, international reactions, and domestic pressures. Unfortunately, there are no objective rules for deciding whether the numerical balance has shifted against the United States to the point where risks might be intolerably increased or for estimating the countermeasures that might be needed to respond to Soviet strategic actions. Indeed, the means of measuring the static strength of strategic forces is itself vague and variable. In a press conference in late 1973, after SALT II had been under way for over a year, Secretary of State Kissinger indicated that, while the goal of "total equality" made sense, the precise meaning of this goal was not apparent. Kissinger asked, for example, whether "total equality" would be measured in terms of throw-weight, warheads, or "comparative numbers of missiles or bombers in opposing arsenals."[34]

THREE STATIC MEASURES

Despite the difficulties outlined above, it is possible to approach the problem of strategic parity on a systematic basis. To begin with, offensive power has generally been given more attention than defensive power, and this will undoubtedly remain the case in the future because of the SALT ABM treaty. Offensive capabilities can, of course, be assessed in many ways. Perhaps the most prominent static index of strategic force strength is the number of deployed delivery vehicles or launchers. This is politically understandable, since missiles and aircraft are visible and verifiable items capable of being easily appreciated by national leaders and by the public at large. Militarily, the number of launchers provides the basis for striking power and the potential for qualitative improvements but is not as important as survivability, penetrability, accuracy, payload capacity, and other characteristics of a strategic force. In many cases, comparisons can be made with respect to specific categories of launchers, such as the ICBM balance between the

34. Cited by Murrey Marder, *Washington Post*, December 23, 1973.

United States and the USSR. For the most part, however, a launcher comparison on an aggregate level is generally considered to be the simplest political index of "superiority" or "inferiority"—terms that may have little military significance but have become part of the strategic lexicon.

A second numerical index, more sophisticated than launcher counts, is the number of nuclear warheads deployed on each side's strategic forces. This measure draws the attention of many analysts, principally because the number of warheads delivered against urban-industrial targets correlates well with assured destruction capabilities—the main mission of strategic forces. During the sixties, Secretary McNamara often claimed that the number of warheads represents the least misleading static measure of the relative strength of U.S. and Soviet strategic forces. Bombers have always carried multiple weapons in the form of bombs and air-to-surface missiles, but with the introduction of MIRVs to missile forces the number of warheads has had increased importance as a static index during the past few years. In analyzing the question of warheads, some experts have made distinctions between the types of missiles that might carry MIRVs, such as SLBMs or ICBMs, and have attempted to highlight the specific characteristics of warheads on both sides—thus introducing a degree of refinement into warhead comparisons. Despite the significance of warhead indices, it is difficult to verify the precise number of warheads deployed by each side; if technological comparability is assumed, the United States and the USSR could eventually match each other in the number of warheads deployed on equivalent launcher types. This suggests that, as a practical matter, launcher comparisons may remain more useful than warheads as a measure of strength.

A third numerical index, related to the number of launchers and warheads, is the payload, or throw-weight, associated with a nation's strategic posture. Whether aggregated or calculated by system type, throw-weight is usually measured in thousands of pounds of carrying capacity of strategic delivery vehicles. This capacity is directly related to the yield of nuclear weapons carried by a strategic force and correlates with the damage potential of a strategic force against cities as well as military targets. Payload is sometimes expressed in equivalent megatonnage (EMT), a more precise measure of the ability of a nuclear weapon to destroy targets. All other factors aside, the more payload a force can deliver, the more destructive potential it gains and the more warheads it can carry. The actual military effectiveness of a strategic force, however, remains dependent on qualitative features such as accuracy, survivability, and the sophistication of MIRV-related technologies.

The three most significant static measures—the number of delivery vehicles, the number of warheads, and the payload—can provide guidelines for future decisions affecting our force posture and the U.S. position during the SALT negotiations. If the Vladivostok agreement becomes a permanent accord, it will codify U.S.-Soviet equality in total numbers of strategic launchers and in levels of MIRV-carrying missile systems. Within these constraints, the United States will hold a numerical advantage in warheads ·and bombers, while the Soviet Union will lead in long-range land- and sea-based missiles. Although the USSR's missile throw-weight is greater than that of the United States, our accuracies are superior, and America's bomber superiority brings the total payload capacity of both nations' strategic forces into approximate equivalence. As the USSR deploys MIRVs on its ICBMs, the U.S. warhead edge could begin to be narrowed by the end of the decade, and the Soviet Union could widen its missile throw-weight advantage still further through qualitative improvements. On the other hand, before that time, the United States will undoubtedly seek to negotiate an additional SALT measure that establishes a more durable and equitable balance between U.S. and Soviet strategic capabilities. Whether through negotiated accords or unilateral actions, however, U.S. policy at the very least should seek to avoid inferiority in the total number of intercontinental strategic launchers and, preferably, to prevent the USSR from gaining a lead in any two of the static indices. It might also be possible to incorporate the three indices into a single composite measure of strategic strength—perhaps the sum of launcher numbers, warhead numbers, and throw-weight—and set as a U.S. goal the maintenance of overall equality based on this combined figure of merit.

Whatever approach is used to maintain parity, sensitivity to the significance of numerical relationships should not be permitted to dominate strategic planning. Cost-effectiveness and performance factors consistent with military requirements should continue to dictate major weapon requirements, and tight controls should be placed over programs in order to prevent major arms procurements with questionable military value or dubious technical features from being undertaken in the name of numerical equality. In the final analysis, a prudent and practical concern over the static balance may not add requirements to programmed U.S. strategic forces, since conservative military planning can itself create strategic force requirements that automatically satisfy numerical criteria. In any case, under no circumstance should the United States procure strategic weapons *primarily* for numerical balance reasons—whether as "bargaining chips" for SALT negotiations or on broader foreign policy grounds—nor should American leaders overstate the significance of shifts in the U.S.-Soviet nuclear relationship or the danger that Moscow might be able to exploit a marginal strategic advantage.

As a final point, it is important to recognize that there can be conflicts between decisions related to the strategic characteristics of our deterrent posture measured in military terms and decisions regarding the requirements for numerical equality. When these conflicts occur, the goal of maintaining a confident and stabilizing strategic posture should, to the extent possible, be given more weight than "force matching." An example of such a conflict is when the gains of phasing out highly vulnerable ICBM systems in order to preserve a reliable deterrent posture by avoiding crisis instabilities must be balanced against the possibility that a unilateral reduction of ICBMs might place the United States in a numerically unfavorable strategic position. In this case, if U.S. ICBMs clearly become endangered and mutual ICBM reductions cannot be negotiated, American leaders should plan to eliminate all of our ICBMs unilaterally—on the grounds that the disadvantages of conceding to the USSR a monopoly in ICBMs and greater numerical superiority are outweighed by the gain of greater deterrent stability associated with eliminating vulnerable U.S. systems. To mitigate the potentially adverse consequences of such an action, it would be wise to gradually reduce our ICBMs following a phased program. As an additional means of offsetting the loss of our ICBMs, the United States could "shift" some ICBMs to sea by deploying Trident submarines carrying intercontinental-range missiles as supplements to the existing fleet within limits imposed by SALT accords. Although these actions could be taken unilaterally, it would be desirable for the United States to attempt to negotiate bilateral ICBM reductions combined with an extended "freedom-to-mix" arrangement that would permit increased SLBM levels—an issue that will be analyzed further in discussions of strategic arms control possibilities.

Strategic Forces and Overseas Commitments

U.S. strategic forces—in conjunction with our tactical nuclear and conventional forces and the forces of NATO—will continue to serve the purpose of deterring nuclear as well as nonnuclear aggression by the

Soviet Union against Western Europe. America's security commitments to Japan and other allies in Asia also place a burden on U.S. strategic forces to counter potential threats from China as well as from the Soviet Union. One particular function of America's strategic forces is to provide a nuclear umbrella to states lacking nuclear weapons in order to reduce the likelihood of the proliferation of such weapons. During the coming decade, as American officials continue to reevaluate our worldwide security policies, as domestic pressures to cut defense spending continue to increase, and as the U.S.-Soviet nuclear balance reaches a higher degree of stability through détente diplomacy and further SALT arrangements, questions involving the extended purposes of our strategic forces will increase in relative importance.

Extended Deterrence

Ever since the Soviet Union first acquired the ability to inflict unacceptable retaliatory damage on the United States, the U.S. pledge to use our strategic nuclear weapons to respond to Soviet attacks on our allies, risking what might be termed national suicide, has not seemed wholly credible. The growth of Soviet strategic power during the late 1950s aroused concern regarding the reliability of our nuclear guarantee to Western Europe. Moscow's recent attainment of visible parity, which was ratified by SALT, has highlighted this problem and has stimulated renewed discussions of the nuclear dilemma that has plagued NATO for well over a decade. Many commentators have concluded that the U.S. nuclear guarantee to NATO has already become largely irrelevant and incredible. Many foreign diplomats and a growing number of American policymakers are echoing Charles de Gaulle's well-known observation that the United States is unlikely to risk New York to save Paris—or any other European city.

The most crucial aspect of our extended deterrent policy is the prospect that the United States might use nuclear weapons against the Soviet Union *before* the latter attacked us directly. An American response to a Soviet nuclear strike against our NATO allies, for example, could involve the use of U.S. theater nuclear weapons against USSR military forces located in Eastern Europe, as well as the launching of strategic nuclear strikes at targets within the Soviet Union itself. In this case, the United States, of course, would not be initiating the use of nuclear weapons and would at least be following its retaliatory deterrent doctrine—particularly if U.S. troops or bases were exposed to the USSR's nuclear strikes.

Whether the United States would actually use its nuclear weapons to respond to Soviet nuclear attacks on Western Europe and risk escalation to a full strategic exchange if the USSR retaliated with strikes against the American homeland obviously is unknown. But the controversial contingency that is the focus of attention on both sides of the Atlantic is the possible use of U.S. nuclear weapons to counter a Soviet *conventional* military attack against Western Europe—that is, a contingency involving the *first use* of nuclear weapons by the United States to defend its allies and the one that most of all causes the dependability of the American guarantee to be questioned.

Although analyses show that NATO can muster the conventional strength capable of coping with a wide range of sizable conventional attacks by the USSR and its Warsaw Pact allies, the prevailing attitude in Europe places a heavy burden on nuclear responses to deter non-nuclear aggression.[35] The contingency of nuclear first use is currently the backbone of NATO defense policy, and the United States in turn is pledged to initiate nuclear strikes, if necessary, as part of its NATO commitment. Such U.S. actions might be limited to the battlefield use of nuclear weapons but could also involve theater nuclear strikes against Soviet cities or interior-based military forces. It is unlikely that the United States would use its strategic nuclear forces before launching tactical and theater nuclear weapons, yet this option has never been foreclosed.

To be more specific, U.S. nuclear policies in regard to Europe are tied to NATO's nuclear policy. NATO strategy calls for possible selective nuclear strikes in the event a Soviet conventional penetration into Central Europe cannot be contained by conventional means, for example, and also includes plans for a general nuclear response in other unspecified contingencies that undoubtedly cover the possibility of a massive Soviet conventional thrust into Western Europe.[36] For conflicts limited

35. See, for example, "Report of Secretary of Defense James R. Schlesinger to the Congress on the FY 1975 Defense Budget and FY 1975–1979 Defense Program" (March 4, 1974; processed), pp. 87–91; and Enthoven and Smith, *How Much Is Enough?*

36. The U.S. commitment to NATO has always included the possible first use of nuclear weapons. For a summary of the U.S. role in NATO nuclear strategy, see *U.S. Security Issues in Europe: Burden Sharing and Offset, MBFR and Nuclear Weapons*, a Staff Report prepared for the Subcommittee on U.S. Security Agreements and Commitments Abroad of the Senate Committee on Foreign Relations, 93 Cong. 1 sess. (1973).

to the European arena, American forward-based nuclear forces assigned to NATO are under dual control and would not be released without presidential approval, but the specific application of these weapons within certain guidelines would be left to the Supreme Allied Commander in Europe. On the other hand, as reported in a recent congressional study, "the responsibility for carrying out NATO's general nuclear response falls on U.S. strategic forces based outside Europe," since such a major action "would not be undertaken by theater nuclear strike forces alone but only in conjunction with the execution of the Single Integrated Operations Plan" of the United States.[37]

Aside from the question of credibility, America's extended nuclear commitment to NATO can conflict with the requirements of strategic stability vis-à-vis the USSR and preclude productive progress in SALT negotiations. The clear implication that the United States might be prepared to use both its strategic and tactical nuclear forces first in a crisis could be viewed by the Soviet Union as a threatening American policy. The Kremlin could react by making corresponding changes in USSR defense plans and perhaps by attempting to exploit Soviet nuclear power for political purposes. In addition, our extended deterrent objectives might make the United States more prone to develop destabilizing counterforce damage-limiting capabilities for its strategic forces or to attempt to acquire some form of strategic superiority within the constraints of the SALT agreements in order to improve the military effectiveness of its nuclear first-strike doctrine and enhance the political credibility of its overseas commitments. These policies would run counter to the concept of mutual stability and the principles of strategic arms control.

Notwithstanding the many weaknesses and disadvantages associated with our extended deterrent policy, it is difficult to discover preferable alternatives. Despite signs of discomfort and disillusionment, it may not be entirely valid to dismiss either the value or the efficacy of nuclear guarantees as an instrument of U.S. foreign policy in the decade ahead. For reasons of credibility and stability, it might be desirable for the United States to dispense with the role played by its nuclear forces in contributing to extended deterrence, but it is by no means clear that such a policy change would in fact be productive. Because of mounting pressure to reduce U.S. conventional forces in Western Europe, as well as the continuing reluctance of NATO allies to undertake the force build-

37. Ibid., pp. 21–22.

ups required for credible defense against Soviet conventional attacks, ensuring a continuation of the U.S. nuclear guarantee to NATO could become more essential as an American foreign policy goal in the future than it has been in the past. Success in negotiating mutual force reductions with the Warsaw Pact nations could cushion the impact of U.S. troop withdrawals, and a restructuring of NATO conventional forces could improve effectiveness at lower manpower levels, but many analysts believe that in either case U.S. nuclear capabilities would be needed to supplement nonnuclear defenses in Western Europe. The small British and French nuclear forces operating independently or possibly jointly may help offset the conventional asymmetries between East and West, but they do not offer viable alternatives to the U.S. strategic deterrent when balanced against the Soviet Union's nuclear capacity, and it is highly unlikely that a European nuclear force of any kind will emerge within the next decade.[38]

The maintenance of an American extended deterrence policy is not only desirable, but possible. Even in the present era of parity, it seems reasonable to believe that uncertainty regarding the use of U.S. nuclear power will deter the Soviet Union from attacking Western Europe with nuclear weapons and will inhibit Soviet leaders from seriously contemplating conventional aggression against NATO. A U.S. strategic posture along the lines suggested earlier—a diverse, survivable force structure, some options for limited strikes, and the absence of obvious numerical inferiorities—should remain militarily and politically credible. In any case, movements toward either a minimum U.S. strategic posture or a large-scale buildup in American strategic forces would only exacerbate European security problems. The initial SALT accords and future directions in U.S.-Soviet strategic arms limitations relate to the problem of U.S. extended deterrence policies and raise many issues central to the NATO alliance. These issues will be discussed further in chapter 6 in the context of U.S. strategic arms control policies.

The role of America's strategic forces vis-à-vis Japan is to offer Tokyo protection against nuclear attack or blackmail from China as well as the Soviet Union. Our strategic forces play no practical part in dealing with the possibility of Chinese *conventional* aggression against the Japanese

38. For an excellent analysis of the prospects for European nuclear cooperation, see Ian Smart, "Future Conditional: The Prospect for Anglo-French Nuclear Cooperation," Adelphi Papers, no. 78 (London: Institute for Strategic Studies, July 1971).

mainland or certain other areas in Asia such as Taiwan. Under present defense plans, U.S. forces available for Asian contingencies, in combination with allied forces, should be able to meet virtually all conceivable contingencies without resort to nuclear weapons. Only in the case of a massive North Korean attack against the South with large-scale Chinese involvement might it prove difficult to handle conventional aggression with conventional forces alone, but in this case tactical nuclear weapons might well be used.[39] Although nuclear threats against Japan from either Moscow or Peking are remote, the U.S. guarantee fills a security need and reduces the likelihood of an independent Japanese decision to acquire nuclear weapons. As suggested earlier, a deterrence-oriented policy toward China would be adequate to cope with the security problems raised by the growing Chinese nuclear force, and our capability to deter Chinese aggression is covered by our strategic policy toward the USSR.

Efforts to strengthen our counterforce capability against China in an attempt to increase our extended deterrent power would not only be unnecessary and destabilizing in the U.S.-Soviet context but would undercut movements toward cooperation and the stabilization of relations with China. This, in turn, could lead to a tense situation in Asia that could actually undermine confidence in U.S. security ties, perhaps prompting Japan and other nations in the region to establish independent policies toward China—either through military buildups or greater accommodation. A reversal of U.S. policy toward anti-Chinese ABMs might result in the abrogation of the ABM treaty, which bans nationwide missile defenses. In any event, if Tokyo questions the U.S. nuclear guarantee in the future, its concern is more likely to relate to our general policy toward Japan and China than to the details of U.S. strategic doctrine or weapon deployments.

On a worldwide level, it would seem unwise to compromise the extended role of our strategic forces, since our nuclear umbrella contributes to U.S. security and international stability by supporting the goal of nonproliferation. In general, the decisions of prospective nuclear powers will probably be less affected by U.S. strategic force developments and the strategic balance than by our overall foreign policy and, ultimately, by the status of their own security and prestige. Nevertheless,

39. For a discussion of U.S. defense policy in Asia, with emphasis on the role of nuclear arms, see Earl C. Ravenal, "The Nixon Doctrine and Our Asian Commitments," *Foreign Affairs*, vol. 49 (January 1971), pp. 201–17.

by following the strategic arms policy outlined above, U.S. strategic forces would be making their maximum contribution to nonproliferation. Extreme policies in either direction—whether a dramatic U.S. arms buildup that would endanger SALT or a major unilateral reduction in U.S. strategic capabilities—could diminish the credibility of our guarantees and increase incentives for other nations to develop their own nuclear arsenals. Nuclear guarantees are tenuous and risky, but in many cases the United States may have no choice but to continue to maintain the paradoxical position of being prepared to risk strategic nuclear war in order to deter nuclear attacks or threats abroad, help reduce the likelihood of conflicts that could escalate to the nuclear level, and forestall the dangers associated with an increased number of nuclear-armed nations.

Lowering the Nuclear Profile

At the same time, the disadvantages of an American extended deterrent policy cannot be ignored, and an important dimension of U.S. strategic policy should be an attempt to minimize these disadvantages. It should be recognized that strategic stability in itself is no guarantee that a nuclear war will not occur in a time of tension or through the escalation of a conventional conflict. To further reduce the likelihood that nuclear weapons might be used, the United States must not only adjust its strategic forces but should pay attention to the overall structure of its defense posture. If the United States maintains strong conventional forces, it may be possible to organize a defense posture that could serve our overseas interests while reducing adverse effects on the U.S.-Soviet strategic balance, avoiding severe setbacks to progress in improving U.S.-Chinese relations, and minimizing the likelihood that an American president would have to face an operational decision to use nuclear arms.

Future defense trends, however, could move the United States toward giving nuclear weapons an *enlarged* role in extended deterrence. If conventional forces were cut significantly in order to reduce the defense budget, the balance between U.S. nuclear and nonnuclear capabilities would be altered. Defense planners might then place increased reliance on modernized tactical nuclear weapons to satisfy U.S. overseas security requirements, unless U.S. policymakers reduced the scope of our commitments or America's allies provided conventional forces to fill the gap.[40] Congressional demands might result in a sizable unilateral reduction of U.S. conventional forces in Europe, despite strong opposition from the executive branch. In this event, NATO might revert to a policy of virtually complete reliance on tactical nuclear weapons for defense, while placing a still greater burden of responsibility on U.S. strategic forces to provide deterrence against a range of possible Soviet aggressive actions. It is also possible that the United States would turn to a nuclear-oriented policy in Northeast Asia if American conventional forces in the region were decreased. Because of our nuclear superiority over China, such a strategy might strike some policymakers as an attractive option, reminiscent of the early 1950s when the United States had a plausible first-strike capability against the Soviet Union and when China, not yet a nuclear power, was allied with the USSR.[41]

The United States need not regain strategic superiority vis-à-vis the Soviet Union in order to adopt a policy of nuclear reliance. The doctrine of massive retaliation in the 1950s, it should be recalled, was initially based on nuclear superiority, but the United States continued to maintain the policy of nuclear reliance even after Eisenhower rejected superiority in favor of sufficiency. As in the 1950s, our willingness to risk nuclear catastrophe to defend U.S. interests could again be used to justify a nuclear-oriented strategy, even in a situation of mutual assured destruction and strategic parity.

However, all the objections to the massive retaliation doctrine that were raised two decades ago are equally or more valid today. Any use of nuclear weapons will remain impracticable and highly dangerous, nuclear threats will continue to have low credibility, and a nuclear-oriented posture will invite rather than deter aggressive acts involving conventional arms. Furthermore, once a crisis began, it would be risky for a U.S. president to be faced with the choice of concessions or nuclear threats. By limiting U.S. options, a nuclear-oriented policy could force the premature use of nuclear weapons, thereby increasing the likelihood of rapid escalation to strategic war. Although intense crises might not necessarily end in all-out strategic exchanges, it would be undesirable to develop a defense policy that increased this possibility. Perhaps ra-

40. See Walter Pincus, "A New Generation of Weaponry: Why More Nukes?" *New Republic*, February 9, 1974, pp. 14–16.

41. Congressional interest in cutting U.S. troops in Europe is documented in John Newhouse and others, *U.S. Troops in Europe: Issues, Costs and Choices* (Brookings Institution, 1971).

tional and deliberate crisis management could minimize this danger, but it should not be forgotten that wars often erupt through miscalculation or inadvertence.

Since the Soviet Union has achieved strategic parity, a strategy of nuclear emphasis in Europe would be a far more dangerous and futile policy to pursue in the future than it was in the past. Moreover, a nuclear-oriented U.S. defense policy would diminish European incentives to build larger conventional forces, would undercut chances for nuclear arms control agreements in Europe, and generally would run contrary to the emerging patterns of détente in Central Europe. In Asia, a U.S. military posture that stressed nuclear rather than conventional forces would lack credibility because of Peking's small but expanding nuclear arsenal. Furthermore, such a policy would increase nuclear risks, stand in the way of improving relations between Washington and Peking, and increase the likelihood of a Japanese nuclear arms decision.

For these reasons, it would be preferable for the United States to attempt to reduce rather than to increase its reliance on nuclear weapons. A basic defense policy embodying the flexible response concept formulated during the early 1960s, which calls for substantial conventional capabilities as well as strong nuclear forces, still remains a sound approach if the United States wishes to maintain its extended security commitments without disrupting the strategic balance, triggering further nuclear proliferation, or unnecessarily raising the risk of nuclear war. Even if the United States cannot wholly reject the option of nuclear first use in Europe or Northeast Asia, sufficient conventional capabilities could be maintained to provide credible deterrence against aggression on all levels. Although the proposed policy would seem to require increased defense spending, some estimates indicate that the United States could make modest reductions in annual expenditures for general purpose forces and still support a reliable nonnuclear option.[42] In any event, the benefits of greater nuclear stability would be well worth the price of maintaining strong conventional capabilities.

Under this basic defense policy, in order to reduce the prominence of nuclear weapons in our defense posture, tactical as well as strategic

42. One conservative estimate suggests that the United States could maintain a credible conventional defense posture with an annual reduction of $3–5 billion in military spending for general purpose forces. See Edward R. Fried and others, *Setting National Priorities: The 1974 Budget* (Brookings Institution, 1973), pp. 365–73.

nuclear forces would be geared primarily to perform a deterrence rather than a warfighting mission, based on the strategic force-planning criteria discussed earlier. A nuclear posture of this kind, designed to be powerful but nonprovocative, would support deterrence and diminish nuclear dangers while offering the flexibility in the use of nuclear weapons needed to strengthen stability and provide the President with a prudent range of choices.

In concert with the proposed force posture, the United States would adjust its policy statements and diplomatic activities to downgrade the role of nuclear weapons. For example, officials would avoid attributing undue significance to variations in the U.S.-Soviet force balance and would refrain from overstating the dangers of the Soviet threat or the problems of nuclear parity. In addition, targeting doctrines that reflected the belief that nuclear forces could be effectively used for military or political purposes would be downplayed, since serious consideration of the practicality of limited nuclear war or the coercive use of nuclear power could be interpreted as a threat and might increase the chance that nuclear weapons would be used. By preserving a strong conventional defense posture and deliberately diminishing the significance of nuclear force, the United States would help to lower the nuclear profile in world affairs, while SALT and other forums could be used to develop multilateral arrangements toward this end. If successful, such a strategy could reduce the risk of nuclear war, contribute to the goal of nonproliferation, and lead to increasingly more comprehensive nuclear arms control agreements, regionally and on the strategic level.

Alternatives to Mutual Assured Destruction

In recent years a group of analysts have begun to question both the desirability and inevitability of the U.S.-Soviet mutual assured destruction relationship, referring to it by the symptomatic acronym MAD.[43] Even though the Moscow ABM treaty seemed to signify an official codification of the MAD philosophy, these experts contend that alternative nuclear doctrines should be sought immediately, since there are major problems associated with accepting mutual assured destruction as a

43. D. G. Brennan was an early critic of the mutual assured destruction, or MAD, doctrine. Other critics include Lewis C. Bohn, Michael M. May, Fred C. Iklé, and Martin J. Bailey.

permanent situation. Because these arguments represent a fundamental challenge to the conventional wisdom that has guided U.S. strategic policies, they must be scrutinized carefully before directions for future policies are firmly established.

Criticisms and Proposals

Those questioning the MAD concept offer a series of objections to demonstrate its absurdity.[44] To begin with, they highlight the fragility of the MAD system by pointing out that, despite the best preparations and policies, deterrence might actually fail—if not through the deliberate use of nuclear weapons then through miscalculation, irrational actions, or an accidental or unauthorized launching by either of the superpowers or a smaller nation. In this event, forces and doctrines designed to inflict assured destruction and to permit an adversary to maintain a comparable capability, it is argued, would lead to a massive destruction of societies with little or no chance of limiting damage. Opponents of the prevailing doctrine also claim that the threat of assured destruction has always been an ineffective and incredible deterrent and that it has become even more so in this age of parity when it can result only in mutual annihilation. Because the MAD doctrine in its most literal form virtually excludes selective response capabilities, critics also question the utility of massive counterpopulation threats in deterring limited strikes and in providing nuclear guarantees.

Following a similar line of reasoning, many analysts question the proposition supported by most arms controllers that the pursuit of damage-limiting capabilities will automatically weaken deterrence. They claim instead that it is unnecessary to maintain huge arsenals of damage-inflicting weapons to deter effectively. Observing that damage limitation as a traditional arms control goal has been severely compromised in favor of the obsession with war prevention, these analysts suggest that alternatives to assured destruction could remove the specter of catastrophic nuclear war without necessarily increasing the likelihood that nuclear weapons would be used. This position runs counter to the arguments against excessive reliance on flexible options or the development of counterforce capabilities presented earlier.

44. For a persuasive criticism of MAD, see Fred C. Iklé, "Can Nuclear Deterrence Last Out the Century?" *Foreign Affairs*, vol. 52 (January 1973), pp. 268–85.

Finally, critics underscore the sheer immorality of a doctrine that legitimizes the goal of maintaining tens of millions of civilians as hostages, stresses the massive slaughter of populations if nuclear war should occur, and gives political leaders power to cause such catastrophes. To make matters worse, it is argued, perpetuation of the present policy leads to the accumulation of weapons designed for mass destruction and fuels the arms race as each side seeks to prevent its opponent from threatening its assured destruction capability. Furthermore, antipopulation threats, combined with continued increases in the capability to carry them out, breed tension and distrust between the United States and the Soviet Union. Indeed, it is emphasized that a distinction should be made between accepting MAD as an unfortunate but unavoidable temporary fact of life in the nuclear age and enshrining this phenomenon by weapons decisions, strategic doctrine, and arms control agreements. If alternatives are freely sought and dogmas are rejected, it is argued, future technical and doctrinal developments may make it possible to replace assured destruction with a more effective, morally preferable, and politically meaningful concept.

It is against this background that strategies for minimizing, if not avoiding, the disadvantages of MAD have been proposed. The most obvious approach to this problem would be to implement the long-standing goal of nuclear disarmament. Critics of MAD, however, regard the total elimination of nuclear weapons as an impractical and probably undesirable objective. Thus, they have suggested three other possible alternatives:

- Reducing offensive arms.
- Constructing large-scale defenses.
- Employing a no-cities strategy.

ARMS REDUCTION

A far more realistic alternative to MAD than nuclear disarmament calls for making substantial reductions in strategic delivery vehicles—either unilaterally by the United States or, preferably, under a bilateral U.S.-Soviet agreement. Some experts contend that, instead of the excessive damage-inflicting capabilities of present assured destruction forces, minimum deterrent forces of perhaps a few hundred invulnerable missiles, based on submarines and designed for counter-city retaliation, would provide an adequate deterrent against nuclear attacks. Neither the U.S. nor the Soviet government, however, seems likely to move unilaterally to a minimum deterrent force, and the prospect for sharp mutual reductions during SALT is dim. This is because the superpowers fear that deterrence would be weakened if retaliatory capabilities were markedly reduced and that the other side might somehow be able to negate a smaller deterrent force or to exploit a strategic advantage for political or military purposes more easily.

If by some chance, the United States and the USSR changed their strategies to permit the negotiation of substantial cuts in force levels, they would still have to solve difficult verification questions. In any event, even if progress were made in developing stable and reliable minimum deterrent postures, the problems associated with MAD would only be alleviated, not eliminated. Only extremely sharp cuts in offensive forces would substantially reduce the damage-inflicting potential of strategic nuclear weapons. A minimum deterrent force of 100 missiles, if launched against cities, would still be capable of inflicting tens of millions of fatalities, and the risk of accidental or unauthorized launchings would remain undiminished.

DEFENSE EMPHASIS

A second alternative to MAD proposed by a number of analysts can be termed the "defense emphasis" approach, whereby the United States would deploy large-scale ABM defenses in an attempt to significantly reduce the ability of the Soviet Union to inflict damage on America.[45] At the same time, the United States would exercise restraint in strategic offensive forces, lowering the damage-inflicting capability of its retaliatory forces to approximately that of the Soviet Union.

The premise for this posture is the belief that deterrence is not necessarily dependent on preserving the capability to inflict a specified high level of fatalities on the Soviet Union but will operate effectively as long as the USSR cannot inflict greater damage on the United States than it would receive in a retaliatory blow. Advocates argue that ABM technology could be developed to make this strategy realizable at costs equivalent to the costs of constructing advanced assured destruction forces. They further contend that the Soviet Union, despite its agreement to ban nationwide ABMs, might nonetheless be sympathetic to a concept that furthers its traditional interest in defense. Therefore,

45. See D. G. Brennan, "The Case for Missile Defense," *Foreign Affairs*, vol. 47 (April 1969), pp. 433–48.

rather than responding to U.S. damage-limiting efforts as predicted by the "action-reaction" model, Moscow might simply match U.S. ABM deployments. Indeed, as a means of increasing the effectiveness of a defense emphasis posture, it has been proposed that the SALT accords should be amended to permit the construction of population-protecting ABMs on both sides, coupled with mutual constraints on offensive forces.

The objective of defense emphasis would be to simulate the effect of drastic offensive force reductions by building up defensive forces to the point where mutual deterrence could be maintained at somewhat lower offensive levels and meaningful damage limitation could take place if deterrence failed. In the extreme, of course, perfect defenses could deter simply by preventing one side from launching a nuclear attack against the other, thus replacing the need to deter through the threat of anti-population retaliation. Proponents of defense emphasis do not claim that such a goal could necessarily be realized in the near term but argue that this approach should be seriously studied by both nations. Ideally, such efforts would involve strategy and weapons posture adjustments that might eventually permit a "mutual assured survivable," rather than a MAD, relationship. As a collateral advantage, it might be noted, advocates of defense emphasis maintain that even modest ABM protection could deter and diminish the danger of nuclear proliferation by negating the effectiveness of smaller strategic forces against powers protected by ABMs.

Despite the superficial attractiveness of defense emphasis, however, this alternative to MAD seems neither possible nor productive. The most crucial flaw in the defense domination approach is its practicality. Based on present or foreseen technologies, including such exotic systems as lasers, defensive systems designed to reduce damage to relatively low levels—below ten million fatalities, for example—will remain extremely expensive to build and will not have high reliability. The experience of the United States with the Safeguard system and of the Soviet Union with the Moscow ABM system support this contention. More important, offensive weapon improvements, both quantitatively and qualitatively, will continue to be able to offset defensive measures at a very favorable cost ratio and with greater confidence than the builders of a defensive system would be able to obtain in the reliability of their protective systems. Efforts by one side to adopt a defense emphasis policy would prove to be economically questionable if the other side took offensive countermeasures, and the act of building ABM systems to protect populations, by directly threatening an opponent's retaliatory capability, could stimulate arms procurements on both sides and create instabilities leading to a breakdown of deterrence in a time of tension. Obviously, these reactions would not occur if both sides rejected assured destruction as the *foundation* of their posture. But the United States is unlikely to do so—whatever flexible options may be introduced—and, while the Soviet Union may not have a pure assured destruction strategy, it seems highly likely that it has adopted a policy that rests on retaliatory threats as at least the basis of its strategic posture.

Even if both sides were willing to cooperate in moving toward defense emphasis through appropriate modification of the ABM treaty, the practical problems they would face suggest that it would be unwise as well as unnecessary to pursue this approach. For one thing, it would be extremely difficult to design ABM deployments that, paired with offensive capabilities, could give both the United States and the USSR comparable damage limitation and damage-inflicting capabilities. The uncertain capabilities of defensive systems invariably force each side to be conservative and to fear an imbalance in its relative assured destruction capability. There would undoubtedly be concern that one side might be able to negate the retaliatory capability of its opponent by improving its ABM system and retaining a retaliatory force. In this sense, real or perceived technological advances could easily upset defense emphasis arrangements and result in increased tension, rapid offensive rearmament, or consideration of preemptive first-strike attacks. Agreed verification systems might help but could not substantially alleviate these problems. ABM performance could not be checked in detail, nor could qualitative improvements in offensive or defensive systems be adequately monitored.[46] The prospect of dual-purpose ABM-ICBM systems could create special verification problems.

Paradoxically, the lower the desired level of damage reduction, the more sensitive the resultant balance would become to possible violations of a defense emphasis agreement, since even small advantages could have a significant effect in altering the relative ability of the two sides to inflict damage in situations where offensive force inventories are slashed and ABM deployments are high. To make matters worse, with ABMs deployed on both sides, neither nation could employ selective

46. For an excellent analysis of U.S. technical intelligence programs, see Ted Greenwood, "Reconnaissance and Arms Control," *Scientific American*, February 1973, pp. 14–25.

strategic options. A defense emphasis approach would force both nations into using their strategic capabilities massively, once deterrence failed, in order to penetrate an opponent's ABM system. If defensive systems then did not work as expected, the result could be *greater* damage inflicted on both sides than if feasible limited response options were available and neither side had ABMs.

Finally, it is unclear whether defense emphasis systems would diminish incentives for other nations to acquire nuclear weapons. In fact, they might have the opposite effect by creating a situation of superpower hegemony. In any event, there is no reason to doubt that deterrence will work against small countries and, conversely, no reason to believe that even large ABM defenses could prevent a small nation from managing to inflict some nuclear damage on one of the two superpowers by circumventing its defensive screen. The dependability of ABM systems against accidental or unauthorized launchings or attacks from smaller countries is also questionable, and any gains in this regard would probably be outweighed by the risks and costs inherent in a defense emphasis approach. Some experts claim that the danger of an accidental detonation or the launching of an ABM system deployed on a large scale might be more serious than the danger of an accidental offensive missile launching.

NO-CITIES OPTIONS

A third proposed alternative to assured destruction—unlike the concept of employing limited strike options as possible supplements to assured destruction—would reverse priorities by placing primary stress on a no-cities philosophy.[47] It may seem difficult to discern the difference between adding flexible options to assured destruction and seeking alternatives to assured destruction by revising targeting plans in an attempt to avoid cities. Nevertheless, although the issue can be considered one of degree, any substantial shift away from a policy of deterrence based on inflicting population damage in massive retaliatory strikes against the Soviet urban-industrial base would represent a significant change in U.S. strategic doctrine—a change that would affect decisions on force levels and types as well as on targeting plans and procedures. Indeed, those supporting the no-cities approach hold out the hope that

47. See, for example, Iklé, "Can Nuclear Deterrence Last Out the Century?" in which the no-cities concept is stressed.

assured destruction will eventually wither away as an operational doctrine, that strategic forces will not be designed with this function in mind, and that a true substitute for assured destruction might be developed. To facilitate such a long-term objective, it has been proposed that the United States, in addition to modifying its unilateral policy, should discuss the question of MAD alternatives with the USSR and seek to structure future SALT accords around this revised no-cities premise.

Under the proposed approach, the United States would retain an invulnerable force capable of destroying cities, but the emphasis on no-cities options, it is claimed, would make both sides prone to avoid attacks on population centers if nuclear war broke out. According to Fred C. Iklé, in an analysis of the no-cities doctrine:

The technical capability to destroy cities, unfortunately, cannot be abolished. This residual risk would make the initiation of any nuclear war still seem to be a terribly dangerous course of action, to be rejected by any prudent planner. But this new strategic order would foster a strong propensity to avoid mass killing, should nuclear fighting ever break out, in contrast to the present strategy with its propensity to do just that.[48]

Deterrence would not be weakened by such a shift in target priorities, it is argued, since threats to destroy war-waging assets would inhibit the initiation of conflicts, thus placing the need to threaten city destruction still further in the background.

To support the proposed policy, it would be necessary to develop technical ability enabling strategic nuclear forces to destroy an adversary's military, industrial, and transportation assets without causing significant collateral population fatalities. This could involve improvements in command and control as well as the acquisition of accurate and "clean" low-yield warheads. It is unclear whether it would be vital to acquire counterforce capabilities permitting the destruction of hard targets, but, as long as missile sites remain part of an opponent's military assets, there seems to be no reason for advocates of a true no-cities concept to reject this particular option. It is interesting to recall that the short-lived no-cities doctrine as presented by Secretary of Defense McNamara in 1962 called for U.S. nuclear strategy to place priority on "the

48. Iklé, in a longer version of his *Foreign Affairs* article, *Can Nuclear Deterrence Last Out the Century?* (California Arms Control and Foreign Policy Seminar, January 1973), p. 38, note 33.

destruction of the enemy's military forces, not of his civilian population," in the event of a nuclear war.[49]

The difficulties and disadvantages of following a no-cities concept— which are identical to those associated with flexible strategic options— were alluded to earlier and need not be recapitulated. In the context of considering flexible strategic options to supplement assured destruction, many of these problems become muted, and a modest movement toward greater flexibility might actually be desirable. However, when a no-cities doctrine is pushed to the point of *replacing* rather than *reinforcing* assured destruction or of even becoming the dominant feature of strategic policies, the risks of pursuing this approach are greatly amplified. Not only would the likelihood of "limited" nuclear war increase dramatically as warfighting doctrines evolved into the central issue determining strategic weapons procurements and affecting attitudes concerning the role of nuclear arms, but placing priority on countermilitary capabilities could create instabilities and exacerbate tensions as each side sought to gain military advantages while preventing its opponent from achieving a counterforce capability that could negate its residual anti-city force. Evidence to date, in any event, suggests that neither the United States nor the USSR would be willing to forgo its reliance on counterpopulation threats as providing the ultimate deterrent to aggression—whatever interest both sides may have in developing nuclear strike capabilities against other targets.

Assessing the Alternatives

Consideration of the three alternatives to MAD leads to the conclusion that critics of the present approach have not offered technically viable or even theoretically preferable choices. At best, they have discussed possibilities that might de-emphasize assured destruction, but they have not even begun to formulate practical schemes that might eliminate the threat of population retaliation and replace it with a system that could deter as well as limit damage more effectively. At worst, they have offered alternatives that could increase the chance of a nuclear war occurring with no guarantee that damage could in fact be reliably

49. Robert S. McNamara, "Defense Arrangements of the North Atlantic Community," Address given at the University of Michigan, June 16, 1962, *Department of State Bulletin*, vol. 47 (July 9, 1962), p. 67.

reduced. On a more fundamental level, it is possible to put aside the question of practicality and argue that MAD is a desirable state of affairs. It may be immoral to hold populations hostage, but it would be less moral if actions by one or both nations to shift away from an assured destruction policy increased the likelihood of nuclear war. A limited nuclear war would not only be destructive but would raise the real danger of escalation to all-out war. Given current and projected technology, MAD appears to be more stable against technological change as well as political misperceptions than other strategic alternatives. Preserving high levels of counterpopulation damage is less difficult than building effective defenses or obtaining meaningful no-city targeting capabilities, for example, and affords a more certain deterrent effect than any of the other alternatives. Furthermore, it may be in our interest to ensure that the Soviet Union retains a confident assured destruction capability—both to reduce the chance of a Soviet preemptive strike against the United States and to minimize the chance that U.S. leaders might believe that nuclear weapons are effective military instruments.

To be sure, the problems inherent in MAD cannot be ignored, but they can continue to be contained. There is no guarantee that the Soviet Union or any other nation will always perceive the power and credibility of our strategic retaliatory forces and refrain from nuclear attacks or threats against the United States or its allies. Nevertheless, through maintaining a confident assured destruction capability supplemented by a range of limited response capabilities and the maintenance of overall numerical equality, the risk of deterrence failing will remain extremely low. Although such a strategy cannot guard against irrational actions or nuclear accidents, no strategy is completely foolproof in these respects. Strategic forces under secure command and control and designed for delayed response, however, reduce the risks of accidental or unauthorized firings and offer the possibility of limiting damage through restraint or war termination in the event a nuclear exchange occurs. Continued consultations and increased understanding between U.S. and Soviet leaders through SALT might offer the most productive path to resolving the contradictions inherent in attempting to minimize the risks and consequences of nuclear conflicts while seeking to maximize mutual deterrence. The recent Washington-Moscow agreements on coping with accidental war, reducing the risks of aggression that might lead to nuclear war, and improving the hot line system represent positive steps in this direction.

CHAPTER FIVE

Arms Interaction and Arms Control

The basic purpose of nuclear deterrence is the protection of the security interests of the United States by preventing the Soviet Union from using its nuclear weapons, threatening to use its nuclear weapons, or profiting diplomatically from its relative strategic position. The deterrence of actual Soviet nuclear attacks during times of tension is clearly of overriding importance, and for this reason the question of developing U.S. forces and strategies capable of enhancing crisis stability has been treated in some depth in earlier chapters. But the problem of dynamic stability—the so-called action-reaction between the size, pace, and character of U.S. and Soviet strategic arms programs—should also be considered in analyzing alternative nuclear policies for the United States.

The strategic arms limitation talks (SALT) and the resultant accords in 1972 reflected a mutual realization that U.S. and Soviet strategic arms policies were inexorably linked and that both sides' security could be improved through cooperative efforts leading to greater nuclear stability.[1] Despite the substantial benefits of these initial SALT accords—and the subsequent Vladivostok agreement in 1974[2]—many important aspects of the strategic arms race were left uncontrolled, and the full implications of SALT for Soviet-American relations, our relations with our allies, and the international political climate generally remain unresolved. The unhappiness of many observers about these SALT agree-

1. Treaty between the United States of America and the Union of Soviet Socialist Republics on the Limitation of Anti-Ballistic Missile Systems; and Interim Agreement between the United States of America and the Union of Soviet Socialist Republics on Certain Measures with Respect to the Limitation of Strategic Offensive Arms, both signed at Moscow, May 26, 1972.

2. Joint Soviet-American Statement on Strategic Arms Limitation, November 24, 1974.

ments, together with uncertainty about the future, makes it essential for the United States to closely examine its strategic arms control objectives and to establish guidelines for continuing negotiations.

In the final analysis, of course, SALT is not the only, or even the primary, path toward greater stability. For one thing, success in reaching negotiated solutions to nuclear arms problems can best be ensured if the negotiations are backed by national policies that pursue the objective of mutual stability. Second, it is possible that continued efforts at SALT may fail or achieve only limited success, and the United States and the USSR may be required to manage strategic policies once again largely on a unilateral basis. Third, under the best conditions of agreement, a wide range of strategic weapons and doctrinal options will be available to both nations.

For these and other reasons, it is imperative for the United States to acknowledge the interrelationship between U.S. and Soviet forces in its strategic arms policies and to seek to strengthen mutual stability through unilateral efforts as well as through arms limitation agreements. Although most experts are concerned about stability, there is little consensus on precisely how U.S. strategic policy can attain this goal. Opinions differ about whether certain strategic weapon decisions are stabilizing or destabilizing, whether the United States has the ability to understand and influence Soviet strategic policies, and whether priority should be given to bilateral stability if it conflicts with other strategic policy objectives. Before exploring negotiated arms limitations, therefore, the question of incorporating mutual stability into U.S. strategic arms decisions should be discussed.

Mutual Stability

The factors influencing decisions on strategic policies and weapons procurements are exceedingly complex and imperfectly understood. U.S. leaders often differ on the meaning of deterrence and stability, on the arms programs needed to meet these goals, and on how our decisions affect Soviet actions. Furthermore, bureaucratic, institutional, and domestic forces affect official stands on national security questions; thus the decisionmaking mechanism may not always produce predictable or even rational results. Relatively little is known about Kremlin strategic policies and decisionmaking mechanisms. Nevertheless, the issues involved in understanding the concept of mutual stability rest on the premise that an action-reaction phenomenon exists between U.S. and Soviet strategic forces and, if not contained, can increase the risks and costs of maintaining a reliable strategic deterrent posture. To the degree that this premise is valid, it would serve U.S. strategic objectives to give serious and systematic consideration to the likelihood, nature, and implications of Soviet reactions to particular American weapon programs and doctrinal decisions.

U.S.-Soviet Arms Interactions

Perhaps the most cogent explanation of strategic arms interaction was offered by Defense Secretary Robert McNamara in 1967 when he described the way in which the United States and the Soviet Union influence each other's strategic plans and how buildups of strategic forces on one side induce reactions on the other side.[3] This "action-reaction" cycle occurs because each nation is uncertain about its adversary's strategic programs and therefore tends to adopt very conservative or "worst-case" planning assumptions in seeking to maintain its assured destruction capabilities. In McNamara's view, this inevitably leads to excessive, or possibly destabilizing, force levels, which induce counteractions on the other side, with the result that the weapon competition continues to be fueled.

During the past few years, however, an increasing number of experts have criticized the action-reaction model as an inadequate representation of the manner in which U.S. and Soviet weapon decisions are made and as offering an insufficient explanation for specific arms programs.[4] These experts believe that U.S. and Soviet strategic decisions and foreign policies have more often than not been determined primarily by internal bureaucratic concessions, organizational pressures, or technical momentum. Thus, in their opinion, one side's weapon decisions may have little relationship to the other side's present or projected program.

3. Robert S. McNamara, "The Dynamics of Nuclear Strategy," *Department of State Bulletin*, vol. 57 (October 9, 1967), pp. 445–46.

4. See Colin S. Gray, "Action and Reaction in the Nuclear Arms Race," *Military Review*, vol. 51 (August 1971), pp. 16–26. For analyses of the so-called bureaucratic model of weapons and foreign policy decisions, see Morton H. Halperin and Arnold Kantor, eds., *Readings in American Foreign Policy: A Bureaucratic Perspective* (Little, Brown, 1973); and Graham T. Allison and Frederic A. Morris, "Armaments and Arms Control: Exploring the Determinants of Military Weapons," *Daedalus*, vol. 104 (Summer 1975), pp. 99–129.

To support the theoretical framework of this so-called bureaucratic politics approach to understanding how arms decisions are made, numerous case studies have been produced that examine in detail the bureaucratic and organizational factors affecting major strategic weapon decisions, including the reasons for U.S. strategic force levels during the Kennedy administration, for the Johnson administration's decisions on Sentinel and multiple independently targetable reentry vehicles (MIRVs), and for President Nixon's decisions on Safeguard and Trident. As a result of these investigations, some arms control experts have concluded that there is little if any action-reaction between U.S. and Soviet weapon programs and have begun to emphasize the theme that "arms control begins at home" rather than to support attempts to dampen the weapon cycle through U.S.-Soviet agreements. Indeed, one analyst suggested that "rather than an arms race in which the decisions of one side are a response to the decisions of the other, the situation seems to be one of parallel unilateral decision-making."[5]

But this line of reasoning should be put in proper perspective. Admittedly, there is no simple model for the U.S.-Soviet arms competition that can fully explain the relationship between past strategic force decisions in each nation or reliably predict what it will be in the future. At the same time, it would be a mistake to conclude that arms policy decisions on both sides are made independently, for a substantial degree of understandable and unavoidable action-reaction between the U.S. and Soviet strategic postures has influenced the decisionmaking processes within each nation, shaped important strategic weapon decisions, and affected U.S.-Soviet relations. Furthermore, strategic policies based on rational objectives have been behind these weapon interactions.

RATIONALE FOR ARMS DECISIONS

In many important cases, neither technological innovation nor organizational pressures have been the primary driving force behind U.S. arms decisions. Rather, policymakers have been in control when decisions have been made to move programs into development, procurement, and deployment stages. To be sure, officials have disagreed over such issues as the emphasis to be placed on various elements of strategic doctrine and the implications of strategy for specific weapon decisions.

5. Franklin Griffiths, cited in Colin S. Gray, "Of Bargaining Chips and Building Blocks: Arms Control and Defense Policy," *International Journal*, vol. 28 (Spring 1973), p. 270.

These disagreements, however, have more often been attributable to real differences of opinion and the imponderable nature of strategic arms questions than to bureaucratic bargaining or clever argumentation designed to influence policies in self-serving directions.

The most significant doctrinal influence on U.S. strategic arms programs since the late 1950s has been the requirement of maintaining an effective retaliatory deterrent posture. Decisions to build the survivable Polaris and hardened ICBM systems reflected a genuine fear that our strategic forces might become vulnerable to Soviet counterforce attacks if the "missile gap" actually occurred. During the 1960s, the logic of deterrence through assured destruction not only led to large-scale U.S. offensive missile programs but was principally responsible for providing impetus to the MIRV program. Perhaps the excessive conservatism characterizing assured destruction requirements can be criticized, but many officials feared that Soviet antiballistic missiles (ABMs) could endanger the reliability of our deterrent and fought for MIRVs as an effective countermeasure that might be less destabilizing than building additional numbers of missile launchers. Despite the prominence given to assured destruction, MIRV and other U.S. strategic arms programs have been motivated by objectives other than retaliatory deterrence—notably, the objective of limiting damage, which is a rational goal supported by serious analysts.

In attempting to discover a logic for nuclear programs, it is fair to consider the many diplomatic and foreign policy factors that have shaped U.S. strategic programs as parts of a plausible doctrinal framework, rather than to dismiss them as clever ploys or artificial arguments designed to justify weapon decisions motivated entirely by bureaucratic or domestic political considerations. American strategic programs of the late 1950s were partly influenced by the desire of U.S. leaders to avoid a numerically unfavorable balance of forces, which in their judgment would have endangered the credibility of our strategic forces. Similar concern caused the United States to expand its Minuteman and Polaris programs in the early 1960s beyond levels that could be explained through strict military calculations and to continue MIRV deployments in the early 1970s. After the SALT talks began, the United States used the maintenance and acceleration of certain strategic programs, such as Trident and Safeguard, as bargaining chips for diplomatic purposes. Again, one might disagree with the importance attributed to the numerical balance or the way in which weapon programs have been linked to negotiations, but both these aspects of strategic policies can certainly be considered rational and subject to policy control.

Given the military and political objectives that seem to have influenced our strategic arms decisions, many prominent experts with policy experience claim that the worst-case planning approach has been responsible for U.S. forces reaching unnecessarily high levels and stimulating the nuclear arms race.[6] There is truth to this contention, for the history of the past twenty years demonstrates how the United States has overreacted to possible Soviet threats that never materialized and supports the view that premature deployments of U.S. weapon systems can induce Soviet reactions. This pattern was evident in various degrees during the missile and bomber gaps of the 1950s and was repeated when the United States expanded its strategic missile programs in the early 1960s. During the last half of the 1960s, the mere prospect that the Soviet Union might deploy ABMs triggered anticipatory U.S. countermeasures in the form of MIRV. Later the United States initiated the Safeguard defense system in response to fears of a Soviet counterforce capability.

These and other U.S. programs were partly responsible for the large-scale Soviet strategic buildup of the late 1960s and help explain the Soviet Union's continued strategic arms programs. The USSR's policy of Sputnik diplomacy in the late 1950s was partially a reaction to America's massive retaliation policy, and the ensuing missile gap fear caused the United States to react by expanding its strategic programs. America's resultant nuclear superiority then motivated Moscow to redress the strategic balance, first by attempting to install rockets in Cuba and later through a major nuclear arms buildup. In the late 1960s, the active development of U.S. MIRV systems, combined with the Sentinel ABM decision, undoubtedly further stimulated the Soviet offensive program. Plans to build the advanced-generation Trident and B-1 systems also are undoubtedly putting pressure on the Soviet Union to maintain momentum in its strategic activities.

Even within the nonrational framework of bureaucratic models, an interplay between U.S. and Soviet strategic postures exists. For one thing, organizations and officials pressing for programs that serve their narrow self-interest may use the adversary's programs and policies as

6. George W. Rathjens, for example, has stated that "the action-reaction phenomenon, with the reaction often premature and/or exaggerated, has clearly been a major stimulant of the strategic arms race." ("The Dynamics of the Arms Race," *Scientific American,* April 1969, p. 19.)

arguments to strengthen their position—a pattern of action emphasized by advocates of the bureaucratic model approach. It is far more difficult for policymakers to succeed in controlling weapon programs that have gained technological or economic momentum if the programs can be justified as necessary to match or counter an adversary's program. Consequently, one nation's strategic programs—whether the outcome of rational debate or blind bureaucratic forces—can affect the weapon decision processes in another nation and generate a series of arms buildups on both sides.

In sum, it is correct to reject a mechanistic military model of the strategic arms race built on the McNamara concept of both sides striving to maintain assured destruction but incorrect to conclude that there is no interaction between U.S. and Soviet nuclear arms decisions, or that if there is, years of analysis are required to understand its dynamics. A bilateral strategic arms race does exist, which, considering both its political and military components, can be understood as an action-reaction phenomenon between two governments.

RISKS OF THE ARMS RACE

Much has been said about the risks of the nuclear arms race, but, in order to put this issue in perspective, two points must be mentioned. First, neither side has pursued an *all-out* competition. Both nations have limited their postures, partly because of budgetary constraints but also because of deliberate strategic policy choices. The numerical limits on U.S. missile delivery systems and America's rejection of a large-scale ABM network come to mind, as does the USSR's decision to build only a relatively small number of long-range bombers. Second, improvements in strategic forces are not always dangerous; many weapon programs enhance deterrence, and some effects of Soviet-American strategic arms interactions have been beneficial and have contributed to stability. For example, the USSR apparently procured survivable deterrent forces, such as hardened ICBMs and Polaris-type submarines, largely in response to U.S. initiatives in these directions.

Nevertheless, substantial military dangers, political problems, and economic costs are related to the U.S.-Soviet arms competition that argue for a U.S. policy of mutual stability designed to minimize these undesirable effects. A U.S. strategic posture that is neither militarily effective nor politically persuasive could lead to Soviet actions that might increase the risk of nuclear war. But an excessively powerful or provocative U.S.

posture might be equally undesirable, since this might also induce Soviet actions and reactions that would diminish U.S. security. If America's strategic posture were seen as threatening the Soviet Union's retaliatory capability, for example, the danger of nuclear war erupting in a crisis could increase. This seesaw effect has been discussed and exemplified in earlier chapters. Furthermore, if U.S. weapon decisions continue to give impetus to Soviet efforts to improve or enlarge the USSR's strategic capabilities, it will become more expensive and more difficult for the United States to maintain a confident nuclear deterrent posture.

Although there may be no strict correlation between political relations and arms competitions, in most instances intense arms races contribute to tensions between nations, and a climate of extreme hostility increases incentives for arms procurement. In the case of the U.S.-Soviet strategic competition, cold war attitudes influenced U.S. arms decisions in the 1950s and early 1960s. More recently, both sides have continued to expand their strategic arsenals despite the SALT agreements and continuing negotiations on many fronts, and a marked reversal of present political trends would undoubtedly lead to still larger weapon procurements. From the opposite perspective, a dramatic upturn in either side's strategic programs could disrupt the present environment of détente, breed uncertainties that could increase tensions, and distort both sides' perceptions of the strategic relationship.

SOVIET STRATEGIC POLICIES

A particularly crucial issue to be considered more closely before designing a detailed U.S. mutual stability policy concerns the question of Soviet strategic arms policies. If the USSR's strategic outlook were dramatically different from ours or if Soviet policies could not be understood by American leaders, the United States would clearly find it difficult to predict Moscow's reactions or to influence Soviet strategic policies through its own stabilizing unilateral decisions. Equally important is the fact that a set of premises shared generally by the United States and the USSR might be the precondition to negotiating effective measures to improve nuclear stability.

In many ways, the Soviet Union's strategic policies have differed from those of the United States. For the most part, Kremlin leaders have viewed strategic forces in more political terms, attempting to exploit strategic power diplomatically in the late 1950s and eventually seeking to gain a clear position of numerical as well as military equality with the United States. In addition, unlike their American counterparts, Soviet officials did not pay primary attention to deterrence in the 1950s but seemed to be more interested in defending the USSR against U.S. nuclear attacks. This defense emphasis approach resulted in *reverse* action-reaction on the Soviet side—that is, the USSR responded defensively to many U.S. programs by deploying a bomber defense network, rather than by improving its offensive retaliatory capability. Finally, Soviet offensive programs, when compared with the strategic systems favored by the United States, have many anomalies, such as the early emphasis on medium-range systems, the stress on large-yield weapons, and the development of unusual systems such as the fractional orbital bombardment system (FOBS). Some of these anomalies may have technical or bureaucratic explanations, but others may stem from the Soviet Union's special needs in regard to Western Europe and China.

On the other hand, there have been many similarities between U.S. and Soviet strategic doctrines and deployments. Before the end of the 1950s, Kremlin leaders had come to appreciate the destructive potential of nuclear weapons and had begun to accept the principle of attempting to avoid war through a strategy of deterrence. In the mid-1960s, the Soviet Union halted ABM deployments and started to deploy sophisticated offensive deterrent forces. The Kremlin's slow progress toward a survivable strategic retaliatory posture was obviously related to a doctrinal lag but also to a lag in acquiring the requisite technology for small missiles and nuclear submarines. By the early 1970s, the Soviet Union had deployed a powerful strategic force built around Polaris-type submarines as well as hardened ICBMs, an action reflecting an appreciation of the importance of maintaining invulnerable retaliatory forces as the cornerstone of an effective strategic posture. That the USSR has now accepted the inevitability, if not the desirability, of a mutual deterrence relationship with the United States is suggested strongly by Moscow's preference for stringent limits on area ABM deployments in the SALT treaty.

There is no solid evidence to indicate that Kremlin leaders have formally accepted an assured destruction doctrine or have officially rejected programs designed to provide counterforce and "warfighting" options in addition to deterrent capabilities. The United States, however, under its policy of strategic sufficiency, is also seeking options to supplement assured destruction. Therefore, granting that doctrinal inferences may not be fully reliable and taking account of bureaucratic and other nonrational factors influencing Moscow's strategic decisions, a persuasive case can be made that U.S. and Soviet strategic policies often have much in common. Although the USSR must cope with potential nuclear threats from the British and French forces as well as from those deployed by China, Soviet needs in these respects can be met with medium-range systems and need not prevent the Kremlin from adopting an independent strategy toward the United States based on intercontinental-range delivery systems.

Stability Principles

If, then, the USSR's strategic doctrine is largely understandable and somewhat comparable to ours, it is possible to establish a relatively effective U.S. policy of mutual stability. It must be recognized that the Soviet Union also fails to behave as a rational actor; it, too, makes weapon decisions as the result of debates within the bureaucracy and is constrained by domestic concerns. Nevertheless, important Soviet strategic force decisions can be influenced by U.S. weapon decisions. Moreover, against the historical pattern of force relationships, the continued interplay of strategic weapon efforts on both sides seems clear enough for policymakers to consider the mutual stability implications of their strategic force decisions.

A mutual stability approach, in the broadest sense, rests on the premise that the United States is benefited if the Soviet Union maintains a strategic deterrent capability comparable in overall strength to our own; it is an acceptance of both the mutual assured destruction relationship and numerical parity. Accordingly, while maintaining and improving its own strategic posture to meet the objective of retaining a confident deterrent force, the United States should also seek to avoid posing a threat to the USSR's deterrent or, more generally, should attempt to avoid causing Soviet leaders to fear that the United States is seeking a form of strategic superiority. It is hoped that this policy would promote both crisis stability and dynamic stability by increasing our sensitivity to potential Soviet reactions to U.S. strategic force decisions, by fostering restraint in responding to Soviet strategic force programs, and by creating a political climate suitable for productive arms control discussions.

STABILIZING VERSUS DESTABILIZING SYSTEMS

In order to establish a mutual stability policy, it is necessary to classify strategic systems as either stabilizing or destabilizing and to avoid the latter. Generally speaking, the *stabilizing* category includes relatively invulnerable weapons and programs designed to enhance surviv- ability, such as missile-firing submarines, the hardening of missile silos, the dispersion of bomber bases, and missile-site ABM defenses. Systems that have little or no ability to threaten an opponent's strategic forces but are designed to improve countervalue retaliatory capabilities would also fall in the stabilizing group and should be procured as necessary to maintain deterrence. They include systems geared to offset population defenses, such as missile penetration aids, clustered or multiple war- heads or inaccurate MIRVs, and air-to-surface missiles, as well as strate- gic bombers and cruise missiles that have a long flight time and there- fore have no meaningful counterforce role against "time-urgent" targets such as ICBM sites or bomber bases. Warning systems to alert retalia- tory forces, survivable command posts, and command and control systems to guard against accidental or inadvertent launches all contrib- ute to stability.

Systems and strategies geared to negate an opponent's retaliatory capability and having no direct bearing on the preservation of a depend- able deterrent should be rejected as *destabilizing*. This category encom- passes offensive weapon programs, such as warhead accuracy and yield improvements, which could provide land- or sea-based missiles with the ability to launch counterforce strikes against Soviet intercontinental ballistic missiles (ICBMs). If the United States pursued major counter- force programs, the USSR's fear that its ICBM force would become vulnerable or that America might be able to negate a large fraction of the Soviet retaliatory capability would work counter to our interest by increasing the risk of an inadvertent breakdown of nuclear deterrence and by stimulating an even greater Soviet procurement program. On the defensive side, ABM systems and bomber defense networks deployed to protect populations should be avoided on stability grounds, since they can directly negate an opponent's deterrent capability. Strategic anti- submarine warfare (ASW) programs should also be viewed in this light. Vulnerable offensive systems, such as soft ICBMs or shipborne missile systems, are destabilizing as well, since they can introduce first-strike incentives and increase the risk of nuclear war.

UNILATERAL DETERRENCE AND BILATERAL STABILITY

In many cases, it is fairly easy to follow the guidelines of mutual sta- bility. But there are two complicating issues to be considered.

First, in addition to minimizing the militarily destabilizing consequences of weapon systems, U.S. leaders should also recognize that programs they consider strategically stabilizing might well trigger reactions based on Moscow's political attitude or psychological outlook. Even if certain U.S. weapons, such as Trident or the B-1, might not literally threaten the Soviet Union's retaliatory capability, their deployment could evoke undesirable Soviet responses, particularly if the Kremlin concluded that the United States was seeking a major quantitative or qualitative advantage. To help forestall such conclusions, the United States should be wary of overstating the significance of numerical measures of comparison or of heralding any edge it might acquire in strategic forces. Furthermore, U.S. officials should refrain from procuring strategic systems solely for reasons of numerical equality. These policies would support mutual stability as well as the unilateral strategic policies discussed earlier. At best, however, attempts to shape U.S. strategic weapon decisions on the basis of highly subjective political factors will remain difficult, uncertain, and controversial.

Second, and more important, it may not always be possible to avoid seeming to threaten the Soviet Union's deterrent while improving our own deterrent. Many strategic systems have dual-purpose functions or are inherently ambiguous. Although the MIRVs currently installed on U.S. missiles are designed principally to strengthen our retaliatory capabilities and may not be accurate enough for a credible first strike against hardened targets, Soviet planners, seeing our capabilities and doubting our intentions, might view these weapons as a threat to their land-based missiles. Similarly, a maneuvering reentry vehicle (MARV) could enhance missile penetrability and strengthen stability but, if given precision accuracy, could become a destabilizing counterforce weapon. Even the acquisition of selective strategic strike capabilities for prudential reasons and based on a controlled response objective might nonetheless be viewed by the Soviet Union as representing a provocative first-strike policy. Technically speaking, U.S. sea-based missiles might not be designed for hard-target kill, but if fired at close range from submarines, they could become counterforce weapons—as in the case of the Trident advanced SLBM. As another example, if the ABM treaty had not prevented the United States from constructing the planned Safeguard system, Soviet strategic planners might have perceived large-scale deployments of ABMs to protect our ICBMs as the first step toward a nationwide population defense.

The goal of minimizing threats to the USSR's deterrent may also conflict with U.S. strategic objectives unrelated to the bilateral balance. In the early 1960s, U.S. commitments to the North Atlantic Treaty Organization (NATO) gave impetus to counterforce and damage-limiting strategies against the USSR, while the objective of building an anti-Chinese ABM, a U.S. policy from 1967 until banned by the ABM treaty, could have posed a danger to the Soviet Union's deterrent. Although the United States should not relinquish its extended deterrent commitments or diminish its efforts to deter China, it should attempt to stress bilateral stability in its strategic decisions. A stable U.S.-Soviet nuclear relationship can actually further U.S. alliance and China policies.

In the final analysis, it will be impossible to completely avoid the conflicts between unilateral deterrence and bilateral stability. It will often be necessary, therefore, to balance these two objectives on a case-by-case basis, weighing the need to strengthen the U.S. deterrent against the potential benefits of a more stable nuclear relationship with the USSR.

To aid in these assessments, it would be useful if the type, timing, and scope of strategic development, testing, and procurement programs were systematically evaluated with likely Soviet reactions in mind. A serious policy of mutual stability could require the United States to be less conservative in strategic force planning and to constrain its strategic programs in an attempt to maintain a confident deterrent without threatening the Soviet Union's nuclear forces. Since Soviet ABMs are limited by treaty, it may be possible to practice unilateral restraint without compromising deterrent requirements. In many instances, however, reliance on high-confidence measures to ensure survivability or penetrability against unlikely future threats might have to be forgone in favor of measures that are less reliable but also less provocative. It would be particularly important to prevent potentially destabilizing weapon projects from gathering excessive momentum as a result of budgetary investments, bureaucratic commitments, or mere "technological drift."[7] More serious consideration might be given to programs and policies that could strengthen strategic stability. Perhaps stabilizing criteria, such as desired *inaccuracies*, could be included in weapon specifications.

A particularly difficult question to be resolved in executing a mutual stability policy is how to respond to Soviet actions that might not reflect

7. For a discussion of the process of "technological drift" and other nonrational factors affecting U.S. and USSR strategic arms, see Abram Chayes, "An Inquiry into the Workings of Arms Control Agreements," *Harvard Law Review*, vol. 85 (March 1972), pp. 905–19.

a comparable concern. Disregarding stability principles simply in order to maintain symmetry represents an unnecessary as well as a potentially risky approach. On the other hand, if the Soviet Union moved rapidly toward a major counterforce capability or other highly provocative force deployments or doctrines, U.S. leaders might well decide that certain compromises must be made—perhaps accepting a broader range of limited-strike options or placing more weight on the numerical balance. Furthermore, if Soviet strategic programs continue to evolve in the directions identified by pessimistic but plausible intelligence projections, the United States might have no choice but to initiate a series of new strategic arms procurements to maintain the survivability of its strategic posture and to sustain a position of strategic comparability. Before taking such steps, however, it would be well to make a determined effort to negotiate further SALT arrangements with the USSR that could strengthen the structure of strategic stability and offer improved opportunities for satisfying America's strategic objectives through cooperation rather than through competition in the nuclear field. The Vladivostok agreement is a step—but only a first step—toward this end. Even if priority is placed on restraining weapon programs and seeking substantial progress in SALT, it must be acknowledged that striking a balance between strengthening our unilateral posture and furthering bilateral stability will be the most difficult challenge facing the United States in setting a nuclear policy course for the 1970s.

Strategic Arms Control: Background Issues

The United States and the USSR are continuing bilateral discussions to ensure the effective operation of the initial SALT agreements and to seek more permanent, comprehensive, and stabilizing restrictions on strategic forces, building on the Vladivostok agreement. But progress in reaching such accords will occur only if both governments make a determined effort to formulate equitable, stable, and verifiable agreements that take into account the differences between U.S. and Soviet weapon systems and that satisfy each nation's security needs. It is essential, therefore, to examine the purposes, premises, and principles of strategic arms control before discussing U.S. policies toward arms limitation possibilities and the long-term direction for SALT.

Purposes of Arms Control

Even the best efforts to practice a unilateral policy fostering mutual stability cannot succeed fully, given the ambiguities of many weapons, the uncertainties typically associated with threat estimates, and the difficulty of estimating an opponent's policy intentions. The character of the U.S.-Soviet strategic competition shows how weapon programs can develop dangerous momentum and suggests that neither nation is capable of pursuing a purely stabilizing policy unilaterally. Even if one country adopted such a policy, moreover, nuclear risks and demands for increased arms would persist unless the other country followed suit. Security considerations aside, political and bureaucratic pressures for expanded arms programs are difficult to contain as long as a nation's opponent is continuing its arms efforts.

Against this background, it seems reasonable to conclude that *the primary purpose of strategic arms control is to attempt to introduce greater stability into the nuclear balance through cooperative efforts and negotiated arrangements affecting nuclear systems.* Other purposes of strategic arms control include:

- Reducing the consequences of nuclear war.
- Building mutual confidence.
- Lowering the costs of strategic programs.

IMPROVING STABILITY

Bilateral arrangements between the United States and the USSR can improve each nation's security by controlling the size, nature, and direction of arms programs and policies on both sides. Limitation agreements can dampen the competition by imposing restrictions on an opponent's forces, thus reducing security needs for new systems geared to counter threats and blunting internal pressures for military programs to match adversary efforts. As weapons are brought under mutual control and as arms inventories change less rapidly, perceptions should move more in line with reality, many uncertainties should be eliminated, tensions should be alleviated, and the danger of conflicts leading to nuclear war should diminish. Stability in crises should be strengthened through the elimination of vulnerable systems on both sides and the prohibition of weapons that might threaten the survivability of deterrent forces. In this way, the difference between a first and second strike should be narrowed, and incentives for launching a preemptive attack should decrease. Although the possession of nuclear weapons by other nations can complicate the balance, strategic stability can be fully realized only if the two superpowers limit their own arms.

A number of analysts point to an apparent contradiction in strategic arms control.[8] Why, they ask, must arms limitations accords be pursued if the strategic balance is relatively unaffected by changes in weapon levels or technology and if both the United States and the USSR are able to counter any threats to their deterrent capabilities through unilateral actions? In other words, if the arms race is neither risky nor necessarily excessively costly, these analysts claim, there may be little need for negotiated agreements. This arms control paradox can be easily resolved. For one thing, as suggested earlier, it is far from clear that the arms competition does not endanger the stability of the U.S.-Soviet strategic relationship or that the nuclear balance is in fact insensitive to comparisons of relative force capabilities. Nuclear advantages might well be translatable into political or diplomatic gains, despite the limited military utility of strategic forces. In any event, each side may misperceive the other's intentions or capabilities, design its posture extremely conservatively as a result of these misperceptions, and attempt to gain advantages whenever possible. One expert has said that "the objective reality of the arms competition, insofar as it can be judged, is quite different from the subjective conceptions of that competition held by many observers."[9]

Arms control arrangements cannot be expected to solve all strategic problems or to result in a completely stable strategic environment, and technical problems as well as practical negotiating constraints will inevitably limit the scope and substance of any accord. But it is equally clear that an uncontrolled arms environment is not free from uncertainty or potential dangers. Accordingly, arms limitation agreements should not be judged on an absolute scale, but by a "relative risk" standard— that is, satisfactory arms control measures should produce only a *net* improvement in security compared with the improvement that could be made in the absence of controls. This leaves open the possibility of negotiating an undesirable arms limitation agreement that could lead to a

8. See Benjamin S. Lambeth, "Deterrence in the MIRV Era," *World Politics*, vol. 24 (January 1972), pp. 221–42.

9. Herbert Scoville, Jr., *Toward a Strategic Arms Limitation Agreement* (Carnegie Endowment for International Peace, 1970), p. 6.

decrease in nuclear stability. In addition, while removal of uncertainty is an important arms control objective, some types of uncertainty, such as doubt about the success of a first-strike attack, can strengthen deterrence. These factors must be considered in evaluating any agreement using the relative risk concept.

To take a specific case, the SALT agreements of 1972 were imperfect from the standpoint of optimizing the U.S. strategic position, controlling the arms race, and eliminating nuclear problems. Despite their many inadequacies and imperfections, however, these accords helped to control the strategic arms competition and contributed favorably to U.S. security. The most significant accord in 1972 was the ABM treaty, which limits ABM deployments in the United States and the USSR to extremely low levels, restricts radar parameters and ABM-related test activities, and commits both nations to refrain from deploying nationwide missile defense systems. Because of the stringent limits on Soviet ABMs imposed by the treaty, the need for the United States to improve or enlarge its offensive forces diminished. The prospect of large ABM deployments by the USSR should no longer dominate defense planning, variations in offensive force levels and uncertainties over qualitative improvements should have less significance, and the potential for seriously destabilizing actions by either side should be reduced.

Although some experts criticized the ABM treaty, most of the American objections to the initial SALT accords centered on the Interim Agreement on offensive forces. There were legitimate grounds for concern, and even strong supporters of the agreement pointed to its potential long-term instabilities, which argued against establishing the accord on offensive weapons in treaty form without alteration.[10] On the other hand, if no constraints had been placed on Soviet offensive forces, the USSR might have continued deploying strategic missiles, perhaps reaching a level of 2,000 ICBMs and 80 nuclear-powered missile submarines by 1980. Faced with expanding Soviet programs, the United States would undoubtedly have reacted by producing a substantial force of new-generation offensive systems even more rapidly and on a larger scale than currently planned in order to maintain a numerical balance. Then the Soviet Union would almost surely have increased its offensive

10. For a discussion of the need to modify the Interim Agreement to ensure long-term stability, see statement of Jerome H. Kahan in *Strategic Arms Limitation Agreements,* Hearings before the Senate Committee on Foreign Relations, 92 Cong. 2 sess. (1972), pp. 201–19.

missile forces still further while improving the quality of its forces. These offensive missile buildups would have put pressure on both sides to expand their defensive networks, and even if ABM limitations had been negotiated, treaty abrogation would have become likely.

Other analysts contend that limitation accords can have such a pernicious effect on the arms race that negotiated agreements might be considered less desirable than an uncontrolled competition that frees both nations to manage their unilateral postures sensibly and with restraint. A number of American arms control advocates have suggested that the SALT I process undercut attempts at unilateral restraint by providing the Nixon administration with arguments in favor of continuing major strategic programs capable of exploiting the loopholes left in the Interim Agreement. These analysts claim, for example, that congressional opposition to administration strategic programs, such as the Safeguard ABM, Trident, and the B-1, would have succeeded in canceling or sharply curtailing U.S. arms procurements if it had not been for SALT. Instead, they argue, the administration disarmed its critics by justifying weapons as bargaining chips and hedges and, in order to gain support for an agreement that only marginally constrained the arms competition, the administration itself was forced to make concessions to the U.S. military and to conservative congressmen, involving commitments to systems that might not have been pressed otherwise. One observer even proposed that, all things considered, "protracted negotiations on arms control are likely to have a negative [i.e., destabilizing] impact upon the weapons competition."[11]

This argument is only partially persuasive and should not necessarily be accepted as valid. It goes without saying that neither nation should abuse the legitimate strategy of negotiating from strength and fulfilling the need for prudent hedges, but even if certain U.S. programs did receive undue impetus because of SALT I, there is a strong possibility that America's strategic arms activities and related budgets would have

11. Gray, "Of Bargaining Chips and Building Blocks," p. 271. At an Arms Control Panel meeting, Paul C. Warnke, former assistant defense secretary, was quoted as saying that the SALT I offensive arms limitation accord signed in Moscow was "slightly worse than having none at all," since it will be "as much of an encouragement" for new arms spending as "a brake" on the arms race. (Cited by Michael Getler, *Washington Post*, June 9, 1972.) Shortly after the arms talks began, Jeremy J. Stone questioned the value of negotiated restraint and argued that arms control should "begin at home." ("U.S. Military Policy: When and How to Use SALT," *Foreign Affairs*, vol. 48 [January 1970], pp. 262–73.)

reached *higher* levels without the arms limitation discussions and agreements. Despite the opposition to Safeguard, it is difficult to conclude with confidence that Congress would have been able to hold the line against deployment year after year as the Soviet Union increased its offensive power, as China began to test an ICBM, and if the USSR had begun to develop and perhaps to deploy an ABM system of its own.

It is also important to note that success at SALT, both in 1972 and in 1974, strengthened the pro-arms control factions in both nations through a consensus-building process and an institutional commitment to maintaining, as well as improving, the initial accords. In terms of bureaucratic politics, the signing of an arms limitation accord can be considered a transnational political activity, representing the outcome of a battle between the hawks and the doves on each side who were attempting to forge an implicit alliance with their counterparts on the other side.[12] As a result of the SALT negotiations, therefore, it appears that bargaining chip and hedging pressures are countered by widespread awareness throughout the bureaucracy and in the Congress of the benefits of SALT and of the need to further stability through unilateral decisions. The sustained Senate opposition to administration requests for improved missile accuracy throughout 1969–73 was one manifestation of congressional interest in strategic arms control. Within the Defense Department and in interagency deliberations, the impact of strategic programs on SALT has gradually become an institutionalized concern of the executive branch that affects many weapon decisions even though it may not be the dominant factor. Similar patterns undoubtedly exist in the USSR, and some signs of battles between proponents and opponents of arms control have surfaced in Soviet publications.

It is certainly possible that even without any limitations agreement the Soviet Union might not have built a strategic missile force larger than the levels permitted under the Interim Agreement, and it is also possible that the United States would not have moved forward with major strategic programs. While both nations ought to exercise unilateral restraint and pursue purely stabilizing strategic policies, however, experience shows that neither nation has taken such initiatives. In this sense, the Moscow accords—or any strategic arms limitation agreement—can be

12. Chayes analyzed the positive effects SALT can have on the bureaucratic mechanisms for arms decisions in the United States and the USSR in "An Inquiry into the Workings of Arms Control Agreements," pp. 919–69.

said to have the unique effect of forcing both sides to do together what they are unlikely to do separately.

REDUCING THE CONSEQUENCES OF NUCLEAR WAR

One commonly held view is that strategic arms control should help to reduce the consequences as well as the likelihood of nuclear war. Unfortunately, these two objectives may not always be compatible and, in fact, are often inversely related. For example, attempts to limit damage by constructing large-scale missile defense systems can create instabilities that increase the chances of deterrence failing. When faced with the dilemma of choosing between these goals, however, most U.S. officials place higher priority on deterrence than on damage limitation. Mutual assured destruction has been the foundation of the accords to date and undoubtedly will be the basis for future accords—despite the questionable contention that an alternative premise should be adopted. It makes sense to emphasize war prevention, since effective protection against nuclear attacks continues to be a costly and difficult problem, and even negotiated agreements to construct defenses on both sides do not appear workable. On the offensive side, moreover, only extremely sharp cuts in existing force levels, beyond the range of realistic negotiations for some time to come, could contribute to a meaningful reduction in damage. The goal of damage limitation, however, can be pursued through U.S.-Soviet agreements aimed at preventing nuclear escalation.

BUILDING MUTUAL CONFIDENCE

On the political plane, successful agreements in the strategic arms field can build confidence between the United States and the USSR and lead to further progress in other aspects of arms control. This confidence was evident when the Moscow SALT accords were signed, was reflected in the declaration of basic principles[13]—which underscored the determination of both governments to avoid confrontations and to seek a peaceful resolution of their differences—and helped make possible the Vladivostok agreement. Clearly, certain prerequisites in political relations between Washington and Moscow were required before either side could engage in serious SALT negotiations. But some analysts fear that the SALT framework may not further relations and express concern that the process of negotiation could evolve into a political conflict.

13. Basic Principles of Relations between the United States of America and the Union of Soviet Socialist Republics, signed at Moscow, May 29, 1972. For the text of the principles, see *New York Times*, May 30, 1972.

Furthermore, it is often argued that any diminution of U.S.-Soviet tensions is due to factors outside the nuclear field, that détente is fragile, and that the Soviet Union might exploit any arms control accords and America's interest in reaching more equitable agreements to our disadvantage. Even conceding many of these points, however, the negotiation of the SALT agreements in 1972 and 1974 symbolized improved relations between the two sides and has had a positive political effect in contributing to a coordinated U.S.-Soviet approach to nuclear security problems. The personal diplomacy involved in the presidential-level SALT interventions and summit visits, the confidence and mutual respect developed between members of the negotiating teams, and the continued use of private "back-channel" contacts all seemed to demonstrate the determination of both nations to pursue a productive pattern of discussions.

Against the background of the continuing Middle East crisis, strains in the Western alliance caused by the energy shortage, and the steady spiral of weapon buildups on the strategic level, the future of SALT now assumes greater international political significance. The success of Washington and Moscow in overcoming the many difficulties standing in the way of negotiating comprehensive strategic arms control agreements that satisfy the security interests of both nations but honor commitments to their respective allies would serve to signal the durability of détente and could stimulate efforts to reduce tensions in other areas, notably Central Europe. Failure to conclude and follow up on the Vladivostok agreement, on the other hand, could strengthen the hand of the hawks in the United States and the USSR, provide a political climate for intensifying the nuclear competition, and endanger the slow but steady progress toward East-West cooperation.

LOWERING THE COSTS OF STRATEGIC PROGRAMS

Arms control proponents frequently claim that agreements can lower the costs of strategic programs. To the extent that agreements such as the ABM treaty prevent the deployment of expensive systems that are destabilizing or unnecessary, substantial savings can be realized. But the Interim Agreement did not affect MIRV installation programs, for example, nor did it rule out modernization programs or restrict qualitative improvements in offensive weapons. After the Moscow accords were signed, the USSR mounted a substantial missile test program, and the U.S. strategic offensive weapons budget increased slightly owing to decisions to modernize existing systems and to institute "assurance" programs in order to provide hedges. This suggested that both sides would maintain high levels of strategic expenditures under any limitation measures likely to be reached in the near future—measures that would not involve steep arms reductions or strict controls over qualitative improvements and force modernization. The Vladivostok agreement seemed to bear out this expectation. Although there is the obvious danger that SALT could contribute to unnecessary spending on strategic weapon procurement, the preservation of a stable and secure strategic posture *within* the framework of arms control accords can require considerable investments.

Pending Kremlin restraint or substantially larger arms reductions than are apt to be achieved in SALT in the near future, the United States can preserve a confident deterrent built on a diversified and survivable strategic posture only if it develops options for improving the survivability and overall effectiveness of its force against likely future Soviet strategic threats. In addition, certain U.S. strategic programs might legitimately be expanded as a result of the SALT I agreements, the Vladivostok guidelines, or any future SALT arrangements. For instance, it could prove necessary to place greater emphasis on national verification efforts needed to monitor Soviet compliance with strategic arms accords. Moreover, it might well be important to develop specialized hedges against potentially undetectable Soviet weapon improvements and to establish a stand-by capacity permitting rapid deployments of U.S. systems barred by SALT agreements in the event the accords were abrogated for any reason. Apart from their prudential value, these programs could help the administration and Congress gain a sense of confidence in the new environment created by continuing SALT negotiations and lower the likelihood that false alarms might generate tensions between Washington and Moscow.

In relative terms, of course, even if strategic spending continues to rise despite the SALT agreements, the costs of U.S. strategic forces would almost surely be greater without the agreements. One estimate indicated that annual spending for U.S. strategic forces over the years 1973–79 would have run $3 billion higher than projected expenditures under the SALT I accords.[14] In this sense, budgetary savings resulting

14. See Charles L. Schultze and others, *Setting National Priorities: The 1973 Budget* (Brookings Institution, 1972), pp. 93–109. This estimate was based on the assumption that, without the restrictions of the Moscow treaty, the United States

from SALT agreements are likely to continue to arise from forgoing future increased expenditures rather than from appreciable cuts in present levels of spending. In the last analysis, however, the lack of substantial savings should not be permitted to obscure the primary potential value of SALT agreements in reducing nuclear risks, stabilizing the balance, and strengthening political relations between the superpowers.

Verification Issues

The question of verification has impeded U.S.-Soviet attempts to negotiate arms control agreements, because Moscow has refused to accept Washington's demands for on-site inspection. This impasse has been partly overcome through the formulation of limited arms control agreements that can be verified by national means—primarily by satellite reconnaissance systems and externally based sensors. The decision to seek less comprehensive accords, combined with improvements in national verification capabilities, resulted in the partial test ban treaty of 1963[15] and made possible the negotiation of the Moscow SALT accords and the Vladivostok guidelines. In contrast to the U.S. "freeze" proposal of 1964, which called for extensive inspection and was nonnegotiable in large part for this reason, America's expressed willingness to consider strategic limitations without on-site inspection contributed greatly to the Soviet Union's decision to enter into SALT discussions. With few exceptions, the various U.S. plans presented during the negotiations of 1969 and 1970 emphasized reliance on national means of verification, and as anticipated, the SALT agreements of 1972, like the 1974 Vladivostok agreement, contained no provisions for on-site inspection. The terms of the Moscow agreements formally acknowledged that each party would use "national technical means of verification . . . for the purpose of providing assurance of compliance with the provisions."[16] It is even more significant that the accords legalized this situation by prohibiting any interference with these verification systems as long as they operated in accordance with the principles of international law. In addition, both

would move forward with the full Safeguard ABM deployment and continue the Trident and B-1 modernization programs at a rapid rate.

15. Treaty Banning Nuclear Weapon Tests in the Atmosphere, in Outer Space and under Water, signed at Moscow, August 15, 1963.

16. See Article XII of the ABM treaty in "Documentation on the Strategic Arms Limitation Agreements" (U.S. Department of State, Bureau of Public Affairs release, June 20, 1972; processed), p. 27.

sides unexpectedly agreed not to undertake "deliberate concealment measures" that would hamper effective verification. Provisions in the 1972 accords regarding verification will probably be retained in any arms control accord based on the Vladivostok agreement.

TECHNICAL INTELLIGENCE CAPABILITIES

To support its unilateral strategic policy requirements, the United States maintains a substantial technical intelligence program designed to monitor Soviet weapon activities.[17] Reconnaissance satellites that overfly the USSR and gather photographic data of remarkable coverage and accuracy are the most effective, but a variety of other systems operating outside the Soviet Union are essential in identifying and evaluating Soviet strategic arms efforts. This latter category includes ground-based radars as well as airborne and shipborne electronic surveillance systems. The Soviet Union maintains similar programs to supplement the wealth of publicly available material dealing with U.S. strategic weapons.

Although the Moscow accords and the Vladivostok agreement make no provision for on-site inspection, the United States would be able to verify the restrictions with a high degree of confidence through national means. The distinctive size of major strategic systems, such as ICBM launchers, submarine-launched ballistic missiles (SLBMs), missile-firing submarines, and ABM launchers and associated radars, and their long construction time, permit the United States to detect their deployment patterns. For example, it takes almost two years for a hardened ICBM launch complex to progress from the first stage of visible construction to fully operational status, and the deployment of a force of hundreds of these systems could span a period of years. To complete the construction of an ABM site can take at least five years, mainly because of the difficulty of building large radar installations. In principle, the Soviet Union could attempt to disguise its deployment activities, but this would involve considerable technical difficulty as well as a high risk of discovery with its attendant political costs. In addition, there would be little payoff for Soviet leaders in undertaking an evasion program unless they could be reasonably certain of gaining a meaningful advantage. This is a most unlikely prospect, for the United States would be certain

17. See Ted Greenwood, "Reconnaissance, Surveillance, and Arms Control," *Adelphi Papers*, no. 88 (London: International Institute for Strategic Studies, June 1972).

of identifying Soviet violations before they became significant enough to pose a threat to our deterrent or to dramatically alter the numerical balance.

ABMs offer the most worrisome prospect for Soviet cheating, since clandestine efforts to upgrade missile defenses could seriously threaten the U.S. retaliatory deterrent capability. Given the stringent limitations of the Moscow treaty, however, it is highly improbable that the Soviet Union could successfully conceal the deployment of substantial numbers of ABM launchers or could convert air-defense systems into missile-defense functions without early detection by the United States. In any case, with the full installation of MIRVs and continued qualitative improvements, the United States would have a cushion against uncertainties and could tolerate delay and ambiguity in detecting possible Soviet violations. Consequently, the USSR would be unable to suddenly abrogate the treaty by rapidly deploying defensive or offensive systems on a scale that would threaten U.S. security before appropriate counteractions could be taken.

In addition to readily verifiable launcher limitations, the initial SALT I accords also imposed controls on certain qualitative improvements and developmental activities. The Interim Agreement, for example, prohibited the replacement of small ICBMs with larger systems and barred major increases in the size of missile silos, while the ABM treaty restricted the characteristics of missile-defense components permitted to be deployed and placed constraints on ABM-related testing. Both sides apparently concluded that such controls were necessary and could be adequately monitored through national means. Problems of definition have arisen, however, particularly on the distinction between light and heavy ICBMs. But the scope of qualitative as well as quantitative limitations contained in the Moscow accords suggests that a variety of additional measures could be negotiated without facing the question of on-site inspection. Indeed, by relying on its technical intelligence capabilities, the United States could verify Soviet compliance with many controls that might be included in future strategic arms agreements that could result in more comprehensive restrictions than the Vladivostok guidelines, such as reductions in deployed missile forces and prohibitions on full-scale testing of new types of launching systems.

On the other hand, national verification systems would be incapable of monitoring many important strategic programs and activities. It is difficult for such systems to fully discern specific weapon performance characteristics, such as precise accuracy and penetration effectiveness, and some experts even question whether a ban on MIRV testing could be adequately verified.[18] Relatively reliable inferences regarding the extent and nature of MIRV deployments could be drawn from indirect evidence, such as the flight-test patterns and basing characteristics of newly developed missile systems associated with MIRV programs. This general approach has been incorporated in the Vladivostok guidelines, which limit the number of MIRV-equipped missiles each side can field. But only direct observation can verify with complete confidence the presence or absence of multiple warheads on operational missiles and the precise number of warheads. Finally, neither satellite cameras nor externally based radars could be relied on to adequately monitor weapon production rates, the quality of critical components, or research and development efforts housed in laboratories and factories.

Accordingly, the search for long-term stability might make it necessary to extend strategic arms agreements into areas that cannot be monitored by national means alone and that would require supplementary verification arrangements. Thus, research projects must be continued in an attempt to discover effective, nonintrusive, and negotiable inspection concepts.

Serious practical problems, however, are associated with developing viable on-site inspection schemes. If the USSR were to permit the United States to check Soviet missiles in order to monitor a MIRV deployment ban, for example, evasion and harassment could degrade the reliability of this procedure. Trained inspection teams outfitted with technical devices could improve the effectiveness of an inspection system, but even if inspectors had free access, their ability to determine the characteristics of complex strategic weapons simply by observing components and equipment is highly questionable. Furthermore, it would be difficult to design workable procedures whereby inspectors could monitor controlled activities without inadvertently becoming aware of secret information about the host's weapon systems. Thus, on-site inspection arrangements could provide one side with classified information that might threaten the reliability of the other side's deterrent forces. For these reasons, it is doubtful that the United States would allow Soviet representatives access to our systems.

18. See ibid. for a comprehensive and balanced discussion of MIRV verification; and Herbert Scoville, Jr., "Verification of Nuclear Arms Limitations: An Analysis," *Science and Public Affairs*, October 1970, pp. 6–11.

In order to avoid the problems of on-site inspection, other aids to unilateral verification could be considered. One approach, based on the principle of adversary cooperation, would require both sides to announce all missile flight tests beforehand and to agree to conduct such activities from specified launch points to designated impact areas.[19] This procedure would facilitate verification, since national collection systems could concentrate on specific events and areas. Attempts to test outside the agreed ranges or to conduct clandestine firings could be detected with relatively high confidence. A different concept would involve stationing tamper-proof "black boxes" at deployment and test sites within each nation. These sensors could monitor controlled activities and eliminate the need for resident inspectors. Because of the many technical and political complexities associated with inspection, it would be useful if a separate U.S.-Soviet working group could discuss this issue during subsequent SALT negotiations.

PRINCIPLES OF VERIFICATION

Discussions of verification capabilities, while essential to any analysis of strategic arms control, can be misleading if not put in proper perspective. The principal purposes of a verification system are, after all, to assure compliance and to deter violations. In addressing the question of what constitutes adequate verification, it is both unreasonable and unnecessary to demand complete certainty in detecting every possible infraction. To adhere to the concept of relative risk, a nation need only ensure that violations significant enough to pose a threat to its security can be detected in sufficient time to take appropriate counteractions. Whether this criterion can be satisfied in SALT agreements does not depend on verification capabilities alone but is related to the size and character of the strategic balance established by a particular agreement. While security considerations should be paramount in setting verification requirements, it must also be recognized that serious infractions that might not threaten military stability could have adverse political effects and endanger the viability of an accord.

In designing a verification system, careful consideration should be given to the incentives and risks that could influence a nation contemplating a program of evasion. For example, there would be little in-

19. Greenwood discussed the possible use of agreed impact areas in "Reconnaissance, Surveillance, and Arms Control."

centive for the USSR to undertake an evasion program under SALT unless it could be reasonably certain of gaining a meaningful advantage. But the massive effort required to mount a clandestine Soviet deployment program that could pose a military threat to America's retaliatory capability or dramatically alter the numerical balance would be technically difficult and expensive and would run a high risk of detection. Small violations, on the other hand, might remain undetected but would have little significance. The Soviet Union could, of course, decide openly to abrogate the Moscow agreement or any agreement reached on the basis of the Vladivostok guidelines. The United States, however, would undoubtedly continue to improve its forces within the terms of any SALT accord, making it virtually impossible for a sudden abrogation that could threaten U.S. security. The international embarrassment of being accused of violating an agreement and the risks inherent in the resumption of an uncontrolled arms race also inhibit evasive actions. Indeed, rather than evade or abrogate, if either the USSR or the United States decided that continued adherence to an arms limitation accord could endanger its security, it would probably evoke the withdrawal clause in the Moscow agreements, a clause certain to be included in all future treaties.[20]

Recent experience suggests that arms control agreements remain relatively stable. Without clear justification, U.S. and Soviet leaders would be wary of abrogating a SALT accord or of even accusing the other side of cheating, since such actions would have major consequences for international security and relations between the two superpowers. Inadvertent violations and minor infractions of a strategic arms limitation agreement would probably be handled diplomatically, as infractions of the partial test ban treaty are handled.[21] The SALT Standing Consultative Committee permits both nations to discuss precise interpretations of restrictions, clarifies actions by either side that might otherwise generate false alarms regarding compliance, and oversees agreed procedures affecting weapon deployments, modifications, and replacements. At the same time that such efforts are being made to sustain sound agreements, however, each nation should be wary of permitting political commitments or bureaucratic inertia to lead to the perpetuation of an

20. See Article VIII-3 of the ABM treaty in "Documentation on the Strategic Arms Limitation Agreements," p. 22.

21. Chayes discussed the stability of the limited test ban treaty in "An Inquiry into the Workings of Arms Control Agreements," p. 967.

undesirable agreement. Limitations should be adjusted as required to ensure that mutual security and strategic stability will be strengthened through continued participation in an arms control arrangement.

The scope of an agreement is closely related to its verifiability and its susceptibility to evasion. Some specialists contend that relatively comprehensive controls could be safely negotiated, even if individual arms restrictions were not fully verifiable. If all weapon categories were covered and all activities from development to deployment were subject to limitations, it is claimed, the chances of detecting a single prohibited action would increase.[22] Other analysts argue that such agreements would lead to an excessive number of false alarms and, what is more important, would prevent the United States from retaining sufficient unilateral freedom of action to hedge against uncertainties and guard against possible Soviet violations.

All experts share the view that a total ban on an activity can be verified more easily than the mere constraint of certain activities. For example, the complete prohibition of deployments of land-mobile missile systems would be preferable to limitations, since an accurate count of operational missiles deployed by an adversary would be difficult to obtain, but under a total ban only one missile, if detected, would constitute a violation. As another example, strictly from a verification standpoint it would be preferable to ban all missile testing rather than to prohibit only certain types of testing in an attempt to preclude accuracy improvements or to restrict other specific weapon characteristics. Surprising as it may seem, in certain circumstances it might make sense to restrict a relatively unverifiable action. If both sides were not eager to implement a particular weapon program and neither side's deterrent would be endangered if its adversary proceeded with such an effort, a mutual ban could help deter deployment and reduce tension. In essence, this approach was followed in the outer space treaty, which prohibited the stationing of weapons of mass destruction in earth orbit or on celestial bodies.[23]

22. For an analysis of the benefits of a comprehensive freeze on strategic forces and a discussion of a variety of offensive arms agreements, see Herbert Scoville, Jr., "The Limitation of Offensive Weapons," *Scientific American*, January 1971, pp. 15–25.

23. Treaty on the Principles Governing the Activities of States in the Exploration and Use of Outer Space, Including the Moon and Other Celestial Bodies, signed at Washington, London, and Moscow, January 27, 1967.

Important as they may be, however, verification considerations should not be permitted to dominate decisions on strategic arms limitations. Overemphasizing the need to verify all controls not only creates the risk of foreclosing the prospects for reaching agreement but raises the possibility that a useless or potentially destabilizing agreement will be negotiated. For example, easily controllable weapon activities, such as missile-firing submarines, will do little to accelerate the arms race and need not be limited, while potentially destabilizing activities that should be restricted, such as missile accuracy improvements, will prove difficult to limit. In the final analysis, the verifiability of a strategic arms limitation measure should simply be one of many factors to be weighed in evaluating the relative security implications of particular controls.

Forms of Agreement

The form of a strategic arms limitation agreement can influence its effectiveness and durability.[24] Most contemporary agreements have taken the traditional form of a treaty, largely because treaties have recognized political as well as legal obligations and can substantially influence the behavior between nations and the attitudes of leaders within each nation. Although a well-designed treaty contains provisions for consultation and review as well as procedures for modification, it nonetheless conveys a sense of permanence and commitment that other types of agreement do not convey. The Moscow ABM treaty, for example, was a serious, long-term agreement by both nations to forgo the option of nationwide defenses.

On the other hand, if strategic weapon limitations are incomplete, controversial, or highly sensitive to near-term technological or political development, a less formal arrangement would be more appropriate. An informal arrangement offers greater flexibility than a treaty and can facilitate arms control progress. The five-year Interim Agreement on offensive weapons, for example, permits controls to be placed on certain systems while both sides seek the limitations necessary to secure a more stable and comprehensive set of measures. In addition to such an execu-

24. See George Bunn, "Missile Limitation: By Treaty or Otherwise?" *Columbia Law Review*, vol. 70 (January 1970), pp. 1–47; and Jerome H. Kahan, "Strategies for SALT," *World Politics*, vol. 23 (January 1971), pp. 171–88.

tive agreement, bilateral commitments could be instituted through the less formal mechanisms of moratoriums or reciprocal-action declarations. The temporary nature of the Interim Agreement attested to the fact that neither nation felt completely comfortable with its provisions and might not renew the measure if modifications or additions were not forthcoming.

In the final analysis, however, while less formal limitations can usefully serve as temporary measures, a treaty, because of its precision and political power and the legal obligations it defines, would be best suited to imposing comprehensive controls on the strategic competition over the long term. Thus, the Vladivostok guidelines seek to rectify the shortcomings of the Interim Agreement by establishing the basis for a stronger accord that would last at least ten years. Such an accord could remain sufficiently flexible to accommodate changing technology that might require minor amendments to the basic agreement, the need to negotiate completely new or more comprehensive measures as the political climate permits, and the problem of dealing with nuclear military power in countries other than the United States and the USSR.

On the basis of the SALT experience thus far, it might seem that formal negotiations are useless or counterproductive because, although they create the illusion of progress, real headway toward agreement is made between officials at a higher level than the heads of the delegations, often in private back-channel discussions. Without question, the Nixon-Brezhnev meetings in 1971 helped break a deadlock at SALT, the Moscow summit in 1972 spurred the two sides to find an acceptable compromise, and the Kissinger-Dobrynin meetings were obviously an important element in the SALT equation. The Vladivostok agreement was also reached at a summit in 1974.

The value of formal negotiations, however, should not be underestimated. Through complicated discussions and hard bargaining, the "front channel" produced the foundation for the SALT I agreements—an understanding regarding the need for low ABM levels and quantitative limits on offensive arms. Issues resolved outside the formal channel were not always of fundamental significance and often involved details concerning such matters as final ABM restrictions and the precise limits of SLBMs. Although personal diplomacy and ad hoc contacts can be useful, the systematic, fully staffed, and institutionalized structure of formal negotiations are beneficial in reaching the goal of mutually acceptable measures. At the same time, it should be recognized that major decisions on SALT positions are generally made in Washington and Moscow—not at the negotiating table.[25]

VALUE OF A DIALOGUE

Entirely apart from negotiated measures, discussions of strategic arms and arms control issues between U.S. and Soviet officials can be useful in their own right. The broad and informal exchange of views during the course of SALT has helped reduce mistrust by increasing each side's understanding of the other's programs, policies, and perceived threats. As mutual understanding of strategic matters improves, both nations may feel able to adopt more restrained strategic arms policies and the arms competition might be contained through tacit reciprocal action, without any formal accords. In addition, by first establishing common guidelines and clarifying issues through organized discussions, weapon controls could be more easily reached and agreements would have a better chance of remaining stable. Discussions of such problems as accidental nuclear war, moreover, could lead to arrangements that do not affect arms levels or weapon characteristics but take the form of agreements to establish procedures or principles—as in the case of the agreement to reduce the risk of nuclear war reached in 1971[26]—that can help realize arms control goals.

There are, of course, inherent limitations in a strategic arms dialogue between the United States and the USSR, as SALT has shown. Classified materials, for one thing, restrict the level of detail that can be discussed. This is clearly more of a constraint for Soviet negotiators than it is for U.S. representatives, given the penchant for secrecy in the USSR. But even beyond security requirements, neither nation can be expected to be completely candid in exposing its military objectives or explaining the basis for its arms policies. Weapon decisions are not always made for entirely rational reasons, and nuclear strategies on both sides contain destabilizing elements. Because of the differences in U.S. and Soviet doctrinal attitudes, force structures, and security requirements, it may not be possible for both sides to reach an understanding on all key questions. This problem should be put in perspective, however, by recognizing that, as in the case of the Moscow accords of 1972, it may be

25. John Newhouse discussed the use of the back-channel during the SALT negotiations and the control exerted by Washington policymakers over the delegation in *Cold Dawn: The Story of SALT* (Holt, Rinehart, and Winston, 1973).

26. Agreement on Measures to Reduce the Risk of Outbreak of Nuclear War between the United States of America and the Union of Soviet Socialist Republics, signed at Washington, September 30, 1971.

unnecessary for the United States and the USSR to agree fully on the rationale behind specific limitations in order to be able to strike a mutually acceptable bargain. In fact, undue insistence on common premises as a prerequisite for arms control could undercut prospects for weapon limitation agreements.

In sum, a strategic arms dialogue coupled with attempts to negotiate specific arms agreements is probably the most productive approach to SALT. Weapon agreements reached without a discussion of broader issues can lead to problems in implementing, interpreting, or modifying an accord and might suffer because lack of understanding would prevent both nations from fully appreciating the political significance of a limitation measure. But discussions alone cannot be relied on to curb the arms competition or to enhance nuclear stability. It is doubtful that even an extremely productive strategic arms dialogue can have the practical effect of prompting the United States or the USSR to take initiatives in the direction of arms restraint by halting or delaying weapon development and deployment. During the preliminary phases of the SALT I discussions, neither nation took such initiatives, although many opportunities were present. Instead, both sides continued to enlarge their strategic arsenals as a hedge against the failure of negotiations and as a means of strengthening their negotiating positions. If neither side is prepared to take steps toward restraint, the arms competition cannot be checked. For this reason, explicit bilateral agreements, whether treaties or less permanent arrangements, are ultimately needed to break the action-reaction cycle and to impede the internal momentum for weapon programs.

Bargaining Tactics

Although arms control negotiations can be considered cooperative ventures in which both parties profit from an agreement, it is equally true that each side will seek to maximize its relative advantage within this framework. This can be accomplished either by an agreement that permits one nation to maintain strategic programs yielding advantages to it or by an agreement that curbs an opponent's edge and thereby reduces threats. Each of the superpowers should be willing to accept certain restrictions on its strategic programs if the other is prepared to offer concessions by accepting appropriate restrictions on its strategic programs. The decision to accept mutual limitations involves the judgment that national security objectives are better served by forgoing or limiting a particular program under an agreement that requires an opponent to do the same.[27]

Obviously, neither nation will accept a SALT agreement unless it is consistent with national strategic objectives. But this condition could be satisfied over a wide range of force levels and types, depending on the constraints imposed on the opposing side. In some cases, of course, one side will consider a weapon to be nonnegotiable. This could occur if the program in question has already resulted in intense domestic and bureaucratic commitment or, on more rational grounds, if a system is scheduled to be deployed as an economic replacement for an older system. A new U.S. bomber program, for example, would probably not be subject to negotiation in SALT if the United States desired to maintain aircraft in its strategic posture, although the number of units deployed or possibly certain controls over characteristics could be considered for inclusion in a limitation accord.

The United States and the USSR both have bargaining strength to support their positions in future SALT negotiations—strength derived from adversary interest in controlling certain strategic programs. In theory, as a bargaining lever, perhaps in connection with seeking to formalize the Vladivostok agreement, one side or the other could threaten not to renew the Interim Agreement or, more dramatically, to abrogate the ABM treaty if negotiations collapsed. But this approach to bargaining, while always implicit and occasionally expressed, is too sweeping and self-defeating to be credible, given the security interests at stake on both sides. Rather than threaten abrogation, the United States and the USSR throughout the SALT process have followed a broad strategy of negotiating from strength and have specifically used bargaining chip tactics.[28]

NEGOTIATING FROM STRENGTH AND THE USE OF BARGAINING CHIPS

In negotiating from strength, one side attempts to persuade the other that its strategic position is strong and will remain so even if negotiations fail. Thus, the other side, in principle, will be more willing to compromise and to accept a mutual accord than to delay and risk a less favorable outcome or face the prospect of an uncontrolled arms race. During

27. This discussion draws on Thomas C. Schelling, "A Framework for the Evaluation of Arms Proposals," Discussion Paper 210 (John F. Kennedy School of Government, Harvard University, January 1974; processed).

28. As noted in chapter 3, however, U.S. leaders did suggest that they might decide to abrogate the ABM treaty unless a satisfactory permanent offensive arms accord could be reached in SALT II.

SALT I the U.S. administration attempted to strengthen its negotiating position with a range of strategic programs and campaigned for continuing and expanding programs to support future negotiations. If such programs can be justified as hedges against uncertainty or as necessary to maintain a confident U.S. deterrent, this strategy cannot be faulted. After all, the Soviet Union bargained hard and continued to improve its strategic programs throughout the SALT I talks and maintained an aggressive negotiating position and an active strategic program while possibilities for the Vladivostok agreement were being explored. As the SALT II negotiations progress, the USSR will surely propose measures that the United States will find difficult to accept and will oppose many of our own proposals. Therefore, leverage should be available to strengthen the hand of U.S. negotiators during the difficult discussions that lie ahead. In particular, the United States must develop and demonstrate both the will and the capacity to counter Soviet attempts to achieve military or numerical superiority in order to provide incentives for the USSR to seek equitable negotiated limitations.

The concept of bargaining chips involves a more direct use of weapon programs to persuade an adversary to accept limits on weapon activities. If a weapon on one side is linked to a weapon on the other side—either through direct force matching or through an offense-defense relationship —then the weapon in question is clearly a chip that could logically be given up if the appropriate opposing weapon is limited by agreement. Conversely, statements by one nation to the effect that a particular program will proceed unless the related program on the other side is restricted can become part of the SALT negotiations. During the first round of SALT I talks, the United States linked the Safeguard missile-site ABM program to constraints on the Soviet SS-9 ICBMs, which had the potential of threatening Minuteman. Of course, one side might deliberately overstate the significance of a particular program in an attempt to force the other side to accept certain terms or might initiate weapon programs somewhat sooner than anticipated in order to buttress negotiating positions. At times, these tactics may be justified and lead to a solid agreement. If this bargaining approach results in appropriate agreements that constrain certain Soviet strategic programs, for example, the United States could then modify its strategic plans, taking account of the reduced threat, even if an agreement does not limit the American programs in question.

While the value of intense negotiating strategies cannot be denied, there are disadvantages in pressing the bargaining chip or negotiating-from-strength arguments too far. For one thing, if not kept within bounds, these approaches can reduce the prospects for agreement by stimulating the nuclear competition in uncontrolled areas as each side seeks to acquire more bargaining chips in response to the other side's moves. Of particular concern is the deliberate use of this concept to gain domestic support for programs that run into trouble on military, technical, or cost grounds. This policy can have many pernicious consequences. For example, if weapon systems are deployed for bargaining purposes or if excessive program momentum is built up because of negotiations, it becomes virtually impossible to reverse the process. In addition to foreclosing limitation options, such bargaining strategies can lead both sides to acquire costly or unwanted programs, independent of any agreements that might be reached. Some U.S. observers point to the lack of MIRV restrictions and a total ABM ban in the SALT accords of 1972, the acceleration of the Trident submarine project, and the continuation of the B-1 bomber program as products of the misapplication of bargaining tactics by the Nixon administration. If care is not taken, newer developmental programs with questionable military value, such as the strategic cruise missile or a larger version of Minuteman for installation in existing ICBM silos, could gain undue momentum if tied to alleged negotiating needs and turn into billion dollar efforts.

The use of destabilizing programs as bargaining levers is an especially dubious, if not a dangerous, tactic. There is the risk that employment of this tactic, even to force the other side to drop its destabilizing programs, will stimulate the weapon competition, exacerbate tensions, and defeat the objectives of arms control. If, for instance, the United States were to develop a hard-target kill capability in order to induce the USSR to forgo comparable developments or to coerce the Kremlin into agreeing to reduce its ICBM force under a SALT agreement, the Soviet Union might well respond with an even greater commitment to its own counterforce program. In this case, the U.S. effort would have been worse than self-defeating; both sides would have hard-target kill weapons. Rather than run this risk, the United States should refrain from pursuing a counterforce capability in the interest of following a stabilizing unilateral strategic policy.[29] The disadvantages of compromising mutual stability

29. As discussed in chapter 4, Defense Secretary Schlesinger has argued that the United States must not permit the USSR to obtain a unilateral advantage in counterforce capabilities. Some analysts believe the secretary is attempting to use the threat that the United States will match any Soviet hard-target kill programs as a bargaining tool to persuade Soviet leaders to agree to "essential equivalence" in SALT II. See, for example, John W. Finney, *New York Times*, January 22, 1974.

criteria in the name of negotiations are too great to justify such a strategy.

POLICY OF RESTRAINT

In contrast to aggressive negotiating tactics, it is possible to adopt a policy of restraint in order to support negotiations. Under this policy, the United States not only would abide by the restrictions of any negotiated agreement but would seek to avoid programs that might foreclose future limitation options either by irrevocably committing the nation to a specific weapon system or by threatening the USSR. In order to facilitate opportunities for mutual agreements that could enhance security, the United States would avoid premature commitments to deployments, even at the temporary risk of being unable to maintain a highly confident deterrent or of facing a costly crash program if the agreements did not materialize. On the other hand, if this unilateral strategic policy led to a successful SALT agreement, it might prove unnecessary to procure certain expensive systems at all, since the threats that justified such systems could be removed through an arms control treaty. This line of reasoning motivated many experts to propose that the United States unilaterally halt its MIRV testing during 1969–70, pending attempts to discuss a mutual MIRV ban with the USSR. Similar arguments were used by opponents of the Safeguard ABM program during that period.

Advocates of a policy of restraint claim that it can bring success without the disadvantages of an aggressive tactic. They believe that in principle, as in the case of the nuclear test moratorium, such reciprocal restraint can create the political climate and technical prerequisites for effective strategic arms agreements.[30] Restraint on one side, for example, might induce a restrained response by strengthening the arms control advocates on the other side and might lead to an improved agreement with more comprehensive controls. U.S. negotiators need not escalate the arms race through the use of a bargaining chip tactic, which results in the procurement of unnecessary or destabilizing systems, because America's technological potential and research activities offer sufficient leverage to deal effectively with Soviet negotiators. Indeed, it is claimed that bargaining tactics that exploit the *potential* for deployment, such as

30. See statements advocating restraint by Marshall Shulman and Paul C. Warnke in *Arms Control Implications of Current Defense Budget,* Hearings before the Subcommittee on Arms Control and International Law and Organization of the Senate Committee on Foreign Relations, 92 Cong. 2 sess. (1971), pp. 205–20, 243–74.

congressional authorization to place construction funds in escrow, might be equally effective in supporting a strong negotiating posture without detracting from the ultimate value of the agreements being sought. If the United States had followed a restrained negotiating strategy, some observers claim, it might have been possible to reach a more comprehensive set of initial SALT limitations at lower force levels.

As a practical matter, however, unilateral restraint may not prove to be a persuasive tactic at the SALT table but may weaken the U.S. position. It can be argued, for example, that a complete halt in the Safeguard ABM construction program in 1969 might well have reduced the USSR's incentive to accept SALT limitations, such as the subceiling on SS-9 missiles and strict ABM radar controls, since the USSR apparently was interested in limiting our ABMs above all else. The limits accepted by the USSR in return not only served U.S. security interests but improved the stability of the agreement. In the future, if America were to discontinue active development programs to modernize its strategic forces, the USSR might see less need to agree to limitations sought by the United States. As a related matter, the United States might undercut the chances of negotiating mutual ICBM reductions if it phased out its land-based missile force unilaterally and rapidly—even though this might make sense as a longer-term strategy. Similarly, since the U.S. advantage in long-range bombers can provide an incentive for the USSR to accept cuts in its superior ICBM force, the United States should be wary of reducing its B-52 force levels before a serious attempt has been made to obtain a Soviet quid pro quo. In these and other instances, a policy of unilateral restraint consistent with what may appear to be cost-effective decisions regarding the U.S. strategic posture could decrease the likelihood of reaching productive bilateral limitation accords.

SEEKING A MIDDLE GROUND

It seems clear that neither restraints nor threats represent a totally satisfying SALT negotiating strategy. U.S. leaders must approach negotiations by recognizing the benefits and risks of both positive and negative leverage, by comparing the net effects of mutual limitations and those of no agreements at all, and by seeking the best means to attain the ultimate objective—mutual stability—whether through negotiated measures or unilateral actions. Unfortunately, it will often seem unclear which negotiating tactic is most suitable; to make matters worse, in many cases there will be genuine conflicts between satisfying the requirement of maintaining a dependable retaliatory force and seeking bilateral agreements in the midst of a dynamic and uncertain negotiating environment.

In an attempt to balance deterrence requirements and negotiating needs, the United States might do the following:

• Prevent the bargaining chip rationale from becoming the major motive for pursuing programs that cannot be justified as necessary to support U.S. deterrent objectives, that would otherwise be halted or delayed for cost-effectiveness reasons, and that have no potential trading counterpart on the Soviet side.

• Maintain the momentum of developmental programs designed to offset potential threats to our retaliatory capability or to redress severe strategic imbalances and maintain a confident deterrent posture, but avoid moving these systems into full flight-test or procurement stages simply to strengthen our negotiating position.

• Reject using programs as negotiating levers that might threaten the USSR's deterrent and, while engaged in SALT bargaining, remain aware of the possible destabilizing effect of U.S. strategic policies on Moscow's programs, policies, and perceptions.

• Indicate to the Soviet Union that, pending an acceptable agreement, continued unilateral restraint on our part in developing particular programs will require some form of reciprocity—not necessarily a symmetrical Soviet response but one that reduces the threat our programs are designed to meet.

• Be wary of using the threat of abrogation as a bargaining tool; if implemented and applied to the ABM treaty in particular, this policy would undercut the foundation of SALT by triggering defensive as well as offensive deployments, and there would be no assurance that America's strategic posture could be maintained more effectively in this way than in an arms control environment.

• Recognize that the failure of both sides to reach a more effective offensive arms agreement, or even the USSR's unlikely but possible decision to abrogate the ABM treaty, need not necessarily strengthen the case for new U.S. strategic arms deployments and that arms decisions should continue to be guided by the need to maintain a confident deterrent.

Strategic Arms Limitation Possibilities

It is impossible to prescribe what the precise elements of future SALT agreements should be or to predict the course of SALT negotiations during this decade. The guidelines established by the Vladivostok agreement are relatively broad, and the shape of possible follow-on accords is undetermined. Because of asymmetries in the size, characteristics, and purposes of the strategic forces deployed by each superpower, at best experts can only formulate a range of agreements that make technical sense and that permit the preservation of a stable mutual deterrent relationship. A continuing convergence of positions can be expected only when the dynamics of the negotiating process have taken hold and when mutual internal political needs can be accommodated and foreign policy requirements can be adequately served. The problem is compounded by the danger that attempts to improve, extend, or modify the initial SALT accords can produce inappropriate agreements if limitations are pursued for their own sake, if only those weapons that can be adequately verified are controlled, or if bargaining tactics and concessions are permitted to detract from strategically sound positions.

Despite the many difficulties and dilemmas, it is possible to outline a general approach to the design of further U.S.-Soviet strategic limitations agreements that take practical and political considerations into account. It is assumed that deterrence through the threat of assured destruction will remain the cornerstone of both sides' strategic policies and of future arms limitation measures—although additional military and political requirements will continue to shape U.S. and Soviet strategic doctrines and will influence to some degree the two nations' positions in SALT. To minimize the complications of detailed verification analyses, emphasis will be placed on possible arms limitations that would generally be considered verifiable through national means. Although the USSR's strategic forces and policies are considered, the orientation of the following discussion is that of a U.S. policymaker seeking to establish a set of objectives and a series of specific proposals for SALT. These criteria should be helpful in evaluating not only any detailed agreement that is achieved on the basis of the Vladivostok guidelines but also any follow-on agreements that may be negotiated.

Criteria for SALT Agreements

In SALT II and beyond, the United States must seek to support and strengthen the security objectives of its strategic forces, to put forward proposals acceptable to the Soviet Union, to promote the principles and purposes of arms control, and to do all this in ways that will gain congressional approval. These complicated conditions can be incorporated into two basic objectives that could be applied as criteria for U.S. SALT proposals—*strengthening strategic stability,* and *codifying numerical equality.* Although success cannot be assured, if both sides apply these criteria and seriously seek to negotiate weapon limitations, the chances of reaching militarily meaningful and politically palatable strategic limitation agreements in the future will be greatly improved.

It is not necessary for U.S. and Soviet strategic doctrines to be the same in every detail in order to negotiate sensible arms limitation agreements, but a sharing of basic objectives is essential to continued success in SALT. Whether differences in the interpretation of, or significance attached to, numerical equality or strategic stability will preclude the continuation of serious progress over the coming decade remains to be seen. Nevertheless, it seems reasonable to conclude that a strategically sound and politically acceptable offensive arms agreement will not be negotiated unless the twin criteria of stability and equality are met to the satisfaction of both nations. A closer examination of the issues associated with each of these conditions lends credence to this judgment and also demonstrates the difficulty of translating policy specifications into actual agreements.

STRENGTHENING STRATEGIC STABILITY

Strengthening stability is the single most important goal of strategic arms control and thus is the starting point for a discussion of future SALT options and opportunities. Whether crisis stability or dynamic stability is considered, threats to the survivability of both sides' strategic forces pose particularly serious problems. The stability of the balance can be enhanced by increasing the invulnerability of the forces themselves or by removing the threat to these forces. Therefore, strategic arms limitation measures should be structured to eliminate potentially vulnerable systems or those having a first-strike counterforce capability but should ensure that both sides retain stabilizing strategic systems— that is, survivable systems geared primarily for retaliatory deterrence missions.

Certain systems, however, have counterforce as well as countervalue functions, and it may simply be infeasible to discern the purpose of a weapon being developed or deployed by an adversary. For example, it is difficult to draw a technically meaningful and verifiable line between simple multiple warheads, which are stabilizing, and accurate MIRVs, which are destabilizing, or between hard-point ABM defense and city defenses. It is especially difficult to classify certain systems because of their intrinsic characteristics and ambiguous implications. Land-mobile missiles, for instance, are relatively invulnerable but, unlike submarine-based missile systems, are not easily countable. Consequently, agreed deployments of land-mobile systems could strengthen stability through increased survivability but could contribute to instabilities by creating uncertainty regarding the size of operational missile forces.

Finding ways to resolve the often conflicting goals of lowering the risk of war and seeking to reduce damage if war occurs will, as suggested, continue to plague arms control experts. One specific instance of this dilemma is the question of flexible strategic options and its relation to SALT. If, as part of its unilateral strategic policy, either the United States or the USSR were to develop flexible options limited to command and control improvements and changes in employment plans, mutual stability would not be endangered and there should be no roadblocks to attempts to negotiate stabilizing agreements. But this would not be the case if either the United States or the Soviet Union acquired substantial *counterforce* capabilities as part of its unilateral force structure and insisted on fitting this option into the framework of SALT. As emphasized earlier, the objective of limiting damage through the active means of destroying an opponent's strategic forces—whether involving city-defense ABMs or a hard-target kill capability for offensive missiles —is incompatible with stable deterrence built on a mutual assured destruction relationship and is inconsistent with the underlying premise of SALT as embodied in the Moscow ABM treaty.

In designing the modalities of agreements consistent with the stability criterion, provisions should be made to permit the modernization and replacement of stabilizing systems. Either the survivability of existing strategic weapons could become threatened as a result of technological improvements or it could become excessively costly to maintain older-generation systems. At the same time, procedures should be enacted to facilitate the elimination of destabilizing systems as well as those weapons not needed to support stable deterrence. If successful, this arms control strategy could bring both nations closer to strategic postures that would provide high degrees of stability at lower levels of expenditure. To be specific, the two sides might agree to replace systems only when justified for economic reasons and to work toward postures characterized by fewer forces of greater survivability designed primarily for retaliatory purposes rather than for warfighting. Guidelines could be established to assist both nations in making unilateral strategic force decisions that would not be viewed by the other side as threatening, and replacement systems and schedules could be made subject to agreement.

ESTABLISHING NUMERICAL EQUALITY

A second objective of SALT should be to design future accords that not only enhance stability in the narrow military sense but also ensure that the numerical balance of forces between the United States and the USSR remains approximately equal. This means of containing the arms competition should reduce both political tensions and the costs of nuclear arms. Although numerical comparisons may have little direct bearing on the effectiveness of either side's deterrent forces, the so-called static force relationship is an important aspect of unilateral defense policies. This relationship should be taken into account in SALT negotiations, for it influences U.S.-Soviet perceptions of power and affects the credibility of America's alliance guarantees.

As a practical matter, if numerical relationships are included in the scope of intended agreements, the chances of negotiating effective and durable limitation agreements will be greatly improved. Neither nation will be prone to accept a permanent agreement that contains significant disadvantages in force levels, types of systems limited, or controls imposed over weapon activities. The ABM treaty was clearly based on the principle of symmetry, and despite its many apparent inequities, the Interim Agreement preserved at least a temporary overall balance between U.S. and Soviet strategic offensive weapons. The Vladivostok agreement seeks to formalize a relationship of equality between the strategic forces of the United States and the USSR. It is worth recalling that the attainment of "political parity" with the United States, not merely the acquisition of a militarily adequate deterrent, persuaded Kremlin leaders to agree to hold strategic arms talks, and Soviet negotiators will continue to press hard to ensure that any permanent agreements will codify the USSR's numerical position. As reflected in the continuing debate over the Interim Agreement and the Vladivostok agreement, public opinion in the United States as well as the attention of America's allies seems to be riveted on the apparent numerical imbalance of forces between the two superpowers and the goal of rectifying this disparity in further negotiations.

In seeking to apply the principle of numerical equality it will be useful to focus on the three most prominent numerical indices—the number of delivery vehicles, the number of warheads, and the payload capabilities of strategic systems—and judge whether a SALT agreement establishes equivalencies between these static measures, singly or in combination. A variety of specific approaches within this general framework can be used to design an offensive arms accord capable of being negotiated within the coming decade.[31]

A particularly important issue to be addressed is the relative emphasis to be given to each of the three parameters. In support of the position that numerical parity of long-range delivery vehicles is the primary condition, it can be argued that payload and warheads are qualitative improvements that both sides can obtain and that cannot be effectively controlled or verified; therefore, launcher parity should be the basis for durable equality. Nevertheless, other analysts suggest that to rely solely on launchers is to ignore important differences in U.S. and Soviet strategic capabilities and to distort the static comparisons of power between the two sides. Thus, throw-weight and the number of warheads are also relevant in attempting to establish approximate equivalence in static measures. It would be possible to include restrictions on missile payload capacity, since this parameter correlates with the size of the launch vehicle itself, which in turn can be discerned through satellite photography and flight-test monitoring. Although warhead limits pose difficult verification problems, MIRV capabilities can be estimated within reasonable bounds through test data and from throw-weight and other missile characteristics.

One strategy for applying the principle of numerical equality, taking into account the asymmetries in the U.S. and Soviet strategic postures, is to guarantee equality for each side in at least two of the three categories mentioned above. The U.S. lead in the number of missile warheads and the Soviet lead in missile throw-weight could be retained, for example, but overall equality in the number of intercontinental delivery systems, as well as in the number of MIRV-equipped missiles, would be maintained, leaving decisions on the precise mixture of land-based missiles, sea-based missiles, and bombers to the respective governments. Warheads would not be dealt with directly, on the grounds that warhead limits cannot be easily verified. This is the practical effect of the Vladivos-

31. For an analysis of comparative static measures for U.S. and Soviet forces and implications for SALT II, see Alton H. Quanbeck and Barry M. Blechman, *Washington Star*, December 10, 1972.

tok agreement, under which the United States would give up its advantage in MIRV-equipped missiles and the Soviet Union would give up its advantage in overall missile numbers.

Still another approach would be to include all three indices in a composite factor that could be used as a basis for parity. It is interesting to note, for example, that U.S. and Soviet strategic missile capabilities projected over the next few years will remain approximately equal if each side's total number of launchers and warheads and the throw-weight (measured in thousands of pounds) of land- and sea-based missiles are added and compared. This balancing effect is due to the almost three-to-one U.S. edge in SLBM throw-weight and six-to-one lead in sea-based missile warheads, both of which offset the USSR's overwhelming advantage in ICBM payload and associated land-based MIRV potential.

Soviet writings suggest that the Kremlin, like the United States, is concerned with solving the analytic problem of determining "criteria for the relative strategic value of various means of delivery"—criteria that deal with the asymmetry between U.S. and USSR forces and take into account "both quantitative and qualitative parameters."[32] The difficult problem is to combine static measure criteria with stability objectives. One technique is to formulate SALT packages following the stability approach, on the grounds that this represents the substantive basis for agreement, and then to superimpose static measure constraints. Intuitively, this appears to be a fruitful course, since stability maximization could lead in the same direction as parity proposals. For example, stability incentives argue for ICBMs to be replaced by SLBMs, perhaps as part of a broad freedom-to-mix measure that would place a numerical ceiling on launchers. Taking into account the differences in U.S. and Soviet missile postures, bomber limitations could then be devised to establish overall equality in launchers without compromising stability. Many other approaches could be devised in an attempt to formulate agreements that satisfy both criteria, using sophisticated equations for combining launchers, throw-weight, and warheads into a single "measure of merit" that would also incorporate qualitative and performance characteristics of each type of system in the U.S. and the USSR arsenals.

32. M. A. Milshteyn and L. S. Semeyko, "Strategic Arms Limitation: Problems and Prospects," *Ekonomika, Politika, Ideologiya*, November 19, 1973 (Foreign Broadcast Information Service, *Daily Report: Soviet Union*, December 17, 1973), p. AA 6.

But to structure an agreement on such a complex theory is to risk defeating the political as well as the strategic purposes of SALT and failing in actual negotiations.

Specific Limitation Options

The criteria outlined above suggest several arms limitation options. These options are presented in relation to individual types of systems; comprehensive accords can be formed by combining a variety of weapon controls into packages.

SOLVING THE PROBLEM OF ICBM VULNERABILITY

The most serious threat to strategic stability is the prospect that the survivability of ICBM forces could become endangered if both sides equipped their offensive missiles with accurate MIRVs. Although the United States could respond to Soviet counterforce threats by reducing and possibly eliminating its fixed ICBM force, Washington might hesitate to do so unilaterally since this would leave Moscow with a massive monopoly in land-based missiles and would shift the numerical balance against America. Alternatively, the United States could seek to protect its ICBMs or to replace them with land-mobile missiles, but these unilateral countermeasures are neither economically sound nor desirable from a policy standpoint. At the same time, because of potential instabilities created by the partial vulnerabilities in strategic postures and the first-strike incentives associated with accurate MIRVs, instabilities in the bilateral nuclear balance could occur if the Soviet Union's ICBM force became vulnerable to a U.S. attack. For these reasons, the United States would find it useful, if not essential, to obtain Soviet cooperation and reciprocity in seeking solutions to the problem of ICBM vulnerability.

But the Soviet Union may not share our concern about this problem. Given the USSR's numerical advantage in ICBM launchers and the relatively small yields of U.S. missile warheads, it is plausible that Soviet planners may not fear our potential counterforce threat as much as we fear theirs or may not take seriously the potential dangers associated with vulnerable systems. This may account for the virtual absence of any direct discussion of the dangers or dilemmas of the ICBM vulnerability issue in Soviet literature or speeches. Soviet writers have, of course, made general references to the need for considering the qualitative

characteristics of weapons in future limitation agreements, thus reflecting the statement of basic principles issued by the two governments in
June 1973.[33] In the writers' analyses, the importance of controlling
MIRVs, the fact that these weapons could be used in a first strike
against military forces, and the connection between multiple warheads
and the preservation of a stable nuclear parity relationship are presented
as "U.S. investigations"—not as Soviet interests or with implications for
Soviet arms programs. This is the traditional Soviet style of operation
and may in fact signify thinking in some official quarters. But Soviet
strategic experts may interpret "stability" differently than their American counterparts and may be interested in acquiring a counterforce
capability against the U.S. Minuteman force—if not as part of a first-
strike doctrine, then simply out of the prudential desire to develop a
warfighting capability if deterrence fails. Despite the uncertainties in
Moscow's policy, the question of ICBM vulnerability—which was not
resolved in the Vladivostok agreement—should be discussed with the
Soviet Union during further SALT negotiations in an attempt to find
mutually acceptable measures that could remove or reduce potential
dangers. Even if a formal agreement on this matter cannot be reached
in the future, such discussions could aid in diminishing potential instabilities by improving understanding of each nation's views on the subject.

One approach to solving the problem of ICBM vulnerability would
be to reach agreements designed to eliminate MIRVs. Because the USSR
is already flight-testing MIRVs and the United States is well along in a
deployment program, however, attempts to negotiate comprehensive
MIRV ban measures will probably continue to prove futile.

It might nevertheless be possible to alleviate the destabilizing consequences of MIRVs through a number of indirect techniques, which
could at least slow down the impact of this weapon and allow more time
for both sides to find durable ways of dealing with this problem. The
Interim Agreement, as indicated, prohibits both sides from replacing
small ICBMs with large missiles and bans significant increases in the
size of silos. The Vladivostok agreement calls for limiting the number of
missiles that can be equipped with MIRVs—thus placing some constraints on MIRV capabilities. Additional measures, such as reducing
the number of large ICBMs, limiting the throw-weight of missiles, or

33. The need for qualitative as well as quantitative SALT limits is discussed in
Milshteyn and Semeyko, "Strategic Arms Limitation."

barring MIRVs on certain types of ICBMs could make it more difficult to develop counterforce MIRV capabilities. One approach would be to consider a prohibition on the flight-testing of new or improved missile systems as a means of controlling MIRVs. Each side could be permitted to conduct a set number of annual missile firings of existing systems needed to maintain a reliable deterrent force. In principle, neither nation would then be able to develop highly accurate multiple warhead systems. Verification of this agreement through unilateral means would be facilitated if both sides cooperated in declaring restrictions that have precedents in the ABM treaty.[34]

On the other hand, a missile flight-test agreement could actually decrease stability by preventing both sides from testing new decoy devices or penetration systems and by precluding the development of reliable replacements for obsolete deterrent systems. Furthermore, intense resistance by military officials in both countries to limitations on the testing of offensive weapons would lower the likelihood of success. Even if successfully negotiated, flight-test restrictions, throw-weight limitations, or partial MIRV deployment proposals would not prevent both sides from gradually improving warhead accuracies and yield-to-weight ratios to the point where hard-target kill capabilities could be achieved.[35] Therefore, *the United States and the USSR must learn to live with MIRVs, accept the fact that land-based missiles will eventually become vulnerable, and seek alternative paths to stability.*

In response to this situation, consideration might be given to an agreement permitting the United States and the USSR to deploy ABM defenses at ICBM sites in an attempt to preserve the survivability of land-based missiles through active protection. But this would involve modification of the ABM treaty and, more important, would raise a host of difficult definition and verification problems. If missile defenses were deployed to protect ICBMs, these installations could indirectly provide population protection and might be seen as the first step toward a nationwide ABM system. Despite continuing research efforts to devise improved missile-site defenses, it is doubtful that such programs will be able to provide cost-effective protection of ICBMs against MIRVs. If this is the case, then mutual hard-point defense measures would make little sense on economic grounds alone.

34. Such precedents are discussed by Alton Frye, *Washington Star*, June 18, 1972.
35. Early negotiation of a total ban on underground nuclear weapons testing could delay the acquisition of hard-target kill capabilities by both sides, since explosive tests geared to improve yield-to-weight ratios could not be conducted.

An alternative approach would be to permit both sides to deploy land-mobile ICBMs in place of fixed land-based missiles. This is possible under the Vladivostok agreement, although details remain to be negotiated. As noted earlier, however, the deployment of land-mobile systems might make it difficult to estimate the other side's force level. In addition, many U.S. analysts question the reliability of land-mobile missiles as a means of providing a secure retaliatory capability against large-scale attacks. The Soviet Union has apparently developed prototype mobile missiles and seems interested in retaining the option to deploy them in shorter-range as well as in intercontinental modes.

The most direct solution to ICBM vulnerability would be an agreement *to reduce and eventually eliminate fixed land-based missile forces.*[36] For example, Moscow and Washington could eventually agree to reduce their ICBM forces by 50 percent, while maintaining the freedom-to-mix formula of the Interim Agreement and the Vladivostok agreement. Although reductions of large ICBMs would be preferable, both sides could take at least proportional cuts in large and small ICBM systems. Exchanges between land- and sea-based missiles could be made on a less than one-for-one basis, leading to a reduction in the total number of strategic launchers available to each nation. At lower ICBM levels on both sides, however, counterforce attacks would actually become less difficult in terms of the ability of an attacking nation to reduce the retaliatory capability of its opponent's land-based missile force. But the incentives to strike first would decrease, since ICBMs would represent a smaller percentage of each side's destructive potential—a point made earlier in discussing unilateral U.S. strategic arms options.

The net effect of mutual ICBM reductions would therefore seem to be that of enhancing strategic stability, while offering the political and economic benefits of a partial disarmament measure. Stability would be reinforced further if ICBM reductions were coupled with indirect controls over MIRVs to retard the development of hard-target kill capabilities. If, after agreeing to a reduction in ICBM strength, both sides further agreed to move toward exclusive reliance on sea-based missiles and bombers by gradually eliminating fixed ICBMs following a phased program of reductions, the resultant bilateral strategic configuration

36. The Federation of American Scientists advocated ICBM reductions in *Public Interest Report*, Special Issue on Counterforce and SALT, vol. 27 (February 1974). It was also reported that Fred C. Iklé, director of the U.S. Arms Control and Disarmament Agency, supported such a plan as a long-term goal for SALT. (See Michael Getler, *Washington Post*, February 2, 1974.)

would eliminate the instabilities associated with accurate MIRVs and obviate the disadvantages inherent in counterforce doctrines by removing hard targets from U.S. and Soviet force structures.

From a U.S. perspective, this approach would be consistent with the unilateral policy option discussed earlier of shifting emphasis from a triad to a diad of SLBMs and bombers. The expansion of Soviet sea-based deterrent forces that would result under this plan would be a price worth paying in order to diminish the USSR's ICBM threat, which poses far more serious dangers to the U.S. deterrent and to nuclear stability generally. On the other hand, although Soviet leaders and writers have supported the concept of arms reductions in future SALT agreements and accepted its inclusion in the statement of basic principles in 1973, Soviet negotiators would almost certainly be reluctant to accept ICBM reduction plans and apparently rejected such a proposal in the early phases of SALT and presumably in negotiations leading to Vladivostok as well. The USSR recently completed a buildup of land-based missiles and is continuing to improve its systems. In addition to the bureaucratic momentum behind these programs, Kremlin leaders undoubtedly view ICBM superiority as a crucial element of strategic power that offsets the U.S. advantage in MIRV and submarine technology, long-range bombers, and forward-based systems. Although the USSR now has a numerical advantage in SLBMs, the Soviet sea-based deterrent is inferior to the Polaris-Poseidon fleet in survivability, MIRV deployments, and total payload.

In recent years, however, the USSR has significantly expanded the size and quality of its submarine-based missile forces, and its SALT position indicates apparent recognition of the importance of these systems in the strategic relationship between the two nations. While a cutback in ICBM strength would require the USSR to eliminate more ICBMs than the United States, by the same token it would permit the Soviet Union to construct a proportionally greater number of submarines and widen its numerical lead. Further, the Soviet Union has more to gain than the United States in reducing ICBMs, since land-based missiles represent a larger fraction of the USSR's overall deterrent force, and the inevitable threat to the survivability of these systems would therefore create particularly serious problems for the Soviet Union. But Soviet leaders would probably be prepared to accept severe reductions in land-based missile forces in favor of SLBMs only if they overcome doctrinal tradition and institutional inertia and recognize that the presence of vulnerable ICBMs, even on one side of the strategic balance, could increase the risk of accidental or inadvertent nuclear war and jeopardize their own security.

ANTISUBMARINE WARFARE LIMITS

A long-term stability problem relevant to SALT and perhaps more significant than the ICBM problem is that of sea-based systems. Because submarine-launched missiles will become the basis of future strategic deterrent capabilities and will contribute to a high degree of nuclear stability in the years ahead, the survivability of sea-based forces needs to be guaranteed. At the present time, missile-firing submarines are extremely survivable when operating at sea, and there seems to be no cause for concern over possible breakthroughs in antisubmarine warfare. Nevertheless, negotiated restrictions could reduce the possibility of missile-firing submarine systems becoming less survivable within the next decade.

There are a number of specific dangers in permitting ASW technology to develop without agreed limitations. As both sides continue to explore ASW possibilities, test new technologies, and deploy antisubmarine systems, uncertainties will inevitably arise about the dependability of SLBM forces. Driven by worst-case military assumptions, the United States and the USSR will undoubtedly respond by improving the quality of their SLBMs and submarines. In addition to stimulating a sea-based strategic arms competition, which would waste resources and possibly endanger SALT, this pattern could increase the risk of an accidental nuclear exchange. Even a limited military clash involving sea-based systems, whether the result of a deliberate decision or a series of miscalculations, could threaten the stability of the U.S.-Soviet nuclear balance. During the 1960s, despite the claims of most scientists that effective protection against ballistic missile attacks was unattainable, the fear of a defensive breakthrough by the other side caused the United States (and to a lesser extent the USSR) to expand its offensive forces at the first sign of ABM deployments by its adversary. ABMs ceased to be a stimulus to the arms race only because of the limitations of the ABM treaty. Even though effective ASW defenses may be more difficult to achieve than effective ABM defenses, there is a real possibility that similar fears will take hold in the 1970s and trigger an action-reaction cycle at sea—each side responding with improved SLBM forces to perceived antisubmarine warfare progress on the other side. Both sides should therefore attempt to prevent ASW from becoming "the ABM of the future" by seeking mutual agreements in this area as well.[37]

It should be recognized that formulating meaningful and negotiable agreements to control ASW is substantially more difficult than designing ABM limitations. Many ASW functions, as noted, are carried out by conventional sea and air forces that perform missions unrelated to antisubmarine warfare. Therefore, multiple controls over strategic ASW could adversely affect each nation's conventional ASW capability or prevent the development of techniques to counter ASW. Moreover, potential ASW threats emerging from advanced technological developments are not yet fully defined and cannot be specifically limited. For these reasons, a technical working group might usefully be established within the SALT framework to grapple with the complex long-range problem of ASW limitations. U.S. and Soviet negotiators meanwhile could begin to explore a number of strategic ASW agreements.[38] Although our ASW capabilities are superior to those of the USSR, the fact that the United States relies more heavily on sea-based missiles than does the Soviet Union suggests that such discussions would be in the interest of the United States. At the same time, Kremlin leaders might also find it in their interest to explore ways of constraining the U.S. ASW threat and narrowing our advantage.

One possible agreement would consist of a pair of related measures limiting the number of nuclear-powered attack submarines each side could maintain and prohibiting continuous tracking of missile-firing submarines by surface ships as well as submarines. Verification of compliance with the submarine limit could readily be accomplished through national means. Monitoring the no-tracking agreement would be more complex, but in most instances a missile-firing submarine can detect that it is being trailed. Together, these two measures would greatly alleviate the dangers inherent in tracking without degrading either nation's conventional ASW capability.

A second agreement could prohibit the installation of large-scale sonar arrays in the open seas. This would curtail attempts by either nation to deploy a widespread network of high-energy acoustical com-

37. These issues are discussed in Bernard Feld, "ASW—The ABM of the 1970s," *Stanford Journal of International Studies*, Spring 1972, pp. 87–95.

38. For a comprehensive analysis of ASW arms control measures, see Kosta Tsipis, Anne H. Kahn, and Bernard T. Feld, eds., *The Future of the Sea-Based Deterrent* (MIT Press, 1973).

ponents in order to gain an ASW breakthrough. Adequate verification could be accomplished unilaterally, since oceanwide systems of this scope could not be built without detection.

A third possibility would be to agree to arrange sanctuaries or zones for each side's submarine deterrent forces from which the other side's attack submarines and sonar-carrying surface ships would be barred. Zones would be selected to provide sufficient room for each nation's missile-firing submarine forces to remain secure against detection and attack when deployed within its barriers. At the same time, it would be important to prevent the zones from interfering with free transit through commonly traveled sea-lanes or from adversely affecting conventional ASW capabilities. Once areas were designated, each side could monitor its zones using acoustic and radar systems.

Moving beyond the discernible problems of ICBM and submarine survivability, both nations could attempt to identify new technological trends—such as laser techniques—that might endanger the future stability of the strategic relationship. In accordance with the provisions of the Moscow agreements, the United States and the USSR plan to consider such questions when the application of new technologies to strategic weapons becomes practical and thus will call for modification of the accords. But it would be desirable for both sides to discuss these issues at an earlier stage when it might be more possible to design effective controls to preclude destabilizing weapon deployments.

BOMBER CONTROLS

In regard to weapon limitations not directly tied to stability, those affecting strategic bombers are an obvious item for negotiation. Bombers are less provocative than ICBMs, since they can be made relatively survivable and do not pose serious counterforce threats. Indeed, bombers can be expected to be a crucial supplement to sea-based missile deterrent systems during the decade ahead. But an uncontrolled race in the bomber field could become a source of tension and result in a waste of resources.

The United States holds a numerical edge over the USSR in long-range aircraft and enjoys a decided qualitative advantage in bomber capabilities. In addition, the United States is developing a new-generation strategic bomber, while the USSR has shown no evidence of a comparable program, although the so-called Backfire medium-range bomber may be capable of intercontinental missions. In the Vladivostok agreement, bombers are included with missiles in a full freedom-to-mix plan, with each side free to select its own force mixture subject to the constraint on the total number of launchers. The issue of whether the launcher quota should include air-to-surface missiles (ASMs) could cause problems, but one solution would be to treat all ballistic ASMs above a 300-mile range as separate strategic missiles. Possible limits on strategic-range cruise missiles, however based, would be discussed separately.

Future limitations on bombers could be related to controls over strategic aircraft defenses. For instance, agreements could call for reductions of existing interceptor aircraft, surface-to-air missiles, and associated radars. With ABMs limited to low levels by treaty, it would make little sense for either side to retain large and costly bomber defense networks beyond essential warning and command and control capabilities. Mutual reductions in active air-defense deployments, moreover, would contribute to stability by alleviating remaining fears that an adversary might upgrade its bomber defense systems and acquire a missile defense capability in violation of the ABM treaty. It is equally significant that lowering the levels of air defense would help preserve the reliability of bomber deterrent forces—a benefit that will become increasingly important as ICBMs become less survivable. The Soviet Union might oppose sharp reductions on the grounds that a substantial fraction of its air-defense deployments are designed to cope with aircraft threats from Western Europe and China, and American leverage is weakening as U.S. air-defense installations continue to be reduced for cost-effectiveness reasons. On the other hand, perhaps U.S. negotiators could offer to slow down our bomber modernization programs in order to persuade the Soviet Union, at a minimum, to eliminate most of its early-generation bomber defenses and to accept certain technical constraints on its newer network.

FORWARD-BASED SYSTEMS

Complicating the analysis of the U.S.-Soviet balance and clouding the picture of future progress in SALT is the likelihood that the USSR will continue its efforts to limit U.S. forward-based systems (FBS) as part of a permanent offensive agreement. A major deadlock occurred in SALT I discussions, it should be recalled, when Moscow claimed that all nuclear weapon systems capable of reaching the homeland of the United States or the USSR should be classified as "strategic." Under the

Soviet definition, U.S. forward-based theater aircraft located in Europe or on carriers would be subject to limitations, but the USSR's medium-range missiles and bombers aimed at Western Europe would be excluded from controls. If FBS were incorporated in the American strategic launcher quota, the Soviet Union could then insist that the United States must either reduce its forward-based deployments or cut the number of its intercontinental strategic forces in order to enable the USSR to maintain parity in strategic launchers. Although this interpretation of strategic weapons was logical and understandable from the standpoint of Soviet security, it may well have reflected a Kremlin effort to strain our relations with our allies or to simply acquire bargaining power at the SALT table. After the United States had officially rejected the Soviet Union's definition of "strategic" and Congress had lent its support to the position of the executive branch on this question, the Soviet Union, for its own reasons, dropped its insistence on this point at Vladivostok. But it is possible that the Soviet Union will raise the FBS issue again in follow-on negotiations.

If the FBS problem reappears in SALT, because of the close relationship between FBS and European defense it might be wise for the United States to attempt to cover this topic in discussions of mutual and balanced force reductions (MBFR) at a later phase in these negotiations. Alternatively, a separate series of tactical arms limitation talks (TALT) could be initiated to deal with tactical and theater nuclear arms limitations. Although conducted independently, SALT, MBFR, and TALT negotiations would undoubtedly be related as the superpowers developed their positions in each forum. Even if the political and procedural difficulties of dealing with FBS are overcome, negotiating such an accord would be technically complicated by the number of weapons involved, the problem of dual-purpose systems, and the relationship between tactical nuclear and conventional forces.[39]

Additional SALT Issues

While the prevention of an accidental nuclear war does not necessarily depend on the limitation of weapon systems, it is clearly one of the purposes of strategic arms control. The existence of nuclear forces

39. See *Strategic Survey: 1972* (London: International Institute for Strategic Studies, 1973) for a discussion of the SALT I accords with special attention to forward-based systems and other issues of direct interest to Western Europe.

in the United Kingdom, France, and China extends the risk of accidental war and therefore raises the issue of broadening SALT to include participation by nations other than the Soviet Union and the United States. Although expanded participation is improbable before the superpowers themselves have reached firm and viable agreements, this expansion should be anticipated, for it may prove both necessary and feasible in the future. Meanwhile, the effects of U.S.-Soviet strategic negotiations on our allies should be weighed carefully by the planners of U.S. arms limitations policies, as should the relationship between SALT and the need to prevent additional nations from acquiring independent nuclear arms.

Lowering Nuclear Risks

In 1963, the United States and the USSR signed the hot line agreement establishing a teletype link between Washington and Moscow to enable U.S. and Soviet leaders to communicate directly with each other during periods of international tension.[40] As mentioned earlier, the two nations agreed to modernize the hot line through the use of satellites and signed a SALT accord to this effect in 1971.[41] This rapid and reliable communication system is a valuable tool in reducing the likelihood that the escalation of a crisis or the misinterpretation of an event might trigger a strategic exchange.

During the first series of SALT meetings, the United States and the USSR also negotiated a related measure specifically designed to reduce the risk of nuclear war between the two countries.[42] This accidents accord obligates each nation to ensure that its nuclear weapons cannot be used accidentally or in an unauthorized manner and to notify the other side of any nuclear detonations or incidents that might lead to a nuclear war, such as the detection of unidentified objects on early warning systems, the crash of a strategic bomber, or an accidental missile firing. As a means of minimizing the chance of an inadvertent nuclear exchange,

40. Memorandum of Understanding between the United States and the Union of Soviet Socialist Republics Regarding the Establishment of a Direct Communications Link, signed at Geneva, June 20, 1963.

41. Agreement between the United States of America and the Union of Soviet Socialist Republics on Measures to Improve the USA-USSR Direct Communications Link, signed at Washington, September 30, 1971. For text, see *New York Times*, October 1, 1971.

42. See note 26.

the agreement requires each side to announce any test launchings that extend beyond its national borders in the direction of the other nation's territory.

In June 1973, the two nations strengthened their commitment to prevent nuclear war in an unprecedented accord signed during Chairman Leonid Brezhnev's visit to the United States. This agreement reaffirmed mutual interest in removing the danger of nuclear war, called for the two nations to prevent conflicts that could lead to nuclear war between them or between either superpower and another country, and committed both nations to "enter into urgent consultations" with each other in the event of circumstances that "appear to involve the risk of nuclear conflict."[43] In essence, the agreement simply codifies rules of conduct and, like some other arms control measures, cannot be enforced literally or verified except through actual behavior—whether compliance or breach. Furthermore, the agreement stops short of a nuclear no-first-use obligation, emphasizing the prevention of situations that could lead to nuclear use rather than restraints on the types of weapons to be employed. Nevertheless, the accord is a desirable prelude to future agreements designed to minimize nuclear risks and their consequences. Indeed, if the Middle East crisis of 1973 underscored the limits of détente, it also demonstrated that both superpowers had already managed to develop a political framework and a style of operation that permitted such a crisis to be contained without serious risks of a U.S.-Soviet confrontation.

Building on these agreements, the United States and the USSR could take additional steps to further decrease the likelihood and consequences of accidental or inadvertent nuclear war. To begin with, the two sides might explore in more detail the various ways in which an outbreak of nuclear war might occur. Through discussions, they might reach an explicit understanding on rules for crisis management that could diminish the danger of escalation. For example, the use of strategic bombers as a show of force during periods of tension could be prohibited, since the sudden movement of enemy aircraft toward a nation's border might inadvertently trigger a nuclear exchange. Perhaps each country could provide the other with information on the equipment and procedures it uses for minimizing accidental or unauthorized use of nuclear weapons.

43. Agreement between the United States and the Union of Soviet Socialist Republics on the Prevention of Nuclear War, signed at Washington, June 21, 1973. For text, see *New York Times*, June 23, 1973.

The United States and the USSR could also agree not to overfly each other's territory with strategic missiles in the event of a nuclear exchange with a third nation. This could force the United States to forgo the option of using ICBMs against China, but American sea-based missile and bomber capabilities would provide an adequate deterrent against the Chinese. Other issues affecting the risk of nuclear war—including the disadvantages of retaining vulnerable systems and the dangers of a launch-on-warning doctrine for ICBMs—could usefully be discussed without requiring any explicit agreement.

A second subject of discussion might be the problem of limiting damage in the event of a nuclear exchange. Although damage limitation is a traditional arms control goal, it can conflict with the objective of deterrence. This dilemma itself could be a topic for joint discussions in an attempt to identify procedural and planning arrangements that would reduce damage but would not adversely affect nuclear stability.[44] It is conceivable, for instance, that the United States and the USSR might reach an understanding on the necessity of acquiring flexible targeting capabilities for strategic forces so that both sides would have the option of launching limited strikes and avoiding attacks against cities. Perhaps some form of "equal flexibility" could be negotiated. While these mutual arrangements would not guarantee the avoidance of all-out nuclear war, they could be more effective than purely unilateral policies. In considering such measures, however, it would be vital to develop strict guidelines to prevent selective strike doctrines from evolving into destabilizing counterforce strategies that could increase nuclear risks.

The United States and the USSR might also pay particular attention to the relationship between the strategic forces of other countries and accidental nuclear war. One topic for discussion could be the prospect that soft Chinese strategic systems might increase the chance of an accidental, unauthorized, or preemptive Chinese launch during a crisis. U.S.-Soviet discussions regarding the possible risks associated with Chinese forces would be controversial, but if they fully revealed the potential danger to the USSR of inadvertent or accidental Chinese missile launches and persuaded Soviet leaders to consider the possibility of establishing a Moscow-Peking hot line—to match a possible Washington-Peking hot line—overall nuclear stability could be strengthened.

44. See D. G. Brennan, "Soviet-American Communication in Crises," in *Arms Control and National Security* (Pergamon Press, 1969), pp. 81–88.

A related question for mutual consideration is the danger accompanying the presence of British and French missile-firing submarines in ocean areas traversed by U.S. and Soviet submarine systems. Moscow and Washington could agree on the desirability of each side attempting to establish bilateral hot lines with other nuclear powers—notwithstanding the political difficulties this might create for U.S.-Soviet relations. As a longer-term objective, U.S. and USSR negotiators might give serious consideration to the possibility of including France, the United Kingdom, and China in the hot line and accidental launch agreements. Ultimately, a comprehensive treaty designed to reduce the risks and consequences of accidental nuclear war could be framed and opened to accession by all nations.

Considerations Affecting Other Countries

Strategic arms limitation negotiations and agreements have thus far been restricted to the United States and the Soviet Union. The size and significance of the nuclear arsenals maintained by the two superpowers, in contrast to the small strategic forces owned by the British, French, and Chinese, make such bilateral arrangements appropriate. On strict stability grounds, it would be unnecessary to consider the participation of these other countries in strategic limitation accords for at least a decade. None of the measures likely to be negotiated during the next phases of SALT would so reduce U.S. and Soviet strategic forces that neither side would be able to maintain sufficient power to deter its other adversaries. Because Soviet ABMs are limited and U.S. MIRVs are permitted by SALT accords, the United States will have no difficulty in deterring China without detracting from its strategic requirements vis-à-vis the Soviet Union. Similarly, the USSR will have adequate strategic capabilities and a sizable arsenal of medium-range nuclear delivery systems to cope with China and Western Europe as well as the United States.

At some future time, if not for stability then for political reasons, participation in SALT by other nations for the purpose of negotiating multilateral strategic arms limitations could become a real issue. U.S. and Soviet negotiators might therefore begin to exchange views on this subject. It is of more immediate concern, however, to attempt to involve the United Kingdom, France, and China in arrangements to reduce the risk of accidental nuclear war. Other issues of near-term concern to the

United States include European reactions to U.S.-Soviet strategic arms agreements and the implications of SALT for Asian security and U.S. relations with China.

WESTERN EUROPE

Despite some negative reactions to the codification of parity and the imbalance between the level of Soviet and U.S. missile launchers, America's NATO allies by and large reacted favorably to the Moscow agreements.[45] Most European observers seemed to accept the view that the U.S. deterrent remained viable as a result of the agreements and that the signing of the Moscow accords was more a reflection of nuclear reality than a radical departure from existing trends. Nor has there been any adverse European reaction to the Vladivostok agreement. European reactions to SALT are largely political and are influenced by broader aspects of U.S.-NATO and East-West relations. The fear of a U.S.-Soviet condominium is, of course, always present and was exacerbated in 1973 by the Nixon-Brezhnev agreement on reducing the risk of nuclear war, which raised fears that Washington and Moscow might move toward some form of a no-first-use accord.[46] On balance, however, a dampening of the superpower arms competition has thus far been seen as aiding Western Europe's security. Finally, SALT I served Western Europe's interest, since the Interim Agreement does not affect weapons directly relevant to European defense, while the ABM treaty permits the small British and French nuclear forces to remain effective for a substantial period, and the Vladivostok agreement leaves unaffected the forward-based systems to which European governments attach such importance.

But a number of factors associated with future SALT negotiations create a less positive picture of alliance relations. Although U.S.-Soviet strategic parity may be regarded as both unavoidable and acceptable, perceived American inferiority could raise problems for Europe. If the United States falls behind the USSR in the level or quality of its strategic forces, NATO could begin to seriously question the strategic advantages

45. For analyses of European interests in SALT, see Andrew Pierre, "The SALT Agreement and Europe," *The World Today*, vol. 28 (July 1972), pp. 281–88; and Wilhelm Grewe, "The Effect of Strategic Agreements on European-American Relations," in "Soviet-American Relations and World Order: Arms Limitations and Policy," *Adelphi Papers*, no. 65 (London: International Institute for Strategic Studies, February 1970), pp. 16–24.

46. See, for example, Flora Lewis, *New York Times*, June 25, 1973.

of SALT, and doubts over the dependability of the U.S. guarantee could increase. There would also be difficulties if the Soviet Union revived its proposal that a prohibition on the transfer of strategic offensive systems should be added to the ban on ABM transfers contained in the Moscow treaty.[47] The latter proposition has already brought adverse reactions from Western Europe, for, if accepted, it could prevent the United States from providing technical support to a possible Anglo-French cooperative nuclear defense arrangement or—a less likely but more significant outcome—it could bar the United States from assisting in the development of a European nuclear force. Even if the Soviet delegates merely raised these matters for exploration at future SALT negotiations and the United States continued to oppose them, America's NATO allies would be deeply concerned.

On the other hand, Western Europe could find positive features in future SALT negotiations. The United Kingdom and France would welcome any U.S.-Soviet ASW agreement that could increase the survivability of British and French sea-based deterrent forces. It is also possible that negotiations leading to limitations on Soviet medium-range nuclear delivery systems could receive support in Western Europe, even if obtaining these restrictions required the establishment of a ceiling on the number of U.S. tactical aircraft systems stationed on overseas bases. Perhaps the United Kingdom and France could informally commit themselves to keep their SLBM forces at existing levels in exchange for limits on Soviet strategic capabilities targeted against their weapons and cities. But progress will not be made on these issues unless ways are found to accommodate the legitimate concerns of Western Europe without detracting from the central goal of maintaining U.S.-Soviet strategic stability. Official allied participation in SALT, while a possibility, is not a strategic prerequisite for stabilizing the U.S.-Soviet nuclear relationship at lower levels. In any case, active participation at this time by other nations would complicate the delicate and difficult negotiations facing the American and Soviet delegations during the next few years and would undermine one of the positive features of SALT—separation from multilateral arms control forums. The preferred solution appears to lie in a determined effort by American leaders to consult closely and candidly with our allies during SALT II and subsequent negotiations. For their part, European nations should not lose sight of the positive effects

47. See Soviet statements in "Documentation on the Strategic Arms Limitation Agreements," p. 27; and Newhouse, *Cold Dawn*.

that continued U.S.-Soviet success in managing the superpower strategic competition can have on the security of Western Europe.

ASIA

Asian attitudes toward SALT are substantially less intense than those in Europe, for the obvious reason that the U.S.-Soviet strategic balance has less significance for Asian security. Japan reacted positively to the SALT agreements and generally supports U.S.-Soviet arms control and détente policies. Continued consultation with Japanese leaders about future SALT possibilities is, of course, imperative for political reasons. But for Japan and other Asian allies, the significance of SALT centers on the role of China.

The Chinese have shown no interest in joining SALT and have denounced the talks as collusion between the superpowers. They have referred to the accords as sham agreements that simply legitimized the nuclear arms race and have accused the United States and the Soviet Union of building up their armaments while insisting that other nations forgo nuclear weapons. Aside from the political difficulties Peking would face if it supported limited arms control measures initiated by the superpowers, it has valid security reasons for its negative stance toward SALT.[48] Although China benefits from the SALT treaty banning nationwide ABM systems, neither the Moscow agreements nor any likely follow-on accords will reduce in any meaningful way the nuclear capabilities of the United States or the Soviet Union in relation to China. Both nations will retain powerful strategic offensive systems and tactical nuclear weapons, and, in the case of the USSR, medium-range missiles and bomber systems capable of being targeted against the Chinese homeland. In fact, the United States and the Soviet Union will both retain highly effective counterforce capabilities against the small and vulnerable Chinese nuclear force for at least the remainder of the decade.

While there is no reason for the United States and the USSR to view limits on China's nuclear forces as a prerequisite to progress in SALT, a continued lack of Chinese participation in the SALT talks could produce a number of undesirable consequences. Nations in Asia might become more fearful of China if Peking refused to negotiate limitations on its

48. See Harry G. Gelber, "Nuclear Weapons, the Pacific, and SALT," in Morton A. Kaplan, *Salt: Problems and Prospects* (General Learning Press, 1973), pp. 182–200.

nuclear force, and the United States might find it increasingly difficult to convince other nations of the dependability of our security guarantees. As a result, pressures to acquire independent nuclear forces might increase in such countries as Japan, and India might turn its recently acquired "peaceful" nuclear explosives capability into a major military program. If the Chinese were to actively oppose SALT, the problems faced by Washington and Moscow in pursuing common nuclear stability objectives could be complicated.

One way of minimizing the potentially undesirable consequences of Peking's isolation from SALT and of taking a positive step toward improving Chinese-American relations would be for the United States to attempt to initiate arms talks with China. Bilateral discussions between the United States and China, first perhaps on the question of accidental war, are likely to prove more productive than any multilateral negotiation as a means of drawing the Chinese into serious consideration of nuclear arms control. At some point in these discussions, the United States could consider the possibility of a nuclear no-first-use accord, since this measure has been central to Peking's public position on arms control. Although China's sweeping proposal that the nuclear powers pledge unconditionally never to initiate the use of nuclear arms may be unrealistic, a limited bilateral no-first-use agreement between Washington and Peking could prove to be an effective means of easing tensions between these two nations while reducing the risks of nuclear war. Even an extremely restricted nuclear pledge by American leaders, consistent with our alliance obligations, would have a positive effect on Peking's perceptions of the United States and could enhance the prospects for engaging China in a productive arms control dialogue. This in turn might make Chinese leaders less reluctant to agree to take part in multilateral strategic limitation negotiations in the 1980s.[49]

Relation of SALT to Nuclear Proliferation

Among the many reasons for the initiation of SALT was the need for the United States and the USSR to curb their own nuclear buildups and thus to set a precedent for arms control measures affecting other nations and, more specifically, to diminish incentives for other nations

49. See Ralph N. Clough and others, The United States, China, and Arms Control (Brookings Institution, 1975).

to acquire nuclear weapons.[50] The nonproliferation treaty, it should be recalled, commits all parties—notably the United States and the USSR —to pursue arms reduction schemes.[51] The effect of the various SALT agreements on nonproliferation, however, has been slight. Although most nations welcomed the ABM treaty, the lack of comprehensive controls in both the Interim Agreement and the Vladivostok guidelines and the continuation of the strategic arms competition created a belief that these measures were at best marginal in signifying superpower restraint.

Interestingly, the ABM treaty raises a dilemma in terms of nuclear proliferation. On the one hand, the superpowers' agreement to curb the strategic competition and the resulting potential for further arms control arrangements are two political consequences of the SALT accords that strengthen antiproliferation barriers. Indeed, unrestricted ABM deployments would have intensified the U.S.-Soviet strategic arms race and contributed to proliferation tendencies. On the other hand, by prohibiting nationwide missile defenses, the ABM treaty makes it easier for small countries to acquire nuclear forces capable of inflicting relatively substantial damage on the United States and the Soviet Union. Furthermore, the lack of nationwide ABMs might be perceived by some nations as diminishing the credibility of U.S. and Soviet nuclear guarantees, thus strengthening the arguments of those in certain countries who are urging entry into the nuclear club.

The future direction of U.S.-Soviet strategic arms control, however, can have an even stronger influence on nonproliferation policies. These policies are vital, since one of the keys to long-term stability is the prevention of further expansion of the nuclear club. Washington and Moscow share the goal of decreasing the likelihood of nuclear spread and should explore ways of satisfying this objective beyond simply attempting to persuade all nations to adhere to the nonproliferation treaty. Clearly, many crucial factors affecting the further spread of nuclear weapons are unrelated to ABMs, SALT, and strategic policies in general. Nevertheless, it would be useful if the United States and the Soviet

50. For a discussion of the connection between SALT and the nonproliferation treaty, see George H. Quester, "Implications of the SALT Outcome for 'Nth Powers: Israel, India, and Others," in W. R. Kintner and R. L. Pfalzgraff, Jr., eds., *SALT: Implications for Arms Control in the 1970s* (University of Pittsburgh Press, 1973), pp. 255–80.

51. Treaty on the Non-Proliferation of Nuclear Weapons, signed at Washington, London, and Moscow, July 1, 1968.

Union, through their SALT contacts, could reach an understanding on the elements of a mutual nonproliferation strategy.

One particularly useful nonproliferation policy approach would be for both sides to seek to downgrade the significance of nuclear weapons as a sign of political importance or military power.[52] This would necessitate a reduction in the degree of attention given to the details of the strategic balance in the public rhetoric of U.S. and Soviet officials; a recognition of the need for maintaining sufficient nonnuclear forces; and a serious effort by both sides to negotiate a total nuclear test ban, regional nuclear limitations in Europe and Asia, and selective no-first-use agreements—in addition to more comprehensive controls in SALT.

Success at SALT, it might be noted, could provide impetus for negotiating an underground test ban. Because the initial SALT accords have resulted in progress toward stabilizing the strategic relationship and efforts to reach more complete offensive arms limitations, the United States and the USSR should find continued nuclear weapon testing less essential. At the same time, a constraint on underground testing—whether a total ban or a threshold arrangement—would reduce fears of the possible development of destabilizing weapons and thus support the goals of SALT.

As part of a more general "nuclear de-legitimization" strategy, Washington and Moscow could attempt to enhance the stature of nations in *nonmilitary* terms. For example, Japan might be considered for membership in an expanded UN Security Council. At the same time, both superpowers should understand the disadvantages of attributing undue importance to nations simply because they have acquired a nuclear arsenal, particularly in the case of China. The important thing is to pursue policies that will help freeze the number of nuclear nations at the present level and decrease the danger of nuclear war.

52. For a discussion of worldwide nonproliferation problems and policies, see Joseph Yager and Eleanor Steinberg, *Energy and U.S. Policy* (Ballinger, 1974), chaps. 16, 17, and 20.

CHAPTER SIX

Stable Deterrence: A Strategic Policy for the 1970s

Regardless of the evolution of the strategic arms limitation talks (SALT) or of further shifts in the pattern of international relations, the nuclear threat posed by the Soviet Union and the changing nature of military technology will require the United States to periodically review the adequacy of its strategic capability and of its weapon plans. Past strategic policy debates have focused on the questions of America's "superiority" or "inferiority," and these phrases will inevitably persist as descriptions of the relative military effectiveness of U.S. and Soviet nuclear forces. But it is of crucial importance to recognize that neither the United States nor the Soviet Union can prevent each other from maintaining a strategic force capable of surviving an all-out attack and inflicting "unacceptable" damage against a population center in retaliation. For the United States or the USSR to achieve the ability to deny its opponent a retaliatory capability would require offensive systems capable of destroying a substantial proportion of the adversary's weapons in a first strike, combined with defensive systems capable of blunting strikes from remaining forces. This appears to be infeasible for either side, given the size and quality of their deterrent forces, their ability to detect major threats, and the availability of countermeasures in the form of force improvements or enlargements.

Both the inevitability and the efficacy of this so-called mutual assured destruction (MAD) relationship have been questioned by a number of experts. Nevertheless, U.S. and Soviet policymakers have come to accept the proposition that security in the nuclear age must be based primarily on deterrence rather than on defense or the ability to achieve victory in a strategic exchange, since there are no reliable means of negating the power of nuclear weapons to inflict massive civilian damage. Proposals to replace a deterrence policy based on the threat of counterpopulation retaliation with "defense emphasis" postures or "no-cities" targeting strategies seem to be unworkable and politically undesirable at present. This does not mean that both sides will completely eschew policies and programs designed to use strategic forces for the purposes of damage limitation or war termination in the event deterrence fails. But it does suggest that each nation not only *can* but *will* take whatever actions are necessary to preserve its retaliatory assured destruction capability in the face of deliberate threats or technological progress. At the same time, for political and diplomatic reasons neither nation will wish to project an image of weakness conveyed by a highly unfavorable force balance. Despite the cries of critics, therefore, if the superpowers keep their forces secure and balanced, use SALT to slow down the weapons competition, and continue to cooperate in attempts to minimize the risks of accidental war, MAD appears to represent the sanest way of coping with the problems and paradoxes created by the introduction of nuclear weapons more than twenty-five years ago.

On the other hand, neither numerical parity nor the mutual destruction relationship will automatically guarantee *nuclear stability*—stability against the possible breakdown of nuclear deterrence, the acquisition of excessive and dangerous weapons, or the application of strategic power for political gains. The unilateral strategic posture and policy decisions of the United States and the USSR will influence the outcome of future arms control talks and ultimately will affect the long-term stability of the nuclear balance. Whether Washington and Moscow can manage their differences without running nuclear risks will obviously involve a host of factors independent of strategic arms, including conventional military force levels, national interests and commitments, and decisionmaking processes within each government. Moreover, there is no way to guarantee that if one nation establishes a desirable course to follow the other will proceed on a parallel course, nor is it possible to ensure against accidental or irrational actions on either side. Nonetheless, the United States has a strong national interest as well as a worldwide responsibility to take the initiative in pursuing a stabilizing strategic nuclear policy.

Principles of Stable Deterrence

In designing a strategic posture for the decade ahead, the United States should seek to maximize stability through a policy of stable deterrence built on three principles:

- Maintaining a confident retaliatory deterrent posture comparable in effectiveness and size to that of the Soviet Union.
- Avoiding weapons and doctrines that pose a threat to the USSR's deterrent and seeking security through negotiated arms limitations.
- Reducing the relative reliance on nuclear power in U.S. defense and foreign policy.

These principles and the practical planning and budgetary problems involved in attempting to implement the proposed policy will be discussed below. The brief policy prescriptions offered here are supported by the detailed analyses in previous chapters.

Confident Retaliatory Capability

The first principle of stable deterrence is that preservation of a secure retaliatory capability against the Soviet Union should be the cornerstone of our strategic doctrine and the major determinant of our force posture and budget. The United States should continue to ensure that its strategic forces retain the ability to inflict "unacceptable" levels of damage on the USSR in a retaliatory strike. The guaranteed destruction of at least 20–25 percent of the USSR's population and over 70 percent of its industrial base should be more than sufficient to deter a Soviet nuclear attack. This destruction level should also inhibit Soviet leaders from engaging in actions that run a high risk of ending in nuclear war—regardless of the number of American fatalities the Soviet Union might be able to inflict.

Under stable deterrence, however, the emphasis should be placed on assurance rather than destruction, for an assured retaliatory capability is the key to minimizing the possibility of an inadvertent breakdown in deterrence through Soviet miscalculation. To this end, the United States should maintain a diversified deterrent with every major element of its strategic posture sufficiently survivable to withstand an attack. Vulnerable strategic systems should either be protected to the extent feasible or phased out and replaced by survivable systems. This basic posture, designed as protection against the Soviet Union, would automatically give the United States an assured destruction capability against China, as well as an appreciable counterforce capability that would be sufficient to cope with military or diplomatic threats against the United States or its allies posed by China's relatively small strategic deployments.

Because the problems of nuclear deterrence inevitably involve perceptions as well as reality and include political as well as military considerations, a reliable U.S. strategic posture should reflect an awareness of the importance of numerical force comparisons. In particular, to guard against circumstances in which America's allies might question the efficacy of our nuclear guarantee or Kremlin leaders might attempt to exploit their newly found strategic strength politically, the United States should ensure that the numerical balance between U.S. and Soviet strategic postures does not tilt to our disadvantage. Precise parity with the USSR in launchers, warheads, or throw-weight is unnecessary and infeasible, but some form of equivalence based on these so-called static indices should be maintained, as is envisaged in the Vladivostok agreement.[1] While primary attention should be paid to the military requirements of a deterrent force in shaping U.S. strategic policies, to deny the political importance of the numerical balance is to increase the risk of nuclear war and to make control of the arms race more difficult.

Conflicts can occur between the objectives of maintaining a diversified deterrent and avoiding numerical imbalances. Central to the stable deterrence approach is the concept that the existence of highly vulnerable systems could create serious instabilities and possibly lead to an inadvertent breakdown in nuclear deterrence. As the U.S. Minuteman intercontinental ballistic missile (ICBM) force becomes vulnerable to Soviet counterforce strikes, therefore, the United States should reduce and eventually eliminate these systems, thus removing any incentive for the USSR to attack our land-based missiles. But this unilateral action could upset the numerical balance, since the Soviet Union would retain a massive ICBM force. This suggests that priority should be given to the goal of securing mutual ICBM reductions in SALT III negotiations, after an agreement based on the Vladivostok guidelines has been concluded and has come into force. Nevertheless, if mutual missile reductions cannot be negotiated, it would appear desirable for

1. Joint Soviet-American Statement on Strategic Arms Limitation, November 24, 1974.

the United States to emphasize military stability and to gradually phase out its ICBMs. If the overall numerical balance were judged to be unduly jeopardized by such a move, the United States could compensate by constructing additional survivable systems, such as submarine-launched missiles, to replace the ICBMs. At a minimum, it would be wasteful, if not destabilizing, to improve the present ICBM force or to replace silo-based systems with land-mobile missiles while planning a proper Minuteman reduction program.

Due to the uncertain future survivability of land-based missiles, it is imperative that submarine-launched ballistic missiles (SLBMs) remain dependable during the coming decade and gradually form the foundation of the U.S. strategic posture. This pattern seems assured, since Soviet progress in this field, if not constrained by future SALT agreements, could be countered by qualitative improvements in the present submarine fleet or by eventually building a replacement for the Polaris-Poseidon force. Because Soviet antiballistic missiles (ABMs) are severely constrained by the treaty of 1972,[2] U.S. sea-based missile forces alone could be assured of inflicting high levels of retaliatory damage on the Soviet Union's population. Nevertheless, the United States should procure the extended-range Trident I missile for installation in the Polaris boats as a prudential move to strengthen our sea-based deterrent. Over the longer term, an entirely new submarine system, whether Trident or a less costly alternative such as the smaller Narwhal system, will undoubtedly have to be procured.

Despite the likely continued safety of submarines, however, diversity is essential for stable deterrence. Therefore, the United States should retain strategic bombers as an additional independent and relatively survivable land-based deterrent force. This would permit U.S. policy-makers to seriously consider gradually eliminating our ICBMs if they become severely threatened and developing a suitable replacement bomber for the B-52—the B-1 or a less costly system. Although Soviet development of low-trajectory SLBMs could threaten our bomber bases, countermeasures can be taken to preserve the survivability of our strategic bomber forces. Because of their penetration characteristics, bombers provide a particularly effective hedge against the possibility that

2. Treaty between the United States of America and the Union of Soviet Socialist Republics on the Limitation of Anti-Ballistic Missile Systems, signed at Moscow, May 26, 1972. A 1974 protocol limited both sides to one ABM site.

the Soviet Union might evade or abrogate the terms of the ABM treaty. For this reason, a diad consisting of SLBMs and bombers would offer a confident U.S. deterrent without the dangers and disadvantages of vulnerable ICBMs. A survivable diad would be preferable to preserving the present triad configuration with one weak component. There would appear to be no need to produce entirely new types of systems, such as a long-range cruise missile or an air-launched ICBM, to provide greater diversity in our strategic posture.

Under the proposed deterrent posture, the United States could continue to develop options that would permit the President to use strategic forces selectively against a variety of targets and that would not restrict his choice to launching massive strikes against Soviet cities. Acquiring flexible capabilities as supplements to assured destruction would enable the United States to reply to a possible Soviet limited strategic attack with a limited strike of its own. Thus, Soviet leaders would be less prone to contemplate such actions in the belief that the United States could not match their limited strikes and would not retaliate in a countercity strike for fear of counterretaliation. It would also be advisable to develop selective targeting capabilities in order to limit damage if deterrence failed and to help support our guarantees to our allies. The programs needed to implement a policy of flexible strategic options, however, would primarily be those of command, control, and communications. The United States should *not* permit the desire to improve the flexibility of its strategic forces to dominate its military doctrine or to lead to "warfighting" strategies and the acquisition of a counterforce capability against Soviet ICBMs through the development of hard-target kill capabilities for missile systems carrying multiple independently targetable reentry vehicles (MIRVs) or the procurement of accurate maneuvering reentry vehicles. A variety of other flexible options are available, and any loss in deterrence effectiveness stemming from the lack of U.S. counterforce capabilities would be slight and well worth the net gain in strategic stability resulting from a decision to forgo such a provocative policy. Finally, there would be no need to seek counterforce capabilities in order to prevent the USSR from achieving an advantage in the potential to inflict population fatalities. As long as the United States maintains a confident deterrent posture capable of inflicting high levels of damage, there should be no danger of possible imbalances in U.S. and Soviet damage-inflicting potentials.

Stability through Negotiation

The second principle of stable deterrence is based on the premise that the successful achievement of America's strategic objectives depends on the Soviet Union's strategic arms policies and procurements. Although the USSR's doctrine cannot be inferred with precision, the nature of the Soviet Union's offensive posture and Moscow's acceptance of the ABM treaty strongly suggest that Soviet strategic policy is similar to the U.S. policy, which is built on a secure retaliatory deterrent supplemented by limited options and which reflects concern over numerical comparisons. At a minimum, it seems safe to assume that Kremlin leaders appreciate the danger of nuclear war and the dynamics of deterrence—even if they do place higher priority than their American counterparts on war-fighting strategies. Thus, the United States should attempt to affect the bilateral relationship by avoiding decisions that threaten or appear to threaten the Soviet Union's retaliatory capability. Weapons with a counterforce potential, such as high-accuracy MIRV-carrying ICBMs, should not be procured, while sea-based missile forces and strategic bombers, which are less suited for counterforce missions, should receive higher priority as deterrent forces. Active defenses, including air defense, anti-submarine defenses, and ABMs, should be pursued primarily as research programs designed to provide information about countermeasures needed to improve the survivability of our own systems, or possibly as prudential protection against attacks by countries other than the Soviet Union, rather than as major procurement programs geared to negate Soviet deterrent forces. In making U.S. strategic weapon decisions, care should also be taken to prevent Soviet leaders from concluding that the United States might be seeking some form of numerical superiority.

A unilateral policy of mutual stability can help dampen the U.S.-Soviet arms competition and reduce the risk of nuclear war, but there are severe limits to the effectiveness of such a policy. Indeed, strategic stability can be fully realized only if both sides downgrade defense and emphasize survivable forces that have no meaningful counterforce capabilities. Hence, a purely stabilizing U.S. nuclear policy would be imperfect unless matched by the Soviet Union. Perhaps the USSR will move toward a stable posture on its own, although there are occasional indications that Soviet leaders might be seeking to gain military or political advantages in ways that could endanger the stability of the strategic relationship. Negotiations have the potential of helping both sides attain stabilizing postures through mutual agreements and threat reduction. Therefore, bilateral arms control arrangements resulting from SALT can prove to be a more fruitful means of achieving a stable strategic balance than can purely independent decisions.

In future SALT negotiations, the U.S. position should be consistent with the guidelines for stable deterrence. Accordingly, the ABM treaty should be maintained as envisaged under the Vladivostok guidelines, which also take account of political needs in seeking to guarantee an overall balance between U.S. and Soviet forces in the total number of delivery systems. If these guidelines can be translated into a concrete offensive arms agreement, stability will be strengthened. Post-Vladivostok proposals should be formulated with a view toward removing vulnerable and provocative strategic offensive systems on both sides while ensuring that survivable second-strike systems can be dependably maintained. Unnecessary weapons could be eliminated through mutual agreement, thereby reducing defense expenditures and preventing one nation from building forces simply to match those of the other. One especially productive course for SALT III, as noted, would be the negotiation of mutual ICBM reductions—a measure that could lower arms levels while improving mutual stability.

Just as there is a conflict between removing vulnerable missiles and maintaining numerical comparability, there are conflicts in attempting to follow the first two principles of stable deterrence—parity and stability. In many instances, for example, the objective of designing a confident deterrent force in the face of uncertainties about Soviet strategic programs and likely SALT outcomes can run counter to the objectives of mutual stability. To make matters worse, particular weapons, such as MIRVs, often exhibit both stabilizing and destabilizing characteristics. The United States must seek to strike a balance between strengthening its deterrent posture through unilateral actions and attempting to improve U.S. security through further SALT agreements. On the one hand, it would be wise to avoid arms procurements designed to hedge against extremely remote dangers, to refrain from acquiring weapons solely for the purpose of obtaining "bargaining chips," and to refuse to compromise the second stable deterrence principle by threatening to build destabilizing systems in order to coerce the Soviet Union into accepting specific limitations. On the other hand, the United States should continue weapon activities required to maintain a reliable strategic posture in the event SALT fails to contain major Soviet programs. Moreover, the existence of U.S. strategic arms programs can lead Kremlin leaders to place higher priority on negotiated solutions than on renewed arms competition as a path to greater security at lower cost. Given these countervailing considerations as broad guidelines, specific decisions relating weapon programs to arms negotiations will have to be made on a case-by-case basis.

Reducing the Significance of Nuclear Power

The third principle of stable deterrence is that strategic stability cannot be separated from the broader question of the significance of nuclear weapons in U.S. defense policy and in world affairs generally. In order to enhance nuclear stability, the United States should seek to reduce reliance on nuclear weapons in its military posture. A policy that leaned heavily on strategic nuclear power and emphasized tactical nuclear weapons for general purpose forces would have the disadvantages of limiting U.S. options, forcing the premature use of nuclear weapons, and risking rapid escalation to strategic war. Such a policy could disrupt efforts to achieve the type of U.S.-Soviet strategic relationship recommended above—by forcing the United States to adopt a doctrine that upgraded the importance of a nuclear first-strike option and to procure such weapons as accurate MIRVs and area ABMs. These actions are precisely those the Kremlin could view as threatening the effectiveness of its retaliatory force; thus Soviet leaders would probably react by making corresponding changes in their own defense plans and perhaps by flexing their nuclear muscles in the political arena.

A preferable course of action would be to keep nuclear forces as far as possible in the background—almost always as the ultimate deterrent to nuclear attack—and, in the case of our extended deterrent commitments to the North Atlantic Treaty Organization (NATO), as the last option to be considered if nonnuclear responses failed to stem a massive Soviet conventional attack against Western Europe. Such an approach would be reflected in our policy, in our choice of military doctrine, and in our defense procurements. On the strategic level, the United States would maintain a powerful but nonprovocative posture, following the first two principles of stable deterrence. The clear implication of this course is that strategic forces would need to be complemented by conventional forces adequate to minimize situations in which nuclear weapons might be used. Failing fundamental shifts in U.S. foreign commitments, this would call for maintaining effective nonnuclear general purpose forces—although reductions could be made in theater nuclear forces.

Finally, the United States should include within the SALT framework the objective of forging a common approach with the Soviet Union restricting the role of nuclear weapons and reducing the risk of nuclear conflict. Progress has already been made on the latter,[3] but the United States should continue to work with the Soviet Union to reduce the danger of nuclear war by accident or miscalculation. Further efforts could be made to establish policies and procedures for diminishing the danger of escalation in crises and for bringing the other nuclear-weapon states into a multiple hot line agreement. On a more basic level, the United States and the Soviet Union can use SALT as a forum to discuss defense strategies. Discussions can cover the political value and military utility of tactical as well as strategic nuclear arms. U.S. officials might specifically emphasize the inverse relationship between nuclear and conventional forces and the importance of maintaining sufficient nonnuclear capabilities to minimize the necessity of relying heavily on nuclear weapons for deterrence and defense. The object of such a strategy dialogue would be to develop a common appreciation of the need for reduced reliance on nuclear weapons in military planning and foreign policy. Ideally, Washington and Moscow would agree to follow parallel policies based on the principles of stable deterrence, to develop coordinated approaches to strengthening the nuclear nonproliferation treaty,[4] and to seek arms control arrangements that would support the goal of lowering the nuclear profile.

Stable Deterrence in Practice

The practical applications of any strategic policy are constrained by many factors, including planning uncertainties, the availability of technology, and cost constraints. Systematic procedures and techniques, such as the use of cost-effectiveness calculations, can be used to set re-

3. Agreement between the United States of America and the Union of Soviet Socialist Republics on the Prevention of Nuclear War, signed at Washington, June 21, 1973. For text, see *New York Times*, June 23, 1973.

4. Treaty on the Non-Proliferation of Nuclear Weapons, signed at Washington, London, and Moscow, July 1, 1968.

quirements for overall force levels; to determine whether existing systems should be retained, modernized, or eliminated; and to establish broad directions for new strategic programs. But analytic techniques alone cannot precisely correlate doctrine and weapon programs so that the optimum mix of our strategic posture can be determined, and weapon technology often shapes policy choices. In addition, crucial characteristics of our strategic posture are apt to be shaped by judgmental decisions on such matters as the degree of confidence to be built into our deterrent force—a factor that cannot always be quantified. Furthermore, many U.S. weapon decisions are motivated by diplomatic factors such as the desire to match Soviet forces or to acquire bargaining chips for negotiations. Finally, the pattern and pace of particular U.S. strategic programs often represent concessions to internal bureaucratic and domestic political demands.

Estimating the Threat

A closer examination of the elements of strategic planning exposes many of the difficulties associated with the implementation of a policy of stable deterrence. For example, the formulation of dependable threat estimates is one of the most important aspects of strategic planning. It is imperative to be able to identify future Soviet weapon activities that could endanger our retaliatory deterrent forces or lead to a dramatic shift in the strategic balance. The earlier and more accurately such trends can be detected, the more readily an appropriate set of responses can be implemented. A typical U.S. strategic weapon program takes at least five years to progress from the research and development phase to testing, production, and operational deployment. Given this lead time, it is clearly desirable to be able to assess Soviet threats as reliably as possible to avoid both excessive reactions, which could be wasteful or destabilizing, and underreactions, which might endanger our deterrent capabilities.

The United States maintains an extensive array of reconnaissance programs, including satellites with electronic and photographic capabilities, ground-based radars, a variety of other shipborne and airborne collection systems, and ocean surveillance programs. These technical intelligence programs can provide information to planners and policymakers on important features of Soviet and Chinese strategic weapon efforts. For example, the United States can locate and identify large, long lead-time, fixed installations, such as ICBM sites, submarine yards, bomber airfields, and ABM missile sites and radars, with a high degree of confidence. On the other hand, many uncertainties regarding the nature of the USSR's strategic posture cannot be resolved through U.S. national detection systems. There is no reliable way, for instance, of predicting future levels of deployment. It is equally difficult to discern the precise performance parameters of Soviet systems or the specific technical characteristics of many weapons. In short, while the United States can often detect trends in Soviet weapon activities in time to take appropriate countermeasures, strategic force decisions must often be made on the basis of incomplete intelligence information and thus at the risk of prematurely procuring systems deemed necessary to ensure a viable strategic posture in the future.

It is equally difficult to identify Soviet motivations and goals, but a continuing attempt must be made to do so in order to avoid designing U.S. forces solely on the basis of the USSR's capabilities. While the experience of SALT and recent Soviet policy statements and actions have increased our understanding of the Soviet Union's strategic objectives, it is virtually impossible to assess Soviet strategic policies with confidence. Even if U.S. planners were able to determine that Kremlin leaders had adopted a particular doctrine, they would know little about the specific Soviet forces that might be used to support it. For example, within the broad bounds of the Soviet strategic outlook, which is somewhat comparable to that of the United States, it is unclear whether the USSR will emphasize restraint in order to stabilize mutual deterrence or will build forces that could provide greater damage-limiting capabilities and numerical advantages. Public policy pronouncements by Kremlin leaders are often misleading in conveying the meaning behind Soviet activity and can drive the United States to overreact or underreact to Soviet weapon efforts. Furthermore, Soviet weapon decisions, like those of the United States, are often the result of bureaucratic compromises or sheer technical momentum rather than of actions dictated by a strategic rationale.

Force-Planning Guidelines

The concept of basing U.S. strategic force planning on "worst-case" assumptions regarding future Soviet nuclear threats has been justified as one solution to the problem of uncertainty about the USSR's intentions and capabilities in the nuclear field.[5] This approach involves an attempt to guarantee the effectiveness of U.S. deterrent capabilities in the face of severe but plausible threats while developing hedges against highly unlikely but potentially dangerous Soviet weapon efforts. But worst-case planning can lead to excessive force levels and destabilizing arms decisions. In the future, therefore, it would not only be desirable but possible for the United States to be less strict in its force planning assumptions and still retain an effective deterrent.

Many U.S. strategic deployment efforts, especially the MIRV programs, were planned primarily as responses to Soviet ABM expansion. Since ABMs are limited and MIRVs are permitted under the SALT accords, the U.S. strategic posture will be more adequate than originally contemplated. There will be less need to react rapidly to signs of new offensive Soviet weapon developments, since U.S. deterrent capabilities cannot easily be undermined. Pentagon planners can afford to place greater reliance on increased research and development efforts to reduce lead times to deployment and to wait for clearer signs of an emerging threat before moving into procurement. Major dangers to the U.S. deterrent posture, such as antisubmarine warfare (ASW), would take years to develop after initial Soviet deployments were identified, thereby providing time to mount countermeasures. If necessary, "quick-fix" programs, such as installing missile penetration aids or increasing bomber alert rates, could be instituted rapidly as temporary actions to guard against potentially dangerous threats.

On the other hand, a prudent degree of conservative planning is necessary to guard against uncertainties and to maintain high confidence in the U.S. strategic deterrent. The size and direction of the Soviet Union's ongoing strategic activities strongly suggest the advisability of seriously pursuing programs that are necessary to preserve a diverse and survivable force. If no countermeasures were taken, the USSR's deployment of a full force of accurate multiple warheads on its ICBMs could endanger the survivability of U.S. land-based missiles, the possible development of depressed-trajectory SLBMs could threaten our bomber forces, and, over the long term, progress in Soviet ASW capabilities

5. For background on strategic planning, see Alain C. Enthoven and Wayne K. Smith, *How Much Is Enough? Shaping the Defense Program, 1961–1969;* and Samuel A. Tucker, ed., *A Modern Design for Defense Decision: A McNamara-Hitch-Enthoven Anthology* (Industrial College of the Armed Forces, 1966).

could even cause the credibility of our sea-based missile force to be questioned. In addition to maintaining a multiple deterrent and modernizing force components as necessary, the United States should also continue to use relatively conservative calculations in estimating the damage-inflicting potential of our strategic forces. Such a conservatively designed deterrent force could help ensure that our strategic capabilities would remain visible to Moscow and could minimize possible Soviet misperceptions, thus making it difficult for a "clever briefer" in the Kremlin to demonstrate that serious weaknesses exist in our present or projected strategic posture.

The Moscow SALT accords, the ongoing negotiations to translate the Vladivostok guidelines into an agreement, and the possibility of future agreements with the USSR create a new framework for the conduct of U.S. strategic planning. In particular, an arms control environment can introduce new weapon needs, alter program priorities, and change established weapon procurement patterns. Constraints placed on Soviet forces by a strategic arms limitations agreement have already altered the nature of the threat Pentagon analysts must consider in developing future American force requirements. At the same time, the United States has been constrained in the implementation of certain of its weapon options. Although the attainment of even more comprehensive agreements would further restrict the alternatives available to American defense planners, continued success in negotiating SALT accords can help the United States achieve its strategic policy objectives with greater reliability and at less cost by limiting Soviet forces and narrowing the scope of future threat estimates.

But the Moscow and Vladivostok agreements do not remove the potential Soviet offensive threats to our strategic retaliatory forces that many U.S. programs are designed to meet. The USSR is already demonstrating that it will continue quantitative and qualitative strategic programs permitted by the agreements—not only in anticipation of future U.S. strategic efforts but as a means of further improving its position and strengthening its hand in future negotiations. Unless Soviet restraint or follow-on SALT agreements eliminate or significantly alleviate these dangers, the United States must pursue programs needed to maintain an assured destruction capability, keeping current forces effective and replacing them when necessary. The lack of ASW limitations thus far in SALT makes it imperative for the United States to ensure the security of its sea-based deterrent, and the prospect that our ICBMs might become vulnerable makes the goal of preserving reliable bomber and submarine systems even more important.

Because the achievement of arms limitations can have potential benefits for American security, the United States should use its strategic planning, where possible, to facilitate progress in SALT. As noted above, there are no formulas for balancing unilateral deterrent requirements against mutual stability objectives or of relating force decisions to bargaining tactics. Nevertheless, it is essential to devise systematic procedures for incorporating mutual stability and SALT considerations into all stages of the force-planning process. The aim should be to prevent proposed strategic programs from interfering unduly with U.S. objectives for SALT agreements and to strengthen those U.S. programs that serve the purpose of maintaining stability and supporting the goals of SALT. It would be particularly important to systematically apply the criteria of stable deterrence to individual weapon decisions at a sufficiently early stage to prevent potentially destabilizing programs from gathering excessive momentum. Given the many complex and controversial diplomatic and military issues connecting strategic weapon decisions and SALT, it might be advisable to hold programs in the development stage for longer periods of time than would ordinarily be the case and to subject all procurement requests to careful scrutiny. Perhaps, as some experts have suggested, the Defense Department could be required by Congress to issue arms control impact statements for each strategic program in its annual budget.

Finally, the anticipated growth of China's nuclear capability introduces a new dimension into U.S. strategic planning. China has begun to deploy a small force of intermediate- and medium-range ballistic missiles capable of reaching targets in Asia as well as in the Soviet Union and before the end of the decade might deploy a number of ICBMs with a sufficient range to reach U.S. cities. Because the Chinese strategic deployments will remain extremely limited for some time, the U.S. forces deployed under the stable deterrence policy to deal with the USSR's strategic threat would also be capable of satisfying U.S. objectives vis-à-vis China. U.S. strategic bombers, for example, would be particularly effective against China; a portion of the present B-52 force along with an even smaller portion of the U.S. submarine-based missile force could inflict devastating damage on China's major cities and destroy a considerable number of its strategic weapon installations.

Budgetary Implications

The need to keep military spending in check is one of the most important considerations involved in the practical pursuit of any defense policy. It is essential, therefore, to explore the budgetary consequences of stable deterrence and, in particular, to determine whether this policy can be implemented without substantially increasing the costs of U.S. strategic programs.

Any discussion of strategic budget issues should be put in perspective, however, by introducing the often overlooked point that the level of spending may *not* be a meaningful measure of U.S. strategic policy. For example, many qualitative arms decisions, such as improving missile accuracy, are relatively inexpensive compared with the costs of new procurements. Yet these and other relatively low-cost decisions can adversely affect strategic stability. Conversely, programs designed to enhance the survivability of U.S. forces can be expensive. It is as misleading to automatically associate lower levels of spending with stabilizing strategic policies as it is to assume that increased strategic budgets are reflections of a dangerous escalation of the nuclear arms race.

An additional caveat is that the relationship between weapon programs and strategic budget levels is neither obvious nor unique. For one thing, decisions on particular strategic weapon systems need not have a noticeable effect on the strategic budget as a whole. Such techniques as slowing the schedule under which a new system is introduced, reducing the number of units produced, and phasing out obsolete systems could make it possible to proceed with new procurement programs while staying within a fixed annual expenditure limit.[6] Second, greater research efforts may not have a significant near-term effect on the budget, since research and development activities are substantially less costly than procurement programs. Finally, although investment costs for new procurements can be high, the operating costs of the new systems can be considerably less than the costs of systems they might replace. In certain cases, the acquisition of new and more efficient systems as economic replacements could prove to be less costly over the long term than retaining existing weapons.

6. In fiscal year 1970, for example, the Nixon administration went forward with both the MIRV and the ABM programs, even though the strategic budget was *reduced* by $2 billion.

During the past decade, the annual cost of U.S. strategic forces, including their proportional share of support costs, has averaged approximately $18 billion in current dollars, absorbing about 20 percent of the overall defense budget. For budgetary purposes, U.S. strategic forces are generally taken to encompass the triad of long-range bombers, ICBMs, and SLBMs on the offensive side, and continental air defense (including warning and control) and antiballistic missile systems on the defensive side. If expenditures are allocated by system, spending for offensive systems has constituted three-quarters of the strategic budget, and over 40 percent of total expenditures have been for land- and sea-based ballistic missile systems. Strategic bombers and air defense have been the two most expensive programs, although major reductions in air defense are scheduled for the next few years. In the missile age, it may seem surprising that these programs account for almost 50 percent of the U.S. strategic budget. Compared with missile systems, however, bomber and air-defense programs are expensive to maintain because of high manpower levels and other operating costs.

Expenditures for antisubmarine warfare and forward-based systems are not included in the strategic budget. Because of the multipurpose nature of ASW systems and the fact that they are rarely procured solely for strategic purposes, antisubmarine warfare is funded as part of the general purpose forces program. Nuclear-capable aircraft deployed in Western Europe and Asia or on carriers at sea are primarily programmed for theater operations and are also budgeted as part of general purpose forces, but some theater nuclear systems may be assigned secondary strategic attack roles.

The figure displayed in the official U.S. strategic force budget usually accounts for only the *direct* cost of strategic systems that are deployed or being procured. This figure includes investment costs—which cover the procurement, construction, development, and testing of approved systems—and operating costs, which include materiel and personnel. To obtain the *total* cost of strategic forces, allowance must be made for *indirect* costs, including associated intelligence and communication programs, basic research and development efforts, and a variety of support costs. In addition, annual atomic energy costs of some $1 billion are attributable to strategic programs. When all indirect costs are calculated, they amount to more than direct costs. Many indirect costs are constant and relatively independent of deployed force levels. Thus, budget variations due to the acquisition of new strategic weapons or the elimination of existing systems would not necessarily cause proportionate changes in indirect costs.

Not surprisingly, it is difficult to estimate the cost of particular U.S. strategic weapon programs with precision. The timing, scope, and phasing of weapon projects are often uncertain, and cost growth is certain to occur owing to inflation, modifications, and mismanagement. A useful technique for analyzing the cost of a weapon system, however, is to compute its ten-year systems cost. This calculation generally includes complete research and development costs, expenditures for producing and deploying a specified number of units, and operating costs over an assumed ten-year lifetime. Typical systems costs for major strategic weapon programs currently under development fall in the range of $15–20 billion. But regardless of uncertainties, there is no choice but to use current expenditure estimates and a cost projection as a baseline for analyzing the budgetary consequences of alternative strategic postures and the specific implications for stable deterrence.[7]

Starting with the ICBM force, the total expenditure for U.S. land-based missiles was approximately $3 billion in fiscal year 1974. Over two-thirds of this figure covered investment costs for force improvements—the MIRV-equipped Minuteman III missile, the silo upgrade program, and the command data buffer. Conversion of 550 Minuteman I missiles to the model III will be completed by 1975 at a total cost of $6 billion. The remaining Minuteman force might also be converted, but annual costs associated with the U.S. land-based missile deterrent will probably remain below $2 billion during the second half of the decade. Reductions in the number of operational ICBMs, through unilateral action or mutual agreement, could obviously lower this funding level, while a decision to deploy hard-point defenses or mobile ICBMs or to accelerate the development of a new-generation land-based missile could lead to substantial increases.

The prominence of submarine-based deterrent systems is reflected in the high annual level of expenditures for these forces—almost $5 billion in fiscal year 1974 and projected to nearly $6 billion by 1980. Although the costs associated with the program to install Poseidon SLBMs in Polaris submarines will total nearly $10 billion by the time of its completion in 1976, the Trident project will account for the bulk of U.S.

7. Information on strategic weapon costs and schedules are drawn from Alton H. Quanbeck and Barry M. Blechman, *Strategic Forces: Issues for the Mid-Seventies* (Brookings Institution, 1973). Costs are given in 1974 dollars.

investment in sea-based forces during the rest of the decade. Early
estimates put the cost of developing and producing ten Trident boats at
over $13 billion, with annual expenditures for the planned accelerated
program approaching $3 billion by the middle of the decade, but acquisi-
tion costs are certain to rise. Annual operating costs for the U.S. submarine fleet, it might be noted, will probably remain at slightly above
$1 billion. A major slowdown of the Trident effort could, of course, result
in substantial savings in the near term. Similarly, a decision to reduce
the number of Trident systems procured and to build the less expensive
Narwhal submarine could yield substantial savings.

The strategic bomber force, as suggested, is the most expensive component of our strategic posture. In 1974, the United States spent over
$5.5 billion to support its bomber capabilities, with $3.5 billion attributable to operating costs. A sizable fraction of the costs of maintaining
bombers derives from the need for a fleet of tanker aircraft used in aerial
refueling. Future expenditures for strategic bombers will rise as investment costs for the new B-1 aircraft enter the picture toward the late
1970s, with total annual expenditures for the bomber force likely to exceed $8 billion by 1980. A fleet of 200 B-1 bombers could in itself involve
cumulative outlays of about $18 billion for research and development
and procurement, and annual investments for this system would average
about $2 billion. Reducing the U.S. bomber force would be one way to
rapidly curtail defense spending, and long-range spending could be
limited if the United States decided to build a less sophisticated bomber
than the B-1. One estimate indicates that savings of $10 billion could
accrue over the years 1974–83 if such a plan were adopted. Alternatively,
introduction of the B-1 could be delayed, some of the high-cost features
of the aircraft could be eliminated, or only 100 units could be procured.

Although primary attention is usually paid to U.S. strategic offensive
forces, strategic defenses constitute a substantial fraction of the U.S.
strategic budget. Possible programs to modernize the U.S. air defense
include the airborne warning and control system (AWACS), an improved manned interceptor to replace existing fighter interceptors, and
the advanced surface-to-air missile SAM-D. If the United States went
forward with a program to fully modernize air defenses in an attempt
to acquire improved damage-limiting capabilities against Soviet bomber
attacks, the new acquisition costs could be substantial. For example,
under a modernization program, air defense costs would average over

$4 billion annually throughout the late 1970s. But a minimum air-defense network for the surveillance of U.S. airspace and the prevention of over-flights, composed of F-106 interceptors and necessary warning and control systems, could be sustained with expenditures of as little as $1 billion annually. However, with the exception of AWACS, which is being pursued primarily for tactical missions, interest in modernizing strategic air defenses has diminished greatly. Expenditures for air defenses have been sharply reduced during the past few years through the gradual elimination of obsolescent systems such as Nike-Ajax and Hercules batteries, and this trend seems likely to continue.

The cost of ABM programs will, of course, be contained because the Moscow treaty prevented the United States from spending at least $15–20 billion for the complete Safeguard system during the last half of the 1970s. The completion of the Safeguard site at Malmstrom Air Force Base—permitted by the treaty—could cost almost $4 billion. Independent of ABM programs, yearly expenditures for research on improved site and area ballistic missile defenses will probably average between $100 million and $500 million for the remainder of the decade.

The funding levels for warning, control, and reconnaissance systems that are vital to the U.S. strategic posture are difficult to estimate. Official strategic arms budget estimates do not indicate expenditures for programs such as the ballistic missile early warning system, satellite warning systems, or Spacetrack, nor are the figures given for the array of electronic and photographic systems used to provide intelligence vital to unilateral defense planning and to the verification of strategic arms limitations accords. Other unknown items are the precise costs of the command, control, and communication systems for U.S. ICBMs, bombers, and submarines and of the programs designed to secure the presidential nuclear chain of command and America's worldwide military communication network. Taking into account the fact that many of these systems serve tactical as well as strategic missions, perhaps annual costs of $3 billion for warning, control, and reconnaissance could reasonably be allocated to strategic forces. Most experts agree that the United States should continue to invest the resources necessary to maintain effective capabilities in these fields.

In drawing implications from the foregoing discussion, it is important to realize that, although it is possible to construct alternative strategic postures costing anywhere between $10 billion and $30 billion annually, it is probable that future U.S. strategic budgets will stay within the somewhat narrow range of $16 billion to $23 billion in constant dollars.[8] Major increases in the strategic budget will almost certainly be precluded by continued demands to reduce overall defense spending; large unilateral cutbacks seem equally implausible, given the momentum behind modernization programs and the continuing need to preserve a reliable deterrent. Furthermore, the likelihood of early and substantial cuts in strategic spending as a result of further arms limitation agreements is small; the Vladivostok guidelines do not provide for force reductions. At best if somewhat more comprehensive SALT accords are eventually reached, calling for limited reductions and partial qualitative controls, annual savings of a few billion dollars could be realized toward the late 1970s or early 1980s.

A number of weapon options consistent with stable deterrence could be accommodated within these likely budget boundaries. If modest programs were undertaken to enhance the survivability of our land and sea-based systems, and if new systems were introduced slowly, spending for strategic forces could drop slightly below present levels as ongoing procurement programs reached completion. If, in the late 1970s the United States continues to procure Trident as planned, the average annual budget could remain constant at approximately $19 billion over the decade, although it could rise to $23 billion if a new strategic bomber is also procured. This increase could be partially offset by reducing the size of the B-52 force to be retained until replaced in the early 1980s. The financial costs of improving our offensive forces could be made more bearable by continuing to reduce bomber defense force levels, to refrain from air-defense modernization programs, and to reject excessive expenditures for research on ABM systems. Downgrading strategic air and missile defenses, as called for by the second principle of stable deterrence, would permit the United States to maintain a confident strategic diad composed of a secure sea-based deterrent and a relatively survivable bomber force at a reduced budget level of approximately $16 billion (in constant 1974 dollars) for strategic armaments.

In sum, it appears that the United States could pursue a stable deterrence policy without escalating the annual strategic arms budget. If the Soviet Union's strategic force improved qualitatively more rapidly

8. For the projected costs (in 1974 dollars) of strategic forces through 1980, see Edward R. Fried and others, *Setting National Priorities: The 1974 Budget* (Brookings Institution, 1973), p. 314.

than expected within the constraints of the Moscow accords and the Vladivostok agreement, the United States might find it necessary to increase spending to preserve a confident retaliatory capability. Alternatively, a modest decrease in strategic spending could be anticipated if the Soviet threat diminished, perhaps as a result of a series of future follow-on SALT agreements. In any case, with strategic spending kept under control, the United States could better afford to sustain the conventional forces needed for an effective nuclear stability strategy. Indeed, with less pressure on the strategic budget, the overall U.S. defense budget could be kept constant or could even be reduced without necessarily diminishing our ability to maintain sufficient nonnuclear defenses.[9]

The three principles of stable deterrence outlined above could enable the United States to preserve a secure and dependable deterrent in the new environment in the 1970s. Equally important, a nuclear policy based on these principles may evoke a military response from the Soviet Union. If the United States and the USSR were to move toward parallel policies of stable deterrence, the prospects for long-term stability would be greatly improved, and U.S. security would ultimately be enhanced. The initial Moscow and Vladivostok SALT agreements should contain the nuclear competition by helping both sides maintain a credible deterrent force and by offering the opportunity to manage strategic policies within a bilateral framework. But these agreements signify only the beginning of the search for stability. Sustained efforts on the part of the superpowers will be needed to maintain a mutually secure nuclear relationship during the coming years.

9. For analyses of U.S. force postures capable of minimizing the role of nuclear weapons without increasing defense spending, see Charles L. Schultze and others, *Setting National Priorities: The 1973 Budget* (Brookings Institution, 1972), pp. 116–21; and Leslie H. Gelb and Arnold M. Kuzmack, "General Purpose Forces," in Henry Owen, ed., *The Next Phase in Foreign Policy* (Brookings Institution, 1973), pp. 203–24.

The Brookings-Carnegie Strategic Arms Policy Study Group (1969–71)

Organizations are those with which members were affiliated in 1969.

E. Ross Adair *U.S. House of Representatives*
John B. Anderson *U.S. House of Representatives*
Howard H. Baker *U.S. Senate*
A. Doak Barnett *Brookings Institution*
Charles Bolté *Carnegie Endowment for International Peace*
Harold Brown (chairman) *California Institute of Technology*
Jeffery Cohelan *U.S. House of Representatives*
Hedley Donovan *Time, Inc.*
Lee A. DuBridge *Science Adviser to the President*
Philip J. Farley *U.S. Arms Control and Disarmament Agency*
John S. Foster, Jr. *Department of Defense*
Philip Geyelin *Washington Post*
Kermit Gordon *Brookings Institution*
Morton Halperin *Brookings Institution*
Daniel K. Inouye *U.S. Senate*
Joseph E. Johnson *Carnegie Endowment for International Peace*
Jerome H. Kahan *Brookings Institution*
Franklin A. Lindsay (vice-chairman) *Itek Corporation*
James McCormack *Aerospace Corporation*
Edmund S. Muskie *U.S. Senate*
Henry Owen *Brookings Institution*
James B. Pearson *U.S. Senate*
Otis G. Pike *U.S. House of Representatives*
George W. Rathjens *Massachusetts Institute of Technology*
Matthew B. Ridgway *General, U.S. Army, Retired*
Herbert Scoville, Jr. *Carnegie Endowment for International Peace*
Gerard C. Smith *U.S. Arms Control and Disarmament Agency*
John A. Wheeler *Princeton University*
Herbert F. York *University of California, San Diego-La Jolla*

Index

Abel, Elie, 111n
ABM. *See* Antiballistic missile
ABM treaty, 3n, 152–53, 179, 186–87, 292, 305, 310, 326, 333, 335
Adequacy, doctrine of strategic. *See* Sufficiency strategy
Airborne warning and control system (AWACS), 346, 347
Air Force: missile development, 36, 37, 39, 44, 70; policy of superiority, 31, 33, 223
Air-to-surface missile (ASM), 316
Allison, Graham T., 80n, 82n, 85n, 88n, 103n, 111n, 154n, 265n
Alsop, Joseph, 196n
Anderson, V. C., 212n
Antiballistic missiles (ABMs): ability to detect, 287; cost of U.S., 347; "defense emphasis" approach and, 256–59; early efforts to limit, 121–22, 126; effect on mutual stability policy, 273, 274; McNamara opposition to, 101–03, 107; SALT and, 152–53, 159, 165, 172, 178–80, 182–83, 184, 185, 186, 279; Soviet, 98, 99, 100, 114–15, 117, 131, 340
Antisubmarine warfare (ASW): effect on mutual stability policy, 273; limitations on, 313–15, 341; Soviet, 150, 212, 220, 340; U.S. expenditures for, 344
Armacost, Michael H., 37n
Arms Control and Disarmament Agency, 171
Army: under Kennedy administration, 75; missile development, 37; support for finite deterrence, 33, 34; training for nuclear conflicts, 16
ASM. *See* Air-to-surface missile

Assured destruction: capability, 141; damage levels required for, 96, 201–02, 230; effect of threat of, 224; explanation of, 94, 157; force characteristics, 205–11; as McNamara objective, 94–95; policy, 2, 200; Soviet, 136, 271; worst-case planning for, 130–32
ASW. *See* Antisubmarine warfare
Atlas (missile), 36, 44, 46, 47
Atoms for Peace plan, 56, 64
AWACS. *See* Airborne warning and control system

B-1 (aircraft), 3, 155, 166, 173, 176, 206, 213
B-47 (aircraft), 29, 38, 43, 47, 48, 78, 98, 120
B-52 (aircraft), 29, 30, 35, 38, 43, 47, 48, 69, 75, 98
B-70 (aircraft), 97
Bader, William B., 64n
Bailey, Martin J., 253n
Ball, D. J., 85n, 86n
Ballistic missile early warning system (BMEW), 38–39, 42, 71, 208
Bargaining chip diplomacy, 244, 267, 281, 301, 335; disadvantage of, 175, 297–98; effect on congressional decisions, 177; explanation of, 297
Barnett, A. Doak, 205n
Baruch Plan, 1
Bay of Pigs invasion, 77
Bechhoefer, Bernard G., 55n
Beecher, William, 126n, 127n, 148n, 156n, 157n
Berlin crisis, 17; during Eisenhower administration, 23–26, 62; during Kennedy administration, 17, 75, 77–79, 89

Bethe, Hans A., 104n
Blechman, Barry M., 148n, 165n, 203n, 206n, 207n, 213n, 222n, 306n, 345n
BMEW. See Ballistic missile early warning system
Bohn, Lewis C., 253n
"Bomber bonfire" plan, 120
Bomber gap, 30–31, 34, 47, 52, 268
Bombers, 29; ability to recall, 208; cost of, 346; limitations on, 315–16; penetration capability, 206; Soviet, 30, 48, 50, 120; survivability of, 213; U.S.-Soviet balance, 35, 48. See also specific bombers
Bottome, Edgar M., 40n, 45n, 65n
Brennan, D. G., 253n, 256n, 320n
Brenner, Michael, 151n
Brezhnev, Leonid, 113, 184, 188, 319
Brinkmanship strategy, 15, 54, 62
Brodie, Bernard, 4n
Brooke, Edward, 161
Brower, Michael, 79n
Brown, Seyom, 15n, 26n
Brzezinski, Zbigniew, 11n, 240n
Bulganin, Nikolai, 48
Bundy, McGeorge, 89n, 109
Bunn, George, 292n

Caldwell, Lawrence T., 168n
Carter, Barry, 155n
Central Intelligence Agency (CIA), 30
Chase, Harold W., 86n
Chayes, Abram, 275n, 281n
China: future nuclear capability, 342; ICBMs, 104, 151, 158, 159; and Korean truce negotiations, 18, 19; reaction to U.S. massive retaliation policy, 21, 23, 63; SALT and, 321, 324–25; threats against offshore islands and Taiwan, 20–23, 63; U.S. counterforce capability against, 234–35, 331; U.S. deterrence against, 137, 139, 140, 141, 148, 249, 320
Chou En-lai, 21
Clifford, Clark, 108, 124, 127, 128
Clough, Ralph N., 325n
Coblentz, Gaston, 19n, 28n, 24n
Coffey, Joseph I., 104n, 238n
Command Data Buffer program, 227
Congress: action on ABM program, 191; action on weapon program expenditures, 177, 192. See also Senate
Controlled response strategy, 90, 99, 223; in alliance strategy, 92; departure from, 93, 234; objective of, 91
Cost-effectiveness, 74; of MIRV, 100,

133; in weapon evaluation, 132–33, 190, 211, 243, 337–38
Council on Foreign Relations, 19n
Counterforce capability: against China, 331; controlled response approach to, 91, 93; destabilizing effect of, 161, 233–34; flexible response strategy and, 228–30; future need for, 333; MIRV and, 105; for NATO, 141; Nixon administration development of, 157, 158; Soviet, 116, 150, 166–69, 203, 267
Crisis stability, 149, 156–57, 162, 263, 272
Cuba: missile crisis, 2, 77, 80–84, 89–90, 110–13; Soviet attempt to install submarine base in, 148, 163, 166
Czechoslovakia, 2, 128, 143

Damage limitation strategy, 94–96, 105, 132, 136; flexible strategic options and, 225–26; McNamara opposition to, 95–96, 130, 132
Defense expenditures: effect of SALT agreements on, 284–85, 348–49; Eisenhower efforts to reduce, 11, 33, 61; Kennedy administration, 74–75, 78; 1950s and 1960s compared, 64; Nixon administration, 146–47; for research and development, 343; for strategic forces, 16, 343–49
de Gaulle, Charles, 245
Department of Defense, 76, 106, 143; post-SALT weapon program, 177; risk analysis, 140; role in SALT, 171; systems analysis techniques, 95
Deterrence, 2, 12, 15, 145, 328; adequacy of, 32–34, 95; anti-China, 199, 200, 205, 275; through assured destruction, 95–96, 200–205; confident, 96–98; cost of stable, 343–49; diversified, 219–23, 330, 331; evaluation of policy, 68–69, 71; extended policy of, 245–50; finite, 33, 34; flexibility and, 224–25, 232–34, 237; "mobile reserve" for, 13–14; mutual, 120–21, 132, 135, 167; principles of stable, 330–37, 349; purpose of, 263; by retaliatory capability, 149, 150–51, 156, 200, 205, 223, 267, 300–33, 334; sea-based, 150, 155, 219–20. See also Assured destruction; Massive retaliation; Mutual assured destruction
DEW line. See Distant early warning line
Diad (SLBMs and bombers), 222–23, 312, 333

Dinerstein, Herbert S., 79n
Disarmament, 55, 56, 59, 61. *See also* Strategic arms control; Strategic arms limitation talks
Disarmament Commission, 56
Distant early warning (DEW) line, 28, 38
Dobrynin, Anatoliy, 81
Dominican Republic, 77
Drummond, Roscoe, 19n, 24n, 28n
Dulles, Allen, 30, 35n
Dulles, John Foster, 14, 18, 57, 61; on massive retaliation, 12, 13; threatened action against China, 19, 20, 21

Eighteen Nation Disarmament Committee, 119
Eisenhower administration: defense expenditures, 11, 16, 33, 47; defense policy, 11–47, 62–65, 68–73; lack of progress on arms limitation, 60–61, 63; massive retaliation policy, 2, 12, 13, 15, 17, 29, 34, 62, 63, 64, 73; reliance on nuclear power, 11–12, 15, 17–18; strengthening of U.S. delivery capability, 29–30
Eisenhower, Dwight D., 12n, 14, 35n, 65n; action on offshore islands, 20–23; Atoms for Peace plan, 56; in Berlin crisis, 23–26; on disarmament, 61; justification for strategic programs, 43–44; Open Skies proposal, 56–58; priority on missile system development, 37, 42; threatened use of nuclear weapons by, 18, 19, 20, 22, 62
Electronic surveillance systems, 286, 338
Emme, Eugene, 36n
Enthoven, Alain C., 17n, 75n, 84n, 95n, 102n, 107, 108, 123n, 136n, 137n, 246n, 340n
Erickson, John, 112n, 165n

FBS. *See* Forward-based systems
Feld, Bernard T., 212n, 213n
Finney, John W., 114n, 139n, 173n, 188n, 196n, 298n
Fisher, Adrian, 126
Flexible response strategy, 2, 147; counterforce capability and, 228–30; in Cuban missile crisis, 81; effect on nuclear deterrence, 224–25, 232–34, 237, 333; effect on weapon budget and procurement, 234; evaluation of, 235–37; explanation of, 74, 90, 223–24; to limit damage to U.S., 225–26; NATO and, 77, 224, 234; objective of, 76; SALT and, 304; targeting and,

226–28; U.S.-Soviet capability for, 232
Forward-based systems (FBS), 178, 179, 180, 316–17, 344
Foster, John S., Jr., 99
Fractional orbital bombardment system, 213, 271
France, 321, 322
Freedom-to-mix formula, 244, 311, 316
"Freeze" proposal, 119–20, 126, 285
Fried, Edward R., 16n, 147n, 252n, 348n
Frye, Alton, 188n, 310n

Gaither Report, 40–42, 71, 72
Galosh ABM (Soviet), 98, 100, 115
Garthoff, Raymond L., 112n
Garwin, Richard L., 104n, 212n
Gates, Thomas, 45, 65, 95
Gelb, Leslie H., 349n
Gelber, Harry G., 324n
George, Alexander L., 82n
Getler, Michael, 237n, 280n, 311n
Gilpatric, Roswell, 79, 89, 109
Glassboro, Johnson-Kosygin meeting, 115, 122, 126
Gray, Colin S., 31n, 32n, 65n, 265n, 266n, 280n
Greenwood, Ted, 99n, 100n, 106n, 127n, 154n, 258n, 286n, 289n
Grewe, Wilhelm, 322n
Griffiths, Franklyn, 266n
Grinev, O., 167n
Gromley, Dennis M., 148n
Gromyko, Andrei, 79

Halberstam, David, 88n
Hall, David K., 82n
Halperin, Morton H., 6n, 17n, 22n, 23n, 40n, 104n, 173n, 190n, 204n, 265n
Hammond, Paul Y., 9n
Hard-target kill capability, 161, 191, 192, 229, 233, 235, 236, 310, 333
Harriman, Averell, 26n
Hersh, Seymour M., 227n
Hilsman, Roger, 79, 89n, 135n
Holst, Johan J., 59n
Horelick, Arnold, 26n, 48n, 49n, 51n, 79n, 89n, 109n, 111n
Hot line communications link, 129, 207; possible inclusion of other nations in, 321; treaty, 113, 118, 318; use of satellite for, 185, 318
Howe, Jonathan T., 22n, 23n
Hsieh, Alice Langley, 22n
Humphrey, Hubert, 129n
Hungarian uprising, 19
Huntington, Samuel P., 32n

ICBM. *See* Intercontinental ballistic missile

Iklé, Fred C., 253n, 254n, 259n, 260, 311n

India, 325

Intercontinental ballistic missile (ICBM): Chinese, 104, 151, 158, 159, 281; cost of U.S., 345, 347; effect on mutual stability policy, 273; effect of SALT on, 152, 172, 175, 184, 185; hard-target kill capability, 233, 235, 236; retargeting capability, 227; Soviet, 25, 26, 35, 36, 38, 39, 41, 45, 47, 54, 55, 57, 58, 65–68, 86, 87, 112–14, 163, 229; suggested phaseout of U.S., 244, 331–32, 335; survivability of, 210; U.S., 36–37, 39, 44, 46, 47, 75, 85–87, 227; vulnerability of, 214–19, 308–13

Intelligence information: to guide weapon and budget decisions, 97; reliability of, 65–68, 338–39; by satellite, 131, 208, 286; on Soviet ABM system, 98; on Soviet bomber strength, 35; on Soviet ICBM strength, 45, 46, 66–67, 85, 87, 165; for verifying strategic arms control, 286–89. *See also* U-2 program

Interim Agreement, 3n, 164, 193, 279, 280, 281, 283, 305; effects of, 194–95; flexibility of, 292, 293; freedom-to-mix formula, 311; on ICBMs, 187, 214, 287; lack of MIRV restrictions in, 193, 283

Intermediate-range ballistic missile (IRBM): Killian Committee recommendation for, 36–37; Soviet, 35, 45, 80, 179; U.S., 37, 42, 44, 80, 97

Italy, 80

Jackson, Henry, 187, 196

Japan, 252, 327; reaction to SALT, 324; U.S. nuclear commitment to, 248–49

Johnson administration, 2; emphasis on strategic superiority, 106, 108, 141

Johnson, Lyndon B., 104, 108, 120n, 129n; efforts to pursue arms negotiations, 121–22; meeting with Kosygin, 115, 122; SALT proposal, 116, 125, 126–27

Joint Chiefs of Staff, 104, 121, 123, 126, 128, 132, 138, 139, 176

Jupiter (missile), 37, 44, 46

Kahan, Jerome H., 80n, 83n, 279n, 292n

Kahn, Anne H., 213n

Kahn, Herman, 69n, 72n, 204n

Kaiser, Robert O., 189n

Kantor, Arnold, 265n

Kaplan, Morton A., 324n

Kaufman, William W., 75n, 89n

Kaysen, Carl, 215n

Kennedy administration, 2; arms control, 117–19; attempt to revise military policy, 74–75, 84; defense expenditures, 74–75, 78; emphasis on nonnuclear forces, 77, 79; emphasis on strategic superiority, 79, 89, 94, 141; missile program, 85–87, 97–98; policy of deterrence, 84, 94

Kennedy, John F., 42n; in Berlin crisis, 78–79, 89; in Cuban missile crisis, 80–84, 89–90; on missile gap, 47, 85

Kennedy, Robert, 81, 82

Khrushchev, Nikita, 48, 49, 109; action on arms control, 58–59; in Berlin crisis, 24–26, 77–79; in Cuban missile crisis, 80–84, 110–13; strategic arms policy, 53; threats against U.S. and allies, 19, 51, 52, 60, 63

Killian Committee, 36

Kintner, William, 168n, 326n

Kissinger, Henry, 144n, 149, 217; in SALT negotiations, 159, 182, 184, 187, 193

Klass, Philip J., 36n, 46n, 65n, 67n, 79n, 86n, 126n

Kolkowitz, Roman, 53n, 168n

Korea, 18, 62

Kosygin, Alexei, 113, 115, 122

Kraft, Joseph, 38n

Kurth, James R., 99n

Kuzmack, Arnold M., 349n

Kuznetsov, Vasily, 112, 134

Laird, Melvin, 144n, 146, 148, 149n, 150, 152, 154, 158, 161, 183, 191

Lambeth, Benjamin S., 238n, 278n

Laos, 77

Lerman, Allen H., 86n

Lewis, Flora, 322n

Licklider, Roy, 39n

London Disarmament Conference, 57

Long, Anne K., 80n, 83n

Lowe, George E., 29n, 31n

McElroy, Neil H., 17, 43, 45n

McNamara, Robert, 74, 76n, 105, 119n, 134n, 135n, 136n, 260, 261n; on ABM development and controls, 101–03, 104, 121–24, 132–33; concept of deterrence, 94–98, 116; and controlled response doctrine, 91–94, 223, 234; on dangers of strategic arms race, 117; on missile program, 85, 86, 87; strategy policy, 106, 130–33, 265

McNaughton, John, 117, 118, 134

MAD. *See* Mutual assured destruction

Malenkov, Georgi, 49

Malinovsky, Rodion, 109, 114

Marder, Murrey, 241n

Massive retaliation policy, 2, 31; bomber forces for, 29; China's reaction to, 21, 23, 63; criticism of, 63–64, 68–70, 73, 251; explanation of, 12; limits of, 20; potential use of, 13; reaffirmation of, 34; Soviet reaction to, 54

Matsu, 20

May, Michael M., 253n

Medium-range ballistic missiles (MRBMs), Soviet, 45, 51, 54, 179, 271, 317; in Cuba, 80, 110–11

Middle East, 149, 170, 283, 319

Milshteyn, M. A., 307n, 309n

Minuteman (missile), 2, 37, 39, 47, 75, 85, 86, 87, 88, 97, 100, 127, 131, 140, 142, 152, 183, 218

MIRV. *See* Multiple independently targetable reentry vehicle

Missile gap, 34, 35, 46, 47, 53, 268; controversy over, 40–43; elimination of, 78, 85, 86; SALT and, 196

Missile systems, U.S.: deterrent capability, 37, 43–44; development of, 36–37; efforts to reduce vulnerability of, 39; expansion of, 85–87, 97–98; liquid-fuel versus solid-fuel, 70; measurement of destruction capability, 96. *See also* specific missiles and missile systems

Moorer, Thomas, 163, 177n

Morris, Frederic A., 85n, 88n, 103n, 154n, 265n

Multiple independently targetable reentry vehicle (MIRV), 2, 75, 142; ability to detect deployment of, 288, 306; cost-effectiveness of, 100, 133; evaluation of, 101; mutual stability and, 274; Nixon administration commitment to, 153–54, 165–66; as response to Soviet ABM system, 98, 99, 114, 115, 117, 131, 138, 163, 340; SALT and, 127–28, 153, 172, 173, 174, 180–82; Soviet development of, 151, 165, 188, 233; strategic balance and, 137–39; threat to ICBMs, 308–12; U.S. missile superiority through,

106, 107, 108, 140, 141; vulnerability of, 218

Murphy, Charles J. V., 66n

Murphy, Robert, 19

Mutual assured destruction (MAD): advantages of policy of, 262, 328–29; arms reduction as alternative to, 255–56; "defense emphasis" as alternative to, 256–59; objections to, 254–55

Mutual and balanced force reduction, 317

Mutual strategic stability, 120; conflict between unilateral deterrence and, 273–76; effect on international relations, 238; effect of various weapon systems on, 272–75; negotiations for, 334–36; SALT and, 276, 303–05, 307; Soviet reaction to, 133–37; sufficiency criteria and, 189–92; U.S. approach to, 129, 130, 131; U.S.-Soviet arms interaction and, 265–69

Narwhal submarine, 212, 332, 346

National Command Authority, 208, 227

National Security Council, 9, 36, 40; Executive Committee, in Cuban crisis, 81, 83; guidelines, 1953, 15; SALT and, 171

NATO. *See* North Atlantic Treaty Organization

Navy: proponent of finite deterrence, 33, 34; submarine-launched missile development, 37, 44

Newhouse, John, 103n, 107n, 115n, 122n, 123n, 126n, 129n, 170n, 182n, 251n, 294, 323n

New Look defense policy. *See* Massive retaliation

Nike ABM system, 102, 103, 104

Nitze, Paul H., 9n, 89n, 105n

Nixon administration, 3; commitment to MIRV, 153–54, 165–66; defense policy, 143–49; hard-target projects, 161; rationale for strategic options, 159–61, 223

Nixon, Richard M.: SALT and, 128–29; on sufficiency doctrine, 149, 156, 157, 158, 159–61, 162, 191, 192; visit to China, 148; visits to Moscow, 3, 164, 185, 293

No-cities doctrine, 91, 141, 227, 231, 259–61, 329

Nogee, Joseph L., 55n

North Atlantic Treaty Organization (NATO), 12, 58; controlled response strategy and, 92; effect of FBS limi-

tations on, 180; effect on U.S.-Soviet
arms balance, 141, 275; flexible response strategy and, 77, 224; reaction
to SALT, 322–23; U.S. ICBMs and,
123; U.S. nuclear commitment to, 16,
245–48, 336
Nuclear arms: buildup, 2, 9–10, 135,
269–70; burden of deterrence on, 15;
limited use of, 230–32, 233; preferred
U.S. trends in, 250–53; reliance on,
11–12, 15, 17–18, 77, 336–37; tactical, 14, 15, 76
Nuclear nonproliferation treaty, 115,
129, 326, 327
Nuclear test ban proposals, 60, 113, 129,
285
"Nuclear umbrella" plan, 120, 146, 245,
249
Numerical balance: effect on bargaining
power, 239–40, 267; as SALT objective, 305–07; significance of, 238–40;
static indexes for, 241–43; strategy of
sufficiency and, 149, 162–63, 190

Offshore islands, 20–23, 52
Ognibene, Peter J., 156n
On-site inspection, 285, 286, 288
Open Skies proposal, 56–58, 59, 60
Organization of American States, 80
Osgood, Robert E., 17n, 61n, 79n
Owen, Henry, 111n, 349n

Packard, David, 144, 174n
Panofsky, Wolfgang K. H., 152, 229n
Parity, in U.S.-Soviet strategic strength,
3; indexes of, 241–43, 305–06, 331;
President Nixon's acceptance of, 144;
significance of, 237; Soviet efforts to
achieve, 113, 114, 135, 169, 252. See
also Numerical balance
Pavlov, V., 167n
Payload: explanation of, 242; as index
of strategic force, 242–43, 306
Peaceful coexistence, 50
Pen-X Project, 99
Perry, Robert L., 36n, 71n
Pfaltzgraff, Robert, 168n, 326n
Pierre, Andrew, 322n
Pincus, Walter, 251n
Polaris (missile), 2, 34, 37, 39, 44, 46,
47, 75, 85, 86, 87, 88, 100, 131, 165
Poseidon (missile), 100, 101, 105, 127,
140, 345
Powers, Francis Gary, 26n
Powers, Thomas S., 72
President's Air Policy Commission, 9

Quanbeck, Alton H., 203, 206n, 207n,
213n, 222n, 306n, 345n
Quarles, Donald A., 32n, 33, 34, 144n
Quemoy, 20, 22, 23, 63
Quester, George H., 9n, 27n, 28n, 55n,
65n, 326n

Radar, intelligence information provided
by, 65, 286
Radford, Arthur W., 13n, 14n, 19, 32
RAND Corporation, 36, 38
Rathjens, George W., 101n, 212–13n,
268n
Ravenal, Earl C., 249n
Reconnaissance satellites. See Satellites,
reconnaissance
Regulus (missile), 39, 43
Retargeting capability, 227
Rhinelander, John B., 67n, 174n
Rice, Berkeley, 156n
Richardson, Elliot L., 227n
Roberts, Chalmers, 48n, 122n, 144n
Ruina, Jack P., 213n
Rush, Myron, 26n, 48n, 49n, 51n, 79n,
89n, 109n, 111n

SAC. See Strategic Air Command
Safeguard program, 151–53, 159, 173,
175, 178, 183, 191, 193, 347
SAGE. See Semi-automatic ground environment warning and control sys-
tem
Salinger, Pierre, 85
SALT. See Strategic arms limitation
talks
Satellites: Discoverer, 67; moderniza-
tion of hot line by, 185, 318; recon-
naissance, 131, 208, 286, 338; warn-
ing system, 228
Schelling, Thomas C., 15n, 55n, 296n
Schelling, Warner R., 9n
Schlesinger, Arthur, 83n, 84, 88n, 134n
Schlesinger, James, 153, 164, 214n, 225,
246n; on targeting capability, 161,
227, 231, 237, 298n; on U.S.-Soviet
strategic balance, 164, 225
Schneider, William, Jr., 59n
Schultze, Charles L., 284n, 349n
Science Advisory Committee, 41n
Scoville, Herbert, Jr., 67n, 138n, 208n,
278n, 288n, 291n
Semeyko, L. S., 307n, 309n
Semi-automatic ground environment
warning and control system (SAGE),
28

Senate: Armed Services Committee, 31, 161; Preparedness Subcommittee, 42; ratification of ABM treaty, 187
Sentinel ABM, 103, 104, 105, 114, 123, 124, 127, 128, 133, 137, 139, 141, 142
Shepley, James, 21n
Silo-hardening program, 39, 157, 190, 209, 214, 215
Simons, William E., 82n
Single Integrated Operations Plan, 227
SLBM. See Submarine-launched ballistic missile
Slocombe, Walter, 83n, 111n, 234
Smart, Ian, 248n
Smith, Gerard, 153, 175n
Smith, K. Wayne, 17n, 76n, 84n, 95n, 102n, 123n, 136n, 137n, 246n, 340n
Snark (missile), 43
SNDV. See Strategic nuclear delivery vehicle
Snyder, Glenn H., 9n
Sokolovskii, V. D., 48n
Soviet Union: ABM system, 98, 99-105, 114-15, 117, 131, 138, 256-57, 340; antisubmarine warfare, 150, 212, 220; assured destruction strategy, 136, 271; attempt to install submarine bases in Cuba, 163, 166; Berlin crisis, 23-26, 77-79, 109-10; bombers, 30, 32, 48, 50, 120; defense policy, 53, 113-15; efforts to obtain strategic parity, 113, 114, 135, 169, 252; emphasis on medium-range missiles, 45, 51, 54; invasion of Czechoslovakia, 2, 128, 142; reaction to Cuban missile crisis, 110-13; reaction to massive retaliation policy, 48-49; reaction to stabilization of nuclear balance, 133-36; role in offshore islands crisis, 22, 23; strategic arms policy, 53-55, 109-10, 113-17, 120, 134-35, 150-51, 165-69, 268; Sputnik diplomacy, 51-54, 113; tactical air-defense system, 98, 127. See also Counterforce capability, Soviet; Intercontinental ballistic missile, Soviet; Sputnik; Strategic arms limitation talks; Submarine-launched ballistic missile, Soviet
Spacetrack system, 208
Spanier, John W., 55n
Sputnik, 22, 24, 26; effect on missile gap, 40; effect on U.S. missile program, 34, 38-39, 52
SS-7 (Soviet ICBM), 112
SS-9 (Soviet ICBM), 113, 114, 165, 167, 190

SS-11 (Soviet ICBM), 113, 114, 165
Stassen, Harold, 56, 61
Steinberg, Eleanor, 327n
Steinbrunner, John, 155n
Stennis, John, 176
Stolley, Richard B., 104n, 123n
Stone, Jeremy J., 280n
Strategic Air Command (SAC): budget, 33; fleet size, 27; improvements in, 1958, 42; vulnerability of, 38, 55, 57, 71, 72
Strategic arms control: bargaining negotiations for, 295-301; to build mutual confidence, 282-83; collateral measures for, 119; to decrease arms expenditures, 283-85; to improve nuclear stability, 277-82; Kennedy administration and, 117-19; Khrushchev and, 58-59; McNamara and, 107, 121-22; obstacles to, 60, 61; problems relating to verification of, 285-92, 306; to reduce risk of nuclear war, 282; types of agreements for, 292-94. See also Interim Agreement; Strategic arms limitation talks; Vladivostok agreement
Strategic arms limitation talks (SALT), 2, 3, 4, 116, 142, 253, 263, 285; ABM negotiations, 152-53, 159, 165, 172, 178-80, 182-83, 184, 185, 186, 279; absence of ASW limits in, 341; bargaining chip diplomacy in, 175-77, 244, 267, 281; criticism of, 175, 187, 280; criteria for, 302-08; effect on defense expenditures, 284-85, 348-49; effect on nonparticipating nations, 321-25; efforts to sustain agreements of, 290-91; evaluation of, 192-96, 281; FBS negotiations, 178, 179, 180, 185; ICBM negotiations, 152, 172, 175, 184, 185; impasse in negotiations, 128-29, 184-85; Joint Chiefs of Staff guidelines for, 176-77; joint commitment to prevent nuclear war, 318-21; MIRV negotiations, 153, 172, 173, 174, 180-82, 193, 194, 195; Nixon approach to, 140, 148, 170-77, 192; nuclear proliferation and, 325-27; possible future agreements, 301-02; possible involvement of other nations in, 321, 323, 324-25; potential benefits from, 125, 349; proposed future programs for, 341-42; and Safeguard program, 152, 153, 159, 175, 193; SLMB negotiation, 185, 186, 187; Soviet attitude toward, 116,

167–69; U.S. proposals for, 116, 125, 126–27. *See also* Interim Agreement; Strategic arms control

Strategic arms parity. *See* Parity

Strategic arms policy, 3; emphasizing combat effectiveness, 84; factors influencing decisions on, 265–69; first-strike capability, 84, 91, 94; issues related to, 4–5; McNamara's objectives for, 94–96; paradoxes in, 129–30; proposed reduced reliance on nuclear weapons, 336–37; role of nonnuclear forces, 77, 79, 146; U.S. and Soviet, compared, 270–72; U.S.-Soviet interplay on, 54–55; for U.S. superiority, 88, 106–09, 144–45. *See also* Assured destruction; Controlled response strategy; Counterforce capability; Damage limitation strategy; Deterrence; Flexible response strategy; Massive retaliation; Mutual assured destruction; Mutual strategic stability; Numerical balance; Soviet Union; Sufficiency strategy

Strategic balance. *See* Crisis stability; Mutual strategic stability; Numerical balance

Strategic Missile Evaluation Committee, 36

Strategic nuclear delivery vehicle (SNDV), 119–20

Strategic Satellite System, 208

STRAT-X study, 106

Submarine-launched ballistic missiles (SLBMs); cost of, 345–46; reliability of, 208; response to ASW with improved, 313–14; Soviet, 114, 150, 151, 165, 166, 190, 226, 312; survivability of, 210; U.S., 27, 75, 154, 332; vulnerability of, 211, 212

Suez crisis, 51

Sufficiency strategy: crisis stability criterion for, 149, 156–57, 162, 189–92; as defense against small attacks, 149, 158–59; in Eisenhower administration, 31, 34; flexible options under, 149, 159–61, 162, 174, 190; in Nixon administration, 3, 144, 149–51, 156–64, 176; numerical balance and, 149, 162–63, 190; relative destruction criterion for, 149, 157–58; retaliatory capability criterion for, 149, 150–56

Surface-to-air missile, 346

Surprise Attack Conference, 58–62

Systems analysis techniques, 74; to compare strategic force capabilities, 95; for cost-effectiveness, 132–33, 337; for weapon program decisions, 136–37, 338; for worst-case planning, 130–32

Tactical arms limitation talks (TALT), 317

Taiwan, 22, 30

Taiwan Strait, 62

Talbott, Strobe, 111n

Tallinn air-defense system (Soviet), 98, 127

Tatu, Michael, 111n

Thermonuclear bomb, 10, 26, 27

Thin-X. *See* Sentinel ABM

Thompson, Llewellyn, 122, 126

Thor (missile), 44, 46

Throw-weight. *See* Payload

Titan (missile), 37, 39, 46, 47, 97

Treaty: on ABM limitation, 3n, 292, 305, 310, 326, 332, 333, 335; on exploration and use of outer space, 115, 291; on hot line communications, 113, 118, 318; limited test ban, 113n, 118, 285; nonproliferation, 115, 129, 326, 337; on prevention of nuclear war, 319. *See also* Interim Agreement; Vladivostok agreement

Triad (bombers, ICBMs, and SLBMs), 221–22, 344

Trident, 3, 154–55, 166, 173, 175, 176, 206, 221, 332, 345–46

Trofimenko, G. A., 232n

Truman administration, 1, 12

Truman, Harry, 10

Tsou, Tang, 22n, 23n

Tucker, Samuel A., 95n, 340n

Turkey, 80, 82

U-2 program, 60; incident over, 26, 46, 53; information on Soviet bomber strength, 35, 46; information on Soviet ICBM strength, 65–68, 85

United Kingdom, 321, 322

United Nations, 80, 119, 327

United Nations Disarmament Commission, 55

USSR. *See* Soviet Union

Van Cleave, W., 178n

Vietnam, 170

Vladivostok agreement, 3, 177, 193, 196, 214, 263, 282, 283; freedom-to-mix formula, 311, 316; guidelines, 195, 287, 293, 302; on ICBMs, 214; to strengthen mutual strategic stability, 276, 305